PRODUCT LIABILITY LITIGATION

The West Legal Studies Series

Your options keep growing with West Legal Studies
Each year our list continues to offer you more options for every area of the law to meet your course or on-the-job reference requirements. We now have over 140 titles from which to choose in the following areas:

Administrative Law	Family Law
Alternative Dispute Resolution	Federal Taxation
Bankruptcy	Intellectual Property
Business Organizations/Corporations	Introduction to Law
Civil Litigation and Procedure	Introduction to Paralegalism
CLA Exam Preparation	Law Office Management
Client Accounting	Law Office Procedures
Computer in the Law Office	Legal Research, Writing, and Analysis
Constitutional Law	Legal Terminology
Contract Law	Paralegal Employment
Criminal Law and Procedure	Real Estate Law
Document Preparation	Reference Materials
Environmental Law	Torts and Personal Injury Law
Ethics	Will, Trusts, and Estate Administration

You will find unparalleled, practical support
Each book is augmented by instructor and student supplements to ensure the best learning experience possible. We also offer custom publishing and other benefits such as West's Student Achievement Award. In addition, our sales representatives are ready to provide you with dependable service.

We want to hear from you
Our best contributions for improving the quality of our books and instructional materials is feedback from the people who use them. If you have a question, concern, or observation about any of our materials, or you have a product proposal or manuscript, we want to hear from you. Please contact your local representative or write us at the following address:

West Legal Studies, 3 Columbia Circle, P.O. Box 15015, Albany, NY 12212-5015

For additional information point your browser at
www.westlegalstudies.com

WEST
★
™
THOMSON LEARNING

Product Liability Litigation

Mark A. Kinzie

STINSON, MAG & FIZZELL, P.C.

Christine F. Hart

DIRECTOR OF LEGAL STUDIES
WEBSTER UNIVERSITY

CHRISTINE F. HART, P.C.

WEST

THOMSON LEARNING ™

Australia Canada Mexico Singapore Spain United Kingdom United States

WEST

THOMSON LEARNING

WEST LEGAL STUDIES

Product Liability Litigation
by Mark A. Kinzie and Christine F. Hart

Business Unit Director:
Susan L. Simpfenderfer

Executive Editor:
Marlene McHugh Pratt

Senior Acquisitions Editor:
Joan M. Gill

Developmental Editor:
Andrea Edwards Myers

Editorial Assistant:
Lisa Flatley

Executive Production Manager:
Wendy A. Troeger

Production Manager:
Carolyn Miller

Production Editor:
Betty L. Dickson

Executive Marketing Manager:
Donna J. Lewis

Channel Manager:
Nigar Hale

Cover Designer:
Dutton and Sherman

Library of Congress Cataloging-in-Publication Data

Kinzie, Mark A.
    Product liability litigation / by Mark A. Kinzie and Christine F. Hart.
        p. cm.
    "West Legal Studies series."
    Includes index.
    ISBN 0-7668-2035-1
    1. Products liability—United States. I. Hart, Christine F. II. Title.
KF1296 .K553 2001
346.7303'8—dc21   2001026300

NOTICE TO THE READER

To
Duncan Matthew Reynolds Kinzie
and
Reneé

Contents

CHAPTER   4

Strict Liability   97

S E C T I O N   T W O

THEORIES OF DEFENSE   147

CHAPTER   5

Defenses and Responses   149

Statutes, Restatements, and Codes

Preface

THE PRACTICAL APPLICATION OF PRINCIPLES IN PRODUCT LIABILITY CASES

Just as all areas of law embrace change, so does product liability. Here especially, product liability has been through common law development, adoption, and modification of statutes by state legislatures, and honorable mention in older restatements, such as the well-recognized § 402A of the *Restatement (Second) of Torts* (1965). Even as recently as May 20, 1997, the American Law Institute unanimously adopted the *Restatement (Third) of Torts: Products Liability,* codifying the most recent development of black letter law on the subject. Without incorporating these recent changes and understanding their visceral impact across the entire chronology of this practice area, this study would be incomplete.

Product cases also hold a unique position in the trial court. Many of the product liability suits filed in 1998 and 1999 were actually tried before juries in state and federal courts. In fact, three out of the top ten jury verdicts recorded in 1999 were in product liability lawsuits. They were *Anderson v. General Motors Corporation* (burns from an automobile fire—$4.93 billion), *Cowart v. Johnson Kart Manufacturing, Inc.* (burns from a go-kart fire—$1.024 billion, later settled), and *Romo v. Ford Motor Company* (rollover of a Ford Bronco—$295.3 million, later reduced to $5 million). Other high jury trial verdicts included *Washington v. American Home Products* (class action for fen-phen side effects—$150 million), *Henley v. Philip Morris, Inc.*(lung cancer from tobacco products—$51.5 million, later reduced to $26.5 million), *Gordon v. BRK Brands, Inc.* (wrongful deaths from failed smoke detector—$50 million, later settled), *Rodriquez v. Suzuki Motor Corporation* (rollover of Suzuki Samurai—$36.9 million upon retrial in 1997, later settled), *Smith v. Cutter Biological* (wrongful death from contaminated blood products resulting in HIV and AIDS—$35.3 million, simultaneously dismissed; appeal pending). See*National Law Journal,* February 28, 2000 at C1–C22.

Fact issues such as the inherently dangerous quality of the product, misuse, reasonable alternative designs, inadequate and nonexistent warnings, the required standard of care in negligence actions, and the appropriate measure of damages for one's personal injury become the sovereign province of the jury and cannot, despite the urging of some, be resolved in a dispositive motion practice. A comprehensive study of product liability requires some limited instruction in the litigation practices that prepare the product lawsuit for trial, including the use and understanding of written discovery, document production, depositions, expert witnesses, product identification and testing, case management orders, and the trial itself. For practical reasons, the student-soon-to-be-practitioner must be ready to apply the theoretical concepts set forth here and to do so in a way that will advance the discovery of facts that comprise the particular product lawsuit and, ultimately, will maximize the effective representation of the individual or corporate client. Without this practical application, the concepts embraced herein simply remain concepts that do not accomplish these goals and do not further the representation of the client beyond academic and theoretical discussions.

For these reasons, this text does not exclusively embrace the traditional Socratic method of learning typically found in ABA-accredited law schools and para-professional classes. Instead, this field merits an inclusive discussion of the law that gathers case law, statutes, federal regulations, restatements, treatises, and law reviews into a comprehensive approach to grasp this field and, ultimately, to apply it in day-to-day circumstances. Case law remains inherent in this study, but it alone cannot communicate the spectrum of legal issues touched upon in the product liability lawsuit, let alone adequately illustrate its historical development from negligence to warranty to strict liability.

What the product liability student cannot avoid—nor can any practicing professional—is an understanding of this practice area that arises only through the development of theory and its relentless application to facts on a case-by-case basis. The more exposure to more scenarios and their resulting application of principles that derive a finding of fact, a conclusion of law, or the progression of theory, the more embedded the individual practitioner becomes in the concept and its application to day-to-day legal problems. So while the Socratic method may in its own abstract way inherently foist this education upon the student, the practical application of other traditional educational tools makes a realistic departure from typical legal education and offers a valid vehicle for learning the law. But this approach requires that the *student*, then, be responsible for applying principles to scenarios, concepts to hypotheticals, and, ultimately, law to facts. Failure to do so will result in little more than a theoretical education—perhaps memorization—of legal principles that will be of little, or no, use to the practitioner. The outcome will be an incomplete education that will manifest itself in the student's inevitable inability to analyze legal problems, derive fully developed causes of action, define case strategy, seize opportunities for defense, and, most importantly, provide value to the client.

This text endeavors to provide the concept—a black-letter understanding of commonly adopted legal principles in product liability law. It is incumbent on the student to do more. It is the charge of the instructor to make broader challenges. It is essential that the student engage in a relentless pursuit of applying law to facts. The intermittent pursuit of this educational objective is not enough. It must be incessant.

This text endorses an intense study of important case law because these materials have an intrinsic value in the development of strict liability and in the student's need to understand—and develop for themselves—the reasoning of legal scholars that have addressed, ruled upon, and challenged the development of this practice area. Without the input of judges, professors, and commentators such as Prosser, Keeton, Hand, Henderson, Schwartz, Priest, and Twerski, this area of law would not be quite so developed and portions of it would, quite literally be non-existent. We benefit from their insight. There, however, we depart from the recognized norm of learning this practice area. Use of the *Restatements*—particularly the *Restatement*

(Third) of Torts: Products Liability—is fundamental in obtaining the unfolding perspective of the entire practice area. In addition, the practical application of negligence, warranty, and strict liability theories through pleadings, jury instructions, discovery, and trial is essential to bridge the gap between theoretical concepts and service to the client.

This text embraces the student's practical application of fully developed concepts in product liability law. The collective resources of case law study, restatements, jury instructions, discovery, dispositive motion practice, and trial work bring the full force of all these disciplines to bear on the products liability problem. The absence of any one of these leaves empty the full development of the legal student. The celebration of them all creates a greater understanding of the law, a genuine understanding among teaching disciplines, a comprehensive education for the student, and, ultimately, the unbeatable practitioner.

ACKNOWLEDGMENTS

The authors wish to acknowledge and extend their thanks to the research assistants who contributed to the research of the various topics included in *Product Liability Litigation* and are particularly grateful to Bach Hang, Jeffrey Baldas, and Tressa Loya. Mark Kinzie extends his thanks and gratitude to his secretary, Kim Faulkenberry.

The authors gratefully acknowledge the permission of the American Law Institute to reprint the pertinent sections of the RESTATEMENT (SECOND) OF TORTS, copyright 1965, 1977, 1979, and the RESTATEMENT (THIRD) OF TORTS: PRODUCT LIABILITY (1997).

The authors and Delmar also wish to thank the reviewers for their constructive comments in the development of this book.

Rena Denham
Truckee Meadows Community College

Julia Ingersoll
Pierce College

Chris Whaley
Roane State Community College

Mark A. Ciccarelli
Kent State University

Elizabeth Mann
Greenville Technical College

Mardy Chaplin
Cuyahoga Community College

Charles Lawrie
Cuyahoga Community College

Mark A. Kinzie
Christine F. Hart

ABOUT THE AUTHORS

Mark A. Kinzie is a shareholder in the law firm of Stinson, Mag & Fizzell, P.C. where he defends product manufacturers in product liability, class action, and commercial litigation lawsuits. He has represented the manufacturers of aircraft parts, automobile tires, chemicals, pharmaceuticals, medical devices, industrial equipment, computer keyboards, swimming pools, refrigerator compressors, and home appliances in litigation and at trial. Mark earned a bachelor's degree in Business Administration from the University of Central Oklahoma in 1986 and a law degree from the University of Oklahoma in 1989. While in law school, he served as Notes Editor for the Oklahoma Law Review. He is also an adjunct professor in the Legal Studies program in the History, Politics, and Law Department at Webster University.

Christine F. Hart has served as the Director of Legal Studies at Webster University since 1997. She earned a bachelor's degree and a law degree, cum laude, from St. Louis University. She also has a master's degree in education from the University of Missouri, St. Louis. In addition, she obtained a certificate in employment law while in law school. She has practiced law in both small and large firms. At present, she is a part-time sole practitioner. Before embarking on her own practice, she concentrated on commercial and product liability litigation. She now focuses primarily on product liability litigation. Ms. Hart teaches a variety of courses throughout the undergraduate and graduate curricula at Webster University, but especially enjoys teaching courses in Legal Ethics, Constitutional Law, and Litigation.

Chapter One

Introduction to Product Liability

WHAT IS A PRODUCT?

Individuals injured by defective products deserve protection and, ultimately, recovery from product manufacturers, suppliers, or sellers. This area of the law is generally categorized as product liability, which "refers to the legal liability of manufacturers and sellers to compensate buyers, users, and even bystanders for damages or injuries suffered because of defects in goods purchased," BLACK'S LAW DICTIONARY, 1089 (5th ed. 1979).

Civil lawsuits filed to enforce these rights may be based upon negligence, warranty, or strict liability theories, none of which are mutually exclusive. All three theories may be found in any one lawsuit and, together, these three theories comprise the entire scope of product liability litigation. In addition to these common law rights, federal statutes, such as the Magnuson-Moss Act, 15 U.S.C. § 2301-2312 and the Lanham Act, 15 U.S.C. § 1051-1127, and individual state statutes concerning consumer protection issues and deceptive trade practices also govern product manufacturers and sellers. Other common law rights govern such concepts as the misrepresentation of a product, the disparagement of a good, and the likelihood of confusion between products or product packaging. They address ideas about products and not the inherent defectiveness of the product itself. This text is designed to address only product defectiveness; laws concerning ideas about products are not included here.

Historically, individuals injured by defective products have been required to pursue the enforcement of their rights through the proof of fault and proximate cause in a negligence action or through the proof of privity of contract in a warranty action. For example, in a negligence action, a plaintiff must plead and prove that a manufacturer did, in fact, act in an unreasonable manner by producing a defective product that was the proximate cause of plaintiff's injury and damages. In a warranty action, a plaintiff must prove privity of contract, which requires proof of a direct contractual relationship between plaintiff as purchaser and the manufacturer as seller, as well as a breach of an express or implied promise between the two that created the basis of the bargain. Moreover, warranty actions are subject to the disclaimers and requirements of notice of the Uniform Commercial Code (U.C.C.). Under either theory, a plaintiff in a product liability suit was required to overcome these hurdles in order to recover. Although these theories are still available to the individual injured by a defective product, these hurdles were eliminated when the no-fault principles of strict liability were adopted.

Almost all state courts eventually adopted the strict-liability principles cast in *Restatement of Tort (Second)* § 402A (1965), and many state courts are beginning to recognize the evolution of these principles as set forth in the *Restatement of Torts (Third): Products Liability* (1997), both of which provide a clear enunciation of strict liability as it applies to defective products. The *Restatement (Second)* § 402A states the following:

> (1) One who sells a product in a defective condition unreasonably dangerous to the user or consumer or to his property is subject to liability for physical harm thereby caused to the ultimate user or consumer, or to his property, if (a) the seller is engaged in the business of selling such a product, and (b) it is expected to and does reach the user or consumer without substantial change in the condition in which it is sold.
>
> (2) The rule stated in Subsection (1) applies although (a) the seller has exercised all possible care in the preparation and sale of his product, and (b) the user or consumer has not bought the product from or entered into any contractual relation with the seller.

The *Restatement (Third)* at § 1 sets forth a similar, but more concise, general standard that requires the following:

> One engaged in the business of selling or otherwise distributing products who sells or distributes a defective product is subject to liability for harm to persons or property caused by the defect.

In either instance, the imposition of strict liability places the burden of the product user's loss squarely on the manufacturer or seller without the proof of fault, causation, privity, or breach of an express or implied promise. It is here that courts derive the true definition of product for purposes of product liability claims.

The social policy justifications underlying the imposition of strict liability in torts in cases in which a product is defective or otherwise inherently dangerous have their roots in protecting the general public from these defective products and, thus, placing the product user's loss on the manufacturer or supplier. This guiding principle defines *products* for purposes of strict-liability litigation. In *Boddie v. Litton Unit Handling Systems,* 455 N.E.2d 142, 147 (Ill. App. 1 Dist. 1983), an Illinois appellate court enunciated these policy justifications as

1. the public interest in human life and health;
2. the invitations and solicitations of the manufacturer to purchase the product;
3. the justice of imposing the loss on the manufacturer who created the risk and reaped the profit;
4. the superior ability of the commercial enterprise to distribute the risk of injury proximately caused by the defective condition of its product by passing the loss onto the public as a cost of doing business.

Few courts have embraced the common language meaning, but overly broad definition, of the term. In fact, courts have consistently rejected dictionary definitions of the term *product* and instead adopt the policy-based doctrine underlying strict liability. See *Lowrie v. City of Evanston,* 365 N.E.2d 923 (Ill. 1977); *Appleby v. Miller,* 544 N.E.2d 773,

775 (Ill. 1990); *Papp v. Rocky Mountain Oil & Minerals,* 769 P.2d 1249, 1253 (Mont. 1989); *Jackson v. City of Franklin,* 554 N.E.2d 932, 938 (Ohio 1988). Webster's defines "product" as "that which is produced by nature or made by industry or art," WEBSTER'S NEW UNIVERSAL UNABRIDGED DICTIONARY, 1436 (2d ed. 1983). Similarly, the American Heritage Dictionary defines the term as "anything produced by human or mechanical effort or by a natural process," THE AMERICAN HERITAGE DICTIONARY, 1044 (1976). Even Black's Law Dictionary references "product" as "[g]oods produced or manufactured, either by natural means, by hand, or with tools, machinery, chemicals, or the like. Something produced by physical labor or intellectual effort or something produced naturally or as a result of natural process as by generation or growth," BLACK'S LAW DICTIONARY, 1209 (6th ed. 1990).

These definitions define the substantive item at issue in the lawsuit but fail to bring the requisite focus necessary to consider the very purpose of product liability litigation: to protect the public from defective products without proof of fault. The residual effect of this places the burden of producing safe products squarely on the manufacturer or seller. These dictionary definitions fail to endorse this policy-based approach in defining products that fall within § 402A or *Restatement (Third)* protection.

Generally, and for instructive purposes here, a product is ordinarily regarded as tangible personal property, usually a good or chattel. The *Restatement (Third) of Torts: Product Liability* (1997) defines a product as follows:

a. A product is tangible personal property distributed commercially for use or consumption. Other items, such as real property and electricity, are products when the context of their distribution and use is sufficiently analogous to the distribution and use of tangible personal property that it is appropriate to apply the rules stated in this Restatement.

b. Services, even when provided commercially, are not products.

c. Human blood and human tissue, even when provided commercially, are not subject to the rules of this Restatement.

See also definitions of "good" at UCC § 2-105(1) and "product" at § 102(C) Uniform Model Product Liability Act (1979).

That which is ordinarily regarded as a product is constantly being challenged by the plaintiffs' bar in an effort to apply the no-fault principles of strict liability to more and more products. This has created more and more opportunities to avoid the rigid proof requirements of privity and breach of a promise in warranty suits, and fault, causation, and proximate cause in negligence actions. Items such as household appliances, household products, industrial equipment, automobiles, boats, pharmaceuticals, medical devices, chemicals, and foods are typically regarded as products and are often included in *Restatement (Second)* § 402A and *Restatement (Third)* protection. Because the *Restatement (Third)* concerns itself only with product liability, the twenty sections following the general statement of strict liability in defective product cases provide guidance about the application of strict liability principles under specific circumstances, such as categories of product defects (§ 2), compliance with safety regulations (§ 4), bulk suppliers and manufacturers of component parts (§ 5), manufacturers and sellers of pharmaceuticals and medical devices

(§ 6), manufacturers and sellers of defective food products (§ 7), manufacturers and sellers of defective used products (§ 8).

Other items such as electricity, real estate, computer software, water, component parts, houses, and pets have been both regarded and disregarded by courts as products for purposes of applying strict liability principles. Other items such as services, blood and human tissue, and the presentation of ideas and concepts in books, magazines, and reports are not typically regarded as products under a policy-based approach for applying strict liability. *See Restatement (Third)* at § 19.

This text is divided into four central sections, the first two of which address the three central theories of negligence, warranty, and strict liability and their defenses in historical perspective and practical application. The third section focuses on particular product problems, including defective warnings, and the final section applies all of these principles in the civil product liability lawsuit and trial. In each section of the text, the principle question to be answered in studying this topic should not be lost: should the responsibility for producing, selling, or distributing an unsafe product be shifted to the manufacturer, seller, or distributor if the product was inherently dangerous at the time it was placed into the stream of commerce? The key will be your focus on the product itself. This question's answer will always lead you to the objective application of appropriate product liability principles and, thus, the correct result in each product liability case.

WHAT IS A DEFECTIVE PRODUCT?

It is elementary that the defect in a product is the genesis of the product liability claim. But it is also the key to the successful recovery or defense of the claim. In negligence suits, the manufacturer's conduct will prove or disprove the existence of a defect in the subject product. In warranty cases, the promises exchanged between product seller and product buyer will be about the defect in the product. In strict liability actions, the product itself will prove or disprove whether a defect existed in its manufacturing, design, or warning.

The term *defect* is essential to understanding the liability and defense of any facts and circumstances associated with a product liability case, but no definition of the term is generally accepted. Black's Law Dictionary defines "defective condition" as follows:

> A product is in a defective condition unreasonably dangerous to the user when it has a propensity for causing physical harm beyond that which would be contemplated by the ordinary user or consumer who purchases it, with the ordinary knowledge common to the foreseeable class of users as to its characteristics. A product is not defective or unreasonably dangerous merely because it is possible to be injured while using it. BLACK'S LAW DICTIONARY 377 (5th ed. 1979).

Even the courts wrestle with this term and its appropriate definition and application. The origins of strict liability, particularly the concept of a *defective condition* in a product, began with Justice Traynor's opinion in *Greenman v. Yuba Power-Products, Inc.,* 377 P.2d 897, 900 (Cal. 1962). There, the Court first began to recognize that the appropriate focus was the defect in the product and not the details of the sale of the product, which had governed most products claims until *Greenman*. The California Supreme Court held that

> [T]o impose strict liability on the manufacturer under the circumstances of this case, it was not necessary for plaintiff to establish an express warranty as defined in section 1732 of the Civil Code. [Footnote omitted.] A manufacturer is strictly liable in tort when an article he places on the market, knowing that it is to be used without inspection for defects, proves to have a defect that causes injury to a human being. Recognized first in the case of unwholesome food products, such liability has now been extended to a variety of other products that create as great or greater hazards if defective. [Citation omitted.]

> Although in these cases strict liability has usually been based on the theory of an express or implied warranty running from the manufacturer to the plaintiff, the abandonment of the requirement of a contract between them, the recognition that the liability is not assumed by agreement but imposed by law [citation omitted] and the refusal to permit the manufacturer to define the scope of its own responsibility for defective products [citation omitted] make clear that the liability is not one governed by the law of contract warranties but by the law of strict liability in tort. Accordingly, rules defining and governing warranties that were developed to meet the needs of commercial transactions cannot properly be invoked to govern the manufacturer's liability to those injured by their defective products unless those rules also serve the purposes for which such liability is imposed.

* * *

> The purpose of such liability is to insure that the costs of injuries resulting from defective products are borne by the manufacturers that put such products on the market rather than by the injured persons who are powerless to protect themselves. Sales warranties serve this purpose fitfully at best. [Citation omitted.] In the present case, for example, plaintiff was able to plead and prove an express warranty only because he read and relied on the representations of the Shopsmith's ruggedness contained in the manufacturer's brochure. Implicit in the machine's presence on the market, however, was a representation that it would safely do the jobs for which it was built. Under these circumstances, it should not be controlling whether plaintiff selected the machine because of the statements in the brochure, or because of the machine's own appearance of excellence that belied the defect lurking beneath the surface, or because he merely assumed that it would safely do the jobs it was built to do. It should not be controlling whether the details of the sales from manufacturer to retailer and from retailer to plaintiff's wife were such that one or more of the implied warranties of the sales act arose. [Citation omitted.] "The remedies of injured consumers ought not to be made to depend upon the intricacies of the law of sales." [Citation omitted.] To establish the manufacturer's liability it was sufficient that plaintiff proved that he was injured while using the Shopsmith in a way it was intended to be used as a result of a defect in design and manufacture of which plaintiff was not aware that made the Shopsmith unsafe for its intended use.

> The manufacturer contends that the trial court erred in refusing to give three instructions requested by it. It appears from the record, however, that the substance of two

of the requested instructions was adequately covered by the instructions given and that the third instruction was not supported by the evidence.

The judgment is affirmed.

Later, courts acknowledged that a straightforward approach of simply defining *defect* in a product was not enough. In *Todd v. Societe BIC, S.A.*, 9 F.3d 1216, 1220 (7th Cir. 1993), the Seventh Circuit Court of Appeals also wrestled with the term in considering the parent's wrongful death claim of their four-year-old daughter who lit a fire with a cigarette lighter. The Court there noted:

> What, then, does Illinois define as a "defect"? Until recently a state court would have dispatched a case such as ours with the observation that a "dangerous product which bears a warning, and which is safe if the warning is followed, is neither defective nor unreasonably dangerous." [Citation omitted.] The BIC lighter would have been safe had the adults kept it out of Cori's reach, as the warning stated. Jurisdictions that have applied § 402A to cigarette lighters have concluded on this reasoning that the absence of child-resistant features does not make the lighters defective or unreasonably dangerous.
>
> A case decided in 1990 draws this straight forward approach into question. *Lamkin v. Towner*, 128 Ill.2d 510, 528, 150 Ill.Dec. 562, 570, 563 N.E.2d 449, 457 (1990), explains: A plaintiff may demonstrate that a product is defective in design, so as to subject a . . . manufacturer to strict liability for resulting injury in one of two ways: (1) by introducing evidence that the product failed to perform as safely as an ordinary consumer would expect when used in an intended or reasonably foreseeable manner or (2) by introducing evidence that the product's design proximately caused his injury and the defendant fails to prove that on balance the benefits of the challenged design outweigh the risk of danger inherent in such designs.

Standards against which products are measured, such as the risk-utility or consumer expectations standards may exclusively define the *defect*—if any—in a product liability claim. In *O'Brien v. Muskin Corporation*, 463 A.2d 298, 304 (N.J. 1983), the New Jersey Supreme Court considered the appropriate meaning of *defect* in connection with defendant's above-ground swimming pool, which was the subject of that product liability suit. Plaintiff sustained head and neck injuries after diving into the pool filled with three and one-half feet of water and bearing the decal, "DO NOT DIVE." The Court determined the proper *defect* definition as it analyzed plaintiffs' defective design allegations and stated the following:

> Under strict liability, a manufacturer that produces defective products is liable even if those products are carefully produced. Thus, the legal standard for evaluating whether a product is defective becomes the touchstone of strict liability.
>
> Critical, then, to the disposition of products liability claims is the meaning of "defect." The term is not self-defining and has no accepted meaning suitable for all strict liability cases. Implicit in the term "defect" is a comparison of the product with a standard of evaluation; something can be defective only if it fails to measure up to that standard. [Citation omitted.] Speaking generally, defects may be classified as design defects or manufacturing defects. In a manufacturing defect case, defining the standard, and thus

the meaning of "defect," is relatively easy. For example, the injury-causing product may be measured against the same product as manufactured according to the manufacturer's standards. If the particular product used by the plaintiff fails to conform to those standards or other units of the same kind, it is defective. An apt illustration is a mass-produced product that comes off the assembly line missing a part. The question in those cases becomes whether the product as produced by the manufacturer conformed to the product as intended. [Citation omitted.]

The considerations are more subtle when a plaintiff alleges that a product is defect due to any feature of its design, including the absence or inadequacy of accompanying warnings. In design defect or failure-to-warn cases, the product has been manufactured as intended and cannot be "defective" by comparison to a standard set by the manufacturer. [Citation omitted.] Rather, the standard to measure the product reflects a policy judgment that some products are so dangerous that they create a risk of harm outweighing their usefulness. From that perspective, the term "defect" is a conclusion rather than a test for reaching that conclusion. [Citation omitted.]

Although the appropriate standard might be variously defined, one definition, based on a comparison of the utility of the product with the risk of injury that it poses to the public, has gained prominence. To the extent that "risk-utility analysis," as it is known, implicates the reasonableness of the manufacturer's conduct, strict liability law continues to manifest that part of its heritage attributable to the law of negligence. [Citation omitted.] Risk-utility analysis is appropriate when the product may function satisfactorily under one set of circumstances, yet because of its design present undue risk of injury to the user in another situation.

Another standard is the consumer expectations test, which recognizes that the failure of the product to perform safely may be viewed as a violation of the reasonable expectations of the consumer. [Citation omitted.] In this case, however, the pool fulfilled its function as a place to swim. The alleged defect manifested itself when the pool was used for diving.

See also Wade, *On Product "Design Defects" and Their Actionability,* 33 VAND.L.REV. 551 (1980); Birnbaum, *Unmasking the Test for Design Defect: From Negligence [to Warranty] to Strict Liability to Negligence,* 33 VAND.L.REV. 593 (1980); Comment, *The Consumer Expectations Test: A Critical Review of Its Application in California,* 17 Sw. U.L.Rev. 823 (1988).

A product defect may not include an improper use of the product that was not foreseeable by the manufacturer. In *Port Authority of New York and New Jersey v. Arcadian Corporation,* 991 F.Supp. 390, 399 (D. N.J. 1997), the United States District Court for the District of New Jersey struggled with this very issue in its consideration of the February 1993 bombing of the World Trade Center in New York City. In that case, the Court was asked to determine whether certain ingredients of the terrorists bomb, nitrogen chemicals and fertilizer manufactured by defendant Arcadian Corporation, were safe for their intended use when placed by the manufacturer into the stream of commerce. The court considered whether defendant Arcadian had a duty not to place such inherently defective products into the stream of commerce:

Plaintiff's remaining claims allege different theories of products liability. Thus, under New Jersey law, the starting point for whether a duty exists must be the Act. The New

Jersey Supreme Court, in *Zaza v. Marquess and Nell, Inc.* 675 A.2d 620 (N.J. 1996) set forth the relevant legal framework:

Under strict products liability a manufacturer has a duty to ensure that the products it places into the stream of commerce are safe when used for their intended purposes. The focus in a strict liability case is on the product itself.

* * *

The term "defect" is not self-defining and has no universally accepted meaning suitable for every strict products liability case. Defects are classified as design defects, manufacturing defects or inadequate warning defects. Generally, the emphasis in strict products liability analysis is on the safety of the product, not on the reasonableness of the manufacturer's conduct. However, under the Act, as under the common law, the ultimate question to be resolved in design-defect and failure-to-warn cases is whether the manufacturer acted in a reasonably prudent manner in designing and fabricating a product. As we [previously] observed:

When the strict liability defect consists of an improper design or warning, reasonableness of the defendant's conduct is a factor in determining liability. The question in strict liability design-defect and warning cases is whether, assuming that the manufacturer knew of the defect in the product, he acted in a reasonably prudent manner in marketing the product or in providing the warnings given. Thus, once the defendant's knowledge of the defect is imputed, strict liability analysis becomes almost identical to negligence analysis in its focus on the reasonableness of the defendant's conduct.

144 N.J. 34, 47-49, 675 A.2d 620 (1996) (Citation omitted.)

How should the District Court resolve the issue about whether Arcadian's product was inherently defective when it was placed into the stream of commerce? Were the ingredients of Arcadian's nitrogen chemical and fertilizer products defective? Were the ingredients of these products made defective when they were placed into the bomb itself? Does that make a difference in determining whether the final product was defective? At what point in the chain of distribution to the marketplace and in the subsequent chain of ownership after these products were purchased did Arcadian's products become defective, if at all? What is the risk-utility balance for selling nitrogen products?

Academicians have also struggled with the *what is a defect* question, including the architects of the new *Restatement (Third) of Torts: Product Liability* (1997). In 109 Yale L. J. 1087, *Is There a Design Defect in the* Restatement (Third) of Torts: *Products Liability?* George Conk challenged the *Restatement (Third)* on this issue. Conk argued that the American Law Institute's resolve to define the term *defect* in the *Restatement (Third)* brought about an effective end to strict liability because the decided definition of *defect* rejected the consumer expectations test and exclusively endorsed the feasible-alternative safer-design test as the reliable measure of a defective product. Conk believed that this decision shifted the focus of strict liability away from the defective product itself and back into a traditional negligence analysis. *Id.*

Courts have also struggled with the problem of defining *defect* in a product because many doctrines have been available to the court to test whether a product is defective. These doctrines include (1) the consumer expectations test, (2) the risk-utility test,

(3) the reasonably prudent manufacturer test, (4) the alternative safer-design test, (5) the court-as-policymaker test, and (6) the Model Uniform Product Liability Act test. The arguments for and against each test typically hinge on whether a stronger emphasis is placed on the defective product itself or whether a traditional negligence analysis, including a reasonableness standard, is also considered.

Knowing or understanding all of these tests is not the primary objective, however. The focus of your analysis in a product liability claim must be the defect itself. Different jurisdictions will provide different definitions of the term "defect", some of which will change depending on the product itself, the liability theory under which plaintiff's product liability claim is filed, and the continuing development of product liability law. In negligence actions, defendant's conduct will govern the existence of a defective condition in a product. In warranty actions, the promise exchanged will determine whether an actionable defect exists in the product. In strict liability actions, the product itself will determine whether a defect is present. If you become entangled in the familiar and re-occurring fog of legal analysis, always return to the alleged defect in the product. This focus will guide you back into the correct analysis, and ultimately the correct answer, regarding your pending product liability claim.

See also Comment b. to § 2 of the *Restatement (Third) of Torts: Product Liability* (1997) (the nonexclusiveness of the definitions of defect in this section); Comment n. to § 2 of the *Restatement (Third) of Torts: Product Liability* (1997) (the relationship of definitions of defect to traditional doctrinal categories); Comment g. to § 402A of the *Restatement (Second) of Torts* (1965) (defective condition defined as "condition not contemplated by the ultimate consumer"); Stevens, *Strictly No Strict Liability: The 1995 Amendments to Chapter 99b, the Products Liability Act,* 74 North Carolina L.Rev. 2240-2259 (1996).

WHAT IS PRODUCT LIABILITY LITIGATION?

Product liability litigation is the resulting dispute between those injured by defective products and those who manufactured, sold, designed, assembled, labeled, packaged, or installed the product. The Model Uniform Product Liability Act at § 102(D) defines a "product liability claim" as

> any claim or action brought for harm caused by the manufacture, production, making, construction, fabrication, design, formula, preparation, assembly, installation, testing, warnings, instructions, marketing, packaging, storage, or labeling of the relevant product. It includes . . . any action previously based on: strict liability in tort; negligence; breach of express or implied warranty; breach of, or failure to discharge a duty to warn or instruct, whether negligent or innocent misrepresentation, concealment, or nondisclosure, whether negligent or innocent; or under any other substantive legal theory.

Admittedly broad, even the Uniform Act recognized that product liability actions are ordinarily grounded in negligence, strict liability, or warranty theories. *See* Comment D, MODEL UNIF. PRODUCT LIABILITY ACT at § 102. Generally, misrepresentation, disclosure, or concealment issues are regarded as fraud or representational issues that affect the presentation of the product to consumers and not a defect in the product itself that brought about personal injuries or property damage. For that reason, this text does not address that area of the law.

The typical product liability lawsuit is characterized by a plaintiff attempting to prove that he or she has been injured by a defective product and a defendant product manufacturer or a product seller attempting to prove that its product has no such defect or that plaintiff's injury has no relationship to its product. Other product liability litigation also exists. Some class action lawsuits allege that hundreds have been hurt by the same defect in the same product. Examples include the Dalcon Shield and breast implant litigation, and litigation alleging physical and neurological side effects from particular pharmaceutical products, such as Halcion or Fen-Phen. In certain jurisdictions, plaintiffs are required to bring their lawsuits in federal court under alleged circumstances that plaintiff's injuries arose from products such as medical devices, tobacco, boats, insecticides, or airbags. As in many other litigation fields, product liability litigation has particular types of cases that are unique to this area of the law. Three of these areas are class actions, federal preemption, and the appropriate use of circumstantial evidence.

Class Actions

During the 1980s and 1990s, products liability plaintiffs successfully filed cases on behalf of classes, rather than individuals. In some instances, these classes became headline news, such as those targeting pharmaceutical companies, and asbestos or breast implant manufacturers. Certainly, even the limited success of these class actions triggered subsequent litigation that has impacted many corners of American business and government. For example, many states' attorneys general filed suit against tobacco manufacturers to recover the cost of treating diseases caused by cigarette smoking, and many health care insurers pursued pharmaceutical manufacturers for health care costs associated with monitoring and with administering electrocardiograms made necessary by prior use of weight reduction medication. In addition, breast implant and asbestos manufacturers have sought federal court protection for bankruptcy. A successful plaintiffs' class action may threaten the very life of the company itself. These plaintiff successes have fuelled the debate about whether the certification of classes in products liability cases should continue, and if so, under what circumstances. *See generally* Adrogue, *Mass Tort Class Actions in the New Millenium,* 17 Rev. Litig. 427 (1998).

Proponents of class actions believe that certification of classes should continue and should be expanded because class actions reduce waste, promote fairness and uniformity, and encourage corporate compliance with safety regulations and industry standards. Opponents believe that courts certify too many classes, which breeds litigation and misses the true purpose of the class action itself. They also argue that nationwide product liability class actions are so procedurally and substantively complex that neither the individual plaintiffs nor the defendant product manufacturer or seller are afforded a fair trial. Moreover, many believe that attorneys' fees consume more than a fair share of class action settlements, leaving individual plaintiffs with substantially less than they would have received in individual lawsuits.

The filing, maintenance, and certification of class actions in federal court is governed by Rule 23 of the Federal Rules of Civil Procedure. Certification of a class, which is the prerequisite for the plaintiff class to proceed in such an action, must meet all of the following four criteria:

1. the class is so numerous that joinder of all members is impracticable;
2. questions of law or fact common to the class;
3. the claims or defenses of the representative parties are typical of the claims or defenses of the putative class; and
4. the representative plaintiffs will fairly and adequately protect the interests of the class. (Fed. R. Civ. P. 23.)

Plaintiffs must provide evidence, not mere allegations, to prove the second criteria—that there are common questions of law or fact. It is advisable that plaintiffs first analyze and prepare to prove that the representative parties have a common cause of injury. For example, in medical device litigation, each plaintiff may have a unique complaint and unique injuries, and may have received different assurances from his or her treating physician. The challenge for plaintiffs is to provide sufficient evidence that adequately links these plaintiffs' complaints to the allegedly defective product. Also key to the successful certification of a class is the similarity of the applicable products liability law. Success on this issue requires a close examination of the putative class members and the law that applies to each member's claims. This legal analysis must be explored earlier rather than later. Many factors will affect this analysis including the nature of the product at issue, the number and place of the products' manufacturers and sellers, the consolidation of individual plaintiff lawsuits into multidistrict litigation, as well as peculiar requirements of the local rules from each individual federal court.

For defense attorneys, trial courts considering certifying a class of plaintiffs may be receptive to challenges that plaintiffs have only alleged but have not provided evidence of common questions of law or fact. Plaintiffs' putative class may be attacked on the grounds that the plaintiffs' injuries and treatment are unique, and therefore do not provide the common link required for certification. Another successful ground for attack lies in the causation-in-fact issue. For example, a defendant in breast implant litigation may argue that products such as latex are commonly found in numerous products, and that other products may be responsible for the plaintiffs' alleged damages. An argument that the law is too complicated may also succeed in defeating a proposed class action if it convinces a court that the jury instructions and verdict form used to submit the matter to the jury would require the application of too many different states' laws to plaintiffs' various claims.

Preemption

If a federal statute expressly or impliedly preempts a state common law tort action, that action cannot be brought in state court. The ramifications of the preemption doctrine surpass even the supremacy clause. The preemption doctrine, rather than simply allowing the states to act in areas of law not occupied by federal law, strips states of their power to act at all, regardless of any conflicting federal law. Products liability litigation is rife with case law in which defendants invoke the preemption doctrine, often successfully. When successful, plaintiffs' products liability cases based on state common law are never decided on their merits. Although the following discussion cannot possibly address the complexities of the preemption doctrine, it can alert products liability practitioners to some of its dangers.

The state of preemption law is unclear, at best, despite the United States Supreme Court's relatively recent decisions interpreting it. *See Cipollone v. Liggett Group, Inc.,* 505 U.S. 504 (1992); *Medtronic, Inc. v. Lohr,* 518 U.S. 470 (1996). Additional preemption cases are currently being reviewed by the United States Supreme Court. *Shanklin v. Norfolk Southern Railway Company,* 173 F.3d 386 (6th Cir. 1999); *Geier v. American Honda Motor Company, Inc.,* 166 F.3d 1236 (D.C.Cir. 1999); *The International Association of Independent Tanker Owners (INTERTANKO) v. Locke,* 148 F.3d 1053 (9th Cir. 1998). Lower courts have resolved preemption issues with a variety of analysis and results, many of which are conflicting. *See e.g., Lewis v. American Cyanamid Company,* 715 A.2d 967 (N.J. 1998) (Federal Insecticide, Fungicide, and Rodenticide Act, 7 U.S.C. § 136v); *Grenier v. Vermont Log Buildings, Inc.,* 96 F.3d 559 (1st Cir. 1996) (Federal Insecticide, Fungicide, and Rodenticide Act, 7 U.S.C. § 136v); *Irving v. Mazda Motor Corporation,* 136 F.3d 764 (11th Cir. 1998) (National Traffic and Motor Vehicle Safety Act, 15 U.S.C. § 1381); *Harris v. Ford Motor Company,* 110 F.3d 1410 (9th Cir. 1997) (National Traffic and Motor Vehicle Safety Act, 15 U.S.C. 1392(d)).

However, courts do agree that preemption applies in two possible ways: by field preemption or by conflict preemption. Conflict preemption takes place when compliance with both state and federal law is impossible or when state law would thwart Congress' purposes and objectives. Conflict preemption occurs only to the extent that a state law actually conflicts with federal law. Field preemption occurs when a state statute occupies a field that Congress intended for exclusive federal government occupation. For example, numerous courts have concluded that the federal Locomotive Boiler and Inspection Act (BIA) preempts the entire field of locomotive safety, including locomotive design, construction, and materials, thereby mandating the dismissal of state law claims against locomotive manufacturers. *Scheiding v. General Motors Corp.,* 77 Cal. Rptr.2d 339, review granted, 966 P.2d 442 (1998); *Monarch v. Southern Pac. Transp. Co.,* 83 Cal. Rptr.2d 253, 255 (Cal. Ct. App. 2nd Dist., 1999). Plaintiffs' attorneys have argued, usually unsuccessfully, that the BIA's provisions were not intended to preempt the entire field, specifying a particular aspect of locomotives such as locomotive parts or locomotives that are out of service.

The ambiguity of preemption law is illustrated by a recent decision by the Illinois Supreme Court in *Weiland v. Telectronics Pacing Systems, Inc.,* 721 N.E. 2nd 1129 (Il. 1999), which decided whether the plaintiff could sue the distributor of a pacemaker that malfunctioned when implanted in his chest. The preemption issue was whether section 360k(a) of the Medical Device Amendments of the federal Food, Drug and Cosmetic Act preempted the plaintiff's common law claims of breach of warranty and defective design and manufacture of the pacemaker. The Court pointed to standards developed by the United States Supreme Court for determining whether the federal law preempts state common-law claims. That standard provides that for a federal requirement to preempt state law under section 360k, it must contain a specific requirement that applies to a particular device and focuses on the safety and effectiveness of that device. In *Weiland,* the state court concluded that the approval of pacemakers by the Food and Drug Administration did not impose a specific federal requirement on the pacemaker manufacturer because "pacemaker approval imposes no ascertainable, substantive requirement on the manufacturer or design of the device." *Id.* at 1152; *see also Medtronic, Inc. v. Lohr,* 518 U.S. 470 (1996) (resolving federal preemption under Medical Device Amendment under federal Food, Drug and Cosmetic Act, 21 U.S.C. § 360e); compare *R.F. v. Abbott Laboratories,* 745 A.2d 1174, 1176 (N.J. 2000) (finding that federal law impliedly preempts state law in a failure-to-warn suit against the developer of a test to detect the HIV virus in blood because "[t]he extensive control and continuous scrutiny of the test by the Food and Drug Administration was so pervasive").

Circumstantial Evidence

Proof in product liability cases most often provides direct evidence of a specific defect in the product at issue. A witness to the damaging incident, often the plaintiff, testifies about the contact the injured party had with the product. In addition, an expert normally testifies that the product had a manufacturing and/or design defect. However, direct proof of the product defect is not always required. Even the *Restatement (Third)* recognizes that circumstantial evidence could adequately support the inference of a product defect. The *Restatement (Third)* provides:

> **§ 3 Circumstantial Evidence Supporting Inference of Product Defect.**
>
> It may be inferred that the harm sustained by the plaintiff was caused by a product defect existing at the time of sale or distribution, without proof of a specific defect, when the incident that harmed the plaintiff:
>
> (a) was of a kind that ordinarily occurs as a result of product defect; and
> (b) was not, in the particular case, solely the result of causes other than product defect existing at the time of sale or distribution.

In some jurisdictions, it is sufficient for the plaintiff to provide only circumstantial evidence of the product defect. The method of using circumstantial evidence may be provided as follows:

> [T]he plaintiff presents evidence that a product, such as a television set, was new or had no problems under normal usage prior to the incident, that a fire occurred with the heaviest burn pattern near where the TV set was located, that the fire so destroyed the set that it could not be examined for evidence of a defect in the set itself, that an examination occurred after the fire to see if there were possible causes for the fire other than the TV set, and at least one witness is able to exclude these other possible causes of the fire. . . . Thus, the plaintiff offers a well-connected train of circumstances that is as cogent and compelling as an array of direct evidence of the fact sought to be proved the existence of a defect that caused the injury. (Hack, *Circumstantial Evidence of Product Defect in Strict Liability Cases,* J.Mo.Bar. 256 (1990) citing *Russell v. St. Louis County Cab Co., Inc.,* 493 S.W.2d 26 (Mo. App. E.D. 1973).

The use of circumstantial evidence to prove product liability cases closely resembles the doctrine of res ipsa loquitor because recovery is based on the recognition, that accidents do not normally happen with a new or rarely used product unless a defect existed within the product itself." Res ipsa loquitor, which means "the thing speaks for itself," is usually used in cases where the plaintiff would normally plead negligence but does not have access to information that could prove the defendant's negligent conduct. Res ipsa loquitor requires proof that (1) the event that injured the plaintiff was one that does not ordinarily happen except through negligence; (2) the instrument that caused the plaintiff's injury was under the exclusive control of the defendant; and (3) the plaintiff's injuries were not due to his or her own activities.

In comparison, the use of circumstantial evidence in product liability cases generally requires proof of the following three elements: (1) the occurrence resulting in injury does not ordinarily occur if those in control use due care; (2) the instrumentalities involved were managed and controlled by the defendant; and (3) the defendant possesses superior knowledge or means of information regarding the cause of the occurrence. *Balke v. Central Mo. Elec. Coop.,* 966 S.W.2d 15, 26 (Mo. App. W.D. 1997). The difference is that the circumstantial evidence products liability case can be made without proving that the defendant exclusively controlled the product. Product liability cases can be submitted in many jurisdictions using a negligence claim with strict liability or as an alternative to strict liability. The less onerous proof requirements of strict liability using circumstantial evidence would therefore compel a plaintiffs' attorney to include the strict liability theory when possible. However, practitioners should carefully research the requirements in the jurisdiction for pleading a product liability case based on circumstantial evidence.

SECTION ONE

THEORIES OF LIABILITY

Negligence

INTRODUCTION

Negligence is the law's broadest field because it governs individual and corporate conduct in many situations, including the manufacturing, designing, and warning of defective products. Negligence in product liability cases requires a finding of fact that one breached a duty to exercise reasonable care by manufacturing, designing, or selling a defective product, and that the product was the direct and proximate cause of the plaintiff's injuries or damages. Because these elements are established through the development of common law, plaintiffs must plead and prove exceptionally fluid concepts, such as duty, standard of care, foreseeability, and causation.

Definitions

Negligence is the failure to act. It is measured by the common law obligation of the reasonable, prudent person who would have acted differently under similar circumstances and, thereby, would have avoided causing harm to someone or some thing. In product liability cases, negligence is the failure of the product manufacturer, retailer, or distributor to exercise reasonable care in manufacturing, designing, selling, distributing, labeling, or warning about a defective product. These are cases of ordinary negligence. In a few limited instances, negligence is more absolute and, therefore, more akin to strict liability. These instances include (1) res ipsa loquitur (*"the thing speaks for itself"*) in which negligence is inferred because the incident would not occur in the absence of negligence; and (2) negligence per se (negligence *by itself*) in which negligence is manifested in the unexcused violation of a statute or regulation.

Elements of a Cause of Action in Negligence

Negligence is routinely comprised of three essential elements: duty, causation, and harm. Duty is the obligation imposed by law that one will act as expected under the circumstances. The measure of one's duty is determined by the degree of care required in a particular situation and may be described as reasonable or ordinary care. Causation is the direct and foreseeable result brought about by the actions of a person or a company. Causation necessarily includes a finding of foreseeability, which is established by proof that the person or company knew or should have reasonably anticipated that harm or injury would be the likely result of their acts or omissions. Causation always includes two components: (1) evidence of the connection between defendant's negligent act and plaintiff's harm; and (2) defendant's legal obligation to have foreseen plaintiff's harm. Harm is typically the plaintiff's personal injuries or property damage, including economic loss. Harm is discussed further in Chapter Five, Defenses and Responses.

These three elements exist in every negligence action. A manufacturer's failure to manufacture or design a product free from defects must include the following elements in order to make a submissible negligence case at trial:

- the defendant manufactured or designed the product
- the product was defective
- the defendant failed to use reasonable care to manufacture or design the product
- the direct and proximate cause of defendant's failure was the injuries or damages sustained by the plaintiff

A manufacturer's or seller's failure to provide an adequate, legible, and sufficiently available warning about a defective product must include the following elements to make a submissible negligence case at trial:

- the defendant manufactured, designed, or sold the product
- the product was defective
- the defendant failed to use reasonable care to adequately provide, write, or make available a warning about the risk of harm from the defective product
- the direct and proximate cause of defendant's failure was the injuries or damages sustained by the plaintiff.

Types of Actions for Negligence in Product Manufacturing

Negligence actions typically arise in the failure of the product manufacturer to manufacture or design a product that is free from defect. Anyone in the product's stream of commerce—manufacturer to wholesaler to distributor to retailer—may be held liable for this failure to act, particularly if the act is the failure to warn of the defect. Failure to warn actions may manifest themselves in the failure of a person or company to provide any warning, the failure to provide an adequate warning, or the failure to place the warning in a sufficiently recognizable location. Res ipsa loquitur and negligence per se cases provide plaintiffs with a cause of action in which the negligent act is already recognized under more commonly agreed circumstances, such as statutes, regulations, or incidents that could not occur but for the existence of the negligent act.

HISTORY AND EMERGENCE

The Pre-1900 General Rule—No Duty Imposed on Product Manufacturers

Depending on one's perspective, negligence theory as it applies to product liability law can be credited or blamed with the earliest and fastest departure from the buyer-be-damned philosophies reflected in the doctrine of *caveat emptor* that dominated British and American law during the Industrial Revolution. That firmly established law from which negligence departed took the form of the general rule that the original manufacturer of goods was not liable for damages caused by the goods' defects to anyone except the buyer or one in privity with the buyer.

Although courts provided a variety of reasons for invoking the general rule, two reasons dominated. One reason was based on the legal fiction that the manufacturer was legally protected from liability to the consumer or user for injuries or damages caused by the company's defective goods; it could not have anticipated any such harm since an intervening party, the seller, resold the product and therefore *insulated* the manufacturer from liability. The second reason was that it would burden manufacturers and sellers too heavily to hold them liable to perhaps hundreds of distant consumers or users whom they could not identify. Hence, it was better to let the consumer or user bear the burden of the harm suffered.

Gradually, exceptions to the general rule were established and broadened. Most important was the exception that held the seller liable to a third person for negligence in the preparation or sale of an article *imminently* or *inherently* dangerous to human safety. See *Huset v. J.l. Case Threshing Machine Co.,* 120 F. 865 (8th Cir. 1903). The inherently dangerous exception began by recognizing a cause of action for negligently labeled products in *Thomas v. Winchester,* 6 N.Y. 397 (1852). Winchester ran a store that sold various vegetable extracts, including extract of dandelion, a harmless drug, and extract of belladonna, a poison. He sold a bottle of extract of belladonna, mislabeled as extract of dandelion, to a pharmacist who in turn filled a prescription written for extract of dandelion for the plaintiff, Ms. Thomas. She became seriously ill. The Court affirmed a jury verdict against Winchester, stating, "[t]he defendant's duty arose out of the nature of his business, and the danger to others incident to its mismanagement" (*Id.*).

Evolution of the New General Rule—*MacPherson*

For the second half of the nineteenth century, the inherently dangerous exception cried out for clarity and precision. It was sporadically applied, with much dispute over the type of products to which it applied. See *Liggett & Myers Tobacco Co. v. Cannon,* 178 S.W.1009 (Tenn. 1915); *Pillars v. R.J. Reynolds Tobacco Co.,* 78 So. 365 (Miss. 1918) (opposing opinions as to chewing tobacco); *Stone v. Van Noy Railroad News Co.,* 154 S.W. 1092 (Ky. 1913); *Coca Cola Bottling Works v. Shelton,* 282 S.W. 778 (Ky. 1926) (opposing opinions as to beverage bottles). In 1916, Judge Cardozo wrote the majority opinion in *MacPherson v. Buick Motor Co.,* 111 N.E. 1050 (N.Y. 1916) in which the inherently dangerous exception to negligence *swallowed the rule*.

Plaintiff MacPherson had been ejected from his 1909 Buick automobile, while driving prudently at eight miles per hour, due to the crumbling of one wooden wheel. Buick purchased the wooden wheel from its component manufacturer and sold the Buick to a dealer. The dealer sold the Buick to MacPherson. MacPherson alleged that although an automobile is not inherently dangerous, it had become weaker when the wheel was installed. He theorized that the automobile was inherently dangerous due to its weak wheel because the manufacturer is charged with the knowledge of the weak wheel if it might be discoverable by a reasonable inspection and the application of reasonable tests. Judge Cardozo wrote the following in affirming the jury's verdict for MacPherson:

> If the nature of a thing is such that it is reasonably certain to place life and limb in peril when negligently made, it is then a thing of danger. Its nature gives warning of the consequences to be expected. If to the element of danger there is added knowledge that the thing will be used by persons other than the purchaser and used without new tests, then, irrespective of contract, the manufacturer of this thing of danger is under a duty to make it carefully. That is as far as we are required to go for the decision of this case (*Id.*).

Legal theorists eagerly interpreted the case further though. They supplied various justification for the *MacPherson* decision, including the idea that the manufacturer derives an economic benefit from the sale and subsequent use of the good. His duty therefore, is like that of a land possessor toward a business visitor to protect against dangers he knows about and those that he might discover by using reasonable care. The *MacPherson* decision and the cases that followed it also reflected judicial disenchantment with unregulated capitalism. Those cases also pointed out growing judicial skepticism about the validity of traditional moral values, such as vigilance to avoid foreseeable danger as a general civil obligation, at least in the area of supplied goods. Ultimately, however, the duty imposed on manufacturers and sellers by *MacPherson,* is a legal, not a philosophical or moral one. It is based on their conduct in marketing a product, which establishes a relationship with the purchaser, to charge them with the foreseeability of harm if proper care is not used.

Survival of Negligence Actions Against Product Manufacturers after *MacPherson*

The negligence theory of product liability was of particular help to certain plaintiffs before 1960. Before that time persons who were physically harmed or whose property was physically harmed rarely recovered on a breach of warranty theory for two reasons. First, due to strong judicial protection of the concept of contractual freedom, parties could contract out of all liability resulting from the seller's objective manifestations of his intent to assure the buyer that the product was free of defects. Second, the privity requirements of the breach of warranty theory eliminated anyone but the immediate purchaser from recovering damages caused by unreasonably dangerous products. That meant that manufacturers were often completely shielded from liability because they sold their products to intermediaries, such as automobile dealers, before the intermediaries resold the product to consumers.

During the forty years after *MacPherson,* states rapidly adopted its rule resulting in virtually universal acceptance. Liability under a negligence theory was extended during that time to include physical harm to property, as well as to the negligent sale of goods such as animal food, where personal injury is not an issue and the foreseeable dangers are posed not to humans, but to property. Plaintiffs using a negligence theory have also expanded their potential defendants to include manufacturers, designers, sellers of a product, including makers of a component part of the final product, assemblers of parts supplied by a third party, dealers, wholesalers and retailers. After one hundred and fifty years of evolution, the general rule has developed to be that the seller is liable for negligence in the manufacture or sale of any product which may reasonably be expected to be capable of inflicting substantial harm if it is defective.

Despite its universal acceptance, practitioners have gradually come to disregard the negligence theory of products liability law. They perceive the strict liability doctrine that has emerged in the last few decades as more favorable to plaintiffs than negligence, because, as discussed later in this text, it is generally easier to prove and is susceptible to fewer defenses. Often, a negligence claim in a products liability case is dismissed by the court or is voluntarily dismissed by the plaintiff prior to trial or jury deliberation. So, why has it survived?

There are several technical reasons. State statutes of limitations or repose may bar suit based on strict liability but not negligence. Some states' negligence statutes begin accruing at the time of injury rather than at the time of sale or delivery, which is when many strict liability statutes begin accruing. Local rules pertaining to discovery, evidence, or other tactical or strategic advantages may be invoked by negligence plaintiffs, but not by plaintiffs suing in strict liability. In addition, a particular type of claim may be prohibited by a state's product liability act but may be allowed under a negligence theory. For example, a manufacturer who dangerously double-stacked felt roofing rolls that were single-banded rather than double-banded, on a flatbed trailer for hauling by plaintiff could be held liable only in negligence, and not in strict liability, for injuries caused to the plaintiff when the load shifted. *Elk Corp. of Arkansas v. Jackson,* 727 S.W.2d 856 (Ark 1987). The Arkansas Supreme Court remarked: "If Elk was at fault, then it was because Elk negligently loaded Jackson's trailer, not because the rolls of roofing were defective." *Id.*

Perhaps most importantly, negligence theory has survived because it is more palatable to plaintiffs' attorneys, judges, juries, and court observers than the more controversial strict liability theory. Many plaintiffs' lawyers still want to demonstrate the manufacturer's negligence even if the suit is brought under a theory other than negligence. The *fault* of a particular defendant may not be required for a plaintiff's judgment from a jury under a strict liability theory, but it may affect the amount that a jury is willing to award the plaintiff. *See* C. Sklaren. *Products Liability,* Ch. 1,1.04 (Matthew Bender, 1993) *quoting* L. Frumer & M. Friedman, *Products Liability,* Ch. 2, 2.0113] (Matthew Bender, 1987).

THE CRITICAL ELEMENTS—DUTY AND CAUSATION

Duty

Establishing a duty upon which negligence actions against product manufacturers could be made developed only as fast as the common law itself. Originally, manufacturers owed no duty to consumers or users of their products who had no contractual privity with the manufacturer itself. Before 1900, this general rule protected manufacturers for incident-specific reasons that did not require the manufacturer to foresee or anticipate injuries to anyone other than the product purchaser and for society-specific reasons that supported the development of industry and manufacturing that was then only in its infancy.

After 1900, exceptions to the general rule developed, which broadened the duty imposed on product manufacturers. In *Huset v. J. I. Case Threshing Machine Co.*, 120 F. 865, 870-72 (8th Cir. 1903), the Eighth Circuit Court of Appeals recognized exceptions to the general rule. There, plaintiff alleged that defendant negligently manufactured a threshing machine with a cover over the operating cylinder for the band-cutter and self-feeder (*Id.* at 865). The thresher operators routinely walked and stood on the cover. One operator (Huset) sank through the cover and lost his leg in the operating cylinder. *Id.* In establishing the duty of J. I. Case, the court departed from the general rule and recognized the following three exceptions in which a duty would be imposed on the manufacturer:

(1) "[A]n act of negligence of a manufacturer or vendor which is imminently dangerous to the life or health of mankind, and which is committed in the preparation or sale of an article intended to preserve, destroy, or affect human life, is actionable by third parties who suffer from the negligence." *Id.* at 870. [Citations omitted.]

(2) "[A]n owner's act of negligence which causes injury to one who is invited by him to use his defective appliance upon the owner's premises may form the basis of an action against the owner." *Id.* at 870-71. [Citations omitted.]

(3) "[O]ne who sells or delivers an article which he knows to be imminently dangerous to life or limb to another without notice of its qualities is liable to any person who suffers an injury therefrom which might have been reasonably anticipated, whether there were any contractual relations between the parties or not." *Id.* at 871. [Citations omitted.]

The Eighth Circuit Court reversed the decision of the district court, which had dismissed Huset's action based on the reasoning that J. I. Case owed no duty to Huset, and embraced the third exception as establishing a duty upon which the defendant manufacturer owed a duty of care to the plaintiff. *Id.* at 865, 872.

Duty eventually became the general rule, evolving away from the *Huset* exceptions and into the generally recognized elements of today's negligence actions in product liability cases. These principles were formally established in Judge Cardozo's landmark opinion in *MacPherson v. Buick Motor* Co., 111 N.E. 1050 (N.Y. 1916).

 CASE LAW ◆

◆ **establishing the duty of product manufacturers**

MacPherson v. Buick Motor
Co., 111 N.E. 1050 (N.Y.
1916).

Plaintiff MacPherson was injured when his new automobile, which he had purchased from an automobile dealer, collapsed. One of the wheels had been manufactured with defective wood. Although defendant Buick did not manufacture the wheel, it did not inspect the wheel prior to its installation on plaintiffs

automobile. The Court determined whether defendant Buick owed a duty of care to MacPherson.

Cardozo, J.

* * *

The question to be determined is whether the defendant owed a duty of care and vigilance to any one but the immediate purchaser.

The foundations of this branch of law, at least in this state, were laid in *Thomas v. Winchester* (6 N.Y. 397). A poison was falsely labeled. The sale was made to a druggist, who in turn sold to a customer. The customer recovered damages from the seller who affixed the label. "The defendant's negligence, " it was said, "put human life in imminent danger." A poison falsely labeled is likely to injure any one who gets it. Because the danger is to be foreseen, there is a duty to avoid the injury. Cases were cited by way of illustration in which manufacturers were not subject to any duty irrespective of contract. The distinction was said to be that their conduct, though negligent, was not likely to result in injury to any one except the purchaser. We are not required to say whether the chance of injury was always as remote as the distinction assumes.

* * *

We hold, then, that the principle of *Thomas v. Winchester* is not limited to poisons, explosives, and things of like nature, to things which in their normal operation are implements of destruction. If the nature of a thing is such that it is reasonably certain to place life and limb in peril when negligently made, it is then a thing of danger. Its nature gives the warning of the consequences to be expected. If to the element of danger there is added knowledge that the thing will be used by persons other than the purchaser, and used without new tests, then, irrespective of contract, the manufacturer of this thing of danger is under a duty to make it carefully. That is as far as we are required to go for the decision of this case. There must be knowledge of a danger, not merely possible, but probable. It is *possible* to use almost anything in a way that will make it dangerous if defective. That is not enough to charge the manufacturer with a duty independent of his contract. Whether a given thing is dangerous may be sometimes a question for the court and sometimes a question for the jury. There must also be knowledge that in the usual course of events the danger will be shared by others than the buyer. Such knowledge may often be inferred from the nature of the transaction. But it is possible that even knowledge of the danger and of the use will not always be enough. The proximity or remoteness of the relation is a factor to be considered. We are dealing now with the liability of the manufacturer of the finished product, who puts it on the market to be used without inspection by his customers. If he is negligent, where danger is to be foreseen, a liability will follow.

* * *

From this survey of the decisions, there thus emerges a definition of the duty of a manufacturer which enables us to measure this defendant's liability. Beyond all question, the nature of an automobile gives warning of probable danger if its construction is defective. This automobile was designed to go fifty miles an hour. Unless its wheels were sound and strong, injury was almost certain. It was as much a thing of danger as a defective engine for a railroad. The defendant knew the danger. It knew also that the car would be used by persons other than the buyer. This was apparent from its size; there were seats for three persons. It was apparent also from the fact that the buyer was a dealer in cars, who bought to resell. The maker of this car supplied it for the use of purchasers from the dealer just as plainly as the contractor in *Devlin v. Smith* supplied the scaffold for use by the servants of the owner. The dealer was indeed the one person of whom it might be said with some approach to certainty that by him the care would not be used. Yet the defendant would have us say that he was one person whom it was under a legal duty to protect. The law does not lead us to so inconsequent a conclusion. Precedents drawn from the days of travel by stage coach do not fit the conditions of travel today. The principal that the danger must be imminent does not change, but the things subject to the principle do change. They are whatever the needs of life in a developing civilization require them to be.

Case Notes: Duty

1. Explain the transition of the courts' logic in having adopted the *imminently dangerous* condition in the *Huset* exception, only to leave it again in *MacPherson* in favor of the general rule adopting a duty of care owed by manufacturers. Ultimately, product liability law

again embraced *inherently dangerous* products in adopting a no-fault, strict liability rule against manufacturers of defective products.

2. Why did courts in the early 1900s have difficulty leaving the concept of contractual privity in favor of imposing a duty of care on manufacturers in a broader array of circumstances? What was the larger impetus that created the new general rule that imposed a duty of care on manufactures for the injuries sustained by third parties? In *Baxter v. Ford Motor Co.,* 12 P.2d 409 (Wash. 1932), the Court abandoned "the old rule that a manufacturer is not liable to third persons who have no contractual relations with him for negligence in the manufacture of an article [and to this] should be added another exception, not one arbitrarily worked by the courts, but arising . . . from the changing conditions of society."

3. Who makes the determination whether a duty of care exists? What establishes the standard of care under which the duty is derived? What is the relationship between the legal concept of *duty* and the legal concept of *standard of care?* Does the standard of care determine the degree of duty expected under the same or similar circumstances?

4. Some legal theorists cite Judge Cardozo's opinion in *MacPherson* as "a classic modern negligence case, where broad universal duty of care is substituted for particularized obligations owing only to certain persons." *See* C. E. WHITE, *TORT LAW IN AMERICA: AN INTELLECTUAL HISTORY,* (Oxford University Press 1985) at 125. If true, what was to prevent countless suits by consumers and users injured by negligently manufactured products?

5. Eventually, manufacturers were required by the courts to protect product users from patent and latent defects in the product. In *Micallef v. Miehle Company,* 348 N.E.2d 571 (N.Y. Ct. App. 1976), the court refused the defendant manufacturer's argument that encouraged continued recognition and application of the open and obvious danger rule. That rule imposed no duty on a manufacturer to protect a product user from dangers of the product that were open and obvious, well-known in the industry, or even known by the product user. The court in *Micallef* overturned prior court decisions and imposed a duty on the manufacturer. It held that

> The bottom does not logically drop out of a negligence case against the maker when it is shown that the purchaser knows of the dangerous condition. Thus if the product is a carrot-topping machine with exposed moving parts, or an electric clothes wringer dangerous to the limbs of the operator, and if it would be feasible for the maker of the product to install a guard or safety release, it should be a question for the jury whether reasonable care demanded such a precaution, though its absence is obvious. Surely reasonable men might find here a great danger, even to one who knew the condition; and since it was so readily available they might find the maker negligent. [2 HARPER & JAMES, *TORTS,* 28.5.]

* * *

The manufacturer of the obviously defective product ought not to escape because the product was obviously a bad one. The law, we think, ought to discourage misdesign rather than encouraging it in its obvious form.

* * *

We find the reasoning of these cases persuasive. *Campo* [*v. Scofield,* 95 N.E.2d 802 (N.Y. Ct. App. 1950)] suffers from its rigidity in precluding recovery whenever it is demonstrated that the defect was patent. Its unwavering view produces harsh results in view of the difficulties in our mechanized way of life to fully perceive the scope of danger, which may ultimately be found by a court to be apparent in manufactured goods as a matter of law.

* * *

A casting of increased responsibility upon the manufacturer, who stands in a superior position to recognize and cure defects, for improper conduct in the placement of finished products into the channels of commerce furthers the public interest. To this end, we hold that a manufacturer is obligated to exercise that degree of care in his plan or design so as to avoid any unreasonable risk of harm to anyone who is likely to be exposed to the danger when the product is used in the manner for which the product was intended, as well as an unintended yet reasonably foreseeable use. [Citations omitted.] *Micallef v. Miehle Company*, 348 N.E.2d 571 (N.Y. Ct. App. 1976).

6. As a practical matter, the duty of a product manufacturer is comprised of the reasonable conduct expected of manufacturers under the same or similar circumstances and whether the manufacturer's conduct creates a foreseeable risk that the product user would be harmed by a defect in the product. Both parts of the duty element are typically fact questions for the jury.

7. Although the courts took considerable time to impose a duty on manufacturers to make safe products, some now argue that the duty is too large and that manufacturers are required, in effect, to insure their products against all harm. Others believe that manufacturers should do more to make products safer. *See* Wheeler, *The Need for Narrow Tort Reform: Abolishing Strict Product Liability,* in *Product Liability Reform: Debating the Issues,* Kenneth L. Chilton, ed. 1990; Henderson and Eisenber, *The Quiet Revolution in Product Liability: An Empirical Study of Legal Change,* 37 U.C.L.A. L. Rev. (1990).

8. What action was the defendant in *Huset v. J. I. Case* required to take to position the case for dismissal by the district court? Why was that action not successful? What other procedural tool was available to J. I. Case to procure a dismissal from the district court? Would any of these other methods have been more successful for J. I. Case?

9. How does an attorney advise manufacturers to convey product warnings? To whom does the seller owe a duty to warn? What if the user of the product is a minor or a person who does not recognize the inherent danger of the product? See *Moning v. Alfono* (Mich. 1977) (slingshot entrusted to a minor; *Ray v. Suburban Supply Co.* (Tenn. Ct. App. 1982) (wet cement supplied to workers who did not appreciate danger of skin contact).

10. If a party who is not the product seller undertakes its repair, why is negligence the plaintiff's only available theory? See *Watts v. Rubber Tree, Inc.,* 853 P.2d 1365 (Ore. Ct. App. 1993). If there is more than one party defendant who brought about plaintiff's injuries, how can damages be apportioned? Should damages be apportioned in such an instance?

Causation

Actual causation-in-fact requires that the defect that brings about plaintiff's harm be traceable to the defendant. In this sense, causation is a fact question that determines whether the complained-about defect was ultimately responsible for plaintiff's injuries or damages. The phrase *proximate cause* is synonymous with *direct result* when used to communicate the relationship between a defendant's negligent act and the plaintiff's injury. In product liability cases, plaintiff's injuries must be caused by the defect in the product.

Causation is often confused with the legal analysis surrounding negligence itself, especially when considering the foreseeability of a plaintiff's injury or damage. The distinction between the two is as different as fact versus law: causation is an analysis of the facts in each specific case regarding the connection between defendant's negligent act and plaintiff's harm; foreseeability determines whether the law imposes an obligation upon the defendant to have anticipated that a plaintiff would have been harmed by the defendant's acts or omissions. For that reason alone, foreseeability is more appropriately an element of the duty and standard of care analysis. If the legal analysis of foreseeability in a case favorably imposes an obligation on defendant to anticipate plaintiff's injury (ordinarily as part of the duty of care) and if the factual analysis of causation reveals that the product defect brought about plaintiff's injury, a court may properly find that the defendant was negligent in having manufactured, designed, or failed to warn about a product defect. In the absence of either, a plaintiff's negligence action will fail.

Additional confusion is often added to the causation analysis by defendants who properly argue the absence of a causal connection between the alleged defect and plaintiff's injuries as a matter of law. For instance, defendants may argue that a plaintiff's case is without causation because the law does not recognize plaintiff's injuries to be a part of the natural chain of incidents arising from the negligent act. See *Palsgraf v. Long Island R. Co.*, 248 N.Y. 339, 162 N.E. 99 (N.Y. 1928). But these cases merely recognize that specific factual scenarios have already been excluded as a causation-in-fact between a negligent act and plaintiff's injuries as a matter of law by another court's ruling and do not include any specific legal analysis other than setting a precedent based on that particular factual scenario. Conversely, res ipsa loquitur and negligence per se actions recognize factual circumstances that already imply causation-in-fact, and therefore liability, as a matter of law.

 CASE LAW ──◆

◆ **evidence of causation in fact between manufacturer's negligence and plaintiff's harm**

General Motors Corp. v. Davis, 233 S.E.2d 825 (Ga. Ct. App. 1977).

Plaintiff Davis brought wrongful death action against defendant truck manufacturer for allegedly defective alternator in a truck that failed to operate in rush-hour traffic, causing an accident that killed Davis' husband. The truck was operated by a third party, W. L. Brown. Davis' spouse was driving a Volkswagen automobile immediately behind the truck. The trial court denied defendant GM's motion for summary judgment challenging causation.

Stolz, J.

* * *

General Motors argues that, as a matter of law, its alleged negligence was not the proximate cause of the fa-

tal collision. It is the contention of General Motors: (1) that there was no causation in fact linking its alleged negligence to the death of the decedent, (2) that is owed no duty to the decedent in its construction of the faulty alternator, and (3) that the collision was such a remote consequence of its alleged negligence as to break the chain of proximate cause. None of these contentions has any merit when applied to the facts as outlined above.

1. We find first that there was causation in fact linking General Motors' alleged negligence to the freeway death. In other words, the "but for" test mentioned by General Motors in oral argument has been met.

According to Prosser, the "but for" rule may be stated as follows: "The defendant's conduct is not a cause of the event, if the event would have occurred without it." W. Prosser, Law of Torts (4th Ed. 1971), 239. In the instant case, if General Motors had not negligently manufactured the alternator, the truck would not have stalled, and there would not have been a stationary vehicle on the freeway for the decedent to hit. Therefore, causation in fact does exist.

2. General Motors also claims that, under the rule expressed by Judge Cardozo in *Palsgraf v. Long Island R. Co.,* 248 N.Y. 339,162 N.E. 99 (1928), it owed no duty to the decedent because he was outside their "ambit of risk" in construction of the alternator. This contention, too, is without merit.

In the construction of vehicles intended for use on our highways, the entire motoring public is arguably within the ambit of risk. A jury could reasonably find that the malfunction of a piece of automotive equipment would place any person using a highway in danger of property danger or bodily injury. [Citations omitted.]

"It was not necessary that the defendant should have had notice of the particular method in which an accident would occur, if the possibility of an accident was clear to the ordinarily prudent eye." *Munsey v. Webb,* 231 U.S. 150,156, 34 S.Ct. 44, 45, 58 L.Ed. 162. [Citations omitted.]

3. General Motors next alleges, citing *Whitehead v. Republic Gear Co.,* 102 F.2d 84 (9th Cir. 1939), that the principle of remoteness releases it from liability. The principle of remoteness is applicable to situations where an intervening agency, such as the negligence of another, may bring about the plaintiff's injury. [Citations omitted.] In *Whitehead,* a truck became disabled on a highway due to the manufacturer's negligence, and a motorist later collided with the stationary vehicle. The accident was found to have been caused by either the negligence of the plaintiff himself or the driver of the disabled truck, such intervening negligence making the collision a remote consequence of the manufacturer's negligence.

[Here], a jury could find that there was no intervening cause that broke the chain of causation linking the collision to the manufacturer's alleged negligence. A jury could reasonably conclude that the occurrences subsequent to General Motors' alleged negligence were natural and foreseeable results of its negligence that did not insulate the manufacturer from liability. [Citation omitted.]

Case Notes: Causation

1. To what degree do courts consider the fact that the nature of an action is negligent, rather than intentional? Is the level of the defendant's intent pertinent to the question of causation? At least one court considered the first question and made the following comments:

In determining how far the law will trace causation and afford a remedy, the facts as to the defendant's intent, his imputable knowledge, or his justifiable ignorance are often taken into account . . . for an intended injury the law is astute to discover even very remote causation. For one which the defendant merely ought to have anticipated it has often stopped at an earlier stage of the investigation of causal connection. And as to those where there was neither knowledge nor duty to foresee, it has usually limited accountability to direct and immediate results. (Derosier v.

New England Telephone & Telegraph Cot, 130 A. 145 (N.H. 1925)).

2. A defendant's breach of its duty is actionable only if that breach was the proximate cause of plaintiff's injuries. The New Jersey Supreme Court put it this way:

[T]he critical consideration in the context of multiple factors contributing to the cause of the accident, is whether the faulty act was itself too remote or insignificantly related to the accident. If it can fairly be regarded as sufficiently remote or insignificant in relation to the eventual accident then, in a legal sense, such fault does not constitute "a cause of the accident . . . [but] simply prevents the condition under which the injury was received[.] (Latta v. Caulfield, 398 A.2d 91 (N.J. 1979)).

3. Causation is but one element of several that determines an even-handed and fair application

of the law in product liability suits that are lodged in negligence. The New Jersey Supreme Court recognized this role for causation in the following:

> Utilization of [the] term [proximate cause] to draw judicial lines beyond which liability will not be extended is fundamentally . . . an instrument of fairness and policy, although the conclusion is frequently expressed in the confusing language of causation, "foreseeability" and "natural and probable consequences." Many years ago a case in this State hit it on the head when it was said that the determination of proximate cause by a court is to be based "upon mixed considerations of logic, common sense, justice, policy and precedent." *Zaza v. Marquess and Nell, Inc.,* 144 N.J. 34, 64, 675 A.2d 620 (1996) *quoting Caputzal v. Lindsay Co.,* 58 N.J. 69, 77, 222 A.2d 513 (1966).

4. How does the *but for* test prove or disprove plaintiff's causation-in-fact in a negligence action for a defectively made product? In *Davis,* would the decedent have died in the automobile accident even if defendant manufacturer had not brought about the accident? Can there be more than one proximate cause of a plaintiff's injury?

5. Facts that comprise an intervening cause and, thus, sever the chain of causation between the defective product and plaintiff's harm must also be considered in a negligence case. In *McCarthy v. Sturm, Ruger and Co., Inc.,* 916 F.Supp. 366, 372 (S.D.N.Y. 1996), the federal court found that acts by the handgun owner broke all potential causation between the allegedly defective product and plaintiff's harm (wrongful death). There, the court held the following opinion:

> Defendant [ammunition manufacturer] argues that plaintiffs' claims must be dismissed for the separate reason that Ferguson's actions constitute the proximate cause of plaintiffs' injuries. Plaintiffs argue that Ferguson's acts were forseeable, and thus the issue of proximate causation should be left for the finder of fact to resolve. [Citation omitted.]

> In general, questions of whether an intervening act severs the chain of causation depend on the foreseeability of the intervening act and should be determined by the finder of fact. [Citation omitted.] However, in appropriate circumstances, the court may resolve the issue as a matter of law. [Citation omitted.] "Those cases generally involve independent intervening acts which operate upon but do not flow from the original" breach. In *Derdiarian v. Felix Contracting Corp.,* 414 N.E.2d 666, 670 (N.Y. Ct. App. 1980), the Appellate Division held that the seller of a shotgun could not be liable in a wrongful death action because the acts of the killer were the sole proximate cause of the injuries. "The sale of a shotgun merely furnished the condition for the unfortunate occurrence." *Jantzen v. Leslie Edleman of New York, Inc.,* 206 A.D.2d 406, 614 N.Y.S.2d 722 (2d Dep't. 1994). Here, as the *Forni* court found, "Ferguson's conduct was an extraordinary act which broke the chain of causation." [Citation omitted.] Therefore, plaintiffs' complaint fails to state a claim in . . . negligence [.]

6. How does foreseeability assist in determining a defendant manufacturer's negligence? Is foreseeability essential to a finding of causation? Is foreseeability essential to a plaintiff's cause of action for negligence?

7. In a negligence analysis, is foreseeability an element in determining the defendant's duty of care or an element in proving causation-in-fact? Does it make a difference in which category foreseeability fits as long as plaintiff proves that the manufacturing defendant was able to reasonably anticipate that plaintiff's injury would result from defendant's acts or omissions?

8. What sources of proof are available for plaintiff to bring as evidence of her causation-in-fact? What is the best evidence available? How does a plaintiff plead and prove causation? What evidence is sufficient to prove causation? What role should expert witnesses play in proving or disproving causation? Do lay witnesses typically have any available evidence of the rela-

tionship between a defendant manufacturer's breach of its duty of care and plaintiff's injuries? What would that evidence typically be?

9. What evidence is inadmissible to prove causation? Why? How can counsel determine the best source of evidence upon which to prove causation? Under what circumstances can the court determine whether plaintiff has pre-

sented sufficient evidence of causation-in-fact? In what ways can the defendant challenge plaintiff's proof of causation?

10. Given the observations of the court in *Derosier v. New England Telephone & Telegraph, supra*, how might litigants in a negligence action deal with that judicial perspective?

 CASE LAW ——————————————————————————————————◆

Foreseeability

◆ **distinguishing foreseeability from causation**

McCarthy v. Sturm, Ruger and Co., Inc., 916 F.Supp. 366 (S.D.N.Y. 1996).

Defendant manufacturer Olin Corporation moved trial court to dismiss plaintiff's negligent manufacturing claim on argument that Olin had no duty to protect train passengers from the criminal misuse of bullets in a handgun.

Baer, District Judge.

I. Negligence.

Plaintiffs first claim that Olin negligently manufactured and marketed the Black Talon ammunition. *Complaint,* ¶ 117. To state a claim for negligence under New York law, a plaintiff must demonstrate that the defendant owed her a duty of care. [Citations omitted.] "In the absence of a duty, there is no breach and without a breach there is no liability." [Citation omitted.] The existence of a legal duty is a question of law for the court to determine. [Citation omitted.]

A. *Negligent Manufacturing.*

Plaintiff's negligent manufacturing claim alleges that Olin breached a duty because it was foreseeable that criminals would use the Black Talon ammunition to injure innocent people such as the plaintiffs. *Complaint* ¶ 117. While this factual allegation of foreseeability may be true, and for purposes of this motion it must be treated as such, the legal conclusion of negligence does not

follow. The New York Court of Appeals has held that foreseeability must be distinguished from duty. *Pulka,* 40 N.W.2d at 785, 390 N.W.S.2d at 396, 358 N.E.2d at 1022 ("Foreseeability should not be confused with duty."). The issue of foreseeability is only relevant in determining the scope of a preexisting duty; it is not normally used to create a duty. *Id.; see also Strauss,* 65 N.Y.2d at 402, 492 N.Y.S.2d at 557, 482 N.E.2d at 36 ("Duty in negligence cases is defined neither by foreseeability of injury nor by privity of contract.") (Citation omitted).

Plaintiffs argue that because Olin could have foreseen criminal misuse of its product, it should not have manufactured the ammunition. Plaintiffs do not allege, however, that any special relationship existed between Olin and Ferguson that would give Olin the authority and ability to control Ferguson's actions. In the absence of such a relationship, New York courts do not impose a duty to control the actions of third parties. [Citations omitted.] Furthermore, in determining the existence of a duty, New York courts attempt to limit the scope of potential liability to a controllable degree in an effort to protect defendants from infinite liability exposure. [Citations omitted.] To impose a duty on Olin to prevent criminal misuse of its products would make it an insurer against such occurrences. Such liability exposure would be limitless and thus to impose a duty here would be inappropriate.

I am sympathetic to plaintiffs' implications that Olin was under a moral duty not to produce ammunition with the destructive capabilities of the

Black Talon bullets. In setting the scope of legal duty, however, the New York Court of Appeals has held that "[a] person may have a moral duty to prevent injury to another, but no legal duty." *Pulka,* 40 N.W.2d at 785, 390 N.W.S.2d at 396, 358 N.E.2d at 1022. As I can find no grounds upon which to base a legal duty, plaintiffs' negligent manufacturing claim must be dismissed.

Case Notes: Foreseeability

1. Causation is "[t]he fact of being the cause of something produced or of happening. The act by which an effect is produced." 200 Black's Law Dictionary (5th Ed. 1979). Foreseeability is "the ability to see or know in advance; hence, the reasonable anticipation that harm or injury is a likely result of acts or omissions." *Id.* at 584. As an element of proximate cause, foreseeability is typically found where the wrongdoer is responsible for the consequence that is probable according to ordinary and usual experience. *Id.* In this way, foreseeability is a legal concept that is appropriately applied as a matter of law by the court. Conversely, causation is a fact question that will be found or not found by a jury or finder of fact at trial. The exception to this rule is res ipsa loquitur in which causation essentially becomes a legal finding based upon the precedent of a particular occurrence or circumstance.

2. In *McCarthy,* the New York federal district court precisely stated that foreseeability is "only relevant in determining the *scope of a preexisting duty;* it is *not normally used to create a duty.*" *McCarthy,* 916 F.Supp. at 369 (emphasis added). In a negligence analysis, foreseeability should be regarded as an ingredient that defines the scope of the defendant's duty, not the existence of the defendant's duty.

TYPES OF NEGLIGENCE ACTIONS AGAINST PRODUCT MANUFACTURERS AND SELLERS

Negligence actions in product liability cases typically fall into three categories: negligent manufacturing, negligent design, and negligent failure to warn. Failure to warn cases commonly present facts that allege even more distinct actions, which include the manufacturer or retailer's failure to provide any warning at all, a failure to give an adequate and effective warning, or a failure to place an adequate warning in a location that will reach the product's intended users. Finally, product cases also appear as res ipsa loquitur or negligence per se actions, which find the existence of a defendant's negligent behavior based on previously recognized factual circumstances or previously violated statutes or regulations.

Negligent Manufacturing

§ 395 *Restatement (Second) of Torts (1965).* **Negligent Manufacture of Chattel Dangerous Unless Carefully Made.** A manufacturer who fails to exercise reasonable care in the manufacture of a chattel which, unless carefully made, he should recognize as involving an unreasonable risk of causing physical harm to those who use it for a purpose for which the manufacturer should expect it to be used and to those whom he should expect to be endangered by its probable use, is subject to liability for physical harm caused to them by its lawful use in a manner and for a purpose for which it is supplied.

 CASE LAW

◆ **liability for negligently manufactured product**

Stevens v. Durbin-Durco, Inc., 377 S.W.2d 343 (Mo. 1964).

Plaintiff Stevens was injured when a load binder used in truck hauling suddenly released and struck Stevens in the face. Trial court sustained defendant's motion for directed verdict at the end of plaintiff's case, thereby rendering judgment for the defendant manufacturer. Stevens appealed complaining that he had sufficient evidence of Durbin-Durco's negligent manufacturing of the load binder.

HOUSER, Commissioner.

* * *

The manufacturer of a product which is potentially dangerous when applied to its intended use [Citation omitted], or reasonably certain to place life and limb in peril when negligently made [Citations omitted], is under a duty to a remote user to exercise ordinary care in its manufacture, and is liable to a remote user injured thereby if the injury results from a latent defect bespeaking lack of ordinary care in making the product. [Citations omitted.]

But the manufacturer is not liable as an insurer, and he is under no obligation to make the product accident proof or foolproof. [Citation omitted.] Since practically any product, regardless of its type or design, is capable of producing injury when put to particular uses, "a manufacturer has no duty so to design his product as to render it wholly incapable of producing injury." HURSH, *AMERICAN LAW OF PRODUCTS LIABILITY,* Vol. 1, § 2:59, p. 240. The manufacturer of a butcher knife, cleaver, or axe, properly made and free of latent defects and concealed dangers, may not be held liable merely because someone was injured while using the product. Thus a manufacturer is not liable to a man who while using an iron dumbbell drops it on his foot. [Citations omitted.]

The extent and limits of the duty of a manufacturer of a product dangerous because of the use to which it is to be applied depend upon the nature and character of the defect and of plaintiff's knowledge thereof . . . the manufacturer may be held liable if the defect or danger is latent or concealed, but where the danger is open, obvious and apparent, or the user has actual knowledge of the defect or danger, there is no liability on the manufacturer. [Citations omitted.] In Campo v. Scofield, supra, the New York Court of Appeals said: "Suffice it to note that, in cases dealing with a manufacturer's liability for injuries to remote users, the stress has always been upon the duty of guarding against *hidden* defects and of giving notice of *concealed* dangers." The duty of the manufacturer in such case is satisfied by the manufacture of a product which is free of latent defects and concealed dangers. The rule, stated as lately as January 24, 1964 by the Supreme Court of Wyoming, is that "* * * [T]he manufacturer * * * of a machine, dangerous because of the way in which it functions, and patently so, owes to those who use it a duty merely to make it free from latent defects and concealed dangers. * * * Accordingly, if a remote user sues a manufacturer * * * for injuries suffered, he must allege and prove the existence of a latent defect or a danger not known to plaintiff or other users." [Citations omitted.]

If we assume by way of argument that the representations in the manufacturer's literature made the cheater pipe an integral part of the load binder; that the use of a cheater pipe introduced the dangers we have noted and that such dangers were in addition to those inherent in the use of the binder without a cheater pipe, and that the possible dangers by the use of the cheater pipe were in the nature of concealed dangers, such assumptions still would not change the applicable principles or the result under the facts of this case. That is because plaintiff's evidence clearly showed that the addition of the cheater pipe did not play any part in causing of the accident. As noted, the pipe did not slip but fitted tightly at all times as though it were in an integral part of the load binder.

Is the rule as to latent defects and concealed dangers affected by plaintiff's charge that defendant should have equipped the product with a safety ratchet to prevent "kick-back"? We think not in this case. A manufacturer is not obliged to adopt only those features which represent the ultimate in safety or design. [Citations omitted.] A manufacturer is not under any duty "to provide a guard or other protective device to prevent injury from a patent peril or a source manifestly dangerous." Hursh, American Law of Products Liability, Vol. 1, § 2:12, p. 133, citing Strickler v. Sloan, (1957) 127 Ind.App. 370, 141 N.E.2d 863. Accordingly, where the product is free of latent defects and concealed dangers; where the perilous nature of the product and the danger of using it is obvious and not concealed; where its normal functioning creates no danger not known to or appreciated by the user; where it is properly manufactured to accomplish the function for which it is designed, the manufacturer has "satisfied the law's demands" and is under no duty to make it "more" safe by providing a built-in safety device. [Citations omitted.]

Here the load binder was structurally sound. It did not disintegrate, break down, crack or fail. The perilous nature of the product was obvious and apparent to plaintiff; its lack of a safety ratchet was plain to be seen. Its use created no danger not known to and appreciated by plaintiff, an experienced trucker who had used load binders for years and knew and appreciated full well their dangerous characteristics and propensities. Plaintiff, with this knowledge and appreciation, cannot recover from the manufacturer simply because he was hurt through a mishap in the normal use of the load binder, which reacted in the normal and foreseeable manner anticipated by the user. To so rule would be to make an insurer of the manufacturer. The full measure of defendant's duty was to manufacture a load binder structurally sound and free from any latent defect or concealed danger. The evidence affirmatively shows that the device complied with these requirements. Plaintiff's "injury through the medium of such an agency is neither a probable nor natural result of anything done or left undone by the maker." Bohlen, Studies in the Law of Torts, (1926), p. 126.

Since plaintiff failed to show the existence or breach of any duty owed to this plaintiff we do not reach the question whether the court erred in ruling that plaintiff is barred because he assumed the risk.

Judgment affirmed.

Case Notes: Negligent Manufacturing

1. In *Stevens,* the Missouri Supreme Court recognized that a product manufacturer is not an insurer of its goods and that the manufacturer is not liable for open and obvious dangers. See *Campo v. Scofield,* 95 N.E.2d 802 (N.Y. Ct. App. 1950). Later development of the manufacturer's duty of care continued to maintain that the manufacturer was not an insurer of its products but was liable for open and obvious dangers that resulted from defects in the product's manufacturing, design, or labeling. See *Micallef v. Miehle Company,* 348 N.E.2d 571 (N.Y. Ct. App. 1976); *Andrulonis v. U.S.,* 724 F.Supp. 1421, 1492 (N.D.N.Y. 1981).

2. What evidence did plaintiff Stevens lack in order to make a submissible case of negligent manufacturing against defendant Durbin-Durco? Did plaintiff have sufficient evidence of a negligent design case given that his chief complaint was about the safety latch of the load binder? What are the distinctions between a cause of action for negligent design and a cause of action for negligent manufacturing?

3. The subject product need not be inherently dangerous in order for plaintiff to have a viable cause of action against a manufacturer for negligent manufacturing. Comment d of § 395 of the *Restatement (Second) of Torts* (1965) provides the following:

   > Comment d. <u>Not necessary that chattel be inherently dangerous.</u> In order that the manufacturer shall be subject to liability un-

der the rule stated in this Section, it is not necessary that the chattel be "inherently dangerous," in the sense of involving any degree of risk of harm to those who use it even if it is properly made. It is enough that the chattel, if not carefully made, will involve such a risk of harm. It is not necessary that the risk be a great one, or that it be a risk of death or serious bodily harm. . . . The inherent danger, or the high degree of danger, is merely a factor to be considered, as in other negligence cases, as bearing upon the extent of the precautions taken.

4. Manufacturers are typically looked upon to exercise reasonable care in the manufacturing of products. Comment f of § 395 of the *Restatement (Second) of Torts* (1965) provides the following:

> Comment f. <u>Particulars which require care.</u> A manufacturer is required to exercise reasonable care in manufacturing any article which, if carelessly manufactured, is likely to cause harm to those who use it in the manner for which it is manufactured. The particulars in which reasonable care is usually necessary for protection of those whose safety depends upon the character of chattels are (1) the adoption of a formula or plan which, if properly followed, will produce an article safe for the use for which it is sold, (2) the selection of material and parts to be incorporated in the finished article, (3) the fabrication of the article by every member of the operative staff no matter how high or low his position, (4) the making of such inspections and tests during the course of manufacture and after the article is completed as the manufacturer should recognize as reasonably necessary to secure the production of a safe article, and (5) the packing of the article so as to be safe for those who must be expected to unpack it.

5. **Illustration** The John Doe Company manufactured a lawn mower that included a defectively manufactured shield surrounding the cutting blade. The defective lawn mower was sold to the Home and Garden Dealer store, which sold it to Jane Smith. Ms. Smith was injured by the lawn mower. The John Doe Company is subject to liability to Ms. Smith.

6. Even after the *Restatement (Third)* has provided the current enunciation of strict liability principles in product liability suits, some plaintiffs continue to rely upon general negligence allegations, including § 395 of the *Restatement (Second)*, in order to recover from the defendant manufacturer. Evidence of negligent manufacturing comes in varying forms. In *Miller v. E.I. DuPont de Nemours and Company*, 811 F.Supp. 1286 (E.D. Tenn. 1992), plaintiff consumer claimed to be injured by temporomandibular joint implant and brought suit against defendant manufacturer of a component in the implant. The court granted defendant's summary judgment motion because Miller failed to present evidence of the negligently manufactured component about which she had complained. The court stated the following in its opinion:

> This is a products liability action in which the plaintiff Patricia Elain Miller allegedly was injured by a temporomandibular joint implant containing a substance, known as Proplast. The plaintiffs allege that Proplast "was manufactured, processed, placed in the market place, sold, promoted, supplied, distributed, and/or designed by the defendant in this action." The plaintiffs further allege that the defendant DuPont knew or should have known that Proplast was a dangerous substance, and that as a direct result of the defendant's negligence, the plaintiff Patricia Elaine Miller was severely injured.

> In its motion for summary judgment, the defendant says that the plaintiffs sued the wrong defendant, and that the defendant did not manufacture or sell any substance known as Proplast, but merely supplied polytetrafluroethylene (PTFE) fibers to the manufacturer of Proplast. The defendant says further the PTFE fibers and resins have been used in a variety of products such as non-stick frying pans, valve parts,

tubing, wiring, and electrical parts, since the early 1960s. DuPont says that is was merely a raw material supplier for Vitek, Inc., and that Vitek, using its own patented procedures, manufactured and marketed the substance known as Proplast.

The plaintiffs cite the *Restatement of Torts* (2d) § 395 in support of their position. [Citation omitted.] The plaintiffs' reliance on § 395 is misplaced. The plaintiffs fail to provide any evidence that the defendant negligently manufactured the PTFE supplied to Vitek. Moreover, there is no proof the PTFE was a defective "component part" of the allegedly defective Proplast manufactured by Vitek.

* * *

This Court is presented with a dearth of evidence which could provide some legal principle on which the defendant in this case could be held liable for the injuries allegedly suffered by the plaintiff Ms. Miller. Accordingly, under the facts of this case, Magistrate Judge Murrian's Report and Recommendation will be accepted in whole by this Court, and the plaintiffs' claim will be dismissed.

7. In *Miller,* what evidence would have sufficiently proven that the defendant DuPont did negligently manufacture the product that ultimately harmed Ms. Miller? What do you believe was the requisite standard of care?

8. In *Miller,* what liability did DuPont have, if any, as a supplier of raw material that was ultimately incorporated into the final product? Are individual component part manufacturers typically held liable for defective products manufactured by them but ultimately incorporated into a final product or a larger assembly?

Negligent Design

§ 398 *Restatement (Second) of Torts* **(1965). Chattel Made Under Dangerous Plan or Design.** A manufacturer of a chattel made under a plan or design which makes it dangerous for the uses for which it is manufactured is subject to liability to others whom he should expect to use the chattel or to be endangered by its probable use for physical harm caused by his failure to exercise reasonable care in the adoption of a safe plan or design.

 CASE LAW ──────────────────────────────◆

◆ **proof of negligent design measured by industry standards**

◆ **negligent design as the proximate cause of plaintiff's injuries**

Del Cid v. Beloit Corporation, 901 F.Supp. 539 (E.D.N.Y. 1995).

Plaintiff factory worker lost his right leg when he attempted to free the chain hoist on a plastic injection molding machine manufactured and designed by defendant Beloit. At a bench trial of the case, the Court held that the molding machine was defectively designed.

Trager, District Judge.

* * *

Under New York strict product liability law, a plaintiff may recover for injuries sustained as a result of a design defect where "the product 'was not reasonably safe and the design defect was a substantial factor in causing [the] injury.'" [Citations omitted.] To recover on such a claim, a plaintiff must demonstrate that the manufacturer failed "to exercise that degree of care in his plan or design so as to avoid any unreasonable risk of harm to anyone who is likely to be exposed to the danger when the product is used in the manner for which [it] was intended . . . as well as unintended yet reasonably foreseeable use," [Citations omitted] and that the design defect was the proximate cause of his or her injuries. [Citations omitted.]

The determination of whether a product presents an unreasonable risk of harm involves the balancing of the foreseeability and gravity of the harm with the burden of preventing it. [Citations omitted.] Although the foreseeability of the misuse of a product is relevant to the issue of whether the manufacturer adequately designed the product to guard against the risk, the precise chain of events preceding the misuse need not have been foreseen to require the manufacturer to guard against the consequences of that misuse. [Citation omitted.] Rather, "foreseeability includes the probability of the occurrence of a general type of risk involving the loss, rather than the probability of the occurrence of the precise chain of events preceding the loss. . . ." *Tucci v. Bossert,* 53 A.D.2d 291, 293, 385 N.Y.S.2d 328, 331 (2d Dept 1976).

Based on the applicable New York law, this case presents a number of issues for resolution: (1) was the injection molding machine defectively designed, i.e., whether it presented an unreasonable risk of harm to Del Cid? . . . (3)(a) was the design defect a proximate cause of Del Cid's injury.

* * *

1. Design Defect—Unreasonable Risk of Harm

As stated above, whether a manufacturer designed an unreasonably unsafe product involves a balancing of the foreseeability and gravity of the harm created by the product with the feasibility of a more safe design. [Citation omitted.] Only where the foreseeability and gravity of the harm is so slight or where the "product would be unworkable [were] the alleged missing feature added, or would be so expensive as to be priced out of the market," will the manufacturer be able to escape liability for a defectively designed product. [Citations omitted.]

a. Design Defect—Applicable Industry Safety Standards

To determine whether the plastic injection molding machine presented an unreasonable risk

of harm to Del Cid, it is helpful to examine the industry safety standard applicable to the design and manufacture of such machines. Such standards were promulgated "to eliminate injuries to personnel associated with machine activity." ANSI B151.1-1976, Foreword. Compliance or lack of compliance with industry safety standards, however, is not dispositive of the issue of a design defect [citations omitted], and other evidence concerning the design and safety of the machine may be considered. [Citation omitted.]

At trial there was much discussion on the standards applicable to the guarding of plastic injection molding machines. Although both Del Cid's and Beloit's experts disagreed as to which standard applied to the case, both agreed that the most appropriate standards were promulgated by the American National Standards Institute, Inc. ("ANSI"). [Footnote omitted.] ANSI standards are relied upon by the manufacturers of machinery and by experts in the various fields to conduct evaluations of the safety of machinery and processes. Here, two standards were discussed—the Safety Standard for Mechanical Power Transmission Apparatus ("General Standard"), and the Safety Requirements for the Construction, Care and Use of Horizontal Injection Molding Machines ("Specific Standard").

Section 9 of the General Standard is entitled "Requirements for Guarding by Location." ANSI B151.1-1972. That section provides that "[e]quipment guarded by location shall by remoteness from the working areas remove the foreseeable risk of contact by persons." *Id.* at § 9.1. More specifically, § 9.1.1 of the General Standard provides that "[t]o be guarded by location or position any moving part shall be at least 96 inches above the walkway, platform or work-space. Where the equipment has in-running nips, shear points or moving projections, it shall be a minimum of 108 inches above the pertinent floor, platform, or working level." *Id.* at § 9.1.1.

Section 4.3 of the Specific Standard is entitled "General Guarding (Other than Point-of-Operation Guarding)." ANSI B151.1-1976. That section requires, among other things, the use of rear, fixed, and top guards on areas where certain hazards exist—a condition in the machinery which has the potential to cause injury or damage to property. *Id.* at § 4.3.1-4.3.3. More specifically, § 4.3.2, entitled "Fixed Guards," requires that "[f]ixed guards shall be provided over areas where pinching or shearing hazards exist." *Id.* Further, § 4.3.3, entitled "Top Guard," requires that "[a] top guard shall be installed where it would be possible for an operator standing on the floor to reach over the top of the safety gate." *Id.*

* * *

In sum, based on the evidence at trial, it is clear that the design of the plastic injection molding machine in question did not comply with § 9.1.1 of the General Standard or §§ 4.3.2 or 4.3.3 of the Specific Standard. Therefore, the plastic injection molding machine was defectively designed.

b. Feasibility of a More Safe Design

Del Cid would not be entitled to recover for his injuries unless he could prove that he was exposed to a reasonably foreseeable and grievous risk of harm and that a safer design for the machine was feasible. [Citation omitted.] The evidence at trial indicated that a safer design of the injection molding machine was quite feasible.

Cocchiola [plaintiffs expert] testified that there were at least three alternatives through which the machine could have been made safer. First, the mechanical stop bar could have been extended several feet. By extending the stop bar several feet, the end of the bar would never have passed the side of the oil reservoir, thereby eliminating the shear point. Second, a type of fixed guard called a tube lining could have been affixed around the stop bar, which would also have eliminated the shear point. In fact, a tube lining was in place over the opposite end of the stop bar. Third, any number of other fixed or top guards could have been used to eliminate or guard against the shear point. According to Cocchiola, each of the three alternatives would have cost no more than a few hundred dollars and would not have affected the function or productivity of the machine. Beloit introduced no evidence to contradict these assertions or to show that, so equipped, the machine would have been priced out of the market. [Citations omitted.]

* * *

3. Proximate Cause

In order to sustain a claim for damages as a result of a design defect, a plaintiff must also prove that the defect was the proximate cause of his or her injuries. [Citation omitted.] New York courts interpret proximate cause in design defect cases to require the defect to be a "substantial factor" in causing the injury. [Citations omitted.] Given the characteristics of the plastic injection molding machine involved in this case—an inherently dangerous and partially unguarded machine—and Del Cid's unrefuted explanation of how the accident occurred, it is appropriate to conclude that the design defect was a substantial factor in causing the accident. [Citations omitted.] Simply put, had an appropriate guard been in place over the point of operation of the machine, Del Cid would not have been injured.

* * *

Although a plaintiff's or third-party's negligent acts are always relevant to the issue of damages, seldom are they sufficient to preclude a finding that a design defect was the proximate cause of an injury. [Citations omitted.] Under New York law, a manufacturer can escape liability for producing an unreasonably unsafe product only where the intervening negligent act was abnormal, unforeseeable, and the *sole cause* of the injury. [Citations omitted; emphasis in original.]

* * *

Moreover, within the context of this proximate cause analysis, even if Del Cid's alleged negligent misuse of the machine and Majestic's failure to provide an appropriate chain container and to properly train and supervise Del Cid all were unforeseeable, that would not defeat the fact that Beloit's failure to properly guard the pinch point was a proximate cause of the accident. *See* Restatement (Second) of Torts § 435(1) (1977) ("If the actor's conduct is a substantial factor in bringing about harm to another, the fact that the actor [did not foresee] . . . *the manner in which it occurred does not prevent him from being liable.*") [Citation omitted; emphasis in original.] As Professor Twerski notes, where a product has been defectively designed *and* has been unforeseeably misused by the plaintiff:

The defect was a cause of the injury and the misuse was a cause. Cause cannot be apportioned, only fault . . . proximate cause is after all a legal fiction. It is an analytical tool which helps us decide whether the harm is to be placed at the defendant's doorstep. There is no good reason why the issue raised by proximate cause or intervening cause should not be factored into the apportionment [of fault] between the parties. The relative accountability for the end result is something which can be taken into account in a fault apportionment.

TWERSKI [THE MANY FACES OF MISUSES: AN INQUIRY INTO THE EMERGING DOCTRINE OF COMPARATIVE CAUSATION, 29 Mercer L.Rev. 403, 432 (1978).] At most, therefore, Del Cid's and Majestic's actions can be considered additional proximate causes of the accident making the three parties joint tortfeasors. [Citations omitted.]

Case Notes: Negligent Design and Proximate Cause

1. Manufacturing defects differ from design defects. A Kansas federal court acknowledged one way to distinguish between these two types of defects:

   There is a distinction between a manufacturing defect and a design defect. "A manufacturing defect involves one particular product in which, through some malfunction of the manufacturing process, there exists a defect. A design defect involves the whole line of products and is the result of the manufacturer's choice to adopt a particular design." Comment, Torts—Product Liability—Strict Liability for Defect in Design, 43 Mo.L.Rev. 601, 902 (1978). A manufacturer's failure to warn or failure to adequately warn is another claim separate and apart from a design defect claim or a manufacturing defect claim. All three claims may be brought under theories of strict liability or negligence. See, e.g., *Long v. Deere & Co.*, 715 P.2d 1023 (Kan. 1986) (negligent failure to provide adequate warnings); *Mays v. Ciba-Geigy Corp.*, 661 P.2d 348 (Kan. 1983) (manufacturing defect claim based on strict liability in tort—strict liability for failing to warn also recognized); *Lester v. Magic Chef, Inc.*, 641 P.2d 353 (Kan. 1982) (strict liability under Restatement (Second) of Torts section 402A applied to design defect claim); *Garst v. General Motors Corporation*, 484 P.2d 47 (Kan. 1971) (design defect claim brought under a negligence theory); *Jacobson v. Ford Motor Co.*, 427 P.2d 621 (Kan. 1967) (case went to jury on claims of manufacturing defect and design defect under a theory of negligence).

2. Other ways to distinguish between a manufacturing defect and a design defect will arise from (1) studying the manufacturing process, (2) studying the design drawings, (3) inspecting the product itself for flaws in the structural integrity of its materials or in its assembly, or (4) studying the functionality of the product. In any of these instances, the manufacturing defect in the product, if any, will be embedded in something specific to that product alone. The design defect, if any, will be common among all products of a similar make, model, or type.

3. In *Del Cid*, industry standards assisted the court in determining the applicable standard of care owed by Beloit Corporation in designing the plastic injection molding machine. The court described the industry standards set by the American National Standards Institute ("ANSI"):

   ANSI is a not-for-profit body comprised of representatives from manufacturers, employers, insurers, government agencies, and trade and professional organizations all of which have an interest in the standardization of safety requirements for the construction, care, and use of various types of industrial machinery and processes. The specific standards are promulgated by different committees and are reached by consensus.

Del Cid, 901 F.Supp. at 545, n4.

4. Is ANSI an appropriate body through which a finder of fact may find the appropriate standard of care? What other ANSI-like bodies help determine a standard of care? Must the standard of care always be set by an entity that promulgates or regulates industry standards or is it simply a benchmark? Why must the finder of fact determine anything about the standard of care in a negligent design case?

5. Why did the New York court in *Del Cid* consider such elements as "degree of care" and proximate cause if Del Cid pursued his cause of action for Beloit's defective design under a negligence theory? *See Del Cid* at 901 F.Supp. at 544.

6. What was the principle reason given that allowed the court to find Del Cid's injury to be foreseeable? How did the court explain the finding of causation-in-fact between Beloit's defective design and Del Cid's injury? What was the relationship between the legal element of foreseeability in the case and the factual finding of proximate cause?

7. Some jurisdictions view inadequate warning claims as a design defect because the inadequacy of the warning affected all makes, models, or types of the same product on which the warning was inadequate. Some jurisdictions view inadequate warning claims as an entirely separate subsection of negligence against a product manufacturer or seller. These two types of claims are even more closely aligned under a strict liability theory.

8. Why was the *Del Cid* case tried to the judge in a bench trial and not to a jury? What role do you think expert witnesses played in providing evidence about the industry standards? Was their testimony essential in that regard? What other sources of proof were likely available to plaintiff at trial to prove up the industry standards?

9. Why did Del Cid rely upon industry standards at trial? Could Del Cid, as plaintiff, have made a submissible case at trial based upon a cause of action for negligent design without relying on industry standards? How do the concepts of time and space enter into the foreseeability analysis? How do intervening causes affect the question of foreseeability?

10. "The area within which liability is imposed is that which is within the circle of reasonable foreseeability. Using the original point at which the negligent act was committed or became operative, and thence looking in every direction as the semi-diameters of the circle; and those injuries which from this point could or should have been reasonably foreseen, as something likely to happen, are within the field of liability, while those remote possibilities, those only slightly probable, are beyond and not within the circle—in all of which time, place and circumstance play their respective and important parts." *Mauney v. Gulf Refining Co.*, 9 So.2d 780 (Miss. 1942).

Negligent Failure to Warn

§ 388 Restatement (Second) of Torts (1965). Chattel Known To Be Dangerous For Intended Use. One who supplies directly or through a third person a chattel for another to use is subject to liability to those whom the supplier should expect to use the chattel with the consent of the other or to be endangered by its probable use, for physical harm caused by the use of the chattel in the manner for which and by a person for whose use it is supplied, if the supplier

(a) knows or has reason to know that the chattel is or is likely to be dangerous for the use for which it is supplied, and

(b) has no reason to believe that those for whose use the chattel is supplied will realize its dangerous condition, and

(c) fails to exercise reasonable care to inform them of its dangerous condition or of the facts which make it likely to be dangerous.

 CASE LAW

Duty to Warn

♦ **defendant's duty to warn about commonly-known dangers**

Ex Parte Chevron Chemical Company (Re Don Lawley and Derrick Bryant v. Chevron Chemical Company), 720 So.2d 922 (Ala. 1998).

Plaintiff gas company employees sued defendant manufacturer of plastic pipe, Chevron, when pipeline exploded during installation. Plaintiffs alleged, in part, Chevron's negligent failure to warn about the propensity of static electricity to ignite natural gas fumes. The trial court granted Chevron's motion for summary judgment based on Chevron's argument that it had no duty to warn about the commonly-known dangers of static electricity and natural gas fumes. The Alabama Supreme Court affirmed the trial court's summary judgment.

See, Justice.

* * *

II. Requirement to Warn

A summary judgment is appropriate in a case where there is no genuine issue of material fact and the moving party is entitled to a judgment as a matter of law. [Citations omitted.] We review motions for summary judgment in the light most favorable to the non-movant. To determine whether Chevron is entitled to a judgment as a matter of law, we must determine whether Chevron had a duty to warn Lawley and Bryant of the danger that caused the accident. *See Rose v. Miller & Co.*, 432 So.2d 1237, 1238 (Ala. 1983) (stating that the existence of a legal duty is a question of law for the court, not the jury, to decide).

A. Negligent Failure to Warn

Lawley and Bryant argue first that Chevron negligently failed to warn them, the ultimate users, of the dangers involved in installing the plastic pipe. Lawley and Bryant acknowledge that Chevron gave Mobile Gas a bulletin that stated, "Before You Start . . . ground [pipe] with wet cloth to remove static electricity." Nevertheless, they argue that this warning to Mobile Gas was not adequate to notify them of the severity of the danger posed by static electricity. Chevron responds that it had no duty to warn Lawley and Bryant of a danger of which their employer, Mobile Gas, was already aware.

The duty to warn end users of the dangers of products arises in a pure negligence context, from § 388, Restatement (Second) of Torts, as adopted by this Court. [Citations omitted.]

We have held that the duty to warn contemplated by § 388(c) is triggered only when the supplier has "no reason to believe" that the user will realize the "dangerous condition" of the product referred to in § 388(b). [Citations omitted.] Thus, the manufacturer is not required to provide a redundant warning, but only to provide a warning of those dangers that are not obvious to the user.

Lawley and Bryant cite *Hicks v. Commercial Union Insurance Co.*, 652 So.2d 211 (Ala. 1994), in support of their contention that Chevron had a duty to notify Mobile Gas notwithstanding the fact that Mobile Gas was aware of the danger posed by static electricity buildup and the fact that Mobile Gas had informed its employees of this danger. In *Hicks*, the manufacturer of a pipe stopper was sued after the pipe stopper dislodged during a hydrostatic pressure test and struck an employee. The manufacturer had provided an instruction booklet with a warning that pipe stoppers are dangerous and that people should not stand in front of the pipe stopper during pressure testing. *Id.* at 217. The manufacturer presented evidence indicating that the danger of pipe stoppers coming loose was common knowledge among employees who used them. *Id.* This Court, however, focused on the lack of evidence of common knowledge that mismatching of the jaws of pipe stopper would greatly increase the likelihood of an accident. *Id.* This Court held that the evidence indicating common knowledge of a general danger did not relieve the manufacturer of its duty to warn, and that there was a genuine issue of material fact as to the adequacy of the warning provided by the manufacturer. *Id.*

This case is unlike Hicks, however, because the undisputed evidence in this case establishes that among installers of plastic pipe it was common knowledge that the failure to properly ground the pipe during the purging process would greatly increase the danger that static electricity would build up and ignite natural gas and cause a fire. The warning printed in Mobile Gas's manual expressly stated:

> Particular attention to prevention of static electric discharge shall be practiced. When plastic gas lines are broken or being purged, static electric charges have been known to build up and, in some instances, cause a fire. . . . The best grounding device to date appears to be wet rags over the pipe and wet to the earth. . . .

Thus, not only was the specific danger of failure to ground the plastic pipes with wet rags during the purging process known in the industry and known to the employer, Mobile Gas, an experienced user, but it was published by Mobile Gas in a manual given to the very employees who were injured. That manual, with the specific warning, was in the truck by the work site where the injury took place. It is undisputed that had Lawley and Bryant followed the safety procedure described in the manual provided to them, and used wet rags to ground the pipe during the purging process, they would not have been injured. Accordingly, Chevron did not have a duty to provide Mobile Gas or its employees with a warning of a danger of which they already were, or had reason to be, aware.

Case Notes: Duty to Warn

1. Persons who sell or otherwise provide products on the market have an obligation to disclose defects even if the product is not sold to the user. Comment a to § 388 of the *Restatement (Second) of Torts* (1965) provides the following:

   > The words "those whom the supplier should expect to use the chattel" and the words "a person for whose use it is supplied" include not only the person to whom the chattel is turned over by the supplier, but also all those who are members of a class whom the supplier should expect to use it or occupy it or share in its use with the consent of such person, irrespective of whether the supplier has any particular person in mind. Thus, one who lends an automobile to a friend and who fails to disclose a defect of which he himself knows and which he should recognize as making it unreasonably dangerous for use, is subject to liability not only to his friend, but also to anyone whom his friend permits to drive the car or chooses to receive in it as passenger or guest, if it is understood between them that the car may be so used. So too, one entrusting a chattel to a common carrier for transportation must expect that the chattel will be handled by the carrier's employees.

2. The obligation of the product seller to inform about the dangerous nature of the product is limited to those dangers known by the seller. Comment l of § 388 of the *Restatement (Second) of Torts* (1965) provides the following:

   > The supplier's duty is to exercise reasonable care to inform those for whose use the article is supplied of dangers which are peculiarly within his knowledge. If he has done so, he is not subject to liability, even though the information never reaches those for whose use the chattel is supplied. The factors which deter-

mine whether the supplier exercises reasonable care by giving this information to third persons through whom the chattel is supplied for the use of others are stated in Comment n [warnings given to third persons].

3. If the court had imposed a duty to warn on Chevron, was the warning in the Mobile Gas manual adequate? Did plaintiffs have a cause of action for failure to provide an adequate warning in a sufficiently available location? Why or why not?

4. What circumstances would have to change in order to impose a duty to warn upon Chevron? Does Chevron ever have a duty to warn about the hazards of static electricity?

5. Keeton comments that adequate warnings achieve two separate goals: risk reduction and the protection of individual autonomy and decision-making. W. P. Keeton, PROSSER AND KEETON ON THE LAW OF TORTS (West Publishing Co. 1984) at 685. Did the Court in *Ex Parte Chevron Chemical Company* further these two purposes?

6. In addition to establishing that the product manufacturer had a duty to warn, plaintiff bears the burden of proving that the defendant manufacturer failed to warn. This is difficult in some circumstances. Nevertheless, it is essential in proving plaintiff's case. In *Morris v. Shell Oil Company*, 467 S.W.2d 39, 42 (Mo. 1971), the Missouri Supreme Court recognized the burden of proof in a failure to warn case:

> Plaintiff proved that Shell knew of the dangers involved by introducing the excerpts from the "Industrial Hygiene Bulletin" published by Shell. It was plaintiff's burden, and an essential element of plaintiff's case, that she prove that Shell failed to warn of the dangers involved. [Citation omitted.] In cases where the evidence shows that the manufacturer packaged the product in a container received by the consumer, evidence by the consumer that no warning was received on the container may also be evidence that no warning was given. This was not the situation in this case. The product was sold by Shell in carload lots. It was Shell's duty to warn [the

wholesaler] of the dangers involved, with the intention that such warning be given the ultimate consumer. [Citation omitted.] Since there was no evidence that Shell failed to give a warning to [the wholesaler], the plaintiff failed to sustain her burden.

7. Finally, comments to the *Restatement (Second)* provided reassurance that the product seller (and manufacturer) were required to give warnings and, in return, an assumption that if such warnings were provided, that the product user would read the warnings and follow them. *See* comment j to the *Restatement (Second)*.

8. If the product manufacturer had a duty to warning but failed to do so, plaintiff is typically entitled to a presumption of causation. Specifically, absence of a warning will be causation-in-fact evidence that the product manufacturer's breach of the duty to warn did, in fact, result in plaintiff's injury or harm. An Indiana appellate court put it this way:

> Comment j provides a presumption that an adequate warning would be heeded. This operates to the benefits of a manufacturer where adequate warnings in fact are given. Where warnings are inadequate, however, the presumption is in essence a presumption of causation.

Ortho Pharmaceutical Corp. v. Chapman, 388 N.E.2d 541, 553 (Ind. App. 1 Dist. 1979); see also *Jarrell v. Monsanto Co.*, 528 N.E.2d 1158, 1162 (Ind.App. 2 Dist. 1988).

9. Some product liability theorists do not believe that a causation presumption is the logical consequence of comment j to 402A of the *Restatement (Second)*. In their article *Doctrinal Collapse in Products Liability: The Empty Shell of Failure to Warn*, 65 N.Y.U.L.Rev. 265(1990), James Henderson and Aaron Twerski argue that the question of causation is never actually considered because once the defendant has given an adequate warning that is likely to reach many consumers, then it may be assumed that consumers will act on the warning. In this way, defendant proves the discharge of her underlying duty to warn, which brings an end to plaintiff's failure to warn claim without consideration of causation.

Failure to Place Warning in a Recognizable Location

The failure to warn theory comes in as many different forms as the failure to manufacture or design properly. In some instances, the product manufacturer's supposed failure is not the absence of a warning but the inability to place the warning in a place where the product user is likely to see it and adhere to its instructions. Other types of inadequate warnings are discussed later in this text.

 CASE LAW ◆

◆ **failure to provide a warning in a recognizable location**

Lockart v. Kobe Steel Ltd.
Construction Machinery
Div., 989 F.2d 864 (5th Cir. 1993).

Injured plaintiff workers sued manufacturer of excavator, Kobe Steel, claiming that the manufacturer failed to provide a sufficiently located warning about the proper use of defendant's hydraulic excavator. Plaintiffs rigged a chain about the bucket teeth of the excavator to suspend a steel pontoon for repairs. Plaintiffs were injured when the pontoon slipped from the chain. The district court granted summary judgment for the defendant manufacturer, and the Fifth Circuit affirmed on appeal.

Wisdom, Circuit Judge.

* * *

In the operator's manual, as is seen in the diagram below, item number 17 states: "Never lift a load from the bucket teeth." An illustration of a load being lifted by the bucket teeth with an "X" through the diagram is directly underneath this warning. This warning is unequivocal. The plaintiffs assert therefore that it must be a reasonably anticipated use because Kobelco specifically warned against it. In other words, Kobelco is to be hoist by its own petard.

* * *

When a manufacturer expressly warns against using the product in a certain way in clear and direct language accompanied by an easy to understand pictogram, it is expected that an ordinary consumer would not use the product in contravention of the express warning. Here,

however, the owners manual and thus the warning probably never reached the ultimate users.

In a case arising from Mississippi, this Court has held that in addition to a warning in a manual being inadequate because it was not clear, it was also inadequate because placing the warning in the manual as opposed to placing it on the product would not reasonably bring the warning to the attention of the users of the product. [Footnote omitted.]

With regard to the excavator in this case, there are many warnings which are as worthy of display as the admonition not to lift a load from the bucket teeth. The preceding warning for example instructs the operator what to do in the event that the excavator comes into contact with live power lines. This warning to remain in one's seat if at all possible is at least as important as the bucket teeth one. With a piece of machinery as complex as an excavator, there are numerous warnings which might seem to be required to be placed on the equipment, but as the *Broussard* court stated, it is simply impractical to place all these on the product rather than in a manual. Further even if the warning had been placed on the bucket scoop, it would have made no difference in this case, because the original scoop made by Kobelco was replaced with a scoop made by another manufacturer. This would be a different case if the plaintiffs had presented evidence that despite the warnings, Kobelco should have been aware that operators were using the excavator in contravention of certain warnings. No evidence suggests such a scenario.

Even if the warning did not reach the users, the LPLA [Louisiana Products Liability Act] speaks of "an ordinary person in same or similar circumstances." [Footnote omitted.] These users had many years experience mining and working with heavy machinery, and both had taken company courses in equipment handling in 1986. The dangers of using the bucket to suspend a heavy pontoon should have been obvious to the ordinary consumer and certainly to experienced workers.

The district court, therefore, did not err in granting a summary judgment based on its holding that Dixon and Sullivan's use of the excavator to suspend the pontoon was not a reasonably anticipated use within the meaning of the Louisiana Products Liability Act.

Case Notes: Failure to Provide a Sufficiently Located Warning

1. In Lockart, the LPLA provided that

    The user or handler of the product already knows or reasonably should be expected to know of the characteristic of the product that may cause damage and the danger of such characteristic.

    See La.R.S. 9:2800.57 B(2), the Louisiana Product Liability Act, as cited in *Lockart,* 989 F.2d at 868, n13.

    Does this statute provide the basis to determine the product manufacturer's standard of care regarding the adequacy or inadequacy of a product warning? What other bases are available? Is it appropriate to use a strict liability statute as the basis for the product manufacturer's standard of care in a negligence case?

2. The LPLA also provided that

    B. A product is unreasonably dangerous if and only if:

    . . .

    (2) The product is unreasonably dangerous because an adequate warning about the product has not been provided as provided in La.R.S. 9:2800.57[.]

    See La.R.S. 9:2800.54.

    Does this statute apply to a negligence theory? Does the statute provide a basis for the standard of care that should be imposed on the product manufacturer? How should the court distinguish between the proof that a plaintiff must provide in proving a negligence case and the proof that plaintiff must provide in a strict liability case?

3. If a product manufacturer provided a well-worded and sufficiently detailed instruction about the proper use of the product but simply positioned the warning label in a place that was not commonly viewed by the product user, is the manufacturer liable for plaintiff's injuries that result from not having read the warning label? Where does the manufacturer's duty to warn end and the plaintiff's duty to avail herself or himself of all warnings, instructions, and guidelines for use of the product begin? Under these circumstances, does the product manufacturer have a viable affirmative defense for plaintiff's comparative fault?

4. Ultimately, product warnings are literally ineffective unless they are well-written and well-placed by the product manufacturer and well-received by the product user. Can Comment j to 402A of the *Restatement (Second)* realistically apply a presumption that product users can and will correctly understand and follow all product warnings that are properly written and placed by the product manufacturer? Some theorists believe that such a presumption is based upon behavioral assumptions that have proven unreliable and that the more critical legal issue is whether even well-written and well-placed warnings should be accepted as substitutes for safe product designs and fair marketing strategies. See Howard Latin, *"Good" Warnings, Bad Products, and Cognitive Limitations,* 41 U.C.L.A. L. Rev. 1193 (1994).

Res Ipsa Loquitur

§ 328D Restatement (Second) of Torts (1965). Res Ipsa Loquitur.

(1) It may be inferred that harm suffered by the plaintiff is caused by negligence of the defendant when:

    (a) the event is of a kind which ordinarily does not occur in the absence of negligence;

    (b) other responsible causes, including the conduct of the plaintiff and third persons, are sufficiently eliminated by the evidence; and

    (c) the indicated negligence is within the scope of the defendant's duty to the plaintiff.

(2) It is the function of the court to determine whether the inference may reasonably be drawn by the jury, or whether it must necessarily be drawn.

(3) It is the function of the jury to determine whether the inference is to be drawn in any case where different conclusions may reasonably be reached.

 CASE LAW

◆ **proving res ipsa loquitur**

Escola v. Coca Cola Bottling Co. of Fresno, 150 P.2d 436 (Calif. 1944).

Plaintiff waitress was injured when defendant's bottle broke in her hand. Plaintiff pursued negligence case against defendant under doctrine of res ipsa loquitur. Defendant bottling company disputed application of doctrine in this case. This appeal followed.

Gibson, Chief Justice.

* * *

Res ipsa loquitur does not apply unless (1) defendant had exclusive control of the thing causing the injury and (2) the accident is of such a nature that it ordinarily would not occur in the absence of negligence by the defendant. [Citations omitted.]

    Many authorities state that the happening of the accident does not speak for itself where it took place some time after defendant had relinquished control of the instrumentality causing the injury. Under the more logical view, however, the doctrine may be applied upon the theory that defendant had control at the time of the alleged negligent act, although not at the time of the accident, *provided* plaintiff first proves that the condition of the instrumentality had not been changed after it left the defendant's possession. [Cita-

tions omitted.] . . . Plaintiff must also prove that she handled the bottle carefully. The reason for this prerequisite is set forth in Prosser on Torts [1941] at 300, where the author states: "Allied to the condition of exclusive control in the defendant is that of absence of any action on the part of the plaintiff contributing to the accident. Its purpose, of course, is to eliminate the possibility that it was the plaintiff who was responsible. If the boiler of a locomotive explodes while the plaintiff engineer is operating it, the inference of his own negligence is at least as great as that of the defendant, and res ipsa loquitur will not apply until he has accounted for his own conduct." [Citations omitted.] It is not necessary, of course, that plaintiff eliminate every remote possibility of injury to the bottle after defendant lost control, and the requirement is satisfied if there is evidence permitting a reasonable inference that it was not accessible to extraneous harmful forces and that is was carefully handled by plaintiff or any third person who may have moved or touched it. *Cf.* Prosser, *supra,* p. 300. If such evidence is present, the question becomes one for the trier of fact [citations omitted] and, accordingly, the issue should be submitted to the jury under proper instructions.

* * *

    Upon an examination of the record, the evidence appears sufficient to support a reasonable inference that the bottle here involved was not damaged by any extraneous force after delivery to the restaurant by defendant. It follows, therefore, that the bottle was in some manner defective at the time defendant relinquished control, because sound and properly prepared bottles of carbonated liquids do not ordinarily explode when carefully made.

The next question, then, is whether plaintiff may rely upon the doctrine of res ipsa loquitur to supply an inference that defendant's negligence was responsible for the defective condition of the bottle at the time it was delivered to the restaurant. Under the general rules pertaining to the doctrine, as set forth above, it must appear that bottles of carbonated liquid are not ordinarily defective without negligence by the bottling company.

An explosion such as took place here might have been caused by an excessive internal pressure in a sound bottle, by a defect in the glass of a bottle containing a safe pressure, or by a combination of these two possible causes. The question is whether under the evidence there was a probability that defendant was negligent in any of these respects. If so, the doctrine of res ipsa loquitur applies.

* * *

It thus appears that there is available to the industry a commonly-used method of testing bottles for defects not apparent to the eye, which is almost infallible. Since Coca Cola bottles are subjected to these tests by the manufacturer, it is not likely that they contain defects when delivered to the bottler which are not discoverable by visual inspection. Both new and used bottles are filled and distributed by defendant. The used bottles are not again subjected to the tests referred to above, and it may be inferred that defects not discoverable by visual inspection do not develop in bottles after they are manufactured. Obviously, if such defects do occur in used bottles there is a duty upon the bottler to make appropriate tests before they are refilled, and if such tests are not commercially practicable the bottles should not be re-used. This would seem to be particularly true where a charged liquid is placed in the bottle. It follows that a defect which would make the bottle unsound could be discovered by reasonable and practicable tests.

Although it is not clear in this case whether the explosion was caused by an excessive charge or a defect in the glass there is a sufficient showing that neither cause would ordinarily have been present if due care had been used. Further, defendant had exclusive control over both the charging and inspection of the bottles. Accordingly, all the requirements necessary to entitle plaintiff to rely on the doctrine of res ipsa loquitur to supply an inference of negligence are present.

* * *

Case Notes: Res Ipsa Loquitur

1. Res ipsa loquitur follows the Latin phrase "the thing speaks for itself." The phrase must be used sparingly and be taken to mean no more than its English equivalent or it unnecessarily adds obscurity to a relatively simple concept. The commonly cited example is unsecured items that fall from buildings.

2. Justice Traynor concurred in the result in the *Escola* case and assisted in furthering the development of res ipsa loquitur into strict liability against a product manufacturer through his concurring opinion.

> I concur in the judgment, but I believe the manufacturer's negligence should no longer be singled out as the basis of a plaintiff's right to recover in cases like the present one. In my opinion it should now be recognized that a manufacturer incurs an absolute liability when an article that he has placed on the market, knowing that it is to be used without inspection, proves to have a defect that causes injury to human beings. *MacPherson v. Buick Motor Co.*, 217 N.Y. 382, 111 N.E. 1050 L.R.A.1916F, 696, Ann.Cas.1916C, 440 established the principle, recognized by this court, that irrespective of privity of contract, the manufacturer is responsible for an injury caused by such an article to any person who comes in lawful contact with it. [Citations omitted]. In these cases the source of the manufacturer's liability was his negligence in

the manufacturing process or in the inspection of component parts supplied by others. Even if there is no negligence, however, public policy demands that responsibility be fixed wherever it will most effectively reduce the hazards to life and health inherent in defective products that reach the market. It is evident that the manufacturer can anticipate some hazards and guard against the recurrence of others, as the public cannot. Those who suffer injury from defective products are unprepared to meet its consequences. The cost of an injury and the loss of time or health may be an overwhelming misfortune to the person injured, and a needless one, for the risk of injury can be insured by the manufacturer and distributed among the public as a cost of doing business. It is to the public interest to discourage the marketing of products having defects that are a menace to the public. If such products nevertheless find their way into the market it is to the public interest to place the responsibility for whatever injury they may cause upon the manufacturer, who, even if he is not negligent in the manufacture of the product, is responsible for its reaching the market. However intermittently such injuries may occur and however haphazardly they may strike, the risk of their occurrence is a constant risk and a general one. Against such risk there should be general and constant protection and the manufacturer is best situated to afford such protection. [Citation omitted.]

* * *

Escola, 150 P.2d at 440.

3. Res ipsa loquitur applies to specific circumstances and events, most of which have been tested and have precedential value. Comment c of § 328D of the *Restatement (Second) of Torts* (1965) provides the following:

   c. Type of event. The first requirement for the application of the rule stated in this Section is a basis of past experience which reasonably permits the conclusion that such events do not ordinarily occur unless someone has been negligent. There are many types of ac-

cidents which commonly occur without the fault of anyone. The fact that a tire blows out, or that a man falls down stairs is not, in the absence of anything more, enough to permit the conclusion that there was negligence in inspecting the tire, or in the construction of the stairs, because it is common human experience that such events all too frequently occur without such negligence. On the other hand there are many events, such as those of objects falling from the defendant's premises, the fall of an elevator, the escape of gas or water from mains or of electricity from wires or appliances, the derailment of trains or the explosion of boilers, where the conclusion is at least permissible that such things do not usually happen unless someone has been negligent. To such events res ipsa loquitur may apply.

4. **Illustration** Jack purchases a can of green beans at a local supermarket. The green beans were canned by Midwest Farming Company. When eating the green beans one evening for dinner, Jack is injured by a glass shard concealed inside a green bean. Neither Jack nor any other person did anything after the green beans were opened that would account for the presence of the glass. Without other evidence it may be inferred that the presence of the glass shard in Jack's green beans was the negligence of Midwest Farming Company.

5. Plaintiff's evidence of res ipsa loquitur may be circumstantial. Comment b to § 328D of the *Restatement (Second) of Torts* (1965) provides that:

   b. Circumstantial evidence. Negligence and causation, like other facts, may of course be proved by circumstantial evidence. Without resort to Latin the jury may be permitted to infer, when a runaway horse is found in the street, that owner has been negligent in looking after it; or when a driver runs down a visible pedestrian, that he has failed to keep a proper lookout. When the Latin phrase is used in such cases, nothing is added. A res ipsa loquitur case is ordinarily merely one kind of case of circumstantial evidence, in which the jury may reasonably infer both negligence and causation from the mere occurrence of the event and the defendant's relation to it.

6. A defendant's evidence of its own exercise of reasonable care does not disturb the infer-

ence of res ipsa loquitur. *See* comment n to § 328D of the *Restatement (Second) of Torts (1965).*

Negligence Per Se

Negligence per se is the presumption of a defendant's negligence based upon the defendant's violation of a statute or regulation. The court must determine whether the statute or regulation will act as the defendant's standard of care, and the defendant's alleged violation must also be the causation-in-fact of the plaintiff's harm. Negligence per se is a step away from traditional negligence concepts and a step toward the no-fault provisions of strict liability. Although the product manufacturer's acts may have been sufficient to have violated a statute or regulation, these acts may not have been sufficient to have violated industry standards or to have created the fault of the manufacturer. Depending on the language of the statute or regulation at issue, the liability inquiry begins to focus on the product being regulated or governed rather than the acts of the manufacturer that allegedly brought it to a point of being defective or substandard, which is more akin to a strict liability theory than to negligence theory.

 CASE LAW ──────────────────────────────────────◆

◆ **statutes and regulations as the standard of care**

◆ **proving negligence per se**

McNeil Pharmaceutical v. Hawkins, 686 A.2d 567 (D.C. Ct. App. 1996).

Plaintiff, estate of Elva Mae Gilliam, alleged that pharmaceutical product, Parafon Forte DSC, caused decedent's liver failure and death. At trial, a jury awarded plaintiff $1.5 million in compensatory and $2.5 million in punitive damages. Defendant McNeil appealed arguing that plaintiff had failed to make a submissible case.

King, Associate Judge.

At trial, Hawkins contended that McNeil had violated numerous federal statutes and regulations. Over McNeil's objections, the trial court took judicial notice and provided the jury copies of the following federal statutes and regulations. [Citations omitted] The trial court pro-

vided the jury the full text of the statutes, which contained over sixty-seven pages, copied so that some or all of the text of several other sections of the regulations, the relevance or admissibility of which had never been determined, were also included and therefore available to the jury. Moreover, some of the copies of statutes included case annotations following each provision.

* * *

As a general rule, the plaintiff in a negligence action bears the burden of proving "the applicable standard of care, a deviation from that standard by the defendant, and a causal relationship between that deviation and the plaintiffs injury." See *Toy v. District of Columbia,* 549 A.2d 1, 6 (D.C. 1988); [citations omitted]. In the present case, the plaintiff proceeded on theories of negligence per se and strict liability, which are slight variations on this general rule.

To prevail on a negligence per se theory, the plaintiff may, in certain circumstances and under specified conditions as discussed in Part B, rely on a statute or regulation as proof of the applicable standard of care. [Citation omitted.] Proof of "[an] unexplained violation of that standard renders the defendant negligent as a matter of law," [citation omitted] so long as the violation was the proximate cause of the injuries, and the alleged injuries were of the type which the statute was designed to prevent. [Citations omitted.] If, however, the defendant puts forth evidence excusing the violation, the violation may be considered evidence of negligence rather than negligence per se. [Citations omitted.]

* * *

In sum, under either the per se or strict liability theories, the plaintiff must establish the applicable standard of care, show that the defendant violated that standard, and that the violation was the proximate cause of the injury. The standard of care may be established by looking to the conduct of the industry or profession in similar circumstances—in this case a reasonable pharmaceutical company—or by looking to standards embodied in statutes or regulations. [Citations omitted.]

* * *

McNeil further contends that, at the very least, the jury should have been guided, either by the trial court or through expert testimony, in its application of the statutes. Where the statutes and regulations are admitted as the basis for a finding of negligence per se, or as evidence of negligence, the plaintiff must also prove a deviation from the standard of care, i.e., that the statutes were in fact violated. [Citations omitted.]

The trier of fact is sometimes confronted with issues that require scientific or specialized knowledge or experience in order to be properly understood, and which cannot be determined intelligently merely from the deductions made and inferences drawn on the basis of ordinary knowledge, common sense, and practical experience gained in the ordinary affairs of life. [Citations omitted.] On such issues, the general rule in the district of Columbia is that testimony of one possessing special knowledge or skill is required in order to arrive at an intelligent conclusion. [Citation omitted.] . . . Thus, had Hawkins presented proof of the standard of care, and its breach, through traditional negligence analysis, she would most certainly have been required to present that proof through expert testimony.

In addition, this jurisdiction has required expert testimony to explain the applicability of statutes where the statute is relied upon as establishing the standard of care. In *Hecht Co. v. McLaughlin*, 214 F.2d 212 (D.C. 1954), where the plaintiff was injured by a "modern" door, "not the ordinary type," on the defendant department store's property, the trial court instructed the jury that the violation of a building code regulation would be negligence as a matter of law, but rejected the testimony of a liaison officer of the District of Columbia Building Department that the regulation did not apply to the situation before the court. The United States Court of Appeals for the District of Columbia Circuit, in an opinion binding on us, reversed, noting that the installation of the door had been approved by the Department of Building Inspection, and holding that the trial court's "failure to receive expert testimony as to the interpretation, and consequent admissibility and application, of the regulation, and the instruction that its violation would constitute negligence per se require[d] reversal." *Id.*, 93 U.S. App. D.C. at 386, 214 F.2d at 216. In so holding, the court cited *Wright v. Wardman*, 55 App. D.C. 318, 319, 5 F.2d 380, 381 (1925) (dubiously worded zoning regulation) which held that where there is uncertainty about the meaning of a "statute, ordinance, or regulation," the expert or administrative view will generally control its interpretation. *Wright*, supra, 55 App. D.C. at 319, 5 F.2d at 381.

In this case, for the reasons stated below, in the face of defense experts who testified that there was no breach of the standard of care, and statutes and regulations which required expert explication, we hold that Hawkins was required to present expert testimony concerning the interpretation of the statutes and regulations relied upon by her, so that the jury would be guided in its application of those sources to the conduct at issue in this case. The jury then would have been able to determine whether McNeil deviated from the proper standard of care, i.e., whether McNeil's conduct violated the statutes and regulations. [Footnote omitted.]

* * *

In this case the trial court admitted dozens of statutes and regulations. Our examination satisfies us that, with three possible exceptions, all involve use of generalized language which would require expert testimony to explain to jurors how McNeil violated them. One of the remaining three, 18 U.S.C. § 1001, is clearly not applicable, as we said earlier. The last two statutes at first seem capable of lay application. However, though parts of 15 U.S.C.A. §§ 51-57 (1973 & 1993 Supp.) (prohibiting false advertisements) seem straightforward, the definitional section, § 55, is quite intricate and may involve complicated implementing regulations. Likewise, 21 U.S.C. § 352 (1958) appears straightforward on its face. But lay jurors may not understand, since it is not apparent on the face of the statute, that the statute is supplemented in great detail by the regulations of 21 C.F.R. §§ 201.1-201.316 (1990). Although these regulations were submitted to the jury, lay jurors would be unable to assess how the regulations affect interpretation of the statute without expert testimony to help them apply the appropriate standard of care.

A review of the testimony in this case reveals that Hawkins presented no competent expert testimony regarding the violation of the statutes and regulations submitted to the jury. While Hawkins attempted to elicit testimony regarding violations of the regulations from its "expert" witnesses, she was not allowed to do so because her medical experts lacked expertise in assessing submissions to the FDA, and they were not allowed to answer questions incorporating the terms of the regulatory requirements. In contrast, McNeil's experts were qualified to testify that McNeil's labeling was fully adequate to inform physicians about the risks and benefits of the drug, that McNeil was at all times in compliance with FDA regulations regarding chlorzoxazone, and that its labeling for the product was fully adequate. They also testified that there was no need to include rechallenge information in the label for chlorzoxazone, and that there is no regulatory requirement that positive rechallenges be described in drug labeling.

Hawkins maintains that she presented numerous expert witnesses to establish that McNeil's labeling was inadequate, and thus, that McNeil violated the standard of care. In particular, Hawkins cites the testimony of Dr. Golombos, qualified as an expert in the disease of the liver, who testified, inter alia, that based on his review of the NDA [New Drug Application] and the clinical records of Dr. Drew, all significant information necessary to determine the safety of the drug was not submitted by McNeil to the FDA. The trial court, however, precluded Dr. Golombos from testifying whether the information allegedly withheld by McNeil from the

FDA would affect the FDA's approval or constitute a violation of the statutes. Dr. Golombos had not been qualified to opine whether McNeil had breached its statutory or regulatory responsibilities. The trial court explained:

> Why was he [Dr. Golombos] foreclosed from testifying about the Food and Drug Administration [a]nd their requirements? [B]ecause each time that the preliminary foundational question of knowledge came up, he was lacking in it, never having worked for the FDA and been in a position to assess, evaluate and pass on the Food and Drug Administration standards.

The expert testimony presented by Hawkins may have been sufficient had Hawkins presented traditional evidence of the standard of care, [footnote omitted] where the label must merely be proven to be unreasonable under the circumstances. [Citation omitted.] In this case, however, the only evidence of a standard of care offered by Hawkins was that embodied in the statutes and regulations. Therefore, in order to prove her case, it was incumbent on Hawkins to prove a violation of those statutes and regulations. And, in order to do that, Hawkins was required to present an expert who was familiar with the application of the statutes and regulations. [Citation omitted.] She did not do so, therefore she did not present to the jury any evidence that McNeil violated the only standard of care offered, i.e., the statutes and regulations.

We reverse on the negligence per se claim because Hawkins did not present sufficient evidence of the standard of care, or that any such standard had been violated. We also hold that because Hawkins failed to adequately establish a standard of care or a deviation from that standard, she also failed to satisfy the element of proof under § 402A of the Restatement (Second) of Torts, or a "defective condition unreasonably dangerous," required for her strict liability claim. [Citation omitted.] Accordingly, judgment as a matter of law should have been entered in favor of McNeil on both of Hawkin's negligence per se and strict liability claims. [Footnote omitted.]

For all of these reasons the judgments in favor of Hawkins must be reversed and remanded with instructions to enter judgment for McNeil.

Case Notes: Negligence per se

1. What is the standard of care in a negligence per se case? What was the proposed standard of care applied to the defendant manufacturer in *McNeil Pharmaceutical?* Why did the court not allow that standard to apply in this case? What must the statute or regulation accomplish for it to be considered as the defendant manufacturer's standard of care under the circumstances?

2. The court must decide whether the subject statute may act as the standard of care in support of plaintiff's negligence allegations. This is not a finding of fact but a legal decision reached by the court itself. The court analyzed this threshold question in *McNeil Pharmaceutical.*

> The decision to adopt from a statute a standard of care to be applied in determining common law negligence is "purely a judicial one, for the court to make." [Citations omitted.] In fact, a court may decline to apply negligence per se to a particular case "if sufficient policy considerations militate against it." [Citation omitted.] At a minimum, however, the statute or regulation relied on must promote public safety and have been "enacted to protect persons in the plaintiff's position or to prevent the type of accident that occurred. [Citations omitted.] The statute must also "impose specific duties on the defendant." [Citation omitted.]

> Moreover, a statute or regulation offered to establish a standard for negligence per se purposes must not merely repeat the common law duty of reasonable care, but must set forth "specific guidelines to govern behavior." [Citation omitted.] *See also e.g., Thoma v. Kettler,* 632 A.2d 725, 728-29, n.8 (D.C. Ct. App. 1993) (noting that the generality of the regulation providing that '[d]ebris and other loose materials, shall not be allowed on or under stairways' and "[s]lippery conditions on stairways shall be eliminated as soon as possible" did not differ significantly in particulars from the common law standard of reasonable care in the circumstances); *District of Columbia v. Mitchell,* 533 A.2d 629, 639 (D.C. Ct. App.1987) (violation of statute requiring Department of Corrections to be "responsible for the safekeeping, care, protection, instruction, and discipline" of inmates implicitly recognized the common law duty of reasonable care and contained no specifics that could give rise to claim of negligence per se). [Citation omitted].

McNeil Pharmaceutical v. Hawkins, 686 A.2d 567, 579 (D.C. Ct. App. 1996). Did the Court enunciate the supporting purpose of the subject statutes and regulations in *McNeil Pharmaceutical?* What underlying premises were missing for the court to disregard the use of the subject statutes and regulations as an applicable standard of care?

3. Courts typically regard negligence per se as "[t]he unexcused violation of a statute which is applicable." Black's Law Dictionary 932 (5th Ed. 1979). Do negligence per se matters allow governing bodies other than civil courts, such as administrative agencies and criminal courts, to determine the ultimate civil liability of a product manufacturer?

4. Causation is still key in a negligence per se case. The defendant manufacturer's violation of the subject statute or regulation must also be the proximate cause-in-fact of plaintiff's injuries. The Fourth Circuit, having determined that the Food, Drug, and Cosmetic Act was the applicable standard of care under the facts in the case and that the defendant manufacturer had violated the Act, pointed to Virginia law on this same causation issue:

> "The violation of a statute, although negligence per se, will not support a recovery for damages unless such violation proximately causes or contributes to the injury complained of." [Citations omitted.]

> *Orthopedic Equipment v. Eutsler,* 276 F.2d 455, 461 (4th Cir. 1960).

5. Res ipsa loquitur and negligence per se are as close as negligence law comes to the combina-

tion of negligence and warranty law found in strict liability principles. Although technically the court continues to find and apply the appropriate standard of care and to impose the appropriate duty on a defendant manufacturer, the rigidity with which the standard and duty are required to be proven in these negligence cases is significantly weaker than in traditional negligence cases. For example, a defendant's violation of a statute presupposes its fault regardless of whether the subject product was

manufactured under the best quality control system available. In res ipsa loquitur cases, causation of the defendant manufacturer becomes a given based upon the prior findings of other courts that such causation-in-fact circumstances create negligence and impose liability on the defendant. In either instance, defendants are a step closer to bearing liability in certain circumstances and in theory are somewhere between older, traditional negligence and newer, strict liability.

 CASE PROBLEM

Each of the following case problems are designed to provide hypothetical facts so that you may work with pleadings, written discovery, and evaluation of liability, damages, and defenses in the context of a lawsuit. The fact patterns below may change from question to question but only if that particular question requests that you assume additional facts. Even then, assume such additional facts for that question only. Finally, with only slight modifications, the fact patterns do not change from chapter to chapter. You will be drafting pleadings and discovery for these same fact patterns in the next few chapters, but those chapters will focus on warranties, strict liability, or defenses.

Piggly Wiggly, LLC

Formerly a prominent retail chain, Piggly Wiggly, LLC redefined its business and best markets and ventured into manufacturing with a corporate partner to make bacon presses. Piggly was successful in obtaining funding and opening markets for large, industrial bacon presses and, on October 1, 1985, first manufactured the Squealer I. It was designed for use in slicing bacon, ham, and other pork products directly in the supermarket meat department. Piggly sold approximately 400 Squealer I units in 1985 alone. In 1990, Piggly first manufactured the Squealer II and began selling it directly to supermarkets and to industrial meat suppliers, such as Oscar Mayer, Hunter, and Healthy Choice, Ltd. In all instances of manufacturing, Piggly was the principal manufacturing partner and was responsible for manufacturing and design, warnings, instructions, servicing, and repair. Its corporate partner was MeatSlicer, Unlimited, which was responsible for financing, management, facilities, and investments.

On June 1, 1995, Sammy Hoagge was injured in a meat department at a Lindy's supermarket in southern Columbia while he was operating a Squealer I. Two other Lindy employees were present when the accident occurred. Sammy lost his left arm during the accident and suffered mild post-traumatic stress disorder from the incident. He had a hospital stay of approximately 35 days. He continues to receive regular medical care and treatment for the remnants of his left arm and participates in outpatient therapy for the limited psychiatric illness associated with the accident. Upon his return to work, Lindy's moved Sammy to the florist department and then to the bakery, but neither of these transitions were successful for Sammy. He eventually left his employment with Lindy's on December 4, 1996. He is currently unemployed. He is divorced and has two daughters, ages 6 and 8.

Piggly's in-house engineer examined the Squealer I that was in the Lindy store and found it to be in good condition. It was manufactured by Piggly in its initial production in December 1985 and delivered to the Lindy store shortly thereafter. It has been located there ever since. All metal guards for the machine were in place but no guard displayed its usual warning sign: "Caution! For Operation Guards Down." Lindy's internal investigation revealed no information about whether the Squealer I arrived at Lindy's with a warning or ever had a warning sign on the metal guard. The internal supermarket investigation did reveal, however, that Sammy Hoagge had not operated the unit with the guards in some time. Sammy Hoagge provided the supermarket with a recorded statement in which he testified that it was "more efficient" to operate the Squealer I unit without the guards because he "could process more meat per hour that way." Sammy also testified that his supervisor, Lonnie Smith, had verbally approved of this process on at least three separate occasions, the last two of which Smith had encouraged Sammy to "keep up the good work" because Sammy had been "the most efficient meat processor at Lindy in the last 12 years." Trade association information had revealed that industrial consumers of meat processing units had recently ranked the Piggly bacon press products very low among all industry bacon presses because the Piggly units were highly inefficient.

1. You represent Sammy Hoagge. He wants to sue for his personal injuries and related damages. Who are the proper parties to the lawsuit? What essential elements of negligence must exist in the facts of his case in order for you to advise him about his potential for a recovery? What additional fact, if any, do you need to know?

2. Draft a complaint for Sammy Hoagge based upon a negligence theory. Name all potential parties to the lawsuit. How do you allege the requisite legal elements to state a cause of action in negligence? What is Sammy Hoagge's potential to obtain a liability verdict against the defendants?

3. Draft 15 Interrogatories and 15 Requests for Production on behalf of Sammy Hoagge. To whom should you direct this written discovery? What is the most essential information you want to obtain at this time? Who should you first try to speak with about the incident, the product, and the injuries?

4. Assume that Sammy Hoagge died after the accident based upon medical complications that arose from his injuries. Draft a complaint to sue the appropriate parties for his injuries and damages. Who are the plaintiffs? Who are the defendants? What are the essential elements of the case? What facts must be pleaded to demonstrate that those elements exist in the case?

5. How should you plead for damages? List all potential damages incurred by Sammy Hoagge. What is his potential to recover these damages? Who are the parties from whom he would make such a recovery?

Exemplar Blueprint of Hydraulic Cylinders of Industrial Meat Press

FORMING MACHINE

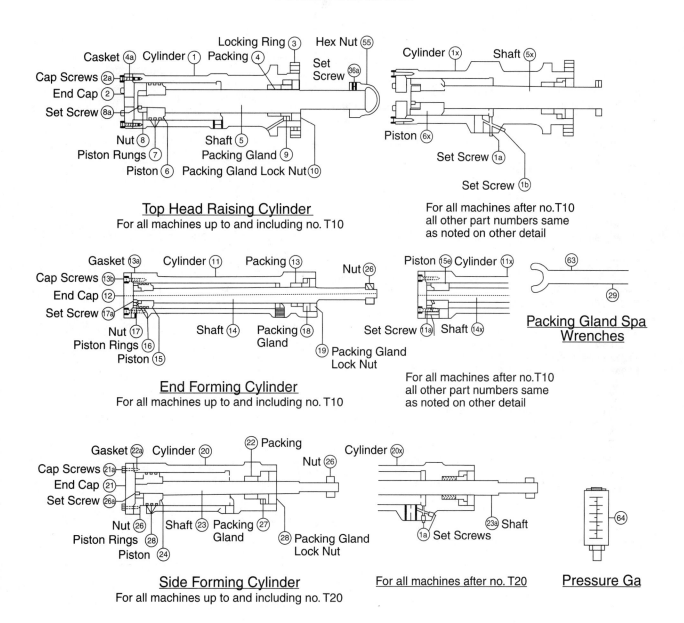

Top Head Raising Cylinder
For all machines up to and including no. T10

For all machines after no. T10 all other part numbers same as noted on other detail

End Forming Cylinder
For all machines up to and including no. T10

For all machines after no. T10 all other part numbers same as noted on other detail

Packing Gland Spa Wrenches

Side Forming Cylinder
For all machines up to and including no. T20

For all machines after no. T20

Pressure Ga

Schematic Piping Diagram for Industrial Meat Press

VALVE 1
Sequence and Check Valve
Vickers RC-108-B-21
Set to 400# pressure

VALVE 2
Sequence and Check Valve
Vickers RC-108-D-21
Set to 600# pressure

VALVE 3
$\frac{1}{4}''$ Check Valve
Vickers C-2-800
Factory set @ 5# pressure

VALVE 4
Solenoid operated spray valve
Vickers C2-2740-SO
No adjustment

VALVE 5
Relief Valve
Vickers C-157-BV
Set to 700-800# pressure

VALVE 6
1" Check Valve
Vickers C-820-S-3
Factory set @ 65# pressure

VALVE 7
Remote Controlled Counterbalance Valve
Vickers RC-108-Z-41
Set 25-50# pressure

VALVE 8
Pilot Valve
Vickers C-2-523-A
No pressure

PUMP
Vickers V135-XH

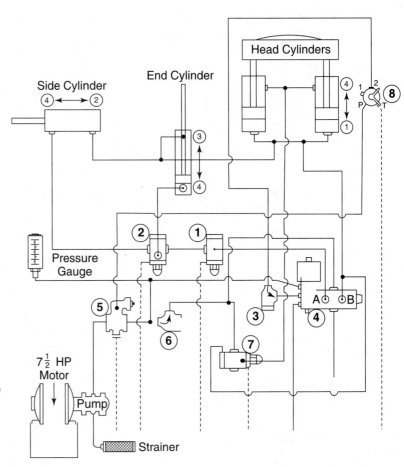

Sample Operating and Warning Language of Signs on Wire Guard

Sample Warning Sign Attached to Outer Housing Below Operating Components of Industrial Meat Press

– PELIGRO –

TODOS LOS INSTRUMENTOS DE SEGURIDAD
DEBEN SER REVISADOS ANTES DE
QUE LA MÁQUINA SEA PUESTA
EN FUNCIONAMIENTO EN CADA TURNO.

– DANGER –

ALL SAFETY DEVICES MUST
BE CHECKED BEFORE MACHINE
IS PUT INTO OPERATION
AT EACH SHIFT.

PELIGRO: PARTES MÓVILES

DANGER: MOVING PARTS

 **CASE PROBLEM**

The Milair Air Scoop

Milair, Inc. manufactures an Air Scoop AMC Cooling device that is a component part designed and manufactured specifically for large passenger aircraft, such as the Boeing 757, 767, 777, and the entire series of Airbus passenger aircraft built from 1988 to June 1992. Milair designed and manufactures its own air scoops according to its own specifications. The Milair Air Scoop attaches to the intake housing on both Rolls Royce and General Dynamic turbine engines. Its function is to facilitate air flow into and around the engine.

On May 28, 1995, Milair sold and shipped 52 air scoops to National Trans Air in St. Louis, Missouri, for installation on several Boeing 757s being operated from Lambert International Airport where National does its maintenance and repair of aircraft. The assistant parts manager at National placed the order with Milair and specified, in writing, that he wanted to purchase 52 Milair Air Scoops, part number M4880. The assistant parts manager did not tell Milair about the engines on which National intended to install the M4880 Air Scoops.

On June 10, 1995, National installed eight of the Milair Air Scoops (P/N M4880) on Rolls Royce turbine engines on its Boeing 757 that was present that day at Lambert International Airport for repairs. On June 11, 1995, the same Boeing 757 was placed back into active service with National and became Flight No. 882 to Miami, Florida. After 1 hour and 23 minutes enroute from St. Louis to Miami, Flight 882 lost power to all engines and crashed. Fifty passengers died in the accident. Another 50 passengers and all crew members survived the crash, all of whom had major or minor personal injuries of some nature.

The National Transportation Safety Board (NTSB) inspected the crash and issued its accident investigation report in which it concluded that the Rolls Royce engines on the Boeing 757 "had failed to maintain requisite rpm (revolutions per minute) during flight due to inadequate air flow." The report stated further that only one engine remained intact after the crash and inspection of that engine revealed "that an M4880 Milair Air Scoop had been installed on the Rolls Royce turbine engine, which required instead the M2213-5 Milair Air Scoop." The report also concluded that the pilot and copilot of Flight 882 had failed to complete their routine preflight inspection of all engines prior to departure, which "would have shown an orange indicator light noting the misinstalled air scoop." The National pilots deny that they failed to complete any part of their preflight inspection.

Attorneys representing several of the injured and deceased passengers retained a mechanical engineer with approximately 19 years of experience in the aerospace industry who also inspected the crash and the remaining Rolls Royce engine. His inspection report confirmed the cause of the crash, confirmed that the correct component part for the engine would have been the M2213-5 Milair Air Scoop, and noted further that "the M4880 Milair Air Scoop had been misinstalled on the Rolls Royce engine because it was backwards, which did not allow the air scoop to capture air and distribute it in and around the engine as designed." The engineer also concluded that the "Milair air scoops were poorly designed in that neither a front or back of the product is designated on the product itself."

Milair's in-house engineer performed the same inspections and issued his final accident inspection report, which made no comment about which air scoop must properly be installed on the Rolls Royce engines of the Boeing 757. Instead, the Milair report stated that "(1) each of the air scoops (M4480 and M2213-5) would properly capture and circulate air in and around the engine if correctly installed (i.e., forward) on each engine; and (2) that the M4880 is not an identical replacement part for the M2213-5." The Milair expert later explained that the M4880 and the M2213-5 are not interchangeable replacement parts for one another and installation of M4880 instead of a M2213-5 requires modification of the Rolls Royce engine upon which the product is being installed.

1. The Millers lost their son in the air crash. They want you to draft a complaint against all parties that have any liability for the accident. Who should you sue? What is the basis for your lawsuit? Can you make a submissible case against Milair in negligence? What are the requisite elements for the negligence count in your Complaint? What facts must you plead to allege a cause of action against Milair in negligence? What individuals or entities

are not specifically identified in the fact pattern that should be considered for a potential lawsuit?

2. Do the Millers have a cause of action against Rolls Royce, National, and Boeing in negligence? What are the requisite elements? What facts must you plead to allege a cause of action against Rolls Royce and National in negligence? Should these be separate counts in your Complaint?

3. Do the Millers have a res ipsa loquitur case? Against which companies?

4. Draft a Complaint for the Millers. How do you allege the requisite legal elements to state a cause of action in negligence? Which parties would you name as defendants? What facts are important to the Complaint? What facts do you still need to know in order to prepare the Complaint? What information would you ask for during discovery?

5. Draft 15 Interrogatories, 15 Requests for Production, and 15 Requests for Admissions on behalf of the Millers. To whom should you direct this written discovery? What is the most essential information you should obtain from these defendants during written discovery? Who should you depose? Who should you interview? Who can you interview?

Manufacturing Blueprint for MilAir Air Scoop AMC Cooling Housing, Part Number M4889

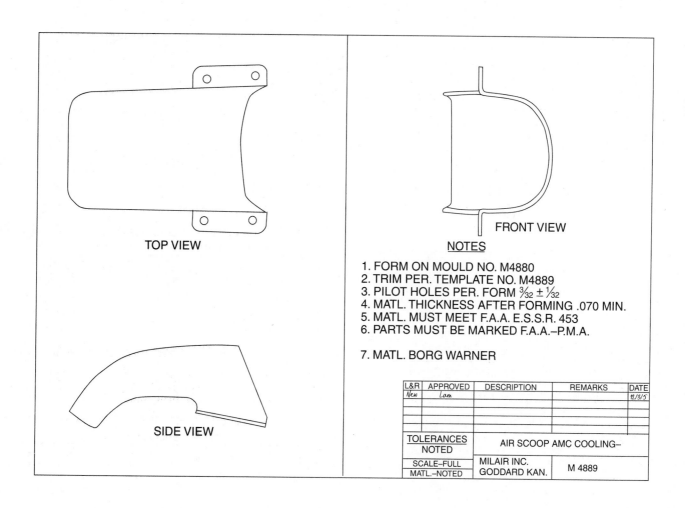

TOP VIEW

SIDE VIEW

FRONT VIEW

NOTES

1. FORM ON MOULD NO. M4880
2. TRIM PER. TEMPLATE NO. M4889
3. PILOT HOLES PER. FORM $\frac{3}{32} \pm \frac{1}{32}$
4. MATL. THICKNESS AFTER FORMING .070 MIN.
5. MATL. MUST MEET F.A.A. E.S.S.R. 453
6. PARTS MUST BE MARKED F.A.A.–P.M.A.

7. MATL. BORG WARNER

L&R	APPROVED	DESCRIPTION	REMARKS	DATE
New	Lam			12/3/5

TOLERANCES NOTED	AIR SCOOP AMC COOLING–	
SCALE–FULL	MILAIR INC.	M 4889
MATL.–NOTED	GODDARD KAN.	

Manufacturing Blueprint for MilAir Air Lower Floor Air Inlet Housing, Part Number M2213-5

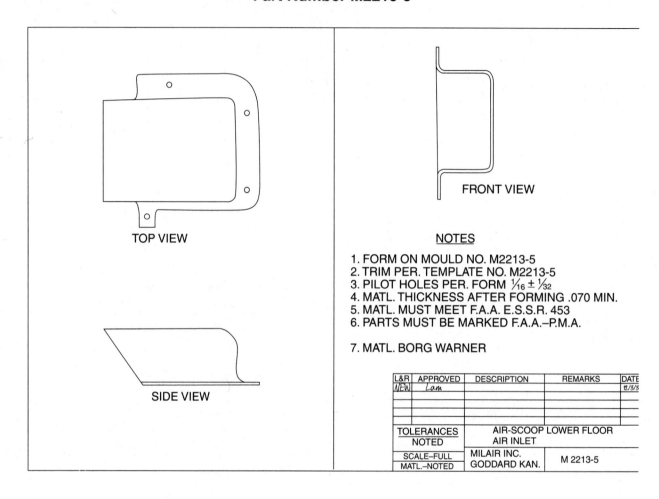

TOP VIEW

SIDE VIEW

FRONT VIEW

NOTES

1. FORM ON MOULD NO. M2213-5
2. TRIM PER. TEMPLATE NO. M2213-5
3. PILOT HOLES PER. FORM $\frac{1}{16} \pm \frac{1}{32}$
4. MATL. THICKNESS AFTER FORMING .070 MIN.
5. MATL. MUST MEET F.A.A. E.S.S.R. 453
6. PARTS MUST BE MARKED F.A.A.–P.M.A.

7. MATL. BORG WARNER

L&R	APPROVED	DESCRIPTION	REMARKS	DATE
NEW	Lam			12/3/3

TOLERANCES NOTED	AIR-SCOOP LOWER FLOOR AIR INLET	
SCALE–FULL	MILAIR INC.	M 2213-5
MATL.–NOTED	GODDARD KAN.	

Chapter 3

Warranties

INTRODUCTION

Product warranties govern the quality, character, or performance of a product but are generally actionable only by the product buyer. Warranty actions bring plaintiffs closer to the no-fault principles of strict liability by not requiring a finding of fault in the manufacture, design, or sale of a defective product but only a breach of the seller's promise that the product be of a particular quality or that it perform in a particular way. Product warranties in this text focus exclusively on the quality or character of a product in a commercial sale, which is generally governed by the Uniform Commercial Code ("U.C.C.") at UCC §§ 2-312–2-318. Warranties—as promises that certain facts are true—also exist in contractual settings (continuing warranties, covenants, personal warranties), real estate (warranties of habitability, warranties of title, construction warranties, general warranty deeds), and insurance (affirmative, express, and promissory warranties), which are not examined here. See UCC §§ 2-312, 2-317. Likewise this text does not examine warranties of title to commercial products, which concerns a warrantor's ownership of veritable title to the product and, therefore, his right to transfer the product in a commercial transaction.

Definitions

A warranty is the promise given by the product seller to the product buyer that forms the basis of the bargain between the two. More simply, a warranty is a promise that certain facts are true. Two critical elements typically define the existence of a warranty. First, privity requires the existence of a relationship between the buyer and seller. Parties to a warranty, or to a cause of action for breach of warranty, cannot be anyone other than the buyer and the seller. Second, the basis of the bargain describes the implicit nature of the exchanged promise that originally induced the sale of the product. The promise must be one that was substantially responsible for the seller having sold or the buyer having bought the product, such as the expected performance or quality of the product. Without the presence of these two elements, a warranty does not exist.

Elements of a Cause of Action for Breach

Generally, a warranty action will require the presence of a promise exchanged in a transaction, a breach of that promise, and the plaintiff's resulting damages. In some instances, the UCC requires that the plaintiff give notice to the defendant in advance of the lawsuit that the product failed in the way in which it was warranted. Ordinarily, a plaintiff must plead and prove the following elements in order to make a submissible case at trial:

- the defendant sold and plaintiff purchased the product
- the defendant promised the product would [or would not] perform in a particular way
- the defendant breached this promise because the product failed to perform in the way promised
- as a direct result of the product's failure to perform in the way promised, plaintiff was damaged
- plaintiff gave notice to the defendant after the product failed to perform in the way promised

Types of Warranties

Product warranties typically present themselves in one of three forms: an express warranty, an implied warranty of merchantability, or an implied warranty of fitness for a particular purpose. Express warranties are stated and become attached to the product when they are written or spoken by the seller in a specific instance for the specific product being purchased. Implied warranties are presumed and become attached to the product without written or verbal communication because they describe the inherent nature of the product, its character, its function, or its purpose.

Statutory Protections

In all states, warranties are governed by that state's adoption of the UCC, which is definitionally uniform among states. In most states, these governing sections of the UCC may be found at §§ 2-312 through 2-318. Each individual state may adopt different language to accomplish similar purposes. Therefore, it is essential to confirm the applicable UCC language before proceeding. Some warranty protections are provided through federal statutes, such as the Magnuson-Moss Act, 15 U.S.C. §§ 2301-2312 (1975).

HISTORY AND EMERGENCE

Caveat Emptor

Prior to the Civil War, American courts generally espoused the doctrine of *caveat emptor,* or *buyer beware,* reflecting the country's economic, political, and social conditions. Economically, the country lacked large-scale mass production until the post-Civil War Industrial Revolution, so Americans were not exposed to the sheer number of products that later became common, if not central, to American life. In addition, the *laissez faire* philosophy permeated American political thought. That philosophy encouraged rewarding the strong and successful in society, such as leaders on the frontiers of the country and business. Society, poor by today's standards to the point of fearing famine and scarcity, approved and encouraged the protection of the proactive producers of manufactured goods and assigned the risks associated with the product to the passive users. See Grant Gilmore, *Products Liability: A Commentary*, 38 U. Chi. L. Rev. 103 (1970).

During the pre-Civil War era, buyers who were daring enough to sue sellers usually lost because there were only two narrow exceptions to the *buyer beware* doctrine. A buyer might prevail if he or she could make a strong showing of (1) the seller's fraud or intentional deception, or (2) the use of precise words guaranteeing some specific characteristic or quality of the product sold. The second exception embodied early express warranty law.

Express Warranties

Express warranty law arose by *operation of law* based on what had been said and done by the seller, independent of any intent on the part of the seller to be bound. Accordingly, express warranty claims reflected the language of contract law, such as *breach of contract* to convey the product that the seller expressly promised. In other words, the seller promised to deliver one thing, but in fact delivered another, as in the following illustration:

+ A horse sold with the representation that is was "sound" and was not. *Hawkins v. Berry*, 10 Ill. (5 Gilm.) 36 (1848).
+ A bill of sale stating the seller is selling "one pair of black geldings sound and kind," but they were not *Hobart v. Young*, 21 A. 612 (Vt. 1891).

Historically, little distinction was made between simple, complex, or warranty cases. Express warranty law applies to subject matter ranging from hay to automobiles, as demonstrated by the following case excerpt:

> An individual seeking to purchase a new car engages in discussions with a salesman during which the salesman represents, among other things, that the car can be safely driven at fifty-five miles per hour. The potential buyer likes the particular model and asks the salesman if he can take it for a test drive. During the test drive the car undergoes a catastrophic mechanical failure at fifty miles per hour. The driver is injured as a result of that failure. . . . The court finds that representations made under these circumstances constitute express warranties *Green v. A.B. Hagglund and Soner*, 634 F. Supp. 790, 793 (D. Idaho, 1986).

Nearly simultaneous with the development of express warranty law in the early 1800s, American courts began to recognize implied warranties, as originated by the British. The distinguishing factor between the two warranties appears to be that express warranty law is based only on what the seller has said or done to induce a sale, whereas implied warranty law is based on what is meant by the seller, but not expressed by him or her.

Implied Warranties

The 1815 case of *Gardiner v. Gray,* 171 Eng. Rep. 46 (K.B. 1815) reveals not only the Court's rejection of the *caveat emptor* doctrine, but the Court's effectuating the "intentions of the parties." In this landmark case, the Court was considering the buyer's claim on contract for his purchase of "waste silk." The buyer's agent had been forwarded samples by the seller, but neither the seller nor the buyer had seen the goods. The Court stated the basic rule of the implied warranty of merchantability as follows:

> I am of opinion, however, that under such circumstances, the purchaser has a right to expect a saleable article answering the description in the contract. Without any particular warranty, this is an implied term in every such contract. Where there is no opportunity to inspect the commodity, the maxim of *caveat emptor* does not apply. He cannot without a warranty insist that it shall be of any particular quality or fineness, but the intention of both parties must be taken to be, that it shall be saleable in the market under the denomination mentioned in the contract between them. The purchaser cannot be supposed to buy goods to lay them on a dunghill. The question then is, whether the commodity purchased by the plaintiff be of such a quality as can be reasonably brought into the market to be sold as *waste silk?* The witnesses describe it as unfit for the purposes of waste silk, and of such a quality that it cannot be sold under that denomination.

Today, product liability law clearly belongs to the world of torts. Its history, though, reflects two separate origins, one in tort law and the other in contract law. It is worth reflecting on those two separate origins at least momentarily because they have left their marks on product liability law as it stands today.

Despite the contractual context of warranty actions that had developed in America by the beginning of the 1800s, American lawyers and courts had transformed the warranty action from its British origins, where it had been a tort. William L. Prosser, *The Implied Warranty of Merchantable Quality,* 27 Mm. L. Rev. 117 (1943). The tort origin of warranty law was advantageous to plaintiffs. It relieved them of the need to prove intentional misrepresentation or even negligence and permitted them to recover damages that were not recoverable under contract law, such as damages for wrongful death.

Privity

The contractual context of warranty actions served to justify the rule of privity, which kept successful contract and tort actions to a minimum, since it prevented anyone but the actual buyer from bringing a case against the seller. Courts explained the privity rule as logical, in that because a warranty action was rooted in contract, it only made sense that a suit based on that contract should be limited to the contracting parties. In addition, courts feared the *slippery slope* that might begin if nonparties to the contract were allowed to recover.

Again, the British courts decided the case, which has since been cited, perhaps often incorrectly, for the establishment of privity in *Winterbottom v. Wright,* 152 Eng. Rep.

402 (Ex. 1842). *Winterbottom* was a suit by an injured coachman against a contractor who had contracted with the Postmaster General to provide, maintain, and repair a mail coach to be used to deliver mail between two towns. During its route, the coach broke down and the coachman was injured. In rejecting the coachman's claims for breach of contract on the basis that only parties to a contract could bring suit, the Court expressed its fear of "the most absurd and outrageous consequences, to which I can see no limit." It put to rest the fears expressed by the defendants' counsel concerning a legal environment without privity that would, in the case of a ship running aground, allow everyone affected to sue "the chain cable manufacturer and even the iron seller."

For most of the twentieth century, the privity rules with regard to warranty law slowly eroded. One of the leading cases causing that erosion was *Henningsen v. Bloomfield Motors, Inc.*, 161 A.2d 69 (N.J. 1960). Ms. Henningsen, the plaintiff, was given a Chrysler automobile by her husband, which he had bought from an automobile dealer, Bloomfield Motors, Inc. Ms. Henningsen was subsequently injured by a sudden failure in the steering. She sued Chrysler as well as the dealer.

Chrysler argued that Ms. Henningsen was not in privity with it, thereby eliminating Chrysler's liability under an implied warranty theory. The Court in *Henningsen* first expressed its concern with manufacturers' maneuvers to avoid liability under the current Sales Act and its judicial interpretations, which held manufacturers liable for injuries caused only to those buyers who purchased items directly from them. To insulate themselves from liability to injured buyers, manufacturers established dealerships so they could transfer liability for manufacturing defects to the dealer. The Court, in finding that Chrysler was not protected by vertical privity from suit by Ms. Henningsen, stated:

There is no doubt that under early common-law concepts of contractual liability only those persons who were parties to the bargain could sue for breach of it. In more recent times a noticeable disposition has appeared in a number of jurisdictions to break through the narrow barrier of privity when dealing with sales of goods in order to give realistic recognition to a universally accepted fact. The fact is that the dealer and the ordinary buyer do not, and are not expected to, buy goods, whether they be foodstuffs or automobiles, exclusively for their own consumption or use. Makers and manufacturers know this and advertise and market their products on that assumption; witness, the "family" car, the baby foods, etc. The limitations of privity in contracts for the sale of goods developed their place in the law when marketing conditions were simple, when maker and buyer frequently met face to face on an equal bargaining plane and when many of the products were relatively uncomplicated and conducive to inspection by a buyer competent to evaluate their quality. . . . With the advent of mass marketing, the manufacturer became remote from the purchaser, sales were accomplished through intermediaries, and the demand for the product was created by advertising media. In such an economy it became obvious that the consumer was the person being cultivated. Manifestly, the connotation of "consumer" was broader than that of "buyer." He signified such a person who, in the reasonable contemplation of the parties to the sale, might be expected to use the products. Thus, where the commodities sold are such that if defectively manufactured they will be dangerous to life or limb, then society's interests can only be protected by eliminating the requirement of privity between the maker and his dealers and the reasonably expected ultimate consumer. In that way the burden of losses consequent upon use of defective articles is borne by those who are in a position to either control the danger or make an equitable distribution of the losses when they do occur.

Since then, UCC § 2-318 provides states with three alternatives in their legislative determination of their state law's privity limits. Most states have opted for Alternative A, which extends express or implied warranties to "any natural person who is in the family or household of his buyer or who is a guest in his home if it is reasonable to expect such person may use, consume or be affected by the goods and who is injured by breach of the warranty. . . . Alternative B extends to". . . any natural person who may reasonably be expected to use, consume or be affected by the goods and who is injured in person by breach of the warranty . . . Alternative C extends to ". . . any person who may reasonably be expected to use, consume or be affected by the goods and who is injured by breach of the warranty."

Warranty Litigation Today

Over the last century, strict liability has been adopted in many jurisdictions, swallowing many portions of warranty law. However, breach of warranty has survived and is quite vibrant in many jurisdictions. In some states, breach of warranty claims have been merged into products liability claims. See Washington (where the Washington Product Liability Act consolidates most of the common law theories of liability, including breach of express or implied warranty). However, in a few states, breach of warranty is the only viable product liability claim besides negligence. For example, Massachusetts had, until the *Restatement (Third) of Torts*, chosen not to recognize the common law tort basis of strict liability as originally embodied in Section 402A of the *Restatement (Second) of Torts*. Instead, it had construed its version of the UCC to provide a warranty remedy "fully as comprehensive" as the strict liability remedy of the Restatement. *Commonwealth v. Johnson Insulation*, 533 N.E.2d 1323, 1326 (Mass. 1997). Importantly, warranty provides the only means under most states' laws to recover for economic loss. In Idaho, for example, recovery of purely economic damages is exclusively limited to breach of warranty, where personal injuries or property damage other than the product itself are absent.

THE CRITICAL ELEMENTS—PRIVITY AND BASIS OF THE BARGAIN

Privity

Privity in warranty actions is the relationship that exists between two or more contracting parties. Thus, a product buyer and a product seller have privity with one another and have obligations imposed by warranty actions that arise from this relationship with one another. More difficult privity problems ensue when the product has passed through a distribution chain (manufacturer to wholesaler to distributor to retailer), and the product buyer seeks to enforce her or his warranty protections against the manufacturer, which did not sell the product directly to the buyer. In this instance, the UCC has recognized that vertical privity exists between the product manufacturer and the product purchaser. In other instances where a party other than the product purchaser seeks to enforce warranty protections, the UCC has recognized that horizontal privity may exist between the product seller or manufacturer and the injured party if the injured party is part of the product purchaser's family or household. If not, the lack of privity may bar an injured party's warranty claims against the seller or manufacturer.

Privity requirements differ from state to state, primarily because the UCC provides varying alternatives for the states' adoption of the UCC § 2-318. The UCC's purpose in offering alternatives was to free the intended beneficiaries of warranty actions from technical privity requirements. The UCC makes explicit the broadening of horizontal privity among product users in the following three alternatives:

UCC § 2-318. Third Party Beneficiaries of Warranties Express or Implied.

Alternative A A seller's warranty whether express or implied extends to any natural person who is in the family or household of his buyer or who is a guest in [buyer's] home if it is reasonable to expect that such person may use, consume or be affected by the goods and who is injured in person by breach of the warranty. A seller may not exclude or limit the operation of this section.

Alternative B A seller's warranty whether express or implied extends to any natural person who may reasonably be expected to use, consume or be affected by the goods and who is injured in person by breach of the warranty. A seller may not exclude or limit the operation of this section.

Alternative C A seller's warranty whether express or implied extends to any person who may reasonably be expected to use, consume or be affected by the goods and who is injured by the breach of the warranty. A seller may not exclude or limit the operation of this section with respect to injury to the person of an individual to whom the warranty extends.

The UCC's Official Comment to § 2-318 explains the anticipated applications of these three alternatives in paragraph 3:

3.   The first alternative expressly includes as beneficiaries within it provisions the family, household and guests of the purchaser. Beyond this, the section in this form is neutral and is not intended to enlarge or restrict the developing case law on whether the seller's warranties, given to his buyer who resells, extend to other persons in the distributive chain.

The second alternative is designed for states where the case law has already developed further and for those that desire to expand the class of beneficiaries. The third alternative goes further, following the trend of modern decisions as indicated by Restatement of Torts 2d § 402A in extending the rule beyond the injuries to the person.

 CASE LAW

◆ **distinguishing horizontal privity from vertical privity**

McNally v. Nicholson Manufacturing Co., 313 A.2d 913 (Me. 1973).

Plaintiff employee brought warranty and strict liability claims against manufacturer of a wood chipper for injuries he sustained when chipper launched wood piece at him through the side of the machine. The wood chipper had been purchased by the employee's employer from the defendant manufacturer. The Maine Supreme Court was asked to decide whether plaintiff employee stated a claim for breach of the implied warranty of merchantability.

WERNICK, Justice.

* * *

Count II focused on the sale transaction between defendant and plaintiff's employer and the "warranties" incident to it. Defendant was said to have expressly, . . . by publication, advertising and salesmen's interviews, . . . represented to the plaintiff's . . . employer that the Nicholson Utilizer II . . . was designed, manufactured, constructed and could be safely used for its intended purpose as a chipping machine.

It was further alleged that by the very act of sale defendant had impliedly represented that said machine was of merchantable quality and reasonably fit for its intended purpose.

Plaintiff claimed to have been injured in his person by breaches of the warranties.

* * *

Subsequently, defendant filed a motion to dismiss Count II on the ground that it failed to state a claim upon which relief can be granted (as authorized by Rule 12(h) M.R.C.P.). [Footnote omitted.] Asserting that the face of the complaint revealed that plaintiff was "not in privity of contract" with the defendant, the motion sought dismissal of Count II because, absent "privity" between the parties, a claim for breach of warranty is [barred by Maine's adoption of UCC statutes].

* * *

[T]he presiding Justice in the Superior Court . . . dismissed Count II of the complaint but sustained Count III as stating a good cause of action.

The basis of the dismissal of Count II was that: "No privity of contract is alleged between plaintiff and defendant."

* * *

We disagree with each of the conclusions of the presiding Justice. We decide that Count II (breach of warranty) does, but Count III (strict liability in tort) fails to, state a claim upon which relief can be granted.

We sustain the "breach of warranty" gravamen of Count II on the basis of 11 M.R.S.A. § 2-318 as enacted in 1963 and in force until entirely rewritten effective October 1, 1969.

Thirty-eight years had intervened between the decision of *Pelletier v. DuPont* (1925) and the 1963 formulation of 11 M.R.S.A. § 2-318 (hereinafter described simply as Section 2-318). During that period there had been major developments in other jurisdictions reflecting a relaxation, or abandonment, of "privity" requirements for breach of warranty recovery. [Footnote omitted.] In Maine, however, no case had come to this Court affording opportunity for thorough reevaluation, in light of developments elsewhere, of the actual decision or doctrine of *Pelletier v. DuPont.* [Footnote omitted.]

Similarly, there had been no intervening attention to the problem by the Maine Legislature. Thus the full significance of the public policy change produced by Section 2-318—adopted as one provision of the Uniform Commercial Code—is best elucidated by a direct comparison of Section 2-318 with *Pelletier v. DuPont.*

Product-wise, in *Pelletier v. DuPont* breach of warranty recovery was sought as to contaminated food. This Court conceded that by 1925 many courts had allowed breach of warranty recoveries, absent privity of contractual relationship between the parties, in cases involving "[t]he sale of drugs and . . . food products . . . intended for human consumption". . . . [Citations omitted.]

Yet, *Pelletier v. DuPont* decided:

. . . this court, . . . finds no good reason for repudiating or modifying, . . . the well-established rule that in order to recover on a warranty, there must be a privity of contractual relations between the parties. [Citations omitted.]

* * *

Although Section 2-318 thus treated products comprehensively, its changes in the *Pelletier v. DuPont* "privity" requirements were narrow. They are best understood when clarified by the frequently discussed distinction between a "vertical" and "horizontal" lack of privity.

Vertical privity lies within the marketing chain and denotes the relationship existing between the parties in the several transactions among the manufacturer, wholesaler, retailer, and ultimate retail purchaser. Where goods are distributed through this four-linked chain, there are three distinct sales transactions. Since the manufacturer sold only to the wholesaler, he is in privity with him alone. The wholesaler, on the other hand, since he purchased from the manufacturer and sold to the retailer is not, however, in privity with the consumer because the consumer had no part in either of the two transactions. Similarly, the retailer is in privity with the wholesaler and the retail purchaser, but not with the manufacturer. The ultimate purchaser, of course, is in privity only with the retailer. Whenever one of these parties attempts to enforce a contractual or sales law obligation, a warranty, for example, vertically along the distributive chain against one with whom he was not dealt, he is said to lack [vertical] privity. . . .

Horizontal privity, so denominated because it does not involve clambering up the marketing chain, arises only after all resales have been completed and one reaches the flat plane spreading outwards from the last purchaser. It refers to the problem presented when the person injured by the products is someone other than the buyer and he seeks to reach the retailer.

* * *

In the present case, however, plaintiff is not claiming authorization under Section 2-318 to skip "vertical" privity links. Here, the issue relates only to a "horizontal" lack of privity, the area which Section 2-318 explicitly covers. Furthermore, for 38 years this Court had not reassessed the public policy of Maine as to lack of privity in breach of warranty cases in any aspects—"vertical," "horizontal" or otherwise. [Footnote omitted.]

* * *

The "particular area" expressly dealt with by Section 2-318 is . . . the extension of person outside the distributive chain, having various "horizontal" relationships to the last buyer, of rights to recover for breach of warranty against the person who was the "seller" to that buyer. Hence, it is as to this area of appropriate "horizontal" relationships that the official Comment to Section 2-313 states that the "policies" underlying Section 2-318 should provide "useful guidance [for] further cases as they arise." [ellipses in original]

On this basis, we conclude that it is intended that the appropriate judicial approach to Section 2-318 be a case by case accommodation to its recognizable policy objectives. . . .

* * *

The benefits of Section 2-318 were afforded only to those within such general calls who, in addition, had such particular relationships, "horizontally", to the last purchaser in the distributive chain as would appropriately reflect the emphasis on consensuality—insofar as the relationships made it highly likely that the last purchaser would *want* (*consensually* intend) the person in such relationships to have the protections of the warranties made to him by his seller.

In light of this fundamental policy approach in Section 2-318, we conclude that section 2-318 imports that the present plaintiff, by virtue of his being an employee of the last purchaser of the "Nicholson Utilizer II" and who in the course of his employment duties was required to be in contact with, or close proximity to, that machine, is to be recognized as a beneficiary of the warranties given to his employer. It is plain that plaintiff's employer would *want* the plaintiff, as a "donee-beneficiary", to be protected by warranties, express or implied, relating to the fitness and safety of the "Nicholson Utilizer II" when used for the purposes for which it was intended. [Citation omitted.] Indeed, in the present circumstances, it takes only the attribution of a figurative bent to the word "family" to bring plaintiff, as an employee of a corporate "buyer", within the policy scope of Section 2-318 since plaintiff may be regarded as a member of such "family" as a corporation may reasonably be said to have. [Footnote omitted.]

Case Notes: Privity

1. A purchaser's guests are recognized in the horizontal privity requirements of UCC § 2-318. In *Handrigan v. Apex Warwick,* 275 A.2d 262, 265-66 (R.I. 1971), the Rhode Island Supreme Court found that privity existed for a purchaser's guest that had been injured by an allegedly defective ladder when the guest was assisting the purchaser in painting his house. Rhode Island had previously adopted Alternative A of the UCC § 2-318, which expressly provided horizontal privity for one "who is a guest in [the buyer's] home[.]"

2. Given the adoption of any one of the three alternatives under UCC § 2-318, how does breach of warranty differ from strict liability in a product liability case?

3. How is the relaxation of horizontal and vertical privity connected to the history and emergence of strict liability? If strict liability provides protection to a product user in the absence of privity, then why is it important to have any warranty protection or to use the distinctions that relax the privity requirements for these warranty protections?

4. Courts sometimes recognize a "diagonal privity," which is the relationship between a party outside the distributive chain who seeks recovery by skipping the last purchaser's seller to reach one standing anywhere higher in the distributive chain. Under this scenario, the injured party may or may not have horizontal privity but seeks in any event to state a claim against a party other than the last immediate product seller. For example, a product purchaser who seeks to collect only against the manufacturer and not the distributor, wholesaler, or retailer, would have diagonal privity. See *McNally,* 313 A.2d 913, 919 fn.8 (Me. 1973).

5. Did McNally's breach of implied warranties action in Count II state a cause of action for which relief could be granted? What was the argument to the contrary by the defendant manufacturer? What impetus did the Court in *McNally* identify for its departure from the narrow privity requirements enunciated in *Pelletier v. DuPont?* What does the *McNally* decision teach litigators they must do in anticipation of litigation involving warranties?

6. Given the Court's extension in *McNally* of horizontal privity to those individuals to whom the purchaser consensually intends to have the protections of the warranties made by the seller, what evidence could the plaintiff present that would tend to prove the buyer's consensual interest? What evidence could the defendant manufacturer present to disprove that intent? What evidentiary problems arise from the "consensual interest" test?

Basis of the Bargain

The promise that comprises the warranty must relate directly to the reason the product buyer originally decided to purchase the product. An express warranty *to sell you red apples,* only to have the purchaser discover upon arriving home that he has purchased green apples will likely be a promise that was the basis of the bargain. An express warranty *to sell you red apples on a Sunday* when the product buyer ultimately made his purchase on Monday will likely not be a promise that constitutes the basis of the bargain, unless the buyer had some specific use for the apples on a Sunday.

As in all warranty actions, it is essential to distinguish statements of fact from opinion. Typically, the basis of the bargain may be derived only from statements of fact. One court described it this way:

> The test of whether a salesman's statement constituted "affirmations of fact" going to the very "basis of the bargain" is whether the salesman was asserting a fact of which the buyer was ignorant or whether he was merely declaring his belief with reference to a matter of which he had no special knowledge and of which the buyer may have been expected to have an opinion. *Valley Datsun v. Martinez*, 578 S.W.2d 485, 490 (Tex. Ct. App. Corpus Christi 1979).

The basis of the bargain is inherent in the analysis of express and implied warranties requiring the determination of a wide array of fact issues, particularly focusing on the knowledge and sophistication of the buyer and seller, as well as the language used in the course of the transaction. This basis of the bargain element is frequently relied upon by courts today to determine the very existence of an express or implied warranty.

 **CASE LAW** ──────────────────────────────────◆

♦ **basis of the bargain**

Yates v. Pitman Manufacturing, Inc., 514 S.E.2d 605 (Va. 1999).

Plaintiff Yates was injured when an outrigger on a crane manufactured by defendant Pitman came loose and crushed plaintiff's left foot. At trial, Yates claimed that Pitman had breached its express warranty to Yates' employer that the crane unit, including the outriggers, met all requirements of the American National Standards Institute ("ANSI") Standard B30.5-1968, which comprised the basis of the bargain between Pitman and Yates' employer when the crane was purchased.

STEPHENSON, Senior Justice.

* * *

Next, we consider whether the trial court erred in striking Yates' evidence relating to his express warranty claim. As previously noted, Pitman certified that, at the time of sale, the crane unit met "applicable design and construction standards as prescribed in ANSI [American

National Standard Institute] B30.5-1968." At that time, ANSI Standard B30.5-1968 required each outrigger to be "visible from its actuating location." Yates, however, presented evidence that, from the actuating station, the crane operator, "[n]ot only [could] not see the outrigger, but he [could not] see that there's a person [who] might come into contact with that hazard."

Pitman contends that the trial court correctly struck Yates' express warranty claim because Yates (1) "offered no evidence that the ANSI certification was part of the bargain in any sales transaction *606 involving the product" and (2) failed to produce any evidence that the crane unit's design and construction violated the ANSI Standard. We do not agree.

Code § 8.2-313, the express warranty statute, provides as follows:

(1) Express warranties by the seller are created as follows:

    (a) Any affirmation of fact or promise made by the seller to the buyer which relates to the goods and becomes part of the basis of the bargain creates an express warranty that the goods shall conform to the affirmation or promise.

(b) Any description of the goods which is made part of the basis of the bargain creates an express warranty that the goods shall conform to the description.

(c) Any sample or model which is made part of the basis of the bargain creates an express warranty that the whole of the goods shall conform to the sample or model.

(2) It is not necessary to the creation of an express warranty that the seller use formal words such as "warrant" or "guarantee" or that he have a specific intention to make a warranty, but an affirmation merely of the value of the goods or a statement purporting to be merely the seller's opinion or commendation of the goods does not create a warranty. An affirmation of fact is presumed to be a part of the bargain, and any fact that would remove such affirmation out of the agreement "requires clear affirmative proof." *Daughtrey v. Ashe*, 243 Va. 73, 78, 413 S.E.2d 336, 339 (1992)

(quoting with approval Official Comment 3 to § 8.2-313). Additionally, a plaintiff is not required to show that he relied upon the affirmation in order to recover under an express warranty claim. [Citation omitted.]

In the present case, Pitman presented no evidence that would take its affirmation out of the agreement. Therefore, its affirmation was a part of the basis of the bargain. [Citations omitted.] Thus, we hold that Pitman's affirmation of fact created an express warranty that applied to Yates even though he was not the purchaser of the crane unit. We also hold that Yates presented evidence from which a jury could reasonably conclude that the crane unit did not comply with ANSI Standard B30.5-1968. Therefore, the trial court erred in striking Yates' express warranty claim.

For the reasons stated, we will reverse the trial court's judgment and remand the case for a new trial consistent with the views expressed in this opinion.

Reversed and remanded.

Case Notes: Basis of the Bargain

1. The UCC recognized the basis of the bargain element as essential in its codification of express warranties and required that it be present in any express warranty. UCC § 2-313 (1) provides that

(a) Any affirmation of fact or promise made by the seller to the buyer which relates to the goods and becomes part of the *basis of the bargain* creates an express warranty that the good shall conform to the affirmation or promise.

(b) Any description of the goods which is made part of the *basis of the bargain* creates an express warranty that the goods shall conform to the description.

(c) Any sample or model which is made part of the *basis of the bargain* creates an express warranty that the whole of the good shall conform to the sample or model. [Emphasis added.]

2. The presence of a basis of the bargain element in a contract negotiation removes any obligation that the product manufacturer or seller have a specific intent to create an express warranty. In other words, the warrantor need not have had a specific intent to create a warranty as long as the resulting contract includes exchanged promises that were part of the basis of the bargain. Comment 3 to § 2-313 provides that [t]he present section deals with affirmations of fact by the seller, descriptions of the goods or exhibitions of samples, exactly as any other part of a negotiation which ends in a contract is dealt with. No specific intention to make a warranty is necessary if any of these factors is made part of the basis of the bargain. In actual practice affirmations of fact made by the seller about the goods during a bargain are regarded as part of the description of those goods; hence no particular reliance on such statements need be shown in order to weave them into the fabric of the agreement.

TYPES OF WARRANTIES

Express Warranty

A product seller, the warrantor, makes or gives a warranty by stating or writing a promise that the product will perform in a certain way. An express warranty does not exist unless it is specifically, overtly, or affirmatively given. A product seller will convey an express warranty by writing or stating a fact about the product in connection with its anticipated sale: "This car has four wheels." "This car is a 1987 Buick and has only 21,000 miles on it." "This lawnmower has a 12 hp engine."

The UCC defines express warranties as follows:

> **UCC § 2-313. Express Warranties. (1)** Express warranties by the seller are created as follows:
>
> **(a)** Any affirmation of fact or promise made by the seller to the buyer which relates to the goods and becomes part of the basis of the bargain creates an express warranty that the goods shall conform to the affirmation or promise.
>
> **(b)** Any description of the good which is made part of the basis of the bargain creates an express warranty that the goods shall conform to the description.
>
> **(c)** Any sample or model which is made part of the basis of the bargain creates an express warranty that the whole of the goods shall conform to the sample or model.

Statements of Fact   In order to comprise an express warranty, the warrantor's statements must be made in connection with the product being shown for sale and must be part of the basis of the bargain. The warranty must also make statements of fact about the product. Although use of specific language, such as *warrant, guarantee,* or *covenant* may assist in signaling the conveyance of an express warranty, this language is not required to appear in the warrantor's statement in order to convey an express warranty.

Conversely, puffery or sales opinions about the product do not comprise express warranties. Not every statement made by a product seller is an express warranty. Although sometimes difficult to distinguish from statements of fact, these opinions may describe the future performance of a product as in, "This car will run for 120,000 miles"; may make outrageous propositions about the product, such as "This kitchen knife will slice tomatoes after having trimmed your hedges and trees"; may be generally vague about the condition of the product, in saying "This camper is in excellent condition"; or may even include *warranty* or *guarantee* language itself, for example, "I guarantee you will be satisfied with this new bubblebath." Distinctions between fact and sales opinion are not always clear. Courts determine these distinctions on a case-by-case basis depending on the knowledge and sophistication of the product buyer, as well as the knowledge and sophistication of the product seller, ultimately judging whether the statement truly formed the basis of the bargain in the sale of the product.

 **CASE LAW**

◆ **establishing an express warranty**

◆ **distinguishing between statements of fact and sales opinion**

Sessa v. Riegle, 427 F. Supp. 760 (E.D. Penn. 1977).

Race horse buyer Sessa sued seller Riegle for breach of warranties, including the breach of an express warranty, when the standardbred race horse became afflicted with tendinitis and thrombosis. Sessa contended that Riegle had promised that "the horse is sound." Sessa testified that Riegle had stated that "[the race horse] can leave like a deer, take a forward position, and if you brush him from the head of the stretch home, he would just jog home in preferred company every week." Sessa sought to return the horse and reclaim his $25,000 after the horse contracted thrombosis, a medical condition that affected the animal's arteries and did not allow it to race to its full potential.

Hannum, District Judge.

* * *

In deciding whether statements by a seller constitute express warranties, the Court must look to UCC § 2-313 [footnote omitted], which present three fundamental issues. First, the Court must determine whether the seller's statement constitutes an "affirmation of fact or promise" or "description of the goods" under § 2-313(1)(a) or (b) or whether it is rather "merely the seller's opinion or commendation of the goods" under § 2-313(2). Second, assuming the Court finds the language used susceptible to creation of a warranty, it must then be determined whether the statement was "part of the basis of the bargain." If it was, an express warranty exists and, as the third issue, the Court must determine whether the warranty was breached.

With respect to the first issue, the Court finds that in the circumstances of this case, words to the effect that "[T]he horse is sound" spoken during the telephone conversation between Sessa and Riegle constitute an opinion or commendation rather than express warranty. This determination is a question for the trier of fact. [Footnote and citations omitted.] There is nothing talismanic or thaumaturgic about the use of the word "sound." Whether use of that language constitutes war-

ranty, or mere opinion or commendation depends on the circumstances of the sale and the types of goods sold. While § 2-313 makes it clear that no specific words need be present, not every statement by a seller is an express warranty.

Several older Pennsylvania cases dealing with horse sales show that similar statements as to soundness are not always similarly treated under warranty law. In *Wilkinson v. Stettler,* 46 Pa.Super. 407 (1911), the statement that a horse "was solid and sound and would work any place" was held not to constitute an express warranty. This result was followed in *Walker v. Kirk,* 72 Pa.Super. 534 (1919), which considered the statement, "This mare is sound and all right and a good worker double."

* * *

However, in *Flood v. Yeager,* 52 Pa.Super. 637 (1912), an express warranty was found where the plaintiff informed the defendant that, "he did not know anything at all about a horse and that he did not want . . . the defendant to make a mean deal with him; whereupon the defendant said that the horse was solid and sound; that he would guarantee him to be solid and sound" [ellipse in original; citations omitted.] While all three of these cases are premised partly on the now displaced rule that specific intent to warrant is a necessary concomitant of an express warranty [footnote omitted], they do show that statements of the same tenor receive varying treatment depending on the surrounding circumstances.

The results in these cases are all consistent with custom among horse traders as alluded to by Gene Riegle. [Footnote omitted.] He testified that it is "not a common thing" to guarantee Tarport Conaway [the horse]. In other words, because horses are fragile creatures, susceptible to myriad maladies, detectable and undetectable, only where there is an "understanding" that an ignorant buyer, is relying totally on a knowledgeable seller not "to make a mean deal," are statements as to soundness taken to be anything more than the seller's opinion or commendation.

The facts suggest no special "understanding" between Sessa and Riegle. Sessa was a knowledgeable buyer, having been involved with standardbreds for some years. Also, Sessa sent Maloney, an even more knowledgeable horseman, as his agent to inspect the horse.

Also militating against the finding of express warranty is the nature of the conversation between Sessa and Riegle. It seemed largely collateral to the sale rather than an essential part of it. Although Sessa testified that Riegle's "personal guarantee" given during the conversation was the quintessence of the sale, the credible evidence suggests otherwise. While on the telephone, Riegle made statements to the effect that "the horse is a good one" and "you will like him." These bland statements are obviously opinion or commendation, and the statement, "The horse is sound," falling within their penumbra takes on their character as such.

Under all the facts and circumstances of this case, it is clear to the Court that Riegle's statements were not of such a character as to give rise to express warranties under § 2-313(1) but were opinion or commendation under § 2-313(2).

Even assuming that Riegle's statements could be express warranties, it is not clear that they were "part of the basis of the bargain," the second requisite of § 2-313. This is essentially a reliance requirement and is inextricably intertwined with the initial determination as to whether given language may constitute an express warranty since affirmations, promises and descriptions tend to become part of the basis of the bargain. It was the intention of the drafters of the UCC not to require a strong showing of reliance. In fact, they envisioned that all statements of the seller became part of the basis of the bargain unless clear affirmative proof is shown to the contrary.

♦

Case Notes: Express Warranties

1. As previously described, the basis of the bargain element is essential in the creation of any express warranty. This element manifests itself in the contract negotiation between product seller and product purchaser in one of three ways: an affirmation of a fact about the product being purchased; a description of the product; or a sample or model of the product. In any one of these three ways, the exchange of information about the product creates an express warranty.

2. A description of the product need not be by words. Comment 5 to § 2-313 provides, in part, that

   A description need not be by words. Technical specifications, blueprints and the like can afford more exact description than mere language and if made part of the basis of the bargain goods must conform with them. Past deliveries may set the description of quality, either expressly or impliedly by course of dealing. Of course, all descriptions by merchants must be read against the applicable trade usages with the general rules as to merchantability resolving any doubts.

3. Samples or models of the product must reflect the product being sold. Comment 6 to § 2-313 provides, in part, that

   [t]he question is whether the seller has so acted with reference to the sample as to make him responsible that the whole shall have at least the values shown by it. The circumstances aid in answering this question. If the sample has been drawn from an existing bulk, it must be regarded as describing values of the goods contracted for unless it is accompanied by an unmistakable denial of such responsibility. If, on the other hand, a model of merchandise not on hand is offered, the mercantile presumption that it has become a literal description of the subject matter is not so strong, and particularly so if modification on the buyer's initiative impairs any feature of the model.

4. The purpose of warranty law is to determine the product that the product seller has agreed to sell and to hold him responsible for that determination. The exchange of promises about the product and the relationship of those promises as a basis of the bargain designates the type and quality of the product involved in the transaction. Because this designation occurs through an affirmation of the product, a description of the product, or a reference to a sample of the product, it is

difficult, if not inherently contradictory, to disavow this designation later by disclaiming "all warranties, express or implied." See Comment 4 to § 2-313, and see § 2-316. Such a disclaimer interrupts the transaction itself by suggesting that when Johnny sells red apples to Mary that the red apples themselves were neither designated for sale by Johnny nor designated for purchase by Mary. Such a suggestion is insulting to both the product buyer and the product purchaser, both of whom likely had an interest in a transaction for a specific type and quality of product.

5. Specific words are not necessary to create an express warranty. UCC § 2-313 (2) provides that

> [i]t is not necessary to the creation of an express warranty that the seller use formal words such as "warrant" or "guarantee" or that he have a specific intention to make a warranty, but an affirmation merely of the value of the goods or a statement purporting to be merely the seller's opinion or commendation of the goods does not create a warranty.

6. If Sessa had stated to Riegle in their prepurchase conversation(s) that he knew little about horses, would the result have been different? How does the requirement that the buyer express ignorance regarding the subject of the purchase compare to the requirements a buyer must meet in order to state a claim under the theory of implied warranty of fitness for a particular purpose.

7. Given the Court's outline of the applicable analysis in the first paragraph, did the Court follow that analysis? Under what theories could Sessa have prevailed? Why did the Court rely upon the language of Pennsylvania U.C.C. to determine whether Riegle had made a statement of fact?

Implied Warranty of Merchantability

Implied warranties are presumed to exist unless specifically disclaimed. They are derived in the law by implication or inference based upon the nature of the transaction and are inherent in the product itself. Existence of the implied warranty of merchantability requires that the seller be a merchant and that the goods be of a merchantable quality. Sellers who are merchants sell products in a commercial setting and are familiar with the nature and type of product. Merchantable goods are products that pass in trade without objection under a contract description; are fit for ordinary purposes for which these products are used; are adequately contained, packaged, and labeled; and conform to the promises made on the container, package, or label.

The UCC defines implied warranties of merchantability as follows:

UCC § 2-314. Implied Warranties of Merchantability.

(1) Unless excluded or modified, a warranty that the goods shall be merchantable is implied in a contract for their sale if the seller is a merchant with respect to goods of that kind.

(2) Goods to be merchantable must be at least such as

    (a) pass without objection in the trade under the contract description;

    (b) in the case of fungible goods, are of fair average quality within the description;

(c) are fit for the ordinary purposes for which such goods are used;

(d) run, within the variations permitted by the agreement, of even kind, quality, and quantity within each unit and among all units involved;

(e) are adequately contained, packaged, and labeled as the agreement may require;

(f) conform to the promises or affirmations of fact made on the container or label if any.

Merchantability passes upon the consumer's presumption that she or he was purchasing a particular product: for example, the purchase of a toaster as described on the product packaging. The breach of this implied warranty occurs upon finding a vegetable steamer in the packaging instead of a toaster. The warranty here is inherent because, in this instance, it forces the obligation upon the manufacturer to place a product on the marketplace shelf that conforms to the packaging. In other instances, it requires the manufacturer to provide a product that is of fair and average quality, is fit for its ordinary purpose, or is typical of most products of this type in the industry.

 CASE LAW

◆ **determining *merchantable* goods subject to implied warranties**

Sessa v. Riegle, 427 F. Supp. 760 (E.D. Penn. 1977).

In the same case, Sessa also alleged that Riegle breached the implied warranty of merchantability, alleging that Riegle was a merchant and that the horse, Tarport Conaway, was a merchantable good.

Hannum, District Judge.

* * *

Plaintiff also seeks relief based on the implied warranty of merchantability of UCC § 2-314(1). The key words in this section are "merchant" and "merchantable." To recover, plaintiff must show that the seller was a "merchant" and that the goods were not "merchantable" at the time of the sale.

In this case there can be no question that Riegle was a merchant. He bought, sold and raced horses for a living. However, because the Court finds that Tarport Conaway was merchantable at the time of the sale, plaintiff cannot recover. First, in accordance with the analysis above, plaintiff failed to prove that any defect in

Tarport Conaway was present on March 23, 1973. Second, even assuming that the defects alleged were present, the horse would still be merchantable.

UCC § 2-314(2) defines merchantable. The standard established does not require that goods be outstanding or superior. It is only necessary that they be of reasonable quality within expected variations and fit for the ordinary purposes for which they are used. [Citations omitted.]

Even with tendinitis and intermittent claudication, Tarport Conaway met this standard. The tendinitis was merely temporary and of no long term effect. The intermittent claudication did not prevent him from becoming a creditable if unspectacular race horse. After rest and recuperation, he won three races in thirteen starts in 1975. Certainly he did not live up to Sessa's hopes for a preferred pacer, but such disappointments are an age old story in the horse racing business. Anyone who dares to deal in standardbreds knows that whether you pay $2500.00 or $250,000.00, a given horse may prove to be a second Hambletonian or a humble hayburner. Consequently, since Tarport Conaway was able to hold his own with other standardbreds, he was reasonably fit for the ordinary purposes for which race horses are used, and was merchantable.

* * *

Case Notes: Implied Warranties of Merchantability

1. The implied warranties described in UCC § 2-314 may be applied only to product sellers who are merchants. UCC § 2-104 (1) describes a "merchant" as

   > [A] person who deals in goods of the kind or otherwise by his occupation holds himself out as having knowledge or skill peculiar to the practices or goods involved in the transaction or to whom such knowledge or skill may be attributed by his employment of an agent or broker or other intermediary who by his occupation holds himself out as having such knowledge or skill.

2. If persons other than merchants make representations about the general condition of the goods, those representations are binding on the non-merchant product seller as an express warranty. Comment 3 to UCC § 2-314 made this point:

   > A specific designation of goods by the buyer does not exclude the seller's obligation that they be fit for the general purposes appropriate to such goods. A contract for the sale of second-hand goods, however, involves only such obligation as is appropriate to such goods for that is their contract description. A person making an isolated sale of goods is not a "merchant" within the meaning of the full scope of this section and, thus, no warranty of merchantability would apply. His knowledge of any defects not apparent on inspection would, however, without need for express agreement and in keeping with the underlying reason of the present section and the provisions on good faith, impose an obligation that known material but hidden defects be fully disclosed.

3. The six attributes of merchantability listed in § 2-314 (2) are not all-inclusive, "and the intent is to leave open other possible attributes of merchantability." Comment 6 to UCC § 2-314. Of the six, however, most cases that rely upon this implied warranty focus on subsection c, that the goods must be "fit for the ordinary purposes for which such goods are used[.]" § 2-314 (2) (c). These ordinary purposes are typically regarded as those that are usual, customary, or reasonably foreseeable for that particular product.

4. The Court in *Sessa v. Riegle* found Tarport Conaway to be "fit for the ordinary purposes for which race horses are used" and, therefore, a merchantable good. Is this the only way to determine whether a good is merchantable? Must all merchantable goods be "fit for their ordinary purpose"?

5. How many theories may a plaintiff pursue in a warranty case? May plaintiff pursue warranty and strict liability theories simultaneously? Does plaintiff recover more than once if she or he proves the liability of a defendant under more than one legal theory? Did Sessa recover for Riegle's breach of an express warranty and for his breach of the implied warranty of merchantability?

 CASE LAW

◆ **establishing a breach of an implied warranty of merchantability**

Southern of Rocky Mount, Inc. v. Woodward Specialty Sales, Inc., 279 S.E.2d 32 (N.C. Ct. App. 1981).

Plaintiff, a processor of peanut and cotton seed oil, purchased an air compressor from defendant, a seller of air compressors. After the sale, a fire destroyed Rocky Mount's shop. Believing the compressor to be the cause and origin of the fire, Rocky Mount filed suit against Woodward Specialties for, among other claims, breach of the implied warranty of merchantability. Upon Woodward Specialties' motion for directed verdict, the Court was required to determine whether Rocky Mount had presented sufficient evidence of a breach.

WHICHARD, Judge.

* * *

Although plaintiff did allege that the fire originated "in the control box of the motor drive unit for the . . . air compressor, " plaintiff also alleged that the air compressor was neither merchantable nor fit for the particular purpose for which plaintiff purchased it, because it contained "latent defects," and "because of the absence of proper safety devices." Under notice pleading theory of Rule 8(a)(1), plaintiff's allegations of latent defects sufficiently raised the issue of breach of implied warranty.

* * *

Defendant contends the court should have granted its motions for directed verdict, judgment notwithstanding the verdict and new trial for one or more of the following reasons: (1) plaintiff failed to show a "sale" by defendant to plaintiff of the air compressor and therefore no implied warranties could have arisen; (2) plaintiff failed to show that a defect existed at the time of sale; (3) the evidence was too speculative to go to the jury. The court properly denied the motions for directed verdict and judgment notwithstanding the verdict if, when it viewed the evidence in the light more favorable to plaintiff and gave plaintiff the benefit of all reasonable inferences, it found "any evidence more than a scintilla to support plaintiff's prima facie case in all its constituent elements." [Citations omitted.] To present a prima facia case of breach of implied warranty under G.S. 25-2-314 plaintiff must produce any evidence more than a scintilla (1) that an implied warranty covered the goods in question, (2) that the seller breached the warranty in that the goods were not merchantable at the time of sale, and (3) that the breach proximately caused the injury and loss sustained by plaintiff. [Citations omitted.]

As to the first element, "[u]nless excluded or modified (§ 25-2-314), a warranty that the goods shall be merchantable is implied in a contract for their sale if the seller is a merchant with respect to goods of that kind." G.S. 25-2-314(1). In its answer, defendant admitted that it was a corporation engaged in the business of whole-

sale and retail selling of air compressors, thereby admitting that it was both a "seller" and a "merchant" of air compressors. [Citations omitted.] Defendant argues no implied warranty arose as between it and plaintiff because the air compressor in question was shipped to plaintiff's plant directly from the manufacturer's factory and did not physically pass from defendant to plaintiff. G.S. 25-2-314(1) does not require a physical passing of goods from seller to buyer, however. The implied warranty arises upon a "contract for . . . sale." G.S. 25-26-314(1) [ellipse in original]. Defendant admitted that the manufacturer "sold" the air compressor in question to defendant and that defendant acquired title to it. [Citation omitted.] Defendant also admitted that plaintiff purchased the compressor from it and that it billed plaintiff for the unit. * * * The fact that the compressor did not pass through defendant's warehouse, but was shipped directly from the manufacturer's factory to plaintiff, does not render the transaction something other than a contract for sale. Defendant had title to the compressor, and the evidence indicated that it contracted to pass title to plaintiff. Plaintiff's evidence indicated that defendant made no express warranties to plaintiff concerning the air compressor, and therefore that the parties did not exclude or modify the 25-2-314 implied warranty. [Citations omitted.] * * *

As to the second element, breach of the implied warranty, plaintiff must offer evidence that the goods in question were not merchantable at the time of sale. [Citations omitted.] Plaintiff can establish lack of merchantability by showing, *inter alia,* that the goods were not fit for the ordinary purpose for which such goods are purchased because they contained a defect at the time of sale. G.S. 25-2-314(2)(c). Plaintiff's [expert] witness, Dr. Zorowski [a mechanical engineer] testified that in his opinion there was a defect in the connection of the service wire to the motor wire inside the terminal or juncture box of the compressor, which could have been aggravated by the vibration of the machine over the two year period of almost continuous operation of the compressor. He also testified that the vibration itself could have caused fatigue at any point where two wires connected. Plaintiff offered evidence from several witnesses that the terminal box was a closed system, and that no one had tampered with or altered any of the electrical wiring of the compressor between the time of the sale and the fire. Viewed in the light most favorable to plaintiff, this evidence indicates breach of the implied warranty of merchantability, in that from it the jury could find existence of a defect at the time of sale and thus lack of fitness for the ordinary purpose for which air compressors are used.

As to the third element, that of proximate cause, Dr. Zorowski testified that in his opinion the fire started as a consequence of electrical arcing across a separated or broken connection between two wires in the terminal box, and that such broken connection resulted from a defect in the wiring or the vibration of the compressor or both. His testimony, viewed in the light most favorable to plaintiff, established as the proximate cause of the fire the alleged defect in or unfitness of the air compressor. Plaintiff's vice president and general manager at the time of the fire testified that the fire completely destroyed plaintiff's shop. He testified that after the fire he supervised an inventory of the shop and the compilation of a list of materials and machinery lost with their values before and after the fire. Plaintiff introduced the list into evidence. Plaintiff's evidence thus indicates both proximate cause and the resultant loss.

A jury could find from the evidence produced each essential element of breach of implied warranty by defendant. The evidence was in no way "too speculative" to allow the jury to decide the question of defendant's liability and the resultant damages. Defendant produced no evidence which negated an element of breach of implied warranty as a matter of law. Therefore, the court did not err in denying defendant's options for directed verdict and judgment notwithstanding the verdict.

The ruling on defendant's motion in the alternative for a new trial rested within the discretion of the trial court. The appellate court will not reverse the action of the trial court as to a matter in its discretion absent an abuse of discretion. [Citation omitted.] We find no abuse of discretion in the court's denial of defendant's motion for new trial. * * *

Case Notes: Establishing a Breach of the Implied Warranty of Merchantability

1. What "elements" does the court in *Southern of Rocky Mount v. Woodward Specialty Sales, Inc.* describe when it refers to the items that plaintiff must prove? Do these elements establish a cause of action for breach of the Implied Warranty of Merchantability under the UCC?

2. Even used goods may qualify as merchantable depending on the product's ability to fit within a contract's description and may be fit for ordinary uses. In *Testo v. Russ Dunmire Oldsmobile, Inc.*, 554 P.2d 349, 353 (Wash. Ct. App. 1976), the court held that

> [h]ence, an implied warranty of merchantability attached to the sale [of the used product]. The Code does not distinguish between new and used good, the sale of which gives rise to implied warranties. We hold that "unless excluded or modified" a warranty of merchantability arises in the sale of a used automobile.

3. Assuming that the facts were available, what other ways could Rocky Mount have established that Woodward Specialty's compressor was not a merchantable product? Where are these other ways found? What is the authority that evidence of these other ways would, in fact, constitute a breach of the implied warranty of merchantability?

4. If Woodward Specialty had to show that a "sale" had not occurred between it and Rocky Mount, would Rocky Mount have been able to prove a breach of the implied warranty of merchantability? What critical element was Woodward Specialty attacking when it argued that a "sale" had not occurred between it and Rocky Mount? Was it convincing? Was there a preponderance of evidence to prove this issue?

5. Why is it important that the appellate court repeatedly use the phrase "a jury could find from the evidence?" With regard to Rocky Mount's evidence of the first element, why does the Court view the evidence "in the light most favorable to plaintiff?" What is the standard of review for defendant's motion for

judgment notwithstanding the verdict? Or for a new trial? At what point are these motions properly raised? Why did Woodward Specialty raise them here?

6. What must Rocky Mount have proven in order to have put on a submissible case that Woodward Specialty breached the implied warranty of merchantability? What level of proof must plaintiff have reached in order to have sufficiently proven Woodward Specialty's breach?

7. Was the testimony of Dr. Zorowski essential to establish a breach of the implied warranty? What was his role at trial? What element(s) did his testimony prove? Could other witnesses have provided testimony that proved the same element(s)?

8. What would the result of the case have likely been if it had been filed in a "fact pleading" jurisdiction?

Implied Warranty of Fitness for a Particular Purpose

Implied warranties of fitness may be found in transactions where the buyer is looking for a product to meet a specific need, the seller knows about the buyer's need, and the buyer relies on the seller to suggest an appropriate product to fulfill the need. In this instance, the product must be fit for the particular purpose suggested by the seller, and the buyer is given implied warranty protection to assure the product's particular purpose. This warranty is narrower than the implied warranty of merchantability and does not apply to all product transactions. It is limited to those instances in which an anticipated particular use of the product was required by the buyer and fulfilled by the seller.

The UCC defines the implied warranty of fitness for a particular purpose as follows:

UCC§ 2-315. Implied Warranty of Fitness for a Particular Purpose. Where the seller at the time of contracting has reason to know any particular purpose for which the goods are required and that the buyer is relying on the seller's skill or judgment to select or furnish suitable goods, there is unless excluded or modified under the next section an implied warranty that the goods shall be fit for such purpose.

Establishing the existence of this implied warranty.   To establish the existence of an implied warranty of fitness for a particular purpose, the product buyer must prove that

1. the seller had reason to know about the buyer's specific need and that the buyer would rely on the seller's skill, judgment, or expertise
2. buyer relied on the seller's skill, judgment, or expertise to select and suggest a suitable product

First, courts ordinarily require that the seller simply be aware that these two "reason to know" requirements are present. The product seller need not have actual knowledge about the buyer's anticipated particular purpose, or use of the product, or that the buyer was relying upon the seller's skill, judgment, or expertise. For example, if a buyer sought to purchase a laptop computer, it is implicit that the buyer's particular purpose is to be able to operate his computer in remote locations, such as on a plane, on the beach, or in the woods. The seller need not know that the buyer actually intends to use the laptop computer while hiking Mount Everest. Furthermore, if the buyer is completely without any computer literacy, he necessarily will rely on the seller's skill, judgment, and expertise to make a purchasing decision about which laptop computer is appropriate for his particular use.

Second, unlike the "reason to know" criteria, the product buyer must actually rely on the seller's skill, judgment, or expertise in selecting and suggesting the appropriate product. In so relying, the seller's knowledge of the product must be demonstrably higher than that of the buyer. If the buyer's own expertise is the equivalent or greater than that of the seller, the buyer may not be able to prove reliance or, therefore, that an implied warranty existed in this transaction at all.

 CASE LAW

◆ **establishing an implied warranty of fitness for a particular purpose**

Lewis v. Mobil Oil Corporation, 438 F.2d 500 (8th Cir. 1971).

Plaintiff Paul Lewis, doing business as a saw mill, company sued defendant Mobil Oil for breach of the warranty of fitness for a particular purpose. Lewis sought to purchase a lubricant from Mobil to use in his new hydraulic power equipment. Lewis' local Mobil Oil dealer, Frank Rowe, contacted Mobil about the proper lubricant to be supplied and began selling Ambrex 810 to Lewis. After Lewis began using Ambrex 810, he began experiencing difficulty with his new equipment. Within six months, complete new equipment had to be installed, and over the next two years, six new pumps were required as they continually broke down.

After 2 1/2 years of difficulty, Lewis was visited by a Mobil Oil representative, who recommended that he use Mobil's DTE 23 and Del Vae Special lubricant. After the change, Lewis experienced no further trouble with his hydraulic equipment. Mobil Oil defended the lawsuit by arguing that Lewis' breakdowns were caused by improper filtration and not by using an improper lubricant.

Gibson, Circuit Judge.

* * *

This evidence adequately establishes an implied warranty of fitness. Arkansas has adopted the Uniform Commercial Code's provision for an implied warranty of fitness. [UCC § 2-315 ('96') omitted.] Under this provision of the Code, there are two requirements for an implied warranty of fitness: (1) that the seller have "reason to know" of the use for which the goods are purchased, and (2) that the buyer relies on the seller's expertise in supplying the proper product. Both of these requirements are amply met by the proof in this case. Lewis' testimony, as confirmed by that of Rowe and Klock [a Mobil engineer who had recommended Ambrex 810], shows that the oil was purchased specifically for his hydraulic system, not for just a hydraulic system in general, and that Mobil certainly knew of this specific purpose. It is also clear that Lewis was relying on Mobil to supply him with the proper oil for the system, since at the time of his purchases, he made clear that he didn't know what kind was necessary.

Mobil contends that there was no warranty of fitness for use in his particular system because he didn't specify that he needed an oil with additives, and alternatively that they didn't give them enough information for them to determine that an additive oil was required. However, it seems that the circumstances of this case come directly within that situation described in the first comment to this [§ 2-315] provision of the Uniform Commercial Code:

1. Whether or not this warranty arises in any individual case is basically a question of fact to be determined by the circumstances of the contracting. Under this section the buyer need not bring home to the seller *actual knowledge of the particular purpose* for which the goods are intended or of his reliance on the seller's skill and judgment, if the circumstances are such that the seller has reason to realize the purpose intended or that the reliance exists. [Citation omitted.] (emphasis added).

Here Lewis made it clear that the oil was purchased for his system, that he didn't know what oil should be used, and that he was relying on Mobil to supply the proper product. If any further information was needed, it was incumbent upon Mobil to get it before making its recommendation. That it could have easily gotten the necessary information is evidenced by the fact that after plaintiff's continuing complaints, Mobil's engineer visited the plant, and, upon inspection, changed the recommendation that had previously been made.

Additionally, Mobil contends that even if there were an implied warranty of fitness, it does not cover the circumstances of this case because of the abnormal features which the plaintiff's system contained, namely an inadequate filtration system and a capacity to entrain excessive air. There are several answers to this contention. First of all, the contention goes essentially to the question of causation—i.e., whether the damage was caused by a breach of warranty or by some other cause—and not to the existence of a warranty of fitness in the first place. Secondly, assuming that certain peculiarities in the plaintiff's system did exist, the whole point of an implied warranty of fitness is that a product be suitable for a specific purpose, and that a seller should not supply a product which is not so suited. Thirdly, there is no evidence in the record that the plaintiff's system was unique or abnormal in these respects. It operated satisfactorily under the prior owner, and the new system has operated satisfactorily after it was adequately cleaned and an additive type oil was used.

While we will discuss these problems more completely in the question of causation, it may be briefly noted here that the proof shows that plaintiff's filtration system was installed and maintained in strict accordance with the manufacturer's recommendations, that this was a standard system, and that any hydraulic system has a certain unavoidable capacity to entrain air. While a "perfect" system which is run 24 hours a day might not have any air in it, in actual practice there are at least two sources of air. One is from minute leaks in packing glands. The other source arises from the fact that when the system is shut down, as at night and over the lunch hour, as well as for repairs, the oil drains out of the system and into the reservoir. When the system is started up again, air which has entered the system to replace the drained oil must be dissipated. This dissipation occurs by running the system for a few minutes and is affected by the capacity of the oil to rid itself of air bubbles. It is sufficient to note here that there was no evidence that the plaintiff's system was in any way unique in this respect. Thus, Mobil's defense that there was no warranty of fitness because of an "abnormal use" of the oil is not appropriate here.

Case Notes: Establishing an Implied Warranty of Fitness for a Particular Purpose

1. It is incumbent on the seller to obtain as much specific information as necessary to determine the buyer's particular purpose. Otherwise, the seller is charged with the burden of having "reason to know" that the buyer generally had an anticipated particular purpose for using the product. See *Lewis v. Mobil Oil Corp.*, 438 F.2d 500, 504 (8th Cir. 1971).

2. Did Lewis rely on Mobil Oil to provide the proper lubricant? Was Lewis' reliance sufficient to establish existence of the warranty? What was Frank Rowe's role in Lewis' reliance on Mobil Oil?

3. Why is it incumbent on the seller to obtain additional information about the buyer's intended particular use of the product? Why not require the buyer to provide additional information about the particular use of the product he seeks to purchase if, in fact, he is going to be given the protection of an implied warranty of fitness for a particular purpose?

4. Did Lewis have adequate proof of Mobil Oil's "reason to know" that he required a particular product for his hydraulic equipment? How did Lewis prove actual reliance? Was a trial necessary in order to present this proof?

5. Courts typically decide the existence of this implied warranty on a case-by-case basis. See comment 1 to UCC § 2-315. A jury (or other finder of fact), however, is not always required to make a decision about whether the product buyer had adequate proof of reliance. Some courts have held that reliance did not exist as a matter of law where the product buyer had

more skill, information, knowledge, or expertise regarding the product. See *H.B. Fuller Co. v. Kinetic Systems, Inc.*, 932 F.2d 681, 689 (7th Cir. 1991); *Binks Manufacturing Co. v. National Presto Industries, Inc.*, 709 F.2d 1109, 1122 (7th Cir. 1983).

6. Reliance is an essential element to this implied warranty. Comment 1 to § 2-315 provides that

> Whether or not this warranty arises in any individual case is basically a question of fact to be determined by the circumstances of the contracting. Under this section the buyer need not bring home to the seller actual knowledge of the particular purpose for which the goods are intended

or of his reliance on the seller's skill and judgment, if the circumstances are such that the seller has reason to realize the purpose intended or that the reliance exists. The buyer, of course, must actually be relying on the seller.

7. The most distinguishing characteristic of the implied warranty of fitness for a particular purpose is the difference between a product's ordinary purpose and its particular purpose. This difference is often difficult to discern because it requires a subjective analysis, which will differ from case to case and from court to court. The difference between these two purposes is described by the next case, *Van Wyk v. Norden Laboratories, Inc.*, 345 N.W.2d 81 (Iowa 1984).

Identifying the Particular Purpose in an Implied Warranty

 CASE LAW

◆ **distinguishing a particular purpose from an ordinary purpose**

Van Wyk v. Norden Laboratories, Inc., 345 N.W.2d 81 (Iowa 1984).

Plaintiff cattle owners sued vaccine manufacturer Norden Laboratories after a number of cattle became sick and died upon being treated with a live-virus vaccine, Resbo-3, serial 54. Within a week of injection, most of 750 cattle became sick with bovine viral diarrhea ("BVD") and almost 50 died. Among other theories, plaintiffs sued the defendant vaccine manufacturer for breach of the implied warranty of fitness for a particular purpose. The Iowa Supreme Court found that a cause of action for breach of this implied warranty did not exist because the vaccine was intended to be used by the plaintiff cattle owners for ordinary purposes.

Larson, Justice.

* * *

The only theory of liability submitted by the court was breach of implied warranty of fitness for a particular purpose. [Citation to Iowa's adoption of UCC § 2-315 omitted.] The implied warranty of fitness for a particular purpose under section 554.2315 is perhaps better understood when viewed with the implied warranty of merchantability, or fitness for ordinary purposes. [Citation to Iowa's adoption of UCC § 2-314 omitted.]

The official comment to the Uniform Commercial Code illustrates the difference between "ordinary" and "particular" purposes under the respective warranties:

> A "particular purpose" differs from the ordinary purpose for which the goods are used in that it envisages a specific use by the buyer which is peculiar to the nature of his business whereas the ordinary purposes for which goods are used are those envisaged in the concept of merchantability and go to uses which are customarily made of the goods in question. For example, shoes are generally used for the

purpose of walking upon ordinary ground, but a seller may know that a particular pair was selected to be used for climbing mountains. [Citing comment 2 of Iowa's adoption of UCC §2-315; other citations omitted.]

The warranty of merchantability, Iowa Code § 554.2314, is based on a purchaser's reasonable expectation that goods purchased from a "merchant with respect to goods of that kind" will be free of significant defects and will perform in the way goods of that kind should perform. It presupposes no special relationship of trust or reliance between the seller and buyer. In contrast, the warranty of fitness for a particular purpose, Iowa Code § 554.2315, is based on a special reliance by the buyer on the seller to provide goods that will perform a specific use envisaged and communicated by the buyer. Thus any recovery under warranty for a specific purpose is predicated on a showing that (1) the seller had reason to know of the buyer's particular purpose; (2) the seller had reason to know the buyer was relying on the seller's skill or judgment to furnish suitable goods; and (3) the buyer in fact relied on the seller's skill or judgment to furnish suitable goods. [Citations omitted.]

The warranty of fitness under section 554.2315 is said to turn on the "bargain-related" facts as to what the seller had reason to know about the buyer's purpose for the goods and about his reliance on the seller's skill or judgment in selecting them. [Citation omitted.] In this case the vaccine was not purchased by the veterinarians to treat these particular cattle but to keep in stock for their general veterinary practice. The plaintiffs, as owners of the cattle, and the defendant, had no direct dealing with regard to the vaccine. The decision as to what vaccine to use was made by the buyers' veterinarians, not by the defendant. There was no evidence that the seller had reason to know of any purpose for the plaintiffs' use of the vaccine, other than its ordinary use, or that the buyer was relying on the seller's skill and judgment in providing it. The implied warranty of fitness for a particular purpose would appear, therefore, to be inapplicable by its terms. [Citations omitted.]

The plaintiffs argue, however, that if the buyer's particular purpose is the same as its general use, a warranty of fitness arises, especially when the product has a specific and limited use. In that case, the other elements of the fitness warranty, i.e., the knowledge of the buyer's purpose, the knowledge of the buyer's reliance, and the buyer's actual reliance, are apparently to be presumed.

* * *

In this case, written material furnished with the vaccine stated that "[f]or reducing the economic loss associated with these viruses, vaccination of healthy animals is recommended before or upon entering the feedlot or dairy herd. Vaccination of stressed animals should be delayed." Use of the vaccine on healthy, unstressed cattle, in accordance with these instructions, is the "ordinary" use for warranty purposes, according to the defendant, and the plaintiffs' evidence was aimed at showing a use in compliance with the instructions, in other words, an "ordinary" use. While there was contradicting evidence presented by the defendant that the cattle were stressed and perhaps not healthy at the time they were vaccinated, there is no claim by the plaintiffs that this deviation from ordinary use is itself a "particular" use. They merely claim that their use here is an ordinary use which we should consider as a particular use for warranty purposes. For the reasons to be discussed, we decline to do so.

Case Notes: Identifying the Particular Purpose

1. Are particular purposes and ordinary purposes the hallmarks of the implied warranties of fitness for a particular purpose and of merchantability, respectively? In other words, is it sufficient to determine the existence of a particular or ordinary purpose, which will in turn determine which of the two implied warranties exist?

On this issue, the Court in *Van Wyk* stated the following:

It is quite another matter, however, to impose an implied warranty of fitness solely on the basis of this identity of purpose. A particular purpose of the buyer is only one of the elements of that warranty; it still turns on what the seller had reason to know—both as to the buyer's particular purpose and as the buyer's reliance on the seller's skill and judgment. 345 N.W.2d at 85.

2. The Court in *Van Wyk* cites a portion of Comment 2 of UCC § 2-315. Comment 2 also states the following:

> A contract may of course include both a warranty of merchantability and one of fitness for a particular purpose.
>
> The provisions of this Article on the cumulation and conflict of express and implied warranties must be considered on the question of inconsistency between or among warranties. In such a case any question of fact as to which warranty was intended by the parties to apply must be resolved in favor of the warranty of fitness for particular purpose as against all other warranties except where the buyer has taken upon himself the responsibility of furnishing the technical specifications.

3. Some courts have held that a buyer's specific use may be the same as the product's general use, thereby allowing both warranties to exist under the circumstances. In *Tennessee Carolina Transportation, Inc. v. Strick Corp.*, 196 S.W.2d 711 (N.C. 1973), the North Carolina Supreme Court rejected the general rule that a particular purpose must be a use not normally expected to be had of goods and allowed both purposes, and therefore both warranties, to exist in and arise from the same transaction. Cases such as these have been criticized as enlarging the fitness warranty beyond the intent of the UCC. See *Van Wyk*, 345 N.W.2d at 85.

4. How do particular purposes differ from ordinary purposes? If particular purposes are typically those in which the buyer envisions a specific use that is peculiar to her or his own business or needs, what is inherent about a product's ordinary purpose? Can they exist at the same time?

5. How does *reliance* help to distinguish the implied warranty of fitness for a particular purpose from the implied warranty of merchantability? Is reliance a requisite element of an implied warranty of merchantability?

6. Given the portion of the case provided, what other theories were available to plaintiffs against the vaccine manufacturer? For what reason did the court reject the submission of these theories to the jury at trial?

7. What proof were plaintiffs lacking in order to make a submissible case that the defendant manufacturer had breached the implied warranty of fitness for a particular purpose? Did that evidence exist? How did the defendant manufacturer go about demonstrating that the trial court had committed error by submitting the implied warranty of fitness for a particular purpose theory? What was the specific error committed by the trial court regarding this theory?

8. Was the defendant manufacturer the proper defendant under the facts alleged by plaintiffs using the theory of implied warranty of fitness for a particular purpose? What defendant(s) could plaintiffs have more appropriately named?

FEDERAL STATUTES PROVIDING WARRANTY PROTECTION: THE MAGNUSON-MOSS ACT

The Magnuson-Moss Act is a federal statute that requires product manufacturers and product sellers to provide written warranties that fully and conspicuously disclose the terms and conditions of the warranty. In most instances, the Act provides relief for damages to the product itself (such as its purchase price) where the product is defective, malfunctions, or fails to conform with the written warranty. The Act has provisions for enforcement through both private and public causes of action. It does not, however, displace or preempt any warranty actions that are available to product consumers by any particular state law.

Magnuson-Moss Act 15 U.S.C. §§ 2301-2312 (1975)

§ 2301. **Definitions** [For the purposes of this chapter]

(1) The term "consumer product" means any tangible personal property which is distributed in commerce and which is normally used for personal, family, or household purposes (including any such property intended to be attached to or installed in any real property without regard to whether it is so attached or installed).

* * *

(5) The term "warrantor" means any supplier or other person who gives or offers to give a written warranty or who is or may be obligated under an implied warranty.

(6) The term "written warranty" means—

(A) any written affirmation of fact or written promise made in connection with the sale of a consumer product by a supplier to a buyer which relates to the nature of the material or workmanship and affirms or promises that such material or workmanship is defect free or will meet a specified level of performance over a specified period of time, or

(B) any undertaking in writing in connection with the sale by a supplier of a consumer product to refund, repair, replace, or take other remedial action with respect to such product in the event that such product fails to meet the specifications set forth in the undertaking, which written affirmation, promise, or undertaking becomes part of the basis of the bargain between a supplier and a buyer for purposes other than resale of such product.

(7) The term "implied warranty" means an implied warranty arising under State law (as modified by sections 2308 and 2304(a) of the title) in connection with the sale by a supplier of a consumer product.

* * *

(10) The term "remedy" means whichever of the following actions the warrantor elects:

(A) repair,

(B) replacement, or

(C) refund;

except that the warrantor may not elect refund unless (i) the warrantor is unable to provide replacement and repair is not commercially practicable or cannot be timely made, or (ii) the consumer is willing to accept such refund.

* * *

§ 2302. Rules governing contents of warranties

(a) Full and conspicuous disclosure of terms and conditions; additional requirements for contents

In order to improve the adequacy of information available to consumers, prevent deception, and improve competition in the marketing of consumer products, any warrantor warranting a consumer product to a consumer by means of a written warranty shall, to the extent required by rules of the Commission, fully and conspicuously disclose in simple and readily understood language the terms and conditions of such warranty. . .

* * *

§ 2303. Designation of written warranties

(a) Full (statement of duration) or limited warranty

Any warrantor warranting a consumer product by means of a written warranty shall clearly and conspicuously designate such warranty in the following manner, unless exempted from doing so by the Commission pursuant to subsection (c) of this section:

(1) If the written warranty meets the Federal minimum standards for warranty set forth in section 2304 of this title, then it shall be conspicuously designated a "full (statement of duration) warranty".

(2) If the written warranty does not meet the Federal minimum standards for warranty set forth in section 2304 of this title, then it shall be conspicuously designated a "limited warranty".

* * *

§ 2304. Federal minimum standards for warranties

(a) Remedies under written warranty; duration of implied warranty; exclusion or limitation on consequential damages for breach of written or implied warranty; election of refund or replacement

In order for a warrantor warranting a consumer product by means of a written warranty to meet the Federal minimum standards for warranty—

(1) such warrantor must as a minimum, remedy such consumer product within a reasonable time and without charge, in the case of a defect, malfunction, or failure to conform with such written warranty;

(2) notwithstanding section 2308(b) of this title, such warrantor may not impose any limitation on the duration of any implied warranty on the product;

(3) such warrantor may not exclude or limit consequential damages for breach of any written or implied warranty on such product, unless such exclusion or limitation conspicuously appears on the face of the warranty; and

(4) if the product (or a component part thereof) contains a defect or malfunction after a reasonable number of attempts by the warrantor to remedy defects or malfunctions in such product, such warrantor must permit the consumer to elect either a refund for, or replacement without charge of, such product or part (as the case may be). The Commission may by rule specify for purposes of this paragraph, what constitutes a reasonable number of attempts to remedy particular kinds of defects or malfunctions under different circumstances. If the warrantor replaces a component part of a consumer product, such replacement shall include installing the part in the product.

* * *

§2310 (d) Civil action by consumer for damages, etc; jurisdiction; recovery of costs and expenses; cognizable claims

(1) Subject to subsections (a)(3) and (e) of this section, a consumer who is damaged by the failure of a supplier, warrantor, or service contractor to comply with any obligation under this chapter, or under a written warranty, or service contract, may bring suit for damages and other legal and equitable relief—

(A) in any court of competent jurisdiction in any State or the District of Columbia; or

(B) in an appropriate district court of the United States subject to paragraph (3) of this subsection.

(2) If a consumer finally prevails in any action brought under paragraph (1) of this subsection, he may be allowed by the court to recover as part of the judgment a sum equal to the aggregate amount of costs and expenses (including attorneys' fees based on actual time expended) determined by the court to have been reasonably incurred by the plaintiff for or in connection with the commencement and prosecution of such action, unless the court in its discretion shall determine that such an award of attorneys' fees would be inappropriate.

(3) No claim shall be cognizable in a suit brought under paragraph (1)(B) of this subsection—

(A) if the amount in controversy of any individual claim is less than the sum of value of $25;

(B) if the amount in controversy is less than the sum or value of $50,000 (exclusive of interests and costs) computed on the basis of all claims to be determined in this suit; or

(C) if the action is brought as a class action, and the number of named plaintiffs is less than one hundred.

 **CASE LAW**

◆ **viable causes of action under the Magnuson-Moss Act**

Todd GORMAN, a minor child, et al. v. SAF-T-MATE, INC., a Michigan Corporation, and North Harbor, Inc., an Indiana Corporation d/b/a North Harbor Marine, 513 F. Supp. 1028 (N.D. Ind. 1981).

Minor child injured by a motor boat brought a cause of action for personal injuries under the Magnuson-Moss Act. The central issue was whether Federal court had proper subject matter jurisdiction for Personal injury action under 15 U.S.C. § 2301-2312.

ESCHBACH, Chief Judge.

This cause is before the court on the September 12, 1980 motion to dismiss filed by defendant Saf-T-Mate, Inc. The motion challenges plaintiffs' complaint on a variety of grounds. One of those challenges raises the question whether the private cause of action created by the Magnuson-Moss Warranty Act (Warranty Act), 15 U.S.C. § 2301 *et seq.,* for breach of consumer product warranties includes damage claims for personal injury. This court concludes that the cause of action created by the federal statute does not, with certain exceptions, extend so far.

* * *

If such personal injury claims are cognizable under the Act, numerous products liability actions which historically have been confined largely to the state courts could be brought in federal court regardless of the locus of citizenship of the parties. This would be a major expansion of the jurisdiction of the federal district courts. Unless the authors of federal legislation clearly convey their meaning, there is a presumption against construing a statute so as to significantly change the federal-state jurisdictional balance. [Citations omitted.] This rule of interpretation calls for a very thorough examination of the statute.

The task, however, poses a very considerable challenge:

A literal reading of the Magnuson-Moss Act is only a departure point for giving meaningful content to the statute which has been variously described as "disappointing", "opaque", and a product of "poor drafting". A review of the legislative history gives but limited solace. That review is the legal equivalent of an archeological dig. Various consumer warranty bills were pending before the House and Senate for four years, during which each body defined, discarded, reintroduced and redefined concepts which in some fashion or another are related to the enacted legislation. Some provisions in the Act are vestigial reminders of concepts buried but not totally forgotten during the ongoing legislative process. Both proponents and opponents of an expansive interpretation have cited compelling, to them, legislative history only dimly related to the language which finally emerged as law. *Skelton v. General Motors Corp.,* 500 F.Supp. 1181, 1184 (N.D.Ill.1980)(footnotes omitted).

The Warranty Act, 15 U.S.C. §§ 2301 to 2312, applies principally to products which sell at retail for more than five dollars and are accompanied by written warranties. The Act does not require written warranties, but if they are given the Act imposes a wide variety of requirements upon the form and content of such warranties. Written warranties for consumer products costing more than ten dollars must be prominently designated as "full" or "limited" warranties. 15 U.S.C. § 2303. A "full" warranty must comply with a list of minimum standards. The party obligated under a full warranty must remedy defective products without charge. *Id.* § 2304(a)(1). Any disclaimer of liability for consequential damages must be conspicuous, *Id.* § 2304(a)(3), and state-law implied warranty liability may not be limited or disclaimed. *Id.* § 2304(a)(2). Although "limited" warranties are not subject to these standards, the Act does provide that the terms of a limited warranty shall not disclaim implied warranty liability for the "duration" of the limited warranty. *Id.* § 2308. Finally, subject to rules promulgated by the Federal Trade Commission, both full and limited warranties must "fully and conspicuously disclose in simple and readily understood language [their] terms and conditions. . . ." *Id.* § 2302(a). These warranty obligations imposed by the Warranty Act are hereinafter alternatively referred to as the Act's "form and content standards" or "substantive obligations."

"The draftsmen believed that warranties on consumer products often were too complex to be understood, too varied for consumers to make intelligent market comparisons, and too restrictive for meaningful warranty protection." Schroeder, *Private Actions under the Magnuson-Moss Warranty Act*, 66 Calif.L.Rev. 1, 2 (1978). Taken as a whole, the Act is concerned primarily with eliminating deceptive warranty practices.

To that end, the "form and content" standards are subject to judicial enforcement. The Justice Department, the Federal Trade Commission and individual consumers are all authorized by separate provisions of the Act to sue to enforce the substantive obligations under the Act. 15 U.S.C. §§ 2310(c) and (d). Section 2310(d)'s private cause of action for individual consumers, however, covers more than just the "form and content" provisions of the Act; it also permits consumers to sue for breach of written or implied warranties pertaining to consumer products. [Footnote omitted.]

The cause of action provision of the Warranty Act refers to three categories of claims: breach of the substantive obligations of the Act, breach of written warranty, and breach of implied warranty. [Footnote omitted.] "The term 'implied warranty' means an implied warranty arising under State law. . . ." *Id.* § 2301(7). Therefore, while this is in large part a federal statutory cause of action, to the extent that it adopts or incorporates state law as the source of liability for implied warranty claims [footnote omitted], it also operates as a hybrid state-federal cause of action.

The private cause of action created by the Act may be asserted in state court and, with certain significant limitations, in federal court. Section 2310 (d)(1)(A) [footnote omitted] affords access to the state courts for such causes of action. Additional requirements must be met to invoke federal jurisdiction under the Act. The total amount in controversy must be at least $50,000, although claims of joined plaintiffs can be aggregated to satisfy this amount, and if a plaintiff class action is to be brought in federal court, the complaint must name at least 100 plaintiffs. 15 U.S.C. § 2310(d)(3).

The novel question presented in this case is whether the cause of action provision includes personal injury claims. The prior reported cases under the Magnuson-Moss Act have involved questions of direct damages (repair, replacement, or refund) as opposed to consequential damages such as those involving personal injuries. [Citations omitted.]

A. Statutory Purpose

Reading § 2310(d) as an integrated whole, it is less than obvious that the cause of action, jurisdiction, and attorney fees provisions were designed to deal with personal injury claims arising out of defective consumer products; its central purpose is to create a new and more effective remedial mechanism for consumer claims involving comparatively small amounts of damages. Congress obviously felt that most aggrieved consumers would go without redress because their individual claims are too insignificant to command representation by counsel or to warrant all the other expenses of invoking the judicial process. "Because enforcement of the warranty through the courts is prohibitively expensive, there exists no currently available remedy for consumers to enforce warranty obligations." S.Rep. No. 93-151, 93d Cong., 1st Sess. 7 (1973). Congress was also of the view that existing federal and state court procedural requirements offered too many impediments to the maintenance of consumer class actions. *See* H.R.Rep. No. 93-1107, 93d Cong. 2d Sess., *reprinted in* [1974] U.S.Code Cong. & Ad. News 7702, 7724 (criticizing requirement of individual notice to potential class members). Accordingly, Congress sought to advance the federal policies expressed in the Warranty Act by fashioning a remedial mechanism for small consumer claims. The court is authorized to award a reasonable sum to defray costs and attorney fees as part of a judgment in favor of a consumer. 15 U.S.C. § 2310(d)(2). This feature obviously was designed primarily for the benefit of consumers having small damage claims. In addition, contrary to the general rule in diversity actions, claims of joined plaintiffs, including members of a plaintiff class, may be aggregated to satisfy the $50,000 federal court jurisdictional amount, as long as each member of the plaintiff class is claiming at least $25. *Id.* § 2310(d)(3). The provision allowing aggregation of such small claims is yet another indication that the cause of action provision contemplates rather small damage claims.

While the provisions for attorney fees and federal court class actions are the most readily apparent clues to the purposes of the cause-of-action provision, there is also some highly corroborative evidence in the report of the House Commerce Committee: "In this context, your Committee would emphasize that this section [2310(d)] is remedial in nature and is designed to facilitate relief which would otherwise not be available as a practical matter for individual consumers." H.R.Rep No. 93-1107,

93d Cong., 2d Sess., *reprinted in* [1974] U.S.Code Cong. & Ad. News 7702, 7724. There is only one variety of consumer complaint for which relief "would otherwise not be available," and that is the small warranty claim seeking repair, replacement or refund. That is the only kind of claim where the amount in controversy is ordinarily so small that individual private enforcement in the courts is "prohibitively expensive."

A personal injury case involving a substantial damage claim is not the type of claim which Congress apparently sought to remedy by § 2310(d). A judicial forum for such cases is not "otherwise unavailable"; they may be pursued without any significant impediments in the state courts, and of course, where diversity of citizenship and the requisite amount in controversy are present, also in the federal courts pursuant to 28 U.S.C. § 1332. In personal injury cases, such as the case at bar, the likelihood of obtaining a substantial damage award is generally sufficient to justify the assumption of all the litigation expenses by the injured party. Even if the personal injury plaintiff is unable to pay these expenses, so long as the claim for relief is arguably meritorious counsel can be retained on a contingent-fee basis. Personal injury claims have always been able to command a judicial remedy.

In sum, the apparent legislative purpose of § 2310(d) is to provide a mechanism for consumer actions involving direct damages; it was not designed to reach personal injury claims.

* * *

C. Scope of Personal Injury Liability

The preceding interpretation of § 2310(d) and (e) is reinforced by the language of Section 2311(b)(2):

Nothing in this title (other than sections 2308 and 2304(a)(2) and (4)) shall (A) affect the liability of, or impose liability on, any person for personal injury, or (B) supersede any provision of State Law regarding consequential damages for injury to the person or other injury.

This provision clearly indicates that the Act creates no new cause of action for personal injury damages except in the case of the specific provisions referred to in § 2311(b)(2).

Thus, the provisions recited in parentheses *do* create additional personal injury liability. Breach of these provisions, however, is actionable under § 2310(d) as violative of the substantive obligations of the Act, rather than merely as breach of warranty, and hence is not limited by § 2310(e)'s "cure" requirement which refers only to actions for breach of warranty. Section 2308 clearly affects a warrantor's potential personal injury liability, because it restricts the power to disclaim or modify implied warranties.

* * *

Section 2311(b)(2) states expressly what §§ 2304 and 2308 fairly imply: Congress was content to let the question of personal injury products liability remain a matter of state-law causes of action, except to the extent that certain substantive provisions in the Magnuson-Moss Act overrule contrary state laws relating to the warrantor's ability to disclaim personal injury liability. One of the prime concerns addressed in the Act was the warranty wherein the large print giveth but the small print taketh away. Prior to passage of the Act, it was not uncommon for manufacturers of consumer products to issue documents which purported to be warranties but had the net effect of eliminating more consumer rights than they conferred. Such instruments typically promised, subject to a plethora of conditions, to repair or replace defective products, but buried in the fine print were terms which effectively disclaimed all liability for personal injury damages. The Magnuson-Moss Congress viewed these practices as deceptive, and by restricting the right to disclaim implied warranties and mandating that disclaimers of personal injury liability be conspicuous, the legislators sought to eliminate the deception. [Citation omitted.] Moreover, Congress did create a federal cause of action and accord the federal courts jurisdiction over actions to enforce the provisions of the Act which "affect" personal injury liability.

Federal jurisdiction over personal injury claims is a function of § 2310(d)'s separate cause of action for breach of the form and content rules. As noted that particular cause of action is not subject to § 2310(e)'s opportunity to cure provision, so personal injury claims brought pursuant to one of the substantive obligations in the Act are not affected by the "cure" limitation. However, the substantive provisions which affect personal injury liability are narrow in scope, and a personal injury claimant seeking to state a claim upon which relief can be granted pursuant to the Magnuson-Moss Act must allege special jurisdictional facts. To satisfy this requirement, the plaintiff would have to be in a position to allege that the defendant sold or supplied a consumer product in violation of 15 U.S.C. §§ 2304(a)(2)-(3) or

2308, and that the plaintiff was a consumer of that product within the meaning of § 2310(d). Of course, to sue in federal court, the complaint must also allege the amount in controversy specified in § 2310(d)(3).

Plaintiffs' present complaint simply alleges breach of warranty as the basis for their Warranty Act claims for personal injury damages; their claims pursuant to the Warranty Act are therefore subject to dismissal for failure to state claims upon which relief can be granted. Since the existing record does not reveal whether plaintiffs would be able to allege the requisite jurisdictional facts, the court will afford them an opportunity to amend the complaint to allege, if they can do so in good faith, a claim for personal injuries that is cognizable for breach of one or more of the Act's pertinent substantive obligations.

Case Notes: The Magnuson-Moss Act

1. The Magnuson-Moss Act simply incorporates well-established contract principles into statutory requirements with which all warrantors must comply. In *Wilbur v. Toyota Motor Sales, U.S.A., Inc.,* 86 F.3d 23, 26 (2nd Cir. 1996), the Second Circuit for the U.S. Court of Appeals noted that

   > The [Act] grants relief to a consumer "who is damaged by the failure of a . . . warrantor . . . to comply with any obligation . . . under a written warranty." 15 U.S.C. § 2310(d) (1) (1994). When drafting a written warranty, Toyota must "fully and conspicuously disclose in simple and readily understood language [its] terms and conditions." 15 U.S.C. § 2302(a) (1994) [Citations omitted.] The accompanying regulations define one such term as "[t]he point in time or event on which the warranty term commences, if different from the purchase date." 16 C.F.R. § 701.3(a) (4) (1995). (*Id.*)

2. Some of the terms and conditions to be incorporated into a written warranty that are required by the Magnuson-Moss Act include a clear identification of the warrantors; an identification of the warrantees; the products or parts covered; a statement about the warrantor's action if the product malfunctions, is defective, or fails to conform; a statement about the consumer's required action if she or he is to act on the warranty; a general description of the legal remedies available; and the time within which the warrantor must act. See 15 U.S.C. § 2302 (a) (1-13).

3. Consumer groups may avail themselves of the Magnuson-Moss Act under 15 U.S.C. § 2310(d, e) to pursue a class action based on a supposedly defective warranty. Generally, the Act requires the following three items to qualify as a consumer class action: (1) no individual claim less than $25, (2) the cummulative amount in controversy must be greater than $50,000, and (3) the consumer class must be comprised of at least 100 named plaintiffs. See 15 U.S.C. § 2310(d); *In re General Motors Corp. Engine Litigation,* 594 F.2d 1106 (7th Cir. 1979). Plaintiff must also comply with the requirements of Rule 23 of the Federal Rules of Civil Procedure. See 15 U.S.C. § 2310(e). See also consumer product warranty suits in federal court under *Magnuson-Moss Warranty—Federal Trade Commission Improvement Act,* 54 A.L.R. Fed 461; Devience, *Magnuson-Moss Act: Substitution for UCC Warranty Protection?* 95 Com.L.J. 323 (1990).

4. The Act restricts the warrantor in the duties it may impose on the consumer. The Act provides that "the warrantor shall not impose any duty other than notification upon any consumer as a condition of securing remedy of any consumer product which malfunctions, is defective, or does not conform to the written warranty[.]" See 15 U.S.C. § 2304 (1). The warrantor may require that the subject

product be made available for inspection and testing. See 15 U.S.C. § 2304 (2).

5. The Act also empowers the U.S. Attorney General to restrain

   (A) any warrantor from making a deceptive warranty with respect to a consumer product, or

   (B) any person from failing to comply with any requirement imposed on such person by or pursuant to this chapter or from violating any prohibition contained in this chapter. 15 U.S.C. § 2310(c) (1).

For purposes of this particular enforcement, a "deceptive warranty" is

   (A) a written warranty which (i) contains an affirmation, promise, description, or representation which is either false or fraudulent, or which, in light of all of the circumstances, would mislead a reasonable individual exercising due care; or (ii) fails to contain information which is necessary in light of all of the circumstances, to make the warranty not misleading to a reasonable individual exercising due care; or

   (B) a written warranty created by the use of such terms as "guaranty" or "warranty," if the terms and conditions of such warranty so limit its scope and application as to deceive a reasonable individual. 15 U.S.C. § 2310(c) (2).

6. Individual warranty actions that properly fall under the umbrella of the Act must be subjected to informal dispute settlement procedures. The Act requires that the warrantor establish such procedures (15 U.S.C. § 2310 (a) (1, 3)). The Federal Trade Commission monitors such procedures and the warrantors compliance with these requirements. 15 U.S.C. § 2310 (a) (2, 4).

7. No provisions of the Act were intended to supplant individual states' laws regarding warranty and sales, particularly under the UCC. See 15 U.S.C. § 2311 (b, c); *Skelton v. General Motors Corp.*, 500 F.Supp. 1181 (N.D. Ill. 1980) (statutory intent was to promote honesty and reliability in entire transaction by requiring specific representations in written warranty).

 CASE PROBLEM ◆

Express and Implied Warranties Associated With Industrial Equipment

Piggly Wiggly, LLC

Assume the facts described in Chapter Two, Negligence, for the Piggly Wiggly Squealer I. Assume further that all Piggly products, including the Squealer I, carry a limited express warranty. The warranty reads as follows: Piggly Wiggly, LLC provides "a limited warranty for all repair, maintenance, and servicing of the Squealer I unit for a period of two years after delivery of the product to your store. This warranty includes replacement parts and the use of a substitute press in the event that your unit must be repaired outside your store." Lindy purchased a three-year extension of the express warranty in March 1987.

1. What warranty claims does Sammy Hoagge have against Piggly Wiggly? List each and explain the basis for each claim. How do you explain these warranty claims to Sammy Hoagge?

2. Assume that you represent Lindy's and that the law of the state of Columbia (where the lawsuits and the accident occurred) allows Lindy an indemnification against the manufacturer under the circumstances in which Lindy has compensated its employee, Sammy Hoagge, for all personal injuries and damages associated with his accident, which occurred during the course and scope of Hoagge's employment. Draft a complaint on behalf of Lindy's to claim indemnification from all proper parties. What theories are available to Lindy's?

What facts must be pleaded in Lindy's complaint in order to state a viable cause of action in warranty against Piggly? Against MeatSlicer?

3. Draft 15 interrogatories and 15 requests for production on behalf of Lindy's. What are the most pertinent details about the product that you want to discover? What are the most pertinent details about the Piggly manufacturing and design process that you want discovered?

The Milair Air Scoop

Assume the same facts described in Chapter Two, Negligence, for the Milair Air Scoop. Assume further that the Milair Air Scoop had no express warranty attached to the product when it was sold to National.

1. Assuming that the law of the state of Columbia (where the lawsuits and the accident occurred) allows National, Boeing, and Rolls Royce an indemnity claim against Milair, and assume further that all of the passengers' wrongful death and personal injury cases have been completed. What warranty claims do National, Boeing, or Rolls Royce have against Milair? What additional facts, if any, do you need in order to determine whether a cause of action in warranty is a viable claim?

2. Assume that you represent National, Boeing, and Rolls Royce and assume the facts in the previous paragraph. Draft a complaint on behalf of each party that has a cause of action in warranty against Milair. What are the essential elements? What facts must be pleaded in the complaint in order to state a viable cause of action in warranty against Milair?

3. Assume that you represent the Millers and that they are furious that you have not alleged a cause of action in warranty in their petition against Milair. What do you tell them? Write a letter to the Millers setting forth your legal and factual reasons for not alleging a cause of action in warranty or setting forth your legal and factual reasons about how you intend to amend the complaint so as to state a cause of action in warranty. What would such a complaint look like?

4. Assume that you represent National, Boeing, and Rolls Royce and assume the facts in paragraph 1. Draft 15 interrogatories, 15 requests for production, and 15 requests for admission on behalf of the Millers. To whom should you direct this written discovery? What is the essential information you should obtain from these defendants during written discovery? Who should you depose? Who should you interview? Who can you interview?

Chapter 4

Strict Liability

INTRODUCTION

Strict liability actions seek to impose liability on a manufacturer or seller who sold a defective product that caused injury to the user of the product. It is typically characterized as no-fault liability because these actions do not consider the conduct of the manufacturer or seller in having prepared, packaged, designed, sold, labeled, or marketed the product. Even if the manufacturer exercised all possible reasonable care in these activities and even if the product complies with the manufacturer's quality control standards and applicable safety regulations, the manufacturer or seller may be liable to an injured plaintiff for having placed a defective product into the stream of commerce that caused harm to its user. Instead of conduct, the focus of the strict liability inquiry is the product itself and whether the product was defective.

Courts often cite an array of rationale for imposing strict liability on manufacturers. These justifications include protecting consumers by creating incentives for manufacturers to make safer products, adopting better product designs, spreading the financial loss of a plaintiff's injury to entities that are better able to bear and insure against such a loss, and meeting consumers' expectations by providing products in the market that function as expected. Similar justifications exist for sellers and distributors, including the incentive for these entities to deal only with reputable and financially responsible manufacturers which, in turn, also protects consumers.

The current state of strict liability law is reflected in the *Restatement (Third) of Torts: Products Liability* (1997). It has arisen from the original statement of strict liability regarding defective products in § 402A of the *Restatement (Second) of Torts,* which has been developed, construed, and interpreted by many state and federal courts since its inception in 1965. This development has brought about three principle strict liability actions against manufacturers and sellers of defective products, including (a) products containing a manufacturing defect; (b) products containing a design defect; and (c) products containing defective warnings.

Definitions

Strict product liability generally references the area of tort law that borrows from negligence and warranty law so as to impose liability on manufacturers and sellers of defective products that cause injury to their users. Strict liability actions are typically regarded as defective product cases, although strict liability has historically been available in other areas of the law, such as one's responsibility for certain animals and in certain real estate actions. These actions are available to all product users. Unlike warranty actions, no privity between the product user and the product seller is required. Unlike negligence actions, neither the manufacturer nor the seller's conduct is evaluated in a strict liability analysis. Instead, the focus of the strict liability inquiry will be the product itself and whether the product was defective.

Elements of a Cause of Action

The first and essential inquiry is whether a defect exists in the product's manufacturing, design, or warnings. Second, any existing defect must have transformed the use of the product into being unreasonably dangerous or, in some jurisdictions, inherently dangerous. Finally, the manufacturing, assembly, design, control, packaging, or labeling of the product by the manufacturer or seller is implied.

These three elements exist in every strict liability action. A strict liability action against the manufacturer or seller of a defective product must include the following elements in order to make a submissible case against the defendants at trial:

- the defendant manufactured or sold the product in the course of defendant's business;
- the product was then in a defective condition that was unreasonably dangerous when put to a reasonably anticipated use;
- the product was used in a reasonable manner by its user;
- the product user was injured as a direct result of the product's defective condition that existed when the product was sold.

Types of Strict Liability Actions

Plaintiffs principally pursue one of three strict liability actions against manufacturers or sellers of defective products for (a) defective manufacturing, (b) defective design, or (c) defective warnings. Manufacturing defects are fundamental flaws in the product itself, which are typically manifested in the composite material or assembly of the product. Design defects are flaws in the specifications of the product, which renders defective an entire line, model, or series of the product. Unlike manufacturing defects, defective designs manifest themselves in the specifications for the product and not in the product itself. Generally, courts have recognized the consumer expectations and the risk-utility tests as standards by which the finder of fact may determine the existence of a defective design. Finally, a product may be deemed defective because it did not include an adequate warning. Manufacturers and sellers of products containing inadequate warnings are strictly liable for injuries caused to product users because the existence of warnings or instructions may have appropriately transferred the product from unsafe to safe, such that the product is regarded as unavoidably unsafe, or from unreasonably dangerous to reasonably dangerous with appropriate instructions and warnings for its use.

HISTORY AND EMERGENCE

Pre-1965—Difficult Hurdles for Products Liability Plaintiffs

If one could compare products liability litigation before 1965 to a track meet, plaintiffs' practitioners would most likely be found negotiating the high hurdles. They could negotiate the field by using one or both of two equally uninviting legal theories—negligence or breach of warranty.

Negligence was rooted in tort theory and was unavailable to the vast number of potential plaintiffs because of its privity requirement. Privity required the plaintiff in a negligence action to have contracted directly with the defendants. Although privity was abolished as a defense in the 1916 landmark case of *MacPherson v. Buick Motor Co.*, 111 N.E.1050 (N.Y. 1916), plaintiff's burden of proving the defendant manufacturer's negligence remained. Consequently, successful cases based on negligence were minimized. For example, evidence that a manufacturer breached the standard of care while designing and producing a product was rarely obtainable. In addition, products were increasingly made with component parts, and plaintiffs bore the burden of proving which component part was negligently manufactured. The manufacturer predominantly controlled information that could prove the manufacturer's negligence and identify the defective component part. The investigation required to obtain information that would prove negligent manufacturing was often prohibitively expensive. Consequently, vast amounts of time, energy, and resources went into the litigation of products liability cases against manufacturers based on negligence. Westerbeke, "The Sources of Controversy in the New Restatement of Products Liability: Strict Liability vs. Products Liability," *The Kansas Journal of Law & Public Policy*, 8 Kan. J. L. & Pub. & Pol'y. 1, 2 Fall, 1998. Further, plaintiffs met with little success in suing retailers using a negligence theory because courts have been reluctant, even currently, to impose a duty on retailers to test or inspect products except on a very limited basis. *Id.*

Breach of warranty did not prove any easier for plaintiffs. Before 1960, privity was as great an impediment under breach of warranty theory as it was in negligence theory. Despite the dropping of the privity requirement for breach of warranty actions by virtue of *Henningsen v. Bloomfield Motors, Inc.*, 161 A.2d 69 (N.J. 1960), plaintiffs continued to face contractually rooted impediments such as notice requirements and express disclaimers. (Schwartz and Behrens, *An Unhappy Return to Confusion in the Common Law of Products Liability—Denny v. Ford Motor Company Should be Overturned*, 17 Pace L. R., 359 [Spring 1997].) In addition, statutes of repose, which began running with the purchase of the product rather than with the injury caused by the product, barred many suits under a breach of warranty theory. Slowly, the judiciary began removing the number and severity of the hurdles facing plaintiffs under both negligence and breach of warranty theories. To smooth the way in negligence actions, courts began, among other techniques, to allow circumstantial evidence more liberally based on the theory of *res ipsa loquitor*. Westerbeke, *The Kansas Journal of Law & Public Policy*, 8 Kan. J. L. & Pub. & Pol'y. at 3. Using circumstantial evidence, a plaintiff could prevail if she or he could prove the following elements:

1. the occurrence resulting in injury does not ordinarily occur if those in control use due care
2. the instrumentalities involved were managed and controlled by the defendant
3. the defendant possesses superior knowledge or means of information regarding the cause of the occurrence

In breach of warranty actions, courts used their ingenuity to avoid the harshness of warranty law by periodically declaring express disclaimers void against public policy and by beginning statute of limitations at the time of the plaintiff's injury, rather than the time of sale. *Id.* at 5.

The Public Policy Underlying the Recognition of Strict Liability

Strict liability now serves as the primary theory against the manufacturers of allegedly defective products. Three foremost public policy reasons provide the impetus for the emergence of strict liability against manufacturers.

The most frequently cited public policy reason is that "it ensures that the costs arising from injuries caused by defective products fall on manufacturers and sellers rather than injured consumers who are powerless to protect themselves." *Keener v. Dayton Electric Manufacturing Co.,* 445 S.W.2d 362, 364 (Mo. 1969). Underlying this reason is the conclusion that manufacturers are in a better economic position than consumers to bear the cost of defective products.

The second reason is based on the idea that holding a manufacturer strictly liable causes the manufacturer to internalize the cost of the injuries brought to bear on consumers by their products. The manufacturer is forced to pass on the cost of liability into the product itself. By passing on the cost of liability, the cost of liability is spread from the single injured plaintiff to all consumers of the product. In addition, this reason includes the belief that the manufacturer will make safer products that reduce the cost of their products in comparison to its competitors.

Proponents of strict liability law believe that it allows more consumers to recover for injuries sustained from defectively manufactured products because consumers do not have to pinpoint the defendant's negligent act, or specifically, to prove causation. Because strict liability brings greater possibilities for liability, a manufacturer is theoretically motivated to produce safer products, and consumers supposedly benefit by sustaining fewer uncompensated injuries. As a practical matter, this theory does not always produce the intended result.

The Recognition of Strict Liability

In 1963, California Supreme Court Justice Traynor wrote his opinion in *Greenman v. Yuba Power Products, Inc.,* 377 P.2d 897 (Cal. 1963), which removed most of the hurdles in both negligence and breach of warranty products liability litigation by recognizing "strict liability." In *Greenman*, Justice Traynor declared that the plaintiff's failure to notify the defendant in a timely manner of its breach of warranty on a power tool that injured him did not bar his claim, stating that a "manufacturer is strictly liable in tort when an article he places on the market, knowing that it is to be used without inspection for defects, proves to have a defect that causes injury to a human being." (*Id.*, 900.) Under Traynor's theory, a plaintiff could establish strict liability by proving that he was injured using the product as it was intended to be used, that his injury was a result of a defect in design or manufacture of the product, and that he was unaware that the product was unsafe for its intended uses. (*Id.*)

The American Law Institute adopted Justice Traynor's strict liability theory the next year, applying it to all products in Section 402A of the *Restatement (Second) of Torts* (1965). Most courts interpreted Section 402A to require the plaintiff to prove the following five elements:

- the product was sold
- the product was defective
- the defective product was the factual and proximate cause of the plaintiff's injuries
- the defect existed at the time the product left the defendant's hands
- the product was manufactured or sold by the defendant

Section 402A relieved the plaintiff of needing to prove negligence and most of its requisite evidence, including that the manufacturer or seller had exercised due care. In essence, the defendant could be held strictly liable without fault. Section 402A became the springboard upon which most United States jurisdictions have crafted their own versions of strict liability law. More than three fourths of the states have incorporated all or part of it. See Frumer and Friedman, *Products Liability*, ch. 1, 1.06[76] (Matthew Bender [1987]).

For the next thirty years or so, strict liability law developed around Section 402A, but not without some criticism. In particular, the new strict liability law ushered in an unprecedented volume of products liability cases, resulting in significant monetary costs to manufacturers and sellers. In addition, strict liability came to be applied in the unanticipated cases alleging failure to warn and defective design. Although many commentators generally viewed Section 402A as well suited for manufacturing defects, they voiced reservations about its use in those unanticipated cases. See Westerbeke, *The Kansas Journal of Law & Public Policy*, 8 Kan. J. L. & Pub. & Pol'y., 6.

Design and warning defects are less susceptible to strict liability. In a warning defect case, the manufacturer is negligent for failure to adequately warn or instruct unless the danger is unforeseeable. Because a manufacturer is deemed an expert concerning its product, a danger is rarely unforeseeable unless it is also unknowable. A manufacturer may be held in strict liability for failing to warn about a particular danger associated with the intended use of the product. Similarly, in a design defect case, a manufacturer may be held in strict liability for failing to adopt a reasonable alternative design that would have eliminated or reduced an existing danger. To address these concerns, the American Law Institute adopted the *Restatement (Third) of Torts* in 1997.

THE CRITICAL ELEMENTS—PROVISIONS OF THE RESTATEMENTS

§ 402A of the *Restatement (Second) of Torts* (1965). Beginning in 1965, the *Restatement (Second) of Torts* enunciated the essential elements for a cause of action in strict liability against sellers of defective products. Since then, the *Restatement (Second)* has served as the sole instrument by which a strict-liability cause of action for defective products is defined. Under the parameters of this section, the seller is subject to liability to a user or consumer of a defective product even though all possible care has been exercised in the manufacturing, designing, preparing, packaging, labeling, and selling of the product. This theory was originally included in the *Restatement (Second)* so that it might be easily identified with comparable negligence theories, although neither strict liability nor negligence causes of action have ever been regarded as mutually exclusive theories. See Comment a, § 402A *Restatement (Second) of Torts* (1965).

Restatement (Second) of Torts § 402A (1965): Special Liability of Seller of Product for Physical Harm to User or Consumer

(1) One who sells any product in a defective condition unreasonably dangerous to the user or consumer or to his property is subject to liability for physical harm thereby caused to the ultimate user or consumer, or to his property, if
   (a) the seller is engaged in the business of selling such a product, and
   (b) it is expected to and does reach the user or consumer without substantial change in the condition in which it is sold.
(2) The rule stated in Subsection (1) applies though
   (a) the seller has exercised all possible care in the preparation and sale of his product, and
   (b) the user or consumer has not brought the product from or entered into any contractual relation with the seller.

Caveat: The Institute expresses no opinion as to whether the rules stated in this Section may not apply:

(1) to harm to persons other than users or consumers;

(2) to the seller of a product expected to be processed or otherwise substantially changed before it reaches the user or consumer; or
(3) to the seller of the component part of a product to be assembled.
   § 402A *Restatement (Second) of Torts* (1965).

Under section 402A, a product seller has a special responsibility to users and consumers of the product, especially toward those who are injured by the product. The general public has a right and an expectation that product sellers will stand behind their goods and that the burden of accidental injuries caused by products will be born by the seller of those products. Moreover, the product seller is better able to bear the loss brought about by accidental injury than is the injured individual because the product seller may obtain liability insurance and may spread these costs into its production and, eventually, pass them back to its consumers. Based upon these principles, many courts have justified their adoption of a strict liability action based on the language of this section of the *Restatement (Second)*. See Comment c, § 402A *Restatement (Second) of Torts* (1965).

Restatement (Third) of Torts: Products Liability §§ 1-2 (1997)

In 1998, the *Restatement (Third)* enunciated the current state of product liability law. In the 33 years since the *Restatement (Second)*, a landslide of individual court decisions have shaped, interpreted, defined, formulated, and construed strict liability actions for defective products. Because many of the elements in § 402A were vague and because many nuances of the strict liability action were not anticipated in 1965, a fine-tuning of the *Restatement* was required.

The *Restatement (Third)* provides a black-letter law for strict liability actions for a product that is allegedly defective in one of three ways: (1) containing a manufacturing defect; (2) containing a design defect; or (3) containing a defective warning.

§ 1. Liability of Commercial Seller or Distributor for Harm Caused by Defective Products

One engaged in the business of selling or otherwise distributing products who sells or distributes a defective product is subject to liability for harm to persons or property caused by the defect.

§ 2. Categories of Product Defect

A product is defective when, at the time of sale or distribution, it contains a manufacturing defect, is defective in design, or is defective because of inadequate instructions or warnings. A product:

(a) contains a manufacturing defect when the product departs from its intended design even though all possible care was exercised in the preparation and marketing of the product;

(b) is defective in design when the foreseeable risks of harm posed by the product could have been reduced or avoided by the adoption of a reasonable alternative design by the seller or other distributor, or a predecessor in the commercial chain of distribution, and the omission of the alternative design renders the product not reasonably safe;

(c) is defective because of inadequate instructions or warnings when the foreseeable risks of harm posed by the product could have been reduced or avoided by the provision of reasonable instructions or warnings by the seller or other distributor, or a predecessor in the commercial chain of distribution and the omission of the instructions or warnings renders the product not reasonably safe.

§§ 1-2 *Restatement (Third) of Torts: Products Liability* (1997).

Section 1 provides the general rule of strict liability that is applicable to product sellers. Section 2 establishes separate standards that determine when a product is defective depending on whether the product was subject to a manufacturing defect, a design defect, or an inadequate warning. If the product is defective in any of these instances, § 2 imposes strict liability on the product seller. See Comment a, § 2 *Restatement (Third)*:

Product Liability (1997). Because the *Restatement (Third)* concerns itself only with product liability, the 20 sections following the general statement of strict liability in defective product cases provide guidance about the application of strict-liability principles under specific circumstances, such as categories of product defects (§ 2), compliance with safety regulations (§ 4), bulk suppliers and manufacturers of component parts (§ 5), manufacturers and sellers of pharmaceuticals and medical devises (§ 6), manufacturers and sellers of defective food products (§ 7), manufacturers and sellers of defective used products (§ 8).

Because the *Restatement (Third)* is only newly published, not many states have adopted these sections and no states have fully analyzed or interpreted the concepts upon which these sections were derived. Nearly every state adopted § 402A as its common-law basis for strict liability actions against sellers of defective products. Construction of the *Restatement (Third)* now takes place as individual state courts begin to weave these newly published standards into their product liability law and begin to grapple with the changing standards for strict-liability actions for defective products.

The Model Uniform Product Liability Act

In 1979, the U.S. Department of Commerce published its Model Uniform Product Liability Act. See 44 F.R. 62,414–62,750. The Department of Commerce was asked to review the Briefing Report of the White House Economic Policy Board's Federal Interagency Task Force on Product Liability and suggest statutory changes to this area of the law. This model act was to be the legislative answer to the Task Force findings. It was never implemented by any national or state legislation but did serve as the template for product liability legislation eventually adopted by state legislatures. It is a societal reflection of the impact that product liability lawsuits were having on courts, insurers, product manufacturers and sellers, and individuals. As stated in its preamble, the act "sets forth uniform standards for state product liability tort law." *Id.* at 62,716. "The principal purposes of the Act are to provide a fair balance of the interests of both product users and sellers and to eliminate existing confusion and uncertainty about their respective legal rights and obligations." *Id.*

Model Uniform Products Liability Act

Sec. 104.   *Basic Standards of Responsibility for Manufacturers.*
A product manufacturer is subject to liability to a claimant who proves by a preponderance of the evidence that the claimant's harm was proximately caused because the product was defective.

A product may be proven to be defective if, and only if:

(1) It was unreasonably unsafe in construction (Subsection A);
(2) It was unreasonably unsafe in design (Subsection B);
(3) It was unreasonably unsafe because adequate warnings or instructions were not provided (Subsection C); or
(4) It was unreasonably unsafe because it did not conform to the product seller's express warranty (Subsection D).

Before submitting the case to the trier of fact, the court shall determine that the claimant has introduced sufficient evidence to allow a reasonable person to find, by a preponderance of the evidence, that one or more of the above conditions existed and was a proximate cause of the claimant's harm.

(A) *The Product Was Unreasonably Unsafe in Construction.* In order to determine that the product was unreasonably unsafe in construction, the trier of fact must find that, when the product left the control of the manufacturer, the product deviated in some material way from the manufacturer's design specifications or performance standards, or from otherwise identical units of the same product line.

(B) *The Product Was Unreasonably Unsafe in Design.*

(1) In order to determine that the product was unreasonably unsafe in design, the trier of fact must find that, at the time of manufacture, the likelihood that the product would cause the claimant's harm or similar harms, and the seriousness of those harms outweighed the burden on the manufacturer to design a product that would have prevented those harms, and the adverse effect that alternative design would have on the usefulness of the product.

(2) Examples of evidence that is especially probative in making this evaluation include:
   (a) Any warnings and instructions provided with the product;
   (b) The technological and practical feasibility of a product designed and manufactured so as to have prevented claimant's harm while substantially serving the likely user's expected needs;
   (c) The effect of any proposed alternative design on the usefulness of the product;
   (d) The comparative costs of producing, distributing, selling, using, and maintaining the product as designed and as alternatively designed; and
   (e) The new or additional harms that might have resulted if the product had been so alternatively designed.

(C) *The Product Was Unreasonably Unsafe Because Adequate Warnings or Instructions Were Not Provided.*

(1) In order to determine that the product was unreasonably unsafe because adequate warnings or instructions were not provided about a danger connected with the product or its proper use, the trier of fact must find that at the time of manufacture, the likelihood that the product would cause the claimant's harm or similar harms and the seriousness of those harms rendered the manufacturer's instructions inadequate and that the manufacturer should and could have provided the instructions or warnings which claimant alleges would have been adequate.

(2) Examples of evidence that is especially probative in making this evaluation include:
   (a) The manufacturer's ability, at the time of manufacture, to be aware of the product's danger and the nature of the potential harm;
   (b) The manufacturer's ability to anticipate that the likely product user would be aware of the product's danger and the nature of the potential harm;
   (c) The technological and practical feasibility of providing adequate warnings and instructions;
   (d) The clarity and conspicuousness of the warnings or instructions that were provided; and

(e) The adequacy of the warnings or instructions that were provided.

(3) In any claim under this Subsection, the claimant must prove by a preponderance of the evidence that if adequate warnings or instructions had been provided, they would have been effective because a reasonably prudent product user would have either declined to use the product or would have used the product in a manner so as to have avoided the harm.

(4) A manufacturer shall not be liable for its failure to warn or instruct about dangers that are obvious; for "product misuse" as defined in Subsection 112(C)(1); or for alterations or modifications of the product which do not constitute "reasonably anticipated conduct" under Subsection 102(G).

(5) A manufacturer is under an obligation to provide adequate warnings or instructions to the actual product user unless the manufacturer provided such warnings to a person who may be reasonably expected to assure that action is taken to avoid the harm, or that the risk of the harm is explained to the actual product user.

For products that may be legally used only by or under the supervision of a class of experts, warnings or instructions may be provided to the using or supervisory expert.

For products that are tangible goods sold or handled only in bulk or other workplace products, warnings or instructions may be provided to the employer of the employee-claimant if there is no practical and feasible means of transmitting them to the employee-claimant.

(6) *Post-Manufacture Duty to Warn.* In addition to the claim provided in Subsection (C)(1), a claim may arise under this Subsection where a reasonably prudent manufacturer should have learned about a danger connected with the product after it was manufactured. In such a case, the manufacturer is under an obligation to act with regard to the danger as a reasonably prudent manufacturer in the same or similar circumstances. This obligation is satisfied if the manufacturer makes reasonable efforts to inform product users or a person who may be reasonably expected to assure that action is taken to avoid the harm, or that the risk of harm is explained to the actual product user.

Sec. 105. *Basic Standards of Responsibility for Product Sellers Other Than Manufacturers.*

(A) A product seller, other than a manufacturer, is subject to liability to a claimant who proves by a preponderance of the evidence that claimant's harm was proximately caused by such product seller's failure to use reasonable care with respect to the product.

Before submitting the case to the trier of fact, the court shall determine that the claimant has introduced sufficient evidence to allow a reasonable person to find by a preponderance of the evidence that such product seller has failed to exercise reasonable care and that this failure was a proximate cause of the claimant's harm.

In determining whether a product seller, other than a manufacturer, is subject to liability under Subsection (A), the trier of fact shall consider the effect of such product seller's own conduct with respect to the design, construction, inspection, or condition of the product, and any failure of such product seller to transmit adequate warnings or instructions about the dangers and proper use of the product.

Unless Subsection (B) or (C) is applicable, product sellers shall not be subject to liability in circumstances in which they did not have a reasonable opportunity to inspect the product in a manner which would or should, in the exercise of reasonable care, reveal the existence of the defective condition.

(B) A product seller, other than a manufacturer, who makes an express warranty about a material fact or facts concerning a product is subject to the standards of liability set forth in Subsection 104(D).

(C) A product, other than a manufacturer, is also subject to the liability of manufacturer under Section 104 if:

  (1) The manufacturer is not subject to service of process under the laws of the claimant's domicile; or

  (2) The manufacturer has been judicially declared insolvent in that the manufacturer is unable to pay its debts as they become due in the ordinary course of business; or

  (3) The court determines that it is highly probable that the claimant would be unable to enforce a judgment against the product manufacturer.

(D) Except as provided in Subsections (A), (B), and (C), a product seller, other than a manufacturer, shall not otherwise be subject to liability under this Act.

Sec. 106. *Unavoidably Dangerous Aspects of Products.*

(A) An unavoidably dangerous aspect of a product is that aspect incapable, in light of the state of scientific and technological knowledge at the time of manufacture, of being made safe without seriously impairing the product's usefulness.

* * *

Sec. 107. *Relevance of Industry Custom, Safety or Performance Standards, and Practical Technological Feasibility.*

(A) Evidence of changes in (1) a product's design, (2) warnings or instructions concerning the product, (3) technological feasibility, (4) "state of the art," or (5) the custom of the product seller's industry or business, occurring after the product was manufactured, is not admissible for the purpose of proving that the product was defective in design under Subsection 104(B) or that a warning or instruction should have accompanied the product at the time of manufacture under Subsection 104(C).

If the court finds that the probative value of such evidence substantially outweighs its prejudicial effect and that there is no other proof available, this evidence may be admitted for other relevant purposes if confined to those purposes in a specific court instruction. Examples of "other relevant purposes" include proving ownership or control, or impeachment.

(B) For the purposes of Section 107, "custom" refers to the practices followed by an ordinary product seller in the product seller's industry or business.

(C) Evidence of custom in the product seller's industry or business or of the product seller's compliance or non-compliance with a non-governmental safety or performance standard, existing at the time of manufacture, may be considered by the trier of fact in determining whether a product was defective in design under

Subsection 104(B), or whether there was a failure to warn or instruct under Subsection 104(C) or to transmit warnings or instructions under Subsection 105(A).

(D) For the purposes of Section 107, "practical technological feasibility" means the technological, mechanical, and scientific knowledge relating to product safety that was reasonably feasible for use, in light of economic practicality, at the time of manufacture.

* * *

Notes: Model Uniform Product Liability Act

1. The Department of Commerce was guided generally by six criteria in developing the model act:
   A. to ensure that persons injured by unreasonably unsafe products receive reasonable compensation for their injuries
   B. to ensure the availability of affordable product liability insurance with adequate coverage to product sellers that engage in reasonably safe manufacturing practices
   C. to place the incentive for loss prevention on the party or parties who are best able to accomplish that goal
   D. to expedite the reparations process from the time of injury to the time the claim is paid
   E. to minimize the sum of accident costs, prevention costs, and transaction costs
   F. to use language that is comparatively clear and concise

2. The model act recognized product liability law as a branch of tort law. This was significant because some courts had considered the field to be a compensation system, such as workers' compensation or social security. The model act sought to impose basic standards of responsibility on manufacturer and sellers of defective products. A product may be proven defective in one of four ways:
   A. The product was unreasonably unsafe in its construction
   B. The product was unreasonably unsafe in design
   C. The product was unreasonably unsafe because adequate warnings or instructions had not been provided
   D. The product was unreasonably unsafe because it did not conform to a product seller's warranty. *Id.,* 62,721.

These are the points propounded in Section 104 of the model act. Although the Department of Commerce properly identified product liability law as a tort, it relied heavily on reasonable standards to determine the defective nature of a product, which continued the infusion of negligence standards into a strict-liability analysis for several more years.

3. The model act made findings (Sec. 101) upon which its proposed legislative action was based. These findings included the following:
   A. Sharply rising product liability insurance premiums have created serious problems in commerce resulting in
      1. increased prices of consumer and industrial products
      2. disincentives for innovation and for the development of high-risk but potentially beneficial products
      3. an increase in the number of product sellers attempting to do business without product liability insurance coverage, thus jeopardizing both their continued existence and the availability of compensation to injured persons

    4. legislative initiatives enacted in a crisis atmosphere that may, as a result, unreasonably curtail the rights of product liability claimants

B. One cause of these problems is that product liability law is fraught with uncertainty [.] The rules vary from jurisdiction to jurisdiction and are subject to rapid and substantial change. These facts militate against predictability of litigation outcome.

C. Insurers have cited this uncertainty and imbalance as justifications for setting rates and premiums that, in fact, may not reflect actual product risk or liability losses.

D. Product liability insurance rates are set on the basis of countrywide, rather than individual state experience. Insurers use countrywide experience because a product manufactured in one state can readily cause injury in any one of the other states. . . . One ramification of this practice is that there is little an individual can do to solve the problems caused by product liability.

E. Uncertainty in product liability law and litigation outcome has added to litigation costs and may put an additional strain on the judicial system.

F. Recently enacted state product liability legislation has widened existing disparities in the law. (*Id.*, 62,716).

4. The model act unnecessarily emphasized the price and availability of insurance, which caused concern about the approach of the model act as a compensation system rather than a branch of tort law. Although insurance was a legitimate concern, it was not instrumental in determining the proper placement of liability on product manufacturers or sellers. The model act also repeatedly mentioned the uncertainty of litigation, but such uncertainty is common in any kind of case. Nevertheless, the model act's provisions became one of many small steps leading to the *Restatement (Third) of Torts: Product Liability* (1997).

TYPES OF STRICT LIABILITY ACTIONS

Depending on the facts in a particular case, a plaintiff may pursue three types of strict liability actions for defective products. These three actions are (1) defective manufacturing, (2) defective design, and (3) defective warnings. Many courts believe that imposing strict liability against manufacturers will foster a greater corporate investment in product safety. This may be true because most strict liability actions are lodged against the manufacturer, as opposed to being lodged against a seller in the chain of distribution.

Defective Manufacturing

A manufacturing defect is a flaw in the product. It is typically seen in products that depart from specifications that are unique to that particular product unit. Common examples of manufacturing defects appear in products that are physically flawed, in the product's composite materials that are structurally incompetent, and in damaged or incorrectly assembled products. Plaintiffs must prove the existence of a manufacturing defect by showing that the product was inherently dangerous when it left the hands of the manufacturer. In this way, strict liability is imposed upon the product manufacturer regardless of fault and regardless whether the manufacturer exercised all reasonable care in the preparation of the product or in its own quality control efforts to satisfy consumer or regulatory standards. Strict liability for a manufacturing defect may also be imposed against a seller in the chain of distribution if the product was damaged during shipment or storage. In that instance, plaintiff must prove that the product was defective when it left the hands of a particular seller in the chain of distribution. See Comment c, § 2 *Restatement (Third) of Torts: Products Liability* (1997).

As defined by § 2(a) of the *Restatement (Third):*

*** A product: (a) contains a manufacturing defect when the product departs from its intended design even though all possible care was exercised in the preparation and marketing of the product.

Causation in Strict Liability—Determining Unreasonably Dangerous Products

The no-fault concept upon which strict liability theories are based, particularly in defective manufacturing cases, does not alleviate the plaintiff's burden to prove that the defectively manufactured product caused the plaintiff's own injury. The absence of this causation in fact between product and harm will be fatal to a plaintiff's strict liability action. Moreover, the causation element is essential in determining the overall existence of an unreasonably dangerous product.

 CASE LAW

◆ **causation and unreasonably dangerous products**

*Jo Ann Allison,
Individually, and Jo Ann
Allison, as Natural Parent
and Guardian of Thomas
Allison, Appellant v. Merck
and Company, Inc.,* 878 P.2d
948 (Nev. 1994).

Tom Allison, an infant recipient of the MMR vaccine (measles, mumps, and rubella) manufactured by Merck and Company, Inc. ("Merck"), brought a lawsuit against Merck alleging a manufacturing defect in the vaccine that brought about the child's encephalitis and his resulting blindness, deafness, and mental retardation. The trial court granted summary judgment in favor of Merck, based on Merck's legal argument that its vaccine was unavoidably unsafe and, therefore, incapable of being made safe. On appeal, the Nevada Supreme Court held that a drug manufacturer may be held liable for dangers that are inherent in drug products even though the product was not negligently prepared or marketed and that the plaintiff infant should be allowed the opportunity at trial to meet his burden to prove the causation between the defective product and plaintiff's resulting injuries.

SPRINGER, J.

* * *

Strict Liability

To establish liability under a strict tort liability theory, Thomas must establish that his injury "was caused by a defect in the product, and that such defect existed when the product left the hands of the defendant." *Shoshone Coca-Cola Co. v. Dolinski,* 82 Nev. 439, 443, 420 P.2d 855, 858 (1966). In this case, whether any defect in the vaccine that might have caused Thomas's disabilities was present "when the product left the hands of the defendant[s]" is not a matter of controversy; so, if the Allisons can prove that Thomas' encephalitis "was caused by a defect in the product," then plaintiffs should be able to recover from Merck.

We have already considered the meaning of the word "defect" in connection with strict products liability. In *Ginnis v. Mapes Hotel Corp.,* we adopted a definition of "defect" that is still useful and applicable to the case at hand: "Although the definitions of the term 'defect' in the context of products liability law use varying language, all of them rest upon the common premise that those products are defective which are dangerous because they fail to perform in the manner reasonably to be expected in light of their nature and intended function." [Citation omitted.] If Thomas can establish that the vaccine caused him to suffer permanent brain damage, then surely the vaccine failed to perform in the manner reasonably to be expected "in light of [its] nature and intended function." The nature and intended function of this vaccine, of course, is to create an immunity to measles, mumps and rubella without attendant blindness, deafness, mental retardation and permanent brain damage. [Footnote omitted.]

Under the law of strict liability in this state, responsibility for injuries caused by defective products is properly fixed wherever it will most effectively reduce the hazards to life and health inherent in defective products that reach the market. Although manufacturers are not insurers of their products, where injury is caused by a defective product, responsibility is placed upon the manufacturer and the distributor of the defective product rather than on the injured consumer. *See Stackiewicz v. Nissan Motor Corp.*, 100 Nev. 443, 448, 686 P.2d 925, 928 (1984).

In *Stackiewicz,* we allowed a strict liability case to go to the jury on the plaintiff's claim of an idiopathic steering defect in an automobile which the plaintiff claimed was the cause of her injuries. We said in *Stackiewicz* that when "machinery 'malfunctions,' it obviously lacks fitness regardless of the cause of the malfunction." [Citation omitted.] In the case before us, plaintiffs are claiming in effect that the vaccine "malfunctioned"; and, if we are to follow *Stackiewicz,* then a vaccine which causes permanent brain damage "obviously lacks fitness regardless of the cause of the malfunction." [Footnote omitted.]

* * *

Unless we are going to abandon longstanding public policy grounds for holding manufacturers and distributors of defective products responsible for injuries caused by manufactured products that prove to be defective, Thomas must be given an opportunity to prove that a malfunctioning vaccine caused his injuries, just as we allowed Ms. Stackiewicz to try to prove that her injuries were caused by a defective steering mechanism. The public policy considerations that support holding the defendants liable in this case (if plaintiffs can prove that the vaccine caused his injuries) were put well by Professor Prosser in the noted law review article, "The Fall of the Citadel":

The public interest in human safety requires the maximum possible protection for the user of the product, and those best able to afford it are the suppliers of the chattel. By placing their goods upon the market, the suppliers represent to the public that they are suitable and safe for use; and by packaging, advertising and otherwise, they do everything they can to induce that belief. . . .

50 Minn.L.Rev. 791, 799 (1966). This concept of "public interest" is the guiding principle of our present opinion.

If we are going to follow *Shoshone Coca-Cola* and *Stackiewicz,* we must send this case back to the trial court. A vaccine that causes blindness and deafness is a defective product. Causation is a factor yet to be determined by a factfinder.

"Unavoidably Unsafe?"

Merck claims that it is free from strict manufacturer's liability by virtue of the dictum stated in comment k to section 402A of the Restatement (Second) of Torts. [Footnote omitted.] This comment suggests that a drug manufacturer should not be held liable for "the unfortunate consequences attending" the use of drugs if: (1) the manufacturer supplies "the public with an apparently useful and desirable product, attended by a known but apparently reasonable risk," (2) the drug is "properly prepared and marketed," and (3) "proper warning is given."

It is not easy to divine just why the framers of the comment thought that a drug manufacturer should be excused in cases in which it manufactured a drug that was "known" to be dangerous. The whole idea behind strict tort liability is that the manufacturer, not the consumer, should bear the responsibility for injuries, even when the product is ostensibly properly prepared and marketed and when the plaintiff is not in a position to prove the origin of the defect. [Citation and footnote omitted.]

What the question in this case really gets down to is whether an exception should be made in a case in which a drug manufacturer injures a consumer with a drug that it knows is dangerous, but not too ("unreasonably") dangerous. That is to say, should a drug manufacturer be allowed to profit with impunity from the distribution of a drug that it knows is capable of resulting in physical injury, so long as the drug can somehow be certified as not being unreasonably dangerous? We answer that question in the negative and say that a drug manufacturer should under the strict liability jurisprudence of this state, be held liable in tort even when the drug is "properly prepared and marketed" (that is to say, non-negligently) and even when the known danger inherent in the drug may be what the comment calls "reasonable."

The apparent rationale of comment k in relieving drug manufacturers from liability is that where the manufacturer is free from fault, that is to say it produces a product that is unsafe because of a claim by the manufacturer that it is "incapable of being made safe," the manufacturer should not be responsible for injuries resulting from use of the drug. The comment itself gives as an example of such an "unavoidably unsafe" drug the Pasteur treatment of rabies "which not uncommonly leads to very serious and damaging consequences when it is injected." We would note, however, that the reason why serious and damaging consequences of the Pasteur rabies treatment do not result in tort liability is not because of the "unreasonably dangerous" doctrine proposed by comment k, but, rather, because the victim chooses to be injected with a drug having known "damaging consequences" rather than to die from rabies. It is the voluntary choice to take the antirabies serum that eliminates tort liability and not the serum's being said to be unavoidably or reasonably dangerous. There is no need to make an exception to the rules of strict liability such as that suggested by comment k in the rabies example because the rabies victim waives tort claims by accepting what the victim knows to be the necessary risk involved in the treatment.

Speaking of "unavoidable" danger or fault-free infliction of harm, or speaking of reasonable (and therefore acceptable) risk of harm, is very much alien to strict liability theory and should have no place in the Restatement provisions relating to strict liability. Mixing concepts of fault-free ("unavoidable") manufacture and "reasonable risk" into the context of non-negligent, strict liability is entirely inconsistent with our products liability cases and with the law established in this state for almost thirty years. The well-accepted principle supporting our products liability cases is expressed in comment c of section 402 A of the Restatement:

> [P]ublic policy demands that the burden of accidental injuries caused by products intended for consumption be placed upon those who market them, and be treated as a cost of production against which liability insurance can be obtained; and that the consumer of such products is entitled to the maximum of protection at the hands of someone, and the proper persons to afford it are those who market the products.

It could not be said any more clearly than this. Merck, not Thomas Allison, must, if the Merck product did in fact cause Thomas' overwhelming misfortune, bear the "burden of the accidental [intended] injuries caused by products intended for consumption." Restatement (Second) of Torts, § 402 A, comment. c (1965).

* * *

Case Notes: Determining "unreasonably dangerous"

1. The finder of fact must determine whether the product was unreasonably dangerous. (*Allison*, 848 P.2d at 956-958.)

   Strict Tort Liability May Be Imposed Even If Merck's Interpretation of Comment K Were Accepted

   This court rejects the idea of freeing drug manufacturers from liability for defective drugs simply because they claim that the drugs are reasonably or unavoidably dangerous. However, even if, like the dissent-

ing justice, we were to accept Merck's interpretation of comment k in this case, Thomas and his mother would still be entitled to a trial. A factfinder could find in this case that the product here, if not defective or dangerous "per se," was "unreasonably dangerous as marketed." *Reyes v. Wyeth Laboratories*, 498 F.2d 1264, 1273 (5th Cir. 1974). Reyes noted that "[i]n terms of the user's interests, a product is 'unreasonably dangerous' only when it is 'dangerous to an extent beyond that contemplated by the ordinary consumer.' " Id. (quoting *Restatement (Second) of Torts* § 402A comment i (1965)). Citing to comment k, the Reyes court thus held that even an "unavoidably" unsafe vaccine may be defective if marketed without an adequate warning. Id. at 1274-78. Accordingly, under the Reyes rationale, even under the broadly exculpatory interpretation of comment k espoused by Merck, liability cannot be avoided by a drug manufacturer and distributor in the marketing of a vaccine unless the vaccine is "accompanied by proper directions and warning." Id. at 1274 (quoting *Restatement (Second) of Torts* § 402A comment k (1965)). [Footnote omitted.]

It would appear that a factfinder in this case could reasonably conclude that the vaccine given to Thomas Allison was not accompanied by a proper warning. [Footnote omitted.] Although Merck does not admit that this vaccine can cause disastrous central nervous system disorders, it announces in its MMR II package circular (which is not distributed to vaccinees) that "significant central nervous system reactions such as encephalitis and encephalopathy occurring within 30 days after vaccination, have been temporally associated with measles vaccine approximately once for every million doses." (In dealing with the mass consumers of the vaccine, the Health District revised this information when it issued its "Important Information" (not a "Warning") flyer prepared by the Center for Disease Control ("CDC"). The "Important Information" flyer is a revision of Merck's package circular, and it contains a much less dissuading statement, namely, that, "[a]lthough experts are not sure," there might be a very remote possibility—a chance in a million—that takers of the vaccine "may have a more serious reaction, such an inflammation of the brain (encephalitis)." The gist of the faulty warning aspect of liability in this case is that none of the prospective vacinees was warned of the actual possibility of permanent brain dam-

age. Rashes, yes; sore throats, yes; "inflammation of the brain," yes; but permanent blindness, deafness, and mental retardation, no. [Footnote omitted.]

Further, there is evidence in the record that Merck underestimated the incidence of serious central nervous system involvement caused by or "temporally associated with" the vaccine. Whether the incidence data be true or not, the information that was ultimately conveyed to Jo Ann Allison could be seen by a factfinder as being slanted and insufficient; and the only information that was actually made available to Ms. Allison was that there was a one in one million [not four in one million] chance that her son "may" have a more serious reaction to the vaccine "such as inflammation of the brain." At no time was Ms. Allison ever made aware that the vaccine might result in her son's becoming an invalid. Accordingly, there is certainly an issue of fact as to whether the warning in this case was "proper"; and, in fact, there appears to be substantial evidence in this case from which a jury could find that the vaccine in question was not "accompanied by proper directions and warning," Reyes 498 F.2d at 1274 (*quoting* Restatement (Second) of Torts § 402A comment k (1965)), especially when that evidence is viewed in the favorable light required on appeal from summary judgment. Consequently, even if we were to accept Merck's version of comment k, the Allisons would still be entitled to a trial on the merits. *Allison*, 848 P.2d at 956-958.

2. What line is drawn between unavoidably unsafe products and products that are inherently and unreasonably dangerous? Can a product be both? What directions must be given to the jury to guide their decision about whether a product is unreasonably dangerous? Can the jury, as users and consumers of products, be left to their own thoughts, expectations, knowledge, and experience to determine whether a product is unreasonably dangerous?

3. What body is responsible for determining whether causation existed between the allegedly defective product and the injury allegedly created by the product? What definitions or instructions guides that body about that determination? What evidence is typically produced jat trial or in support of ja motion for summary judgment that proves causation? What is the best evidence of causation?

4. If causati jon is a fact question to be determined by the jury, how is this similar or dissimilar to negligence suits? If they are similar, does the similarity bring strict liability suits closer to negligence actions? Does that enhance or endanger the strict liability theory? Why is proof of causation required in a strict liability action if strict liability cases are truly based on a no-fault theory?

Illustration: Able Manufacturing made soda bottles that were used by Baker, Inc. in its soda bottling business. Charlie's Soda Outlet sold a six-pack of soda that included these bottles to Joe, who sustained an injury to his hands and face when one of the bottles exploded. Able, Baker, and Charlie are each strictly liable for Joe's injury even though they each may have exercised due care in the manufacturing, packaging, and selling of this product. The inherent flaw in the bottle itself that brought about its explosion and Joe's injury subjects each of the entities in the chain of distribution of the product to strict liability.

Foreseeability in Strict Liability   Just as in negligence suits, foreseeability is a required element of proof in strict liability actions against product sellers and manufacturers. In strict liability actions, plaintiffs must typically prove that the injury produced by the allegedly defective product was foreseeable by the manufacturer under normal use of the product. The focus of this inquiry must be the product and a user's normal use of the product, and not the risk that the product might cause an injury because it was unreasonably dangerous when placed into commerce for sale. That inquiry belongs to negligence suits that seek to evaluate the conduct of the manufacturer based upon the reasonableness of its actions. Thus, foreseeability in strict liability actions must be distinguished from foreseeability in negligence suits. Foreseeability in strict liability suits evaluates the product and the injury arising from that product. Foreseeability in negligence suits evaluates risk and the manufacturer's (or seller's) conduct in that risk by having placed the product into commerce for sale.

 CASE LAW

◆ **foreseeability and unreasonably dangerous products**

Halphen v. Johns-Manville Sales Corporation, 737 F.2d 462 (5th Cir 1984).

Samuel Halphen died from malignant mesothelioma, which he contracted from exposure to asbestos. At trial, the jury found against defendant Johns-Manville and awarded damages to Halphen. On appeal, Johns-Manville argued that it could not be held liable for an alleged failure to warn about its asbestos product because it could not foresee that asbestos would cause Halphen's injury and death. The Fifth Circuit affirmed the jury's verdict in favor of Halphen.

POLITZ, Circuit Judge.

* * *

Stripped to its essentials, Johns-Manville's primary contention is that it cannot be held strictly liable for injuries incurred due to its failure to warn of potential dangers of its product because it could not foresee the particular harm. Specifically, Johns-Manville maintains that it cannot be held strictly accountable for asbestos-related diseases caused by its products because, when it marketed the products, it did not know that asbestos would cause serious illnesses. Johns-Manville urges the "state of the art" defense, asserting that it did not know of the product's defect, nor did anyone else, and furthermore, there was no way that it could have known. The thrust of the state of the art defense is that scientific knowledge and methods of research were not advanced enough to permit discovery of the defect.

In this diversity case we are obliged to apply Louisiana's substantive law. Louisiana law on strict products liability is of relatively recent vintage, but the infant quickly grew to adulthood. This body of law is essentially jurisprudential, although drawing its genesis from revered codical provisions.

The seminal case in which the Supreme Court of Louisiana adopted strict liability for manufacturers in products cases is *Weber v. Fidelity & Casualty Ins. Co. of N.Y.,* 259 La. 599, 250 So.2d 754 (1971). Johns-Manville advances what it perceives to be an inconsistency or confusion in the language of the Weber holding on the critical question of foreseeability. The Louisiana Supreme Court held:

> A manufacturer of a product which involves a risk of injury to the user is liable to any person, whether the purchaser or a third person, who without fault on his part, sustains an injury *caused by the defect in the design, composition, or manufacture of the article, if the injury might reasonably have been anticipated.*

Id. at 755 [emphasis added]. Johns-Manville argues from this language that not only must the injury be foreseeable but the defect must also be foreseeable. However, the Louisiana high court continued:

> If the product is proven defective by reason of its hazard to normal use, the plaintiff need not prove any particular negligence by the maker in its manufacture or processing; for *the manufacturer is presumed to know of the vices*

> *in the things he makes, whether or not he has actual knowledge of them.*

Id. at 756 [emphasis added]. This holding imposes a presumption of knowledge of the defect which requires no showing of foreseeability.

A careful reading of the Louisiana cases reflects the distinction between foreseeability of the defect and foreseeability of the harm that might flow from the defect. For example, in *Hunt v. City Stores, Inc.,* 387 So.2d 585, 589 (La. 1980), the court stated:

> [T]he plaintiff in a products liability suit must only prove that the product was defective, i.e., unreasonably dangerous to normal use; that the product was in normal use at the time the injury occurred; that the product's defect might cause his injury; and that the injury might reasonably have been anticipated by the manufacturer. It is unnecessary to prove that the manufacturer was negligent because he knew or should have known of the dangerous condition of the product at the time of the manufacture or sale. The focus is on the product itself and whether it is unreasonably dangerous to normal use.

These three sentences, which leave a mite to be desired for precision writing, are logically consistent only if the foreseeability element is taken to mean that the injury must be foreseeable when viewed in light of the knowledge of the dangerous defect. The injury must be foreseeable; the defect need not be. That interpretation is internally consistent and is consistent with the holdings in other Louisiana cases. [Citation omitted.]

Foreseeability of the risk, as distinguished from the foreseeability of injury once the risk is actually or constructively known, is the hallmark of a negligence action; it is the antithesis of a strict products liability action: "The distinction between the two theories of recovery lies in the fact that the inability of a defendant to know or prevent the risk is not a defense in a strict liability case but precludes a finding of negligence." Hunt at 588. [Citation omitted.]

The thrust of Louisiana law is certain—in a strict products liability case, the manufacturer is presumed to know the defects of its product. The presumption suffices; no proof is necessary. The injured party need only show that the injury would reasonably be foreseeable to one with knowledge (actual or imputed) of the defect. The Louisiana Supreme Court bright-lined this rule in *Kent v. Gulf States Utilities Co.*, 418 So.2d 493 (La. 1982):

> In products liability cases, the manufacturer is presumed to know the dangerous propensities of its product and is strictly liable for injuries resulting from the product's unreasonable risk of injury in normal use. The claimant nevertheless must prove that the product presented an unreasonable risk of injury in normal use (regardless of the manufacturer's knowledge), thus in effect proving the manufacturer was negligent in placing the product in commerce with (presumed) knowledge of the danger.

Id. at 498 n.6.

* * *

It is our present perception of Louisiana law that a manufacturer is presumed to know the defects in its product. Foreseeability is not an element in that equation. Foreseeability, in a Louisiana products liability case, applies only to the question of injury. [Citation omitted.] The essential inquiry, then, is whether a manufacturer, with knowledge of the defect, should reasonably anticipate the injury. In this case, Johns-Manville was presumed to know that its product was defective, specifically, Johns-Manville was presumed to know that its product would cause, exacerbate or enhance carcinomatous growths. With that presumed knowledge, the suggestion that Johns-Manville could not foresee Halphen's malignant mesothelioma falls of its own weight.

* * *

The Crashworthiness Doctrine The crashworthiness doctrine is a determination about whether a product user's injury has been enhanced by a defect in the product. The doctrine arises from automobile accidents in which the plaintiff arguably would have been injured anyway as a result of the accident itself but sustained more serious injuries as a result of a defect in the automobile itself. The issue is always a determination whether the plaintiff's injuries have been enhanced as a result of the allegedly defective product and a measurement of how much. Typically, crashworthiness is regarded as a product defect that increased the injured plaintiff's harm beyond that of other actual causes. See *Restatement (Third)* § 16(a).

 CASE LAW

◆ **manufacturer's burden to prove crashworthiness**

Poliseno v. General Motors Corporation, 744 A.2d 679 (N.J. Super. Ct. 2000).

Wife brought wrongful death suit against defendant automobile manufacturer alleging that driver's side door, where wife's husband was at time of accident, was defectively manufactured and that this defect prevented the automobile from being crashworthy.

KEEFE, J.A.D.

* * *

The jury returned a verdict in response to special interrogatories as follows:
1. Did the Corvette at the time it left the control of General Motors contain defective driver's side door beam welds that made the car not reasonably safe for its intended use?
Yes—7 No—2

* * *

"Crashworthiness" is defined as the ability of a motor vehicle to protect its passengers from enhanced injuries after a collision. *Barris v. Bob's Drag Chutes & Safety Equip.*,

Inc., 685 F.2d 94, 100 (3d Cir. 1982). The crashworthiness doctrine was first recognized in *Larsen v. General Motors Corp.,* 391 F.2d 495, 504-05 (8th Cir. 1968). It is premised upon the manufacturer's legal duty to design and manufacture a reasonably crashworthy product. [Citations omitted.] Thus, "a manufacturer has to include accidents among the 'intended' uses of its product." *Barris,* supra, 685 F.2d at 100 [Citation omitted]. Strict liability is imposed on a manufacturer for injuries sustained in an accident involving a design or manufacturing defect that enhanced the injuries, but did not cause the accident. [Citations omitted.]

The manufacturer is liable only for enhanced injuries, that is, injuries that would not have occurred absent the alleged defect. *Larsen,* 391 F.2d at 503. "Enhanced injury refers to the degree by which a defect aggravates collision injuries beyond those which would have been sustained as a result of the impact or collision absent the defect." *Barris,* supra, 685 F.2d at 100. The crashworthiness doctrine is also referred to as the "second collision" doctrine, the accident itself being the "first collision," or "enhanced injury" doctrine. [Citation omitted.]

It is generally agreed that the plaintiff in a crashworthy case has the burden of establishing that the alleged defect was a substantial factor in increasing the harm beyond that which would have resulted from the first collision. Restatement (Third) of Torts: Products Liability § 16 comment a (1997). Beyond that agreement, however, there is a split of authority concerning any additional burden a plaintiff may have in apportioning damages between the first and second collision. Apportionment is generally a problem that occurs in crashworthy cases involving an indivisible injury, such as death, where it is often difficult to prove with any precision whether the alleged defect was the sole cause of the injury, or whether the second collision contributed to the injury in a substantial degree. Which party has the burden of proof on that issue can be determinative of whether a plaintiff recovers damages in such cases.

In an effort to predict what New Jersey would do on the subject, the Third Circuit, in *Huddell v. Levin,* 537 F.2d 726, 737-38 (3d Cir. 1976), held that the plaintiff must prove not only that the alleged defect was a substantial factor in causing some increased harm, but must also prove the extent of the increased harm. If a plaintiff is unable to quantify the increased harm, the plaintiff is unable to recover. Huddell, however, has come to represent the minority view. The majority view, referred to as

the Fox-Mitchell [footnote omitted] approach, shifts the burden of proving apportionment to the defendant manufacturer after the plaintiff offers some evidence that the injuries were in fact enhanced because of the defective product. See Restatement (Third) at § 16, Reporter's Note, comment d.

The accuracy of Huddell's prediction of New Jersey law was first questioned in *Crispin v. Volkswagenwerk A.G.,* 248 N.J. Super. 540, 569 n. 1, 591 A.2d 966 (App.Div.) (predicting that a rule placing the burden of proof of apportionment on the defendant would be more in line with recent New Jersey Supreme Court medical malpractice apportionment cases), certif. denied, 126 N.J. 385, 599 A.2d 162 (1991). Despite the caution flag raised by Crispin, the Law Division in 1993 applied Huddell to the case before it. *See McLaughlin v. Nissan Motor Corp.,* 267 N.J.Super. 130, 134, 630 A.2d 857 (Law Div.1993). A year later, Judge Lintner, recognizing that the Fox-Mitchell line of cases expressed the majority view and that the majority view was in accord with our Supreme Court's approach to apportionment in the medical malpractice context, held that the burden of apportionment should be on the defendant. *Thornton v. General Motors Corp.,* 280 N.J.Super. 295, 303, 655 A.2d 107 (Law Div.1994). At the time of trial, the conflict in the Law Division cases had not been resolved.

Here the judge rejected the Crispin dicta and the Thornton decision, and opted for the Huddell approach. The judge charged the jury that plaintiff had the burden of proving by a preponderance of the credible evidence that the alleged defect enhanced the injuries sustained by Mr. Kuhlbars in the accident. There is no claim in this case. . . . that any defect in Michael Kuhlbars' Corvette caused the car to hydroplane, to jump the curb and to hit the tree and the brick wall. For that reason you cannot find General Motors liable for injuries that would have been sustained by him as a proximate result of those events alone. The claim against GM is instead for damages for the enhanced injuries that [plaintiff] claims occurred as the result of the alleged defect in the door beam welds. In order to prove enhanced injury, [plaintiff] must establish, again, by a preponderance of the credible evidence, first of all, what injury, if any, Mr. Kuhlbars would have sustained if the welds had not been defective as alleged and, number two, what injury, if any, was approximately caused [sic] by the defect as alleged in the welds. Recovery can be obtained from GM only for the damages flowing from the enhanced injury.

If you conclude that the injuries sustained by Mr. Kuhlbars would have been the same regardless of the defect, if you find a defect to exist, then you cannot find that there has been an enhancement of the injury.

Subsequent to the trial in this case, the issue of who had the burden of proof of apportioning an indivisible injury between the first collision and the second collision was addressed in *Green v. General Motors Corp.,* 310 N.J.Super. 507, 525-29, 709 A.2d 205 (App.Div.), certif. denied, 156 N.J. 381, 718 A.2d 1210 (1998). Judge Dreier, writing for this court, held that the trial judge in that case erred in following Huddell and in placing the burden of apportionment on the plaintiff. *Id.* at 528, 709 A.2d 205. The court adopted the Fox-Mitchell approach, allocating the burden of apportionment to the defendant manufacturer. *Id.* at 528-29, 709 A.2d 205.

Defendant argues here that the Green court's holding on this issue was dicta, because the jury in that case found plaintiff's paralysis solely attributable to the design defect, and, thus, apportionment was not an issue. We agree with defendant. Nonetheless, we find Judge Dreier's analysis of the doctrine compelling and adopt it as our own.

Therefore, we hold that in a crashworthy case, the plaintiff must prove only that a defect in the vehicle increased or enhanced the injury beyond that which would have resulted had there not been a defect. Thus, contrary to the judge's instruction in this case, plaintiff was not obliged to prove "what injury, if any, Mr. Kuhlbars would have sustained if the welds had not been defective." That is, plaintiff is not required to prove a negative. Plaintiff need only prove that the presence of the alleged defect was a substantial factor in producing an injury that would not have occurred, or would have been substantially diminished, in the absence of the defect. Restatement (Third) of Torts: Products Liability, § 16 comment a; *Sumnicht v. Toyota Motor Sales, U.S.A., Inc.,* 121 Wis.2d 338, 360 N.W.2d 2, 11 (1984). When a plaintiff has sustained that burden, the plaintiff need not quantify to what extent the second collision enhanced the injury. Rather, if the defendant seeks credit against the verdict for an injury that it claims resulted, in part, from the first collision, defendant shall have the burden of proof on that issue.

In this case, the plaintiff satisfied her initial burden of proving that the welding defect caused injuries to Kuhlbars resulting in his death that would not have occurred had there been no defect in the door beam welds. To the extent that defendant contends that the injury (death) is divisible and resulted from both the first collision, for which it is not responsible, and the second collision, it was defendant's burden to quantify the extent to which each collision caused Kuhlbars' death.

Accordingly, the trial judge erred in placing on the plaintiff the burden of quantifying the extent to which second collision damages were enhanced by first collision damages.

Defective Designs

Determining the Existence of a Design Defect

A design defect is a flaw in the product specifications. In the instance of a design defect, the subject product adheres to the unit specifications but the specifications themselves are supposedly defective, which gives rise to a strict liability action against the product seller or manufacturer. Standards determine whether the design is, in fact, defective. Ordinarily, the two standards employed by most courts are (1) the consumer expectations; and (2) the risk-utility standard. The consumer expectation test evaluates whether a product is dangerous beyond that which would be contemplated by the ordinary consumer who has ordinary common knowledge of the community. The risk-utility balancing test weighs the risks and benefits of the product design and requires inquiry into whether a reasonable alternative design at a reasonable cost would have reduced the danger posed by the product. In either instance, the finder of fact must focus on the product in order to make a precise and legitimate determination whether the design is, in fact, defective and, more importantly, to keep intact the no-fault analysis of this strict-liability cause of action.

The *Restatement (Third)* defines defective design in § 2(b) as follows:

A product; (b) is defective in design when the foreseeable risks of harm posed by the product could have been reduced or avoided by the adoption of a reasonable alternative design by the seller or other distributor, or a predecessor in the commercial chain of distribution, and the omission of the alternative design renders the product not reasonably safe.

 CASE LAW

◆ **testing for defective design**

Barker v. Lull Engineering Company, Inc., et al., 573 P.2d 443 (Cal. 1978).

In August of 1970, plaintiff Ray Barker was injured while operating a high-lift loader manufactured by defendant Lull Engineering Company ("Lull"). Plaintiff filed this action against Lull claiming that his injuries were proximately caused by an alleged defective design of the loader which was, among other things, manifested by the absence of seat belts and a roll bar in the loader. At trial, the jury returned a verdict in favor of the defendant manufacturer, which was based upon a jury instruction regarding the jury's consideration and finding of a defective design. On appeal, plaintiff complained that the trial court had erred in instructing the jury "that strict liability for a defective design of a product is based on a finding that the product was unreasonably dangerous for its intended use. . . ."

TOBRINER, C.J.

* * *

In August 1970, plaintiff Ray Barker was injured at a construction site at the University of California at Santa Cruz while operating a high-lift loader manufactured by defendant Lull Engineering Co. and leased to plaintiff's employer by defendant George M. Philpott Co., Inc. Claiming that his injuries were proximately caused, inter alia, by the alleged defective design of the loader, Barker instituted the present tort action seeking to recover damages for his injuries. The jury returned a verdict in favor of defendants, and plaintiff appeals from the judgment entered upon that verdict, contending primarily that in view of this court's decision in *Cronin v. J. B. E.,* the trial court erred in instructing the jury "that strict liability for a defect in design of a product is based on a finding that the product was unreasonably dangerous for its intended use. . . ."

As we explain, we agree with plaintiff's objection to the challenged instruction and conclude that the judgment must be reversed. In *Cronin,* we reviewed the development of the strict product liability doctrine in California at some length, and concluded that, for a variety of reasons, the "unreasonably dangerous" element which section 402A of the Restatement Second of Torts had introduced into the definition of a defective product should not be incorporated into a plaintiff's burden of proof in a product liability action in this state. Although defendants maintain that our *Cronin* decision should properly be interpreted as applying only to "manufacturing defects" and not to the alleged "design defects" at issue here, we shall point out that the *Cronin* decision itself refutes any such distinction. Consequently, we conclude that the instruction was erroneous and that the judgment in favor of defendants must be reversed.

* * *

As *Cronin* acknowledged, in the past decade and a half California courts have frequently recognized that the defectiveness concept defies a simple, uniform definition applicable to all sectors of the diverse product liability domain. Although in many instances—as when one machine in a million contains a cracked or broken part—the meaning of the term "defect" will require little or no elaboration, in other instances, as when a product is claimed to be defective because of an unsafe design or an inadequate warning, the contours of the defect concept may not be self-evident. In such a case a trial judge may find it necessary to explain more fully to the jury the legal meaning of "defect" or "defective." We shall explain that *Cronin* in no way precluded such elucidation of the defect concept, but rather contemplated that, in typical common law fashion, the accumulating body of product liability authorities would give guidance for the formulation of a definition.

* * *

As we explain in more detail below, we have concluded from this review that a product is defective in design either (1) if the product has failed to perform as safely as an ordinary consumer would expect when used in an intended or reasonably foreseeable manner, or (2) if, in light of the relevant factors discussed below, the benefits of the challenged design do not outweigh the risk of danger inherent in such design. * * *

This dual standard for design defect assures an injured plaintiff protection from products that either fall below ordinary consumer expectations as to safety, or that, on balance, are not as safely designed as they should be. At the same time, the standard permits a manufacturer who has marketed a product which satisfies ordinary consumer expectations to demonstrate the relative complexity of design decisions and the trade-offs that are frequently required in the adoption of alternative designs. Finally, this test reflects our continued adherence to the principle that, in a product liability action, the trier of fact must focus on the *product*, not on the *manufacturer's conduct*, and that the plaintiff need not prove that the manufacturer acted unreasonably or negligently in order to prevail in such an action.

* * *

2. *The trial court erred in instructing the jurors that "strict liability for a defect in design . . . is based on a finding that the product was unreasonably dangerous for its intended use."*

Plaintiff principally contends that the trial court committed prejudicial error in instructing the jury "that strict liability for a defect in design of a product is based on a finding that the product was unreasonably dangerous for its intended use. . . ." [Footnote omitted.] Plaintiff maintains that this instruction conflicts directly with this court's decision in *Cronin,* decided subsequently to the instant trial, and mandates a reversal of the judgment. Defendants argue, in response, that our *Cronin* decision should not be applied to product liability actions which involve "design defects" as distinguished from "manufacturing defects."

The plaintiff in *Cronin,* a driver of a bread delivery truck, was seriously injured when, during an accident, a metal hasp which held the truck's bread trays in place broke, permitting the trays to slide forward and propel plaintiff through the truck's windshield. Plaintiff brought a strict liability action against the seller, contending that his injuries were proximately caused by the defective condition of the truck. Evidence at trial established that the metal hasp broke during the accident "because it was extremely porous and had a significantly lower tolerance to force than a nonflawed aluminum hasp would have had" and, on the basis of this evidence, the jury returned a verdict in favor of plaintiff.

On appeal, defendant in *Cronin* argued that the trial court had erred "by submitting a definition of strict liability which failed to include, as defendant requested, the element that the defect found in the product be 'unreasonably dangerous.' " Relying upon section 402A of the Restatement Second of Torts [footnote omitted] and a number of California decisions which had utilized the "unreasonably dangerous" terminology in the product liability context, [footnote omitted] the defendant in *Cronin* maintained that a product's "unreasonable dangerousness" was an essential element that a plaintiff must establish in any product liability action.

After undertaking a thorough review of the origins and development of both California product liability doctrine and the Restatement's "unreasonably dangerous" criterion, we rejected the defendant's contention, concluding "that to require an injured plaintiff to prove not only that the product contained a defect but also that such defect made the product unreasonably dangerous to the user or consumer would place a considerably greater burden upon him than that articulated in *Greenman v. Yuba Power Products, Inc.,* (1963), 59 Cal.2d 57 (Cal.Rptr. 697, 377 P.2d 897, 13 A.L.R.3d 1049), [California's seminal product liability decision].

* * *

In attempting to escape the apparent force of *Cronin's* explicit language, defendants observe that the flawed hasp which rendered the truck defective in *Cronin* represented a manufacturing defect rather than a design defect, and they argue that *Cronin's* disapproval of the Restatement's "unreasonably dangerous" standard should be limited to the manufacturing defect context. Defendants point out that one of the bases for our rejection of the "unreasonably dangerous" criterion in *Cronin* was our concern that such language, when used in conjunction with the "defective product" terminology, was susceptible to an interpretation which would place a *dual burden* on an injured plaintiff to prove, first, that a product was defective and, second, that it was additionally unreasonably dangerous. Defendants contend that the "dual burden" problem is present only in a manufacturing defect context and not in a design defect case.

In elaborating this contention, defendants explain that in a manufacturing defect case, a jury may find a product defective because it deviates from the manufacturer's intended result, but may still decline to impose liability under the Restatement test on the ground that such defect did not render the product unreasonably dangerous. In a design defect case, by contrast, defendants assert that a defect *is defined* by reference to the "unreasonably dangerous" standard and, since the two are equivalent, no danger of a dual burden exists. In essence, defendants argue that under the instruction which the trial court gave in the instant case, plaintiff was not required to prove both that the loader was defective and that such defect made the loader unreasonably dangerous, but only that the loader was defectively designed by virtue of its unreasonable dangerousness.

* * *

As we noted in *Cronin*, the Restatement draftsmen adopted the "unreasonably dangerous" language primarily as a means of confining the application of strict tort liability to an article which is "dangerous to an extent beyond that which would be contemplated by the ordinary consumer who purchases it, with the ordinary knowledge common to the community as to its characteristics." In *Cronin*, however, we flatly rejected the suggestion that recovery in a products liability action should be permitted *only* if a product is more dangerous than contemplated by the average consumer, refusing to permit the low esteem in which the public might hold a dangerous product to diminish the manufacturer's responsibility for injuries caused by that product. As we pointedly noted in *Cronin*, even if the "ordinary consumer" may have contemplated that Shopsmith lathes posed a risk of loosening their grip and letting a piece of wood strike the operation, "another Greenman" should not be denied recovery. [Citation omitted.]

* * *

Thus, our rejection of the use of the "unreasonably dangerous" terminology in *Cronin* rested in part on a concern that a jury might interpret such an instruction,

as the Restatement draftsman had indeed intended, as shielding a defendant from liability so long as the product did not fall below the ordinary consumer's expectations as to the product's safety. [Footnote omitted.]

* * *

Accordingly, contrary to defendants' contention, the reasoning of *Cronin* does not dictate that that decision be confined to the manufacturing defect context. Indeed, in *Cronin* itself we expressly stated that our holding applied to design defects as well as to manufacturing defects and in *Henderson v. Harnischfeger Corp.*, (1974) 12 Cal.3d 663, 670, we subsequently confirmed the impropriety of instructing a jury in the language of the "unreasonably dangerous" standard in a design defect case. [Citation and footnote omitted.] Consequently, we conclude that the design defect instruction given in the instant case was erroneous. [Footnote omitted.]

3. *A trial court may properly formulate instructions to elucidate the "defect" concept in varying circumstances. In particular, in design defect cases, a court may properly instruct a jury that a product is defective in design if (1) the plaintiff proves that the product failed to perform as safely as an ordinary consumer would expect when used in an intended or reasonably foreseeable manner, or (2) the plaintiff proves that the product's design proximately caused injury and the defendant fails to prove, in light of the relevant factors, that on balance the benefits of the challenged design outweigh the risk of danger inherent in such design.*

Defendants contend, however, that if *Cronin* is interpreted as precluding the use of the "unreasonably dangerous" language in defining a design defect, the jury in all such cases will inevitably be left without any guidance whatsoever in determining whether a product is defective in design or not. [Citation omitted.] Amicus California Trial Lawyers Association (CTLA) on behalf of the plaintiff responds by suggesting that the precise intent of our *Cronin* decision was to preclude a trial court from formulating any definition of "defect" in a product liability case, thus always leaving the definition of defect, as well as the application of such definition, to the jury. As we explain, neither of these contentions represents an accurate portrayal of the intent or effect of our *Cronin* decision.

In *Cronin*, we reaffirmed the basic formulation of strict tort liability doctrine set forth in *Greenman*: "A manufacturer is strictly liable in tort when an article he places on the market, knowing that it is to be used without inspection for defects, proves to have a defect that causes injury to a human being. . . ." We held in *Cronin* that a plaintiff satisfies his burden of proof under *Greenman*, in both a "manufacturing defect" and "design defect" context, when he proves the existence of a "defect" and that such defect was a proximate cause of his injuries. [Citation omitted.] In reaching this conclusion, however, *Cronin* did not purport to hold that the term "defect" must remain undefined in all contexts [citation omitted], and did not preclude a trial court from framing a definition of defect, appropriate to the circumstances of a particular case, to guide the jury as to the standard to be applied in determining whether a product is defective or not.

As this court has recognized on numerous occasions, the term defect as utilized in the strict liability context is neither self-defining nor susceptible to a single definition applicable in all contexts. In *Jiminez v. Sears, Roebuck & Co.*, 4 Cal.3d 379, 383, for example, we stated: "A defect may be variously defined, and as yet no definition has been formulated that would resolve all cases or that is universally agreed upon." Indeed, in *Cronin* itself, we expressly recognized "the difficulties inherent in giving content to the defectiveness standard" and suggested that the problem could best be resolved by resort to the "'cluster of useful precedents'" which have been developed in the product liability field in the past decade and a half. [Citation omitted.]

Resort to the numerous product liability precedents in California demonstrates that the defect or defectiveness concept has embraced a great variety of injury-producing deficiencies, ranging from products that cause injury because they deviate from the manufacturer's intended result (e.g., the one soda bottle in ten thousand that explodes without explanation [citation omitted]) to products which, though "perfectly" manufactured, are unsafe because of the absence of a safety device [citation omitted]), and including products that are dangerous because they lack adequate warnings or instructions (e.g., a telescope that contains inadequate instructions for assembling a "sun filter" attachment [citation omitted]).

Commentators have pointed out that in view of the diversity of product deficiencies to which the defect rubric has been applied, an instruction which requires a plaintiff to prove the existence of a product defect, but which fails to elaborate on the meaning of defect in a particular context, may in some situations prove more misleading than helpful. As Professor Wade has written: "[The] natural application [of the term 'defective'] would be limited to the situation in which something went wrong in the manufacturing process, so that the article was defective in the sense that the manufacturer had not intended it to be in that condition. To apply [the term 'defective'] also to the case in which a warning is not attached to the chattel or the design turns out to be a bad one or the product is likely to be injurious in its normal condition . . . [and to] use it without defining it to the jury is almost to ensure that they will be misled." [Citations omitted.]

* * *

Since the rendition of our decision in *Cronin*, a number of thoughtful Court of Appeal decisions have wrestled with the problem of devising a comprehensive definition of design defect in light of existing authorities. [Citations omitted.] As these decisions demonstrate, the concept of defect raises considerably more difficulties in the design defect context than it does in the manufacturing or production defect context.

In general, a manufacturing or production defect is readily identifiable because a defective product is one that differs from the manufacturer's intended result or from other ostensibly identical units of the same product line. For example, when a product comes off the assembly line in a substandard condition it has incurred a manufacturing defect. [Citation omitted.] A design defect, by contrast, cannot be identified simply by comparing the injury-producing product with the manufacturer's plans or with other units of the same product line, since by definition the plans and all such units will reflect the same design. Rather than applying any sort of deviation-from-the-norm test in determining whether a product is defective in design for strict liability purposes, our cases have employed two alternative criteria in ascertaining, in Justice Traynor's words, whether there is something "wrong, if not in the manufacturer's manner of production, at least in his product." [Citation omitted.]

First, our cases establish that a product may be found defective in design if the plaintiff demonstrates that the product failed to perform as safely as an ordinary consumer would expect when used in an intended or reasonably foreseeable manner. This initial standard, somewhat analogous to the Uniform Commercial Code's warranty of fitness and merchantability, reflects the warranty heritage upon which California product liability doctrine in part rests. As we noted in *Greenman*, "implicit in [a product's] presence on the market . . . [is] a representation that it [will] safely do the jobs for which it was built." When a product fails to satisfy such ordinary consumer expectations as to safety in its intended or reasonably foreseeable operation, a manufacturer is strictly liable for resulting injuries. [Citations omitted.] Under this standard, an injured plaintiff will frequently be able to demonstrate the defectiveness of a product by resort to circumstantial evidence, even when the accident itself precludes identification of the specific defect at fault. [Citations omitted.]

As Professor Wade has pointed out, however, the expectations of the ordinary consumer cannot be viewed as the exclusive yardstick for evaluating design defectiveness because "[in] many situations . . . the consumer would not know what to expect, because he would have no idea how safe the product could be made." [Citations omitted.] Numerous California decisions have implicitly recognized this fact and have made clear, through varying linguistic formulations, that a product may be found defective in design, even if it satisfies ordinary consumer expectations, if through hindsight the jury determines that the product's design embodies "excessive preventable danger," or, in other words, if the jury finds that the risk of danger inherent in the challenged design outweighs the benefits of such design. [Citations omitted.]

A review of past cases indicates that in evaluating the adequacy of a product's design pursuant to this latter standard, a jury may consider, among other relevant factors, the gravity of the danger posed by the challenged design, the likelihood that such danger would occur, the mechanical feasibility of a safer alternative design, the financial cost of an improved design, and the adverse consequences to the product and to the consumer that would result from an alternative design. [Citations omitted.]

Although our cases have thus recognized a variety of considerations that may be relevant to the determination of the adequacy of a product's design, past authorities have generally not devoted much attention to the appropriate allocation of the burden of proof with respect to these matters. [Citations omitted.] The allocation of such burden is particularly significant in this context inasmuch as this court's product liability decisions, from *Greenman* to *Cronin*, have repeatedly emphasized that one of the principal purposes behind the strict product liability doctrine is to relieve an injured plaintiff of many of the onerous evidentiary burdens inherent in a negligence cause of action. Because most of the evidentiary matters which may be relevant to the determination of the adequacy of a product's design under the "risk-benefit" standard— e.g., the feasibility and cost of alternative designs—are similar to issues typically presented in a negligent design case and involve technical matters peculiarly within the knowledge of the manufacturer, we conclude that once the plaintiff makes a prima facie case showing that the injury was proximately caused by the product's design, the burden should appropriately shift to the defendant to prove, in light of the relevant factors, that the product is not defective. Moreover, inasmuch as this conclusion flows from our determination that the fundamental public policies embraced in *Greenman* dictate that a manufacturer who seeks to escape liability for an injury proximately caused by its product's design on a risk-benefit theory should bear the burden of persuading the trier of fact that its product should not be judged defective, the defendant's burden is one affecting the burden of proof, rather than simply the burden of producing evidence. [Citations omitted.]

Thus, to reiterate, a product may be found defective in design, so as to subject a manufacturer to strict liability for resulting injuries, under either of two alternative tests. First, a product may be found defective in design if the plaintiff establishes that the product failed to perform as safely as an ordinary consumer would expect when used in an intended or reasonably foreseeable manner. Second, a product may alternatively be found defective in design if the plaintiff demonstrates that the product's design proximately caused his injury and the defendant fails to establish, in light of the relevant factors, that, on balance, the benefits of the challenged design outweigh the risk of danger inherent in such design.

* * *

Case Notes: Testing for Defective Design

1. In *Barker*, the California Supreme Court reaffirmed its "continued adherence to the principle that, in a product liability action, *the trier of fact must focus on the product, not the manufacturer's conduct*, and that the plaintiff need not prove that the manufacturer acted unreasonably or negligently in order to prevail[.]" *Barker*, 573 P.2d at 447. In so doing, the court adopted a dual standard through which a plaintiff may prove a defendant manufacturer's liability for defective design. The court enunciated this standard by holding that

> in design defect cases, a court may properly instruct a jury that a product is defective in design if (1) the plaintiff proves that the product failed to perform as safely as an ordinary consumer would expect when used in an intended or reasonably foreseeable manner, or (2) the plaintiff proves that the product's design proximately caused injury and the defendant fails to prove, in light of the relevant factors, that on balance the benefits of the challenged design outweigh the risk of danger inherent in such design. *Id.*, 452.

These two standards have been generally recognized, respectively, as (a) the consumer expectations test and (b) the risk-utility test.

    a. The *consumer expectations test* is taken directly from comment i of the *Restatement (Second) of Torts* § 402A, which provides, in part, that

> The [product] sold must be dangerous to an extent beyond that which would be contemplated by the ordinary consumer who purchases it, with the ordinary knowledge common to the community as to its characteristics. Comment i, *Restatement (Second) of Torts* § 402A.

Critics of this test note that it is difficult, if not unfair, for the finder of fact to determine the boundaries, skills, and knowledge of the ordinary consumer in a strict-liability analysis, particularly one that is possessed of "ordinary knowledge common to the community." *Id.* This criteria is subjective because it depends upon the reasonable expectations of the ordinary consumer. Although objective, it is less than certain that the average consumer would reasonably anticipate the dangerous condition of the product and for that reason alone, fully appreciate the attendant risk of injury from the product. See *Vincer v. Esther Williams All-Aluminum Swimming Pool Co.*, 230 N.W.2d 794, 798-99 (Wis. 1975). This discrepancy unnecessarily injects subjective criteria into the test. The objective application of the consumer expectations test is one that recognizes the ordinary risks of using the product that are commonly known to the community. The test loses its objectivity when the special knowledge of any one consumer is considered in the analysis or if the general knowledge at issue is not commonly known in the community.

    b. A court engaged in applying *the risk-utility test* also seeks to focus this balancing analysis on the condition of the product and not the conduct of the manufacturer. A similar risk-utility test is available in ordinary negligence cases, but in those circumstances, the condition of the actor, perhaps manufacturer, is at issue and is necessarily the focus of the analysis. In *Barker*, the court held that it was the plaintiff's obligation to make a prima facia showing that his injury had been proximately caused by the product's design, at which point the burden shifted to the defendant to prove that its product was not defective. *Barker*, 573 P.2d at 455.

In applying this test, the trier of fact is asked to weigh the risk of potential harm from the product against its potential social benefit and to make a collective determination about whether the harm outweighs the risk or vice-versa. For example, a car owner derives the utilitarian benefit of quick, accessible transportation in exchange for the risk of being hurled down the road at certain speeds and in a machine that has an operating engine, transmission, wheels, and axles. The benefit is transportation, but it is provided at the risk of being injured by the very benefit it provides.

Some scholars disagree about the factors to be weighed in a risk-utility analysis, particularly whether the manufacturer might have reduced the risk of harm to the plaintiff without having brought about a significant impact to the product's utility, cost to manufacture, functionality, or design. See *Thibault v. Sears, Roebuck & Co.*, 395 A.2d 843, 846 (N.H. 1978). Other facts to be weighed in a risk-utility analysis include causation and foreseeability. *Id.* at 847.

The inclusion of additional factors in this test must be carefully considered because the overindulgence into any one of them will lead to a floating perspective that places an emphasis on the conduct of the manufacturer with the same if not higher emphasis than the inherent defectiveness of the product itself. It is here that the result from this analysis will change because the focus will shift away from the character of the product and to the conduct of the manufacturer. A strict-liability analysis requires that the appropriate application of any test for defective design always focus on the product. To lose this focus is to lose the no-fault element inherent in any strict-liability analysis.

2. Comment I to § 402A of the *Restatement (Second)* provided parameters of an unreasonably dangerous product:

a. *Unreasonably dangerous.* The rule stated in this Section applies only where the defective condition of the product makes it unreasonably dangerous to the user or consumer. Many products cannot possibly be made entirely safe for all consumption, and any food or drug necessarily involves some risk of harm, if only from over-consumption. Ordinary sugar is a deadly poison to diabetics, and castor oil found use under Mussolini as an instrument of torture. That is not what is meant by "unreasonably dangerous" in this Section. The article sold must be dangerous to an extent beyond that which would be contemplated by the ordinary consumer who purchases it, with the ordinary knowledge common to the community as to its characteristics. Good whiskey is not unreasonably dangerous merely because it will make some people drunk, and is especially dangerous to alcoholics; but bad whiskey, containing a dangerous amount of fuel oil, is unreasonably dangerous. Good tobacco is not unreasonably dangerous merely because the effects of smoking may be harmful; but tobacco containing something like marijuana may be unreasonably dangerous. Good butter is not unreasonably dangerous merely because, if such be the case, it deposits cholesterol in the arteries and leads to heart attacks; but bad butter, contaminated with poisonous fish oil, is unreasonably dangerous.

3. Consumer expectations about the product's safety or its reasonably foreseeable operation and performance "are frequently of direct significance to the defectiveness issue, " particularly in determining the existence of any defect in the product. *Barker,* 573 P.2d at 451. Although consumer expectations are a significant consideration in the analysis of a defective design, the product may still retain an inherently defective design in which the risks of danger in that design outweighs the benefits of the product in that design.

4. The *Restatement (Third)* adopts the risk-utility test as the principle test of choice by which a finder of fact must determine the existence of a defective product. See Comment d, § *Restatement (Third) of Torts: Products Liability* (1997). In fact, the *Restatement (Third)* specifically rejects use of the consumer expectations test. "Under Subsection (b), consumer expectations do not constitute an independent standard for judging the defectiveness of product designs." See Comment g, § 2 of the *Restatement (Third) of Torts: Products Liability* (1997).

5. In weighing the risks and benefits of the product design, especially during application of a

risk-utility review, the finder of fact may consider the following:

- any danger posed by the challenged design
- the likelihood that this danger will occur
- the mechanical feasibility of a safer, alternative design
- the financial cost of an improved design
- the adverse consequences to the product consumer from the proposed alternative design

6. In *Barker*, the California Supreme Court extracted the "unreasonably dangerous" language of § 402A of the *Restatement (Second)* from consideration in determining the existence of a defective design. The court expressed concern that a product that was truly defective in design may not be regarded as unreasonably dangerous if it did not fall below the consumers' expectations about safety and foreseeable operation, especially if the product was substantially similar to other items of the same product line. *Id.*

7. The California Trial Lawyers Association (CTLA) represented in their amicus position in *Barker* that the finder of fact cannot appropriately "weigh" or "balance" relevant design defect factors because such a process introduces a negligence analysis into the determination of a defective design, which is far afield from the requisite burden of proof in a strict liability action. *Barker*, 573 P.2d at 456. The California Supreme Court held, however, that the process of weighing competing considerations and, specifically, analyzing the risks and benefits of alternative designs is inherent in determining whether a defective design is present and is not "the equivalent of an instruction which requires the jury to determine whether the manufacturer was negligent in designing the product." *Id.*

8. What are the problems that emerge from applying the reasonably prudent manufacturer test? If the conduct of the manufacturer is considered or if knowledge of the inherent danger in the product is imputed to the man-

ufacturer, how may a trier of fact distinguish between what the manufacturer knew and what the manufacturer truly did not know? Under this test, can a manufacturer's state-of-the-art defense be given fair consideration?

9. For additional insight regarding the consumer expectations test, consult these authorities: Harris, *Enhanced Injury Theory: An Analytic Framework*, 62 N.C.L.Rev. 640, (1984) (crashworthiness and second collision doctrines); Wade, *On Product "Design Defects" and Their Actionability*, 33 Vand.L.Rev. 551, 566-71 (1980); Birnbaum, *Unmasking the Test for Design Defect: From Negligence [to Warranty] to Strict Liability to Negligence*, 33 Vand.L.Rev. 593, 602-18 (1980); Comment, *The Consumer Expectations Test: A Critical Review of its Application in California*, 17 Sw.U.L.Rev. 823 (1988); Henderson, *Judicial Review of Manufacturers' Conscious Design Choices: The Limits of Adjudication*, 73 Colum.L.Rev. 1531 (1973).

10. How can a finder of fact distinguish design defects from manufacturing defects?

In *Barker*, the California Supreme Court carefully distinguished design defects from manufacturing defects. The court noted that "a manufacturing or production defect is readily identifiable because a defective product is one that differs from the manufacturer's intended result or from other ostensibly identical units of the same product line. For example, when a product comes off the assembly line in a substandard condition it has incurred a manufacturing defect" *Barker*, 573 P.2d at 454. Likewise, a "design defect, by contrast, cannot be identified simply by comparing the injury-producing product with the manufacturer's plans or with other units of the same product line, since by definition the plans and all such units will reflect the same design. Rather than applying any sort of deviation-from-the-norm test in determining whether a product is defective in design for strict liability purposes, our cases have employed two alternative criteria[.]" *Id.* These two criteria are: (1) "a product may be found to be defective in design if the plaintiff demonstrates that the product failed to perform as safely as an ordinary consumer would expect when used in an intended or reasonably foreseeable manner;" *Id.* and, (2) "a product may alternatively be found defective in design if the plaintiff demonstrates that the product's design proximately caused his injury and the defendant fails to establish, in light of the relevant factors, that, on balance, the benefits of the challenged design outweigh the risk of danger inherent in such design." *Id.* 455.

What are the other notable differences between defective manufacturing and defective designs? What analysis differs? How does the finder of fact distinguish one type of defect from another?

11. What other methods are available to evaluate whether the product was defectively designed?

12. In *Barker*, the jury returned a verdict at trial in favor of the defendant manufacturer, Lull Engineering Company, and thereafter appealed complaining that the trial court had erred in instructing the jury that strict liability for a defectively designed product was based on a finding that the product was unreasonably dangerous for its intended use. *Barker*, 573 P.2d 443. The challenged instruction read as follows:

> I instruct you that strict liability for the defect in design of a product is based on a finding that the product was unreasonably dangerous for its intended use, and in turn the unreasonableness of the danger must necessarily be derived from the state of the art at the time of the design. The manufacturer or lessor are not insurers of their products. However, an industry cannot set its own standards. *Id.* at 449.

Plaintiffs' challenge [was] limited to the portion of the instruction which provides that "strict liability for the defect in design of a product is based on a finding that the product was unreasonably dangerous for its intended use"[.] *Id.*

13. The California Supreme Court rejected the defective design instruction submitted to the jury in *Barker* because the court believed that the instruction was too narrow in that the finding of a defective design did not rest exclusively upon whether the product was "unreasonably dangerous for its intended use." The court noted that a defective design may be found in any one of a number of considerations, including the dangers posed by the challenged design, the likelihood that those dangers would occur, the feasibility of a safer alternative design, the financial cost of a safer design, the adverse consequences posed to the product and its consumer by the alternative design, and the remaining risks and benefits of the alternative design as weighed against the risks and benefits of the challenged design. *Id.* at 454.

14. A jury instruction is a written "statement made by the judge to the jury informing them of the law applicable to the case in general or some aspect of it" Black's Law Dictionary 769 (5th ed. 1979). The appropriate statement to be given is determined by the judge after all parties have submitted suggested instructions. It is generally regarded as a statement of the law upon which the jury must base its decision if the jury, as the finder of fact, is to find for or against plaintiff or defendant at trial. The instruction will provide, among other things, a listing of the elements necessary for plaintiff to make a submissible case in the cause of action upon which plaintiff has brought its suit.

15. Why are jury instructions important to a finder of fact that is determining the facts in the case and not the law in the case? If a jury instruction simply misstates the applicable law, does the court simply correct the law as applied by the judge in the case? Why or why not?

16. At what point in the trial are jury instructions submitted to the judge? When are the jury instructions submitted to the jury? When should the jury instructions be considered by counsel and their clients in pursuing and defending product liability litigation?

Further consideration of consumer expectations and risk-utility standards

 CASE LAW ──◆

◆ **consumer expectations and risk-utility tests**

Lamkin v. Tower, et al., and
Pace v. Tower, et al., 563
N.E.2d 449 (Ill. 1990).

In 1982 and 1983, Jason Lamkin and Dustin Pace, respectively, each fell from a second story apartment after their mothers had opened a window but left the window screen in place. These minors had depended upon the strength of the window screens to bear their weight when each of these boys leaned against the screen to peer outside. The defendants, including the manufacturer, filed dispositive motions alleging that they were not liable in either case based upon the absence of any legal duty owed to either of the plaintiffs. The trial court granted these defendants' motions, and the appellate court affirmed these decisions. The appellate court granted plaintiffs' motions for an interlocutory appeal and certified four questions to be answered by the Illinois Supreme Court, only one of which concerned the product manufacturer's liability.

CLARK, J.

* * *

The primary issue in this case is whether liability can be imposed under theories of negligence or strict products liability for damages sustained by a child who fell through a window screen.

* * *

All appellants filed motions for summary judgment [citation omitted] in both cases based on the absence of any legal duty on their part on which liability could be predicated. The manufacturer also filed a motion to dismiss pursuant to Section 2—621 of the Illinois Code of Civil Procedure. [Citation omitted.] The trial court denied appellants' motions for summary judgment and the motion to dismiss. On December 18, 1987, the trial court granted appellants' motions for interlocutory appeal in each case pursuant to Supreme Court Rule 308 (107 Ill. 2d R. 308). The cases were consolidated on appeal and the appellate court affirmed the trial court's denial of the motions for summary judg-

ment as well as the motion to dismiss. [Citation omitted.] We granted appellants' petitions for leave to appeal. [Citation omitted.]

In allowing appellants' motions for interlocutory appeal, the trial court certified four questions for review pursuant to Supreme Court Rule 308(a). [Citation omitted.] These questions are as follows:

> "d. Whether, as a matter of law, a window frame and window screen can be defective or unreasonably dangerous because they were not sufficiently strong to support the weight of a child leaning against the window screen so as to serve as the basis for a cause of action for products liability against the manufacturer of such window frames and window screens."

Before proceeding with an examination of these questions, we note that the appellate court opinion failed to address the certified questions individually. Instead, the appellate court reached a general conclusion that there was "liability on the part of the landlord, the builder or renovator, the retailer * * * or the manufacturer" [citation omitted] without first determining whether a separate duty existed on the part of each of these individual appellants. Implicit in the restriction that any appeal pursuant to Rule 308 should be limited to only those questions certified by the trial court [citations omitted] is the requirement that those questions must, in fact, be addressed. We turn therefore to a separate review of each of the questions certified by the trial court.

III. The Retailer's and Manufacturer's Duty

The trial court certified two separate questions focusing on appellees' products liability approach to the retailer's and manufacturer's liability. Because the analysis is the same for both appellants, we consider both issues here.

The court has indicated that strict products liability in Illinois follows the formulation set forth in Section 402A of the Restatement (Second) of Torts (1965), which imposes strict liability upon one "who sells any product in a defective condition unreasonably dangerous to the user or consumer or to his property." [Citation omitted.] A product is "unreasonably dangerous" when it is "dangerous to an extent beyond that which would be contemplated by the ordinary consumer who purchases it, with the ordinary knowledge common to the community as to its characteristics." [Citations omitted.] A product may be unreasonably dangerous in one of two ways: because of (1) a design or manufacturing defect or (2) a failure to warn of a danger posed by the product of which the average consumer would not be aware. [Citation omitted.] A nondefective product that presents a danger that the average consumer would recognize does not give rise to strict liability. [Citation omitted.]

A plaintiff may demonstrate that a product is defective in design, so as to subject a retailer and a manufacturer to strict liability for resulting injuries, in one of two ways: (1) by introducing evidence that the product failed to perform as safely as an ordinary consumer would expect when used in an intended or reasonably foreseeable manner or (2) by introducing evidence that the product's design proximately caused his injury and the defendant fails to prove that on balance the benefits of the challenged design outweigh the risk of danger inherent in such designs. [Citations omitted.]

There has been no evidence presented in the form of affidavits, depositions, testimony or other evidentiary materials to support a finding on a motion for summary judgment that the window screens failed to perform as safely as an ordinary consumer would expect when *used* in an intended or reasonably foreseeable manner. Window screens are designed to allow air and light into an area while preventing insects from entering. (*Scheffler,* 67 Ill. App. 2d at 225 ("[I]t is settled law that a landlord has no duty to furnish screens suitable for anything other than keeping out insects"); *Gasquoine,* 10 Ill. App. 2d at 425 ("[A] primary purpose * * * of screens [is] to keep out insects while letting in light and air").) They may, on occasion, serve to prevent an individual from falling from a window, but this purpose is incidental to their *intended* use. (*Crawford,* 331 Ill. App. at 574 ("'A screen in a window, obviously and of common knowledge, is not placed there for the purpose of keeping persons from falling out of a window'"), quoting *Egan,* 103 N.J.L. at 476, 135 A. at 812.) Virtually any manufactured product can cause or be a

proximate cause of injury if put to certain uses or misuses (*Hunt,* 74 Ill. 2d at 211), but strict liability applies only when the product is "'dangerous to an extent beyond that which would be contemplated by the ordinary [person] * * *, with the ordinary knowledge common to the community as to its characteristics'" (*Palmer,* 82 Ill. 2d at 216, quoting Restatement (Second) of Torts § 402A, comment *i* (1965); see also *Hunt,* 74 Ill. 2d at 211-12).

The window screens were simply serving the purpose for which they were created when the accidents occurred. Even assuming that "the ordinary [person]" may recognize the potential for a screen to restrict a fall from a window, we cannot conclude that, in the event a window screen fails to prevent the fall of a minor leaning against it, "the ordinary [person]" would consider the screen dangerous beyond his original contemplation of the product. A consumer may rightfully expect a product to safely do the job for which it was built or for a foreseeable similar use, but neither a retailer nor a manufacturer can be held strictly liable for injuries resulting from the misuse of its product.

Likewise, there has been no evidence presented in the form of affidavits, depositions, testimony or other evidentiary materials to support a finding on a motion for summary judgment that the window screens' *design* proximately caused appellees' injuries. Appellees allege in their complaints that:

"(a) The screens readily popped out from the frames;
 (b) The screens were not securely fastened within tracks on the windows;
 (c) There are no secure latches, locks or other devices to fix the window screens to the frames."

Appellees fail to provide evidence of how the window screens' design could have been altered to create a safer screen, such as the one described by appellees, or any evidence of the form and feasibility of the alternative screen design. In light of appellees' failure to provide any evidence to support their allegations, we cannot conclude that, as a matter of law, the window screens are "defective or unreasonably dangerous" such as to serve as the basis for a products liability action against the retailer or manufacturer of such window frames and window screens.

* * *

Other Tests for Defective Design   Other tests to determine the existence of a defective design are available. These tests include (1) allowing the jury exclusive control to define whether the product is unreasonably dangerous, (2) the reasonably prudent manufacturer test, (3) the court-as-policymaker approach, and (4) the Uniform Model Product Liability Act approach. Only a minority of courts have embraced these tests because they introduce too many negligence, conduct-evaluating standards into the strict-liability analysis.

 CASE LAW

◆ **allowing the jury to define "unreasonably dangerous"**

Nesselrode v. Executive Beechcraft, Inc., 707 S.W.2d 371 (Mo. banc 1986).

Plaintiff wife and her three daughters brought a wrongful death action against airplane manufacturer alleging that the right and left elevator trim tab actuators of the aircraft's tail section were defectively designed. At trial, the jury found for plaintiffs and awarded $1.5 million. Defendant Beech appealed and argued that the jury had not been properly instructed about the requisite elements necessary to find that the aircraft was defectively designed.

BILLINGS, J.

* * *

The crux of the plaintiffs' theory of defective design focuses on the fact that the right and left actuators, as designed by Beech, are visually identical but functionally distinct, and as such, they are capable of being interchanged—i.e., reversed—during installation. Relying on these facts, plaintiffs contend that the actuators, as designed, were sold in a defective and unsafe condition. In connection with their failure to warn theory of liability, plaintiffs argue essentially that the very nature of the design of the actuators created the need for a warning—and the absence of a warning detailing the possibility of reverse installation and its consequences also caused the actuators to be sold in a "defective condition."

This Court first adopted strict tort liability in *Keener v. Dayton Electric Manufacturing Company*, 445 S.W.2d 362 (Mo. 1969). In *Keener*, which was a case involving a defect in the manufacturing process rather than a problem associated with the way the product was originally de-

signed, we set forth our basic reasons for adopting strict tort liability, [footnote omitted] and we also delineated the initial contours of the doctrine. [Citation omitted.] In the course of doing so, we acknowledged that we were adopting the rule of strict tort liability as set forth in Section 402A of the *Restatement (Second) of Torts*. [Citation omitted.]

Eight years later in *Blevins v. Cushman Motors*, 551 S.W.2d 602 (Mo. banc 1977), we held that the doctrine of strict tort liability applies with equal purpose to products liability cases involving problems caused by the way a product has been designed. *Blevins v. Cushman Motors*, 551 S.W.2d at 607. *See also Duke v. Gulf & Western Manufacturing Co.*, 660 S.W.2d 404, 411-412 (Mo. App. 1983). In *Blevins*, we took care to stress that under a theory of strict tort liability, the focal point of the litigation process is the condition or character of the product and not the character of the defendant's conduct—thereby exercising the concept of reasonable care, the limits test of liability in negligence law, from Missouri's rule of strict tort liability. [Footnote and citations omitted.]

Although the focus of a products liability suit brought under a theory of strict tort liability is on the condition or character of the product rather than on the nature of the defendant's conduct, the doctrine of strict tort liability is not, nor was it ever intended to be, an enveloping net of absolute liability. As Roger Traynor, the eminent California jurist most responsible for pioneering the doctrine, noted in his 1965 article, *The Ways and Meanings of Defective Products and Strict Liability*, "[i]t should be clear that the manufacturer is not an insurer for all injuries caused by his products." 32 Tenn.L.Rev. 363 (1965) [Citations omitted.]

The core concern in strict tort liability law is safety. *See* Comments a through i to Section 402A. Therefore, the primary inquiry in a design defect case is whether the product—because of the way it is designed—creates an unreasonable risk of danger to the consumer or user when put to normal use. [Citation omitted.] To establish liability in a design defect case, the plaintiff bears the burden of demonstrating that the product, as designed, is unreasonably dangerous and therefore "defective," and that the demonstrated defect caused his injuries. Though obviously abbreviated, the foregoing explanation describes the heart and soul of a strict tort liability design defect case—unreasonable danger and causation.

In design defect cases, however, the job of defining and giving content to the legal meaning of "defective" has taxed the creative energies of courts and commentators alike and has led Professor Wade to declare that "the determination of when a product is actionable because of the nature of its design appears to be the most agitated controversial question before the courts in the field of products liability." Wade, *On Product Design Defects and Their Actionability,* 33 Vand.L.Rev. 551, 576 (1980). Under the *Restatement,* a product, as designed, is actionable if the product is dangerous to an extent beyond that which would be contemplated by the ordinary consumer, who either purchases it or uses it, with the ordinary knowledge common to the community as to its characteristics. [Footnote omitted.]

* * *

Under Missouri's rule of strict tort liability, a product's design is deemed defective, for purposes of imposing liability, when it is shown by a preponderance of evidence that the design renders the product unreasonably dangerous. [Footnote and citations omitted.] This Court most recently articulated a formulation of liability for a design defect case in *Elmore v. Owens-Illinois, Inc.,* 673 S.W.2d at 434. In *Elmore,* an asbestosis case brought under a theory of defective design, Judge Higgins, author of the principal opinion, pointed out that the plaintiffs had satisfied their burden of proving the design of the product defective "when they proved it was unreasonably dangerous as designed." [Footnote omitted.] *Id.* at 438.

Though Missouri has adopted the rule of strict tort liability as set forth in the *Restatement,* we have not yet formally incorporated, in any meaningful way, the *Restatement's* consumer expectation test into the lexicon of our products liability law. [Footnote omitted.] Nor have we yet decided to travel or require plaintiffs to travel the path of risks and utilities. And in this connection, we note that none of the parties in the present case, at ei-

ther the trial level or on appeal, has raised as an issue the applicable standard by which to determine when a product, as designed, is defective and therefore actionable. Moreover, the appellate posture of this case strongly militates against considering this issue sua sponte. Because of these two decisional constraints, we choose not to decide this question and instead, limit our discussion to edificatory ends.

Under our model of strict tort liability the concept of unreasonable danger, which is determinative of whether a product is defective in a design case, is presented to the jury as an ultimate issue without further definition. [Citation and footnote omitted.] Accordingly, our approved jury instruction which governs in a design defect case, MAI 25.04 (3rd) does not contain as one of its component elements a definitional paragraph which gives independent content to the concept of unreasonable danger.

Notwithstanding the minority character of this approach, Professor Leon Green, in his 1976 Texas Law Review article, *Strict Liability Under Sections 402A and 402B: A Decade of Litigation,* explains why an approach that avoids the use of an external standard by which to determine unreasonable danger—i.e., defectiveness—is preferable to one which does use an external standard. He points out first that juries do not have "a fictitious standard by which to determine assault, battery, false imprisonment, nuisance, entry upon land, or the taking of a chattel" and then he suggests that "[n]or do juries need an external standard by which to determine the danger of a product in an unreasonably dangerous defective condition." Green, *Strict Liability Under Sections 402A and 402B: A Decade of Litigation,* 54 Tex.L.Rev. 1185, 1206 (1976). He concludes his discussion with the judgment that "the ritual indulged in by the giving of abstract, abstruse standards, impossible to comply with, only perpetuates the mystical trial by ordeal and *may conceal a hook in a transcendental lure that will snag an appellate court." Id.* at 1206 [emphasis added].

As we noted previously, at the trial of a design defect case, the concept of unreasonable danger is treated as an ultimate issue. The jury gives this concept content by applying their collective intelligence and experience to the broad evidentiary spectrum of facts and circumstances presented by the parties. In the present case, Beech's primary argument is that plaintiffs failed, as a matter of law, to make a submissible case concerning their burden of proving that the elevator trim tab actuators were unreasonably dangerous when put to a reasonably anticipated use. To determine whether plaintiffs did make a submissible case, we must examine the sufficiency of the evidence. [Citation omitted.] In so doing, plaintiffs are entitled to the most favorable view of all of the evidence and the benefit of all favorable inferences to be fairly drawn from the evidence. [Citation omitted.]

* * *

As we have already determined, there was sufficient evidence to support a finding that Executive's "abnormal use" of the actuators could have been reasonably anticipated. Beech's real contention, however, is that the actions of Executive's mechanics, as a matter of law, constitute a superseding cause sufficient to relieve Beech of any liability. This argument, however, is one that we cannot in good conscience accept. Plaintiffs' entire stratagem was directed toward proving that the incorrect installation of physically symmetrical but functionally asymmetrical parts was a natural and expected consequence of manufacturing actuators without "murphy proof" design features. We find the evidence legally sufficient to support a finding that Beech's design was a proximate cause of George Nesselrode's death.

In summary, we think a jury composed of reasonable men and women could come to the conclusion that actuators lacking "murphy proof" design features, when put to normal use, do present an unreasonable risk of danger. There was ample evidence from which the jury could infer that the risk of incorrect installation is reduced or eliminated when critical flight components contain "murphy proof" design features. They also could conclude that the way in which these actuators were designed was the efficient cause of the accident, notwithstanding Executive's alleged negligence.

In this connection, the jury was free to disbelieve defendant's evidence to the contrary. The jury was provided a number of feasible alternative "murphy proof" designs. They were free to infer that an alternative design would have been safer and would have prevented this accident. It is the function and duty of the jury to reason upon the evidence presented and to draw inferences and reach conclusions. We think the quantum of evidence which plaintiffs presented allowed the jury to do just that.

* * *

Case Notes: Alternative Tests for Defective Design

1. The Missouri Supreme Court in *Nesselrode* advocated an open-ended approach to the finder of fact's determination of defective design. The court left the jury unconstrained by definitions of any terms or phrases, including "unreasonably dangerous," which allowed the jury to make its own assessment of the aircraft product within the parameters of the jury instruction as submitted by the court.

2. In *Nesselrode*, the court recognized the roots of plaintiffs' strict liability action in negligence but precisely distinguished the applications of typical negligence-type elements. On this issue, the court noted the following:

   Although the negligence-rooted concept of fault has little if any theoretical utility in

   the law of strict tort liability, proximate causation and foreseeability are concepts that factor into the calculus of liability in a strict tort liability action. Foreseeability, however, is a determinant of use; it is not a determinant of harm. *Nesselrode,* 707 S.W.2d at 375, n4.

3. The Missouri Supreme Court adopted a minority approach in *Nesselrode* when it opted to leave undefined the terms and phrases of the jury instruction. The Court knew at the time that other states had opted to define these terms:

   Most states, whether they apply a unitary definitional test or a multifactor analysis, define to some extent the appropriate standard to the jury. [Texas and Kansas citations omitted.] The subject of how the jury should be instructed and what is the proper role for the jury has been given attention by a number of commentators and courts. *See* Owens and Montgomery, *Reflections on the Theory and Administration of Strict Tort Liability for Defective Products,* 27 S.C.L.R. 803, 830-45 (1976); Wade, *On the Nature of Strict Tort Liability for Products,* 44 Miss.L.J. 825, 838-41 (1973); *see also, Phillips v. Kimwood Machine Co.,* 269 Or. 485, 525 P.2d 1033, 1039-40 (1974). *Id.* at 378, n11.

4. Other tests that focus on the product but consider the conduct of the manufacturer.

   A. *The reasonably prudent manufacturer test.* As its name implies, this test requires consideration of the manufacturer's acts in making the product and placing it in the stream of commerce. Its application borders dangerously close to a negligence analysis because the finder of fact must determine the baseline standard for the conduct of a reasonable manufacturer and whether the conduct of the defendant manufacturer deviated from that standard. In essence, the jury must decide what a reasonable manufacturer would have done under the same or similar circumstances. Indeed, many states have adopted jury instructions in strict liability actions that require the finder of fact to determine whether the product was inherently dangerous when it left the manufacturer, which implies a consideration of knowledge on the part of the manufacturer when the product was still within its control. *See* Missouri Approved Instructions.

In *Phillips v. Kimwood Machine Co.,* 525 P.2d 1033, 1037 (Ore. 1974), the Oregon Supreme Court defined the prudent manufacturer test:

A dangerously defective article would be one which a reasonable person would not put into the stream of commerce *if he had knowledge of its harmful character.* The test, therefore, is whether the seller would be negligent if he sold the article *knowing of the risk involved.* [Emphasis in original].

Professors Wade and Keeton developed a list of seven factors to be considered when applying the prudent manufacturer test. These factors are as follows:

(1) the usefulness of the product to the public as a whole;

(2) the safety aspects of the product and its likelihood that it will cause an injury;

(3) the availability of a substitute product that meets the same need and not be unsafe;

(4) the manufacturer's ability to eliminate the unsafe character of the product without impairing its usefulness or making it too expensive;

(5) the consumer's ability to avoid danger by exercising due care;

(6) the consumer's awareness of inherent dangers in the product and their avoidability—the general public's knowledge of the obvious condition of the product; and

(7) the manufacturer's feasibility of spreading the loss from injury by setting the price of the product or by carrying liability insurance. (Wade, *On the Nature of Strict Tort Liability for Products,* 44 Miss. L. J. 825, 837-38 (1974)).

B. *The court-as-policymaker approach.* This approach is more extreme because it requires that the court assert itself into the factual question (traditionally a role for the jury) and justify its ultimate decision as grounded in social policy (again, not a job for the court) to determine the fate of the parties. If the court finds that the utility of the product does not outweigh its danger, it shifts the plaintiff's loss to the manufacturer but for the principle reason that the manufacturer is better positioned to bear the loss.

In *Azarello v. Black Brothers Co.,* 391 A.2d 1020, 1025 (Pa. 1978), the Pennsylvania Supreme Court defined the phrase "unreasonably dangerous" of comment I to § 402A of the *Restatement (Second)* to be a "label to be used where it is determined that the risk of loss should be placed upon the supplier." The court clearly believed that neither the consumer expectations nor the risk-utility tests were the province of the finder of fact because the court advocated this role for itself as

> "a judicial function to decide whether, under plaintiff's averment of the facts, recovery would be justified; only after this judicial determination is made is the case submitted to the jury to determine whether the facts of the case support the averments of the complaint" (*Azarello*, 391 A.2d at 1026).

Not only does this approach derail the faith and trust that the judicial system places in the juries themselves to determine the standards by which products are found to be defective as a matter of *fact*, this approach makes the manufacturer a guarantor of the product's safety. *Id.*, at 1027. That result is inconsistent with the principle purpose of strict liability law in defective product cases, which is to make manufacturers liable for their products that are in a defective condition unreasonably dangerous to their users.

See also Conk, *Is There a Design Defect in the* Restatement (Third) of Torts: Product Liability?, 109 Yale L.J. 1087-1133 (March 2000).

C. *The Model Uniform Product Liability Act Approach (UPLA).* The UPLA was published by the U.S. Department of Commerce in 1979 for voluntary use and adoption by the states. It provides that a manufacturer is liable for a defective product if the injured plaintiff proves that the product was the proximate cause of his injury. The product is defectively designed only if it is determined to be unreasonably dangerous. Under the UPLA, the finder of fact is specifically instructed to balance "(1) the likelihood that the product would cause the claimant's harm or similar harms, and the seriousness of those harms; against (2) the manufacturer's burden of designing a product that would have prevented those harms, and the adverse effect that alternative design would have on the use-

fulness of the product" UPLA, Analysis § 104(B), 44 Fed. Reg. at 62,723.

The jury may consider several items to determine the requisite "unreasonably dangerous" nature of the allegedly defectively designed product. These items include: (1) warnings and instructions; (2) practical feasibility of a product to have prevented plaintiff's injury while serving the user's expectations of the product; (3) the effect of any proposed alternative design on the usefulness of the product; (4) the costs of producing, distributing, selling, using, and maintaining the product; and (5) new risks if the product had been manufactured as alternatively designed. *Id.*, at 62,721.

Although the UPLA's approach adds a degree of predictability to a strict-liability analysis for allegedly defectively designed products, its standards unfortunately adopt a fault analysis that considers the conduct of the manufacturer and leaves a roving commission to the finder of fact to determine the ordinary consumer's expectations. For example, many consumers may not know how safe a product may be made. These standards leave open undefined terms to be decided by the finder of fact, which injects a subjective criteria into the analysis. However, under general application of objective criteria, most juries are likely to require that a product live up to the manufacturer's representations and that the product be free from manufacturing defects.

See also Schwartz, *The Uniform Product Liability Act—A Brief Overview*, 33 Vand.L.Rev. 579 (1980).

5. Because the *Restatement (Third)* necessarily endorses the risk-utility test and requires plaintiff to prove the existence of a reasonable alternative design, the *Restatement (Third)* does not discuss or recommend the use of these minority approaches.

6. The verdict instructor submitted to the jury at *Nesselrode* trial was in substantially the same form as the following:

> Your verdict must be for plaintiff if you believe:
>
> First, defendant sold the product in the course of defendant's business, and

Second, the product was then in a defective condition unreasonably dangerous when put to a reasonably anticipated use, and

Third, the product was used in a manner reasonably anticipated, and

Fourth, plaintiff was damaged as a direct result of such defective condition as existed when the product was sold. (M.A.I. 25.04.)

7. How would the jury have been aided if the phrase "unreasonably dangerous" had been defined by the jury instructions? What latitude was the jury given because the court did not define the phrase for it? What precedent is set by allowing the jury its own reign to determine what constitutes an unreasonably dangerous product?

Defective Designs and Inadequate Warnings   Generally, when a reasonable, alternative design provides a safer product, the manufacturer is required to adopt the alternative design rather than issue a warning that notices but does not remove the risk. But in some instances where a reasonable alternative design is not available, a manufacturer may properly provide adequate instructions and warnings that will render the product reasonably safe. Product sellers cannot substitute warnings for a safer design, but sellers may make efficient use of adequate warnings in the absence of a safer design. See Comment l, § 2 *Restatement (Third) of Torts: Products Liability (1997)*.

 CASE LAW

◆ **warnings and unavoidably unsafe products**

Brochu, et al. v. Ortho Pharmaceutical Corporation, 642 F.2d 652 (1st Cir. 1981).

Judith Brochu alleged that defendant Ortho Pharmaceutical Corporation ("Ortho") defectively designed oral contraceptive by placing too much estrogen in the pill and failed to warn physicians about the inherent dangers and higher risk of cerebral thrombosis from ingesting a pill with two additional milligrams of estrogen. At trial, the jury awarded Brochu and her husband $700,000. On appeal, Ortho argued that it had no duty to provide a warning about its product because its product was unavoidably unsafe. The First Circuit affirmed the jury award and held that Ortho had an obligation to provide an adequate warning about the defective design of the oral contraceptive.

BOWNES, Circuit Judge.

Design Defect

New Hampshire recognizes defective design as a basis for a strict liability claim. *Thibault v. Sears, Roebuck & Co.,* 118 N.H.802, 807, 395 A.2d 843, 846 (1978). In *Thibault* the New Hampshire Supreme Court stated that "[a] design defect occurs when the product is manufactured in conformity with the intended design but the design itself poses unreasonable dangers to consumers." *Id.* New Hampshire, however, has never considered the design defect theory in the context of an ethical drug case. In determining the result we believe the New Hampshire court would reach if presented with that issue, we consider the decisions of other state and federal courts and the general weight of the authority. [Citations omitted.]

In *Thibault* the New Hampshire Supreme Court outlined what the plaintiff in a defective design strict liability case must prove to prevail. Initially, the plaintiff must demonstrate "the existence of a 'defective condition unreasonably dangerous to the user.'" 118 N.H. at 807, 395

A.2d at 846; accord, Restatement (Second) of Torts § 402A(1). Courts are to consider the social utility and desirability of the product as well as its danger in determining if it is unreasonably dangerous. Thibault noted that "[s]ome products are so important that a manufacturer may avoid liability as a matter of law if he has given proper warnings." [Footnote omitted.] 118 N.H. at 807, 395, A.2d at 846.

In its brief, Ortho strenuously objects to the Brochus' theory that a drug . . . might be unreasonably dangerous, with or without warnings. It calls their design defect argument a "semantic ploy." We disagree. We are unwilling to say that under New Hampshire's balancing test no drug can ever be classified as unreasonably dangerous. We do not believe, as Ortho contends, that the New Hampshire Supreme Court would necessarily limit the application of Thibault to mass-produced items sold over the counter.

In Thibault the New Hampshire court listed several factors to consider in balancing product utility and danger. One consideration is whether the risk could have been lessened without significantly affecting effectiveness or cost. The court noted that "liability may attach if the manufacturer did not take available and reasonable steps to lessen or eliminate the danger of even a significantly useful and desirable product." Id. Under New Hampshire law, "when an unreasonable danger could have been eliminated without excessive cost or loss of product efficiency, liability may attach even though the danger was obvious or there was adequate warning." Id. 118 N.H. at 808, 395 A.2d at 847. We think that plaintiffs' first claim based on a design defect inherent in the high content of estrogen and the danger resulting from it states cause of action in strict liability under New Hampshire law. [Footnote omitted.] Ortho has limited its challenge on this claim to its legal basis. We, therefore, note only that there were evidentiary grounds to support a jury finding of liability on this claim. [Footnote omitted.]

Warning

Another consideration specified by Thibault is the presence or absence of warnings: when the risk is not apparent, "the user must be adequately and understandably warned of concealed dangers." Id. 118 N.H. at 808; 395 A.2d at 846. In cases involving ethical drugs, the manufacturer must warn the physician, not the patient. [Citations omitted.]

As noted, Thibault also pointed out that some products are so important that liability may be avoided as a matter of law if adequate warnings are given. Plaintiffs claim that Ortho's warnings were inadequate because, although the company knew that there was a significantly higher risk of cerebral thrombosis from ingesting Ortho-Novum 2 mg. than from ingesting lower-dosage oral contraceptives, it did not so inform physicians. We have previously held that "having embraced strict liability, the New Hampshire court would . . . [impose] upon a drug manufacturer an affirmative duty to warn the medical profession of . . . dangerous side effects." McCue v. Norwich Pharmacal Co., 453 F.2d 1033, 1035 (1st Cir. 1972).

Although not specifically cited in Thibault, the New Hampshire Supreme Court presumably based this duty to warn on Comment k to the Restatement (Second) of Torts, section 402A [.] [Footnote omitted.]

* * *

Basing a strict liability claim on both design defect and inadequate warning is neither illogical nor inconsistent. [Footnote omitted.] The example given in Comment k itself—the Pasteur rabies vaccine—suggests a balancing: certain death is weighted against the high degree of risk posed by the treatment itself. [Footnote omitted.] If the danger is unnecessary, the product, regardless of its utility, is defective. If, as Comment k explains, the danger is unavoidable and the utility is great, liability may be avoided with proper warnings. [Footnote omitted.]

The Fifth Circuit has utilized a similar analysis applying Texas law in a case in which the plaintiff's child contracted polio after receiving the Sabin oral polio vaccine. Reyes v. Wyeth Laboratories, 498 F.2d 1264 (5th Cir.), cert. denied, 419 U.S. 1096, 95 S.Ct. 687, 42 L.Ed.2d 688 (1974). [Footnote omitted.] The court first asked if the vaccine itself was so unsafe that marketing it at all was "unreasonably dangerous per se." Id. at 1273. Such a conclusion is warranted only "if the potential harmful effects of the product—both qualitative and quantitative—out-weigh the legitimate public interest in its availability." Id. at 1274. If the product is not unreasonably dangerous per se, the court then inquires if the product is "unreasonably dangerous as marketed." Id. According to the Reyes opinion, under section 402A and Comment k of the Restatement, "a seller who has reason to believe that danger may result from a particular use of his product" must provide an adequate warning. *Id.* at 1275. Failure to warn in such circumstances constitutes a defect in the product, making it unreasonably dangerous as marketed.

An adequate warning is one reasonable under the circumstances. [Citation omitted.] A warning may be inadequate in factual content, in expression of the facts, or in the method by which it is conveyed. [Citation omitted.]

The adequacy of the warning must be judged in the light of what Ortho knew at the time Mrs. Brochu was actually taking Ortho-Novum 2 mg. [Footnote omitted.] The key document in this determination is a study conducted by Inman, Vessey, Westerholm, and Engelund and published in the British Medical Journal in April 1970. Their research found a "positive correlation . . . between the dose of oestrogen [estrogen] and the risk of . . . cerebral thrombosis."

* * *

Ortho argues that its warnings were adequate because they were drafted by the Food and Drug Administration (FDA) as required uniform labeling for all oral contraceptives. It places a great deal of reliance [footnote omitted] on *Chambers v. G. D. Searle & Co.*, 567 F.2d 269 (4th Cir. 1977) (per curiam), which affirmed a directed verdict for Searle on the opinion of the district court. The plaintiff in *Chambers* sustained her injury in July 1970, but none of her experts appears to have mentioned the April 1970 study that looms so large in this case. Moreover, the district court specifically stated "that approval by the FDA of the language involved is not necessarily conclusive on the question of the adequacy of the warnings." *Chambers v. G. D. Searle & Co.*, 441 F.Supp. 377, 383 (D. Md. 1975)[.] [Citations omitted.] The district court in *Chambers* concluded that the warnings in the package insert approved by the FDA in 1968 were sufficient only after deciding that Searle had no information indicating greater dangers or risks other than that available to the FDA drafting group in 1968. [Citation omitted.]

The absence of any reference to the 1970 British study, which, unlike the four studies actually referred to in the package insert, would have provided numerical data to the physician on the dose-effect relationship between thromboembolic disease and oral contraceptives, was ground for a jury finding that the warnings were factually inadequate. To this is to be added the fact that the inserts for each of Ortho's oral contraceptives

were identical, despite this evidence that higher-estrogen-dose pills might present greater risks to users. [Footnote omitted.] From this, the jury might have concluded that the warnings for the 2 mg. pills were inadequate. The jury might also have considered on the question of warning the fact that the salesperson who regularly called on Dr. Campbell did not orally inform him that the 2 mg. drug appeared to present a higher risk of thromboembolism.

In view of the expert testimony that the April 1970 study did establish the existence of a positive correlation between the dose of estrogen and the risk of cerebral thrombosis, and the admitted fact that the labeling did not refer to this study, Ortho's claim that the Brochus did not provide expert testimony on the inadequacy of the label is untenable.

Causation

A plaintiff in a defective design case must prove that the unreasonably dangerous condition existed when the product was purchased and that this condition caused the injury. The plaintiff must also prove that the manufacturer could reasonably foresee the manner in which the product would be used. [Citation omitted.] Because the absence of proper warnings itself renders a product unreasonably dangerous, [citations omitted] the jury had a basis for finding that the contraceptive was unreasonably dangerous when sold to Mrs. Brochu. There can be no question that Mrs. Brochu was using Ortho's product in a reasonably foreseeable manner.

We next consider whether the failure to warn adequately was a proximate cause of Mrs. Brochu's use of this drug. [Citation omitted.] At trial, the Brochus presented . . . testimony from Mrs. Brochu's prescribing physician, Dr. Campbell[.]

On the basis of this testimony the jury could have concluded that, if Ortho's warnings had been adequate, Dr. Campbell would have switched Mrs. Brochu to a lower-dose oral contraceptive.

At trial and in its brief Ortho stressed that physicians are trained to prescribe the lowest effective doses. It seems to argue that it had a right to rely on this training to ensure that Ortho-Novum 2 mg. would be prescribed only when it was the lowest effective dose. In effect, Ortho is attempting to use the actions of the physician, the "learned intermediary," as an intervening cause. We stated in McCue that a physician's carelessness, even if it takes an unanticipated form, should not relieve a drug manufacturer of liability if the manufacturer's failure to warn adequately may have contributed to that carelessness. *McCue v. Norwich Pharmacal Co.,* 453 F.2d at 1035[.] [Citations omitted.]

Finally the Brochus had to prove that this oral contraceptive was the cause-in-fact of Mrs. Brochu's stroke. [Citation omitted.] At trial, Ortho's counsel skillfully attempted to establish that no study had demonstrated a causal connection between the use of oral contraceptives and an increased risk of stroke. As it did in Chapman, Ortho argues that liability cannot be based on failure to state what has not been proven to be true. *Ortho Pharmaceutical Corp. v. Chapman,* 388 N.E.2d at 554. We agree with the Chapman court that the question of such a causal relationship was properly for the jury to determine. *Id.*

Three of the Brochus' medical experts, Dr. Merwyn Bagan, a Board-certified neurosurgeon, Dr. John H. Altshuler, Board-certified in anatomic and clinical pathology and immunohematology, and Dr. Wendel, testified that the most likely cause of Mrs. Brochu's thrombosis was her ingestion of oral contraceptives. Ortho presented the testimony of Dr. Ebehard F. Mammen, a professor of physiology and pathology, and Dr. Taylor. Dr. Mammen testified that he could not say with reasonable medical certainty that the Ortho-Novum 2 mg. caused Mrs. Brochu's stroke. He further stated that he could not say "with absolute certainty, [that] it was not the cause." Dr. Taylor testified that he did not think Mrs. Brochu's stroke was caused by taking oral contraceptives. The jury was clearly entitled to decide which of the experts it would believe. There was sufficient evidence to support a finding of causation-in-fact.

Case Notes: Design Defects and Inadequate Warnings

1. In what ways would a plaintiff's design defect claim be inconsistent with a plaintiff's claim that the product was provided with an inadequate warning? List the elements of each type of claim. What elements are similar in each cause of action?

2. In some instances, a product may be unavoidably unsafe but because it has a great utility to the public at large, liability for the dangers that product poses may be avoided with a proper warning. See § 402A *Restatement (Second) of Torts* comment k. (1965). In that instance, the product is not regarded as defectively designed or unreasonably dangerous. See also Twerski, *The Use and Abuse of Warnings in Products Liability—Design Defect Litigation Comes of Age,* 61 Cornell L. Rev. 495, 501 (1976) (if proper warning results in nonmarketability of product, true issue is the public's acceptability of the basic design); *cf. Brochu,* 643 F.2d at 657, n6.

3. Comment k to § 402A of the *Restatement (Second)* provided the parameters of unavoidably unsafe products:

   k. *Unavoidably unsafe products.* There are some products which, in the present state of human knowledge, are quite incapable of being made safe for their intended and ordinary use. These are especially common in the field of drugs. An outstanding example is the vaccine for the Pasteur treatment of rabies, which not uncommonly leads to very serious and damaging consequences when it is injected. Since the disease itself invariably leads to a dreadful death, both the marketing and the use of the vaccine are fully justified, notwithstanding the unavoidable high degree of risk which they involve. Such a product, properly prepared, and accompanied by proper directions and warning, is not defective, nor is it *unreasonably* dangerous. The same is true of many other drugs, vaccines, and the like, many of which for this very reason cannot legally be sold except to physicians, or under the prescription of a physician. It is also true in particular of many new or experimental drugs as to which, because of lack of time and opportunity for sufficient medical experience there can be no assurance of safety, or perhaps even of purity of ingredients, but such experience as there is justifies the marketing and use of the drug notwithstanding a medically recognizable risk. The seller of such products, again with the qualification that they are properly prepared and marketed, and proper warning is given, where the situation calls for it, is not to be held to strict liability for unfortunate consequences attending their use, merely because he has undertaken to supply the public with an apparently useful and desirable product, attended with a known but apparently reasonable risk.

4. When is a product unavoidably unsafe? When does the benefit of the product outweigh its risks and inherent dangerousness? What warning to the product's users is adequate so as to alleviate a manufacturer's obligation not to manufacture an unreasonably dangerous product?

5. The principle opinion relied upon by the court in *Brochu* was *Thibault v. Sears, Roebuck & Co.*, 395 A.2d 843, 846 (N.H. 1978). There, the court held that an unavoidably unsafe product, such as a pharmaceutical, was neither defective nor unreasonably dangerous under § 402A if the manufacturer gives an adequate warning of the risks.

6. The relationship between the design and the instructions or warnings provided with the product was also noted in Comment l of § 2 to the *Restatement (Third)* (1988). Comment l provided the following:

   l. Reasonable designs and instructions or warnings both play important roles in the production and distribution of reasonably safe products. In general, when a safer design can reasonably be implemented and risks can reasonably be designed out of a product, adoption of the safe design is required over a warning that leaves a significant residuum of such risks. For example, instructions and warnings may be ineffective because users of the product may not be adequately reached, may be likely to be inattentive, or may be insufficiently motivated to follow the instructions or heed the warnings. However, when an alternative design to avoid risks cannot reasonably be implemented, adequate instructions and warnings will normally be sufficient to render the product reasonably safe. . . . Warnings are not, however, a substitute for the provision of a reasonably safe design.

7. The relationship between a defectively designed product and an inadequate warning was also discussed in *Allison v. Merck*. There, the court noted the following:
   "*Properly* prepared and marketed" means to me simply that the injured consumer is unable to prove that the manufacturer was guilty of negligence. This should not be able to defeat a strict liability action [for an inadequate warning]. "*Proper* warning" is a subject apart and is akin to informed consent. If a consumer uses a dangerous product after having been fairly and *properly* warned of its dangers, we are really not talking about strict liability at all. *See* discussion of comment k and voluntary use of dangerous drugs below. (*Allison*, 878 P.2d at 954, n8 (Nev. 1994).)

Ultimately, Merck was unable to defend its actions in this strict liability lawsuit by embracing the concept enunciated in Comment k of the *Restatement (Second)* that its product was unavoidably unsafe. (*Id.*, 954.)

8. Forseeability. Comment m to § 2 of the *Restatement (Third)* provides the following:
   m. Reasonably foreseeable uses and risks in design and warning claims. Subsections (b) and (c) impose liability only when the product is put to uses that it is reasonable to expect a seller or distributor to foresee. Product sellers and distributors are not required to foresee and take precautions against every conceivable mode of use and abuse to which their products might be put. . . .

* * *

The issue of foreseeability of risks of harm is more complex in the case of products such as prescription drugs, medical devices, and toxic chemicals. Risks attendant to use and consumption by definition cannot specifically be warned against. Thus, in connection with a claim of inadequate design, instruction, or warning, plaintiff should bear the burden of establishing that the risk in question was known or should have been known to the relevant manufacturing community. (Comment m, § 2 *Restatement (Third) of Torts: Products Liability* (1997).)

9. The Court in *Brochu* found sufficient evidence to state a cause of action against Ortho for having defectively designed the oral contraceptive and for having failed to provide an adequate warning. *Brochu*, 642 F.2d at 655, 658. The court also found that plaintiffs had provided sufficient evidence of causation-in-fact between Mrs. Brochu's use of the drug and her resulting injuries. *Id.,* at 660. What is insufficient evidence? What is the result at trial if plaintiff presents insufficient evidence in support of one of its elements of its cause of action?

10. The Court also found a preponderance of evidence from which the jury may have had sufficient support for the jury instruction given by the judge at trial. *Id.,* at 661-62. Although admittedly unclear, the court's jury instruction in the case provided as follows:

> A manufacturer of a prescription drug is not an insurer with respect to its products, and the fact that a person sustained injury through the use of the product does not, of itself, mean that the manufacturer did anything wrong. . . .
>
> The question for you is: Was there adequate warning given which was reasonable under the circumstances of the case?
>
> . . . Now, under the doctrine of liability, one who sells any product in a defective condition, unreasonably dangerous to the user or consumer, is subject to liability for physical harm thereby caused to the ultimate user or consumer if the seller is engaged in the business of selling such a product, and it is expected to and does reach the user or consumer without substantial change in the condition in which it is sold. The rule just stated applies, although the seller has exercised all possible care in the preparation and sale of his product, and the user or

> consumer has not bought the product from or entered into any contractual relation with the seller. . . .
>
> Where, however, he has reason to anticipate that danger may result from a particular use as where a drug is sold which was safe only in limited doses, he, meaning the manufacturer, may be required to give adequate warning of the danger, and a product sold without such warning is in a defective condition.
>
> A drug manufacturer has imposed upon him an affirmative duty to warn the medical profession of the dangerous side effects that might result from the long-term use of its product.
>
> . . . To satisfy its duty to warn, the defendant drug manufacturer must have utilized a method of warning which was effective, in light of the gravity of the risk of danger of ingesting the product.
>
> . . . In determining whether the defendant sold an unreasonably dangerous product for the purposes of contraception, you should consider whether the risk of danger could have been reduced without significant impact on the product's effectiveness. (*Brochu,* 642 F.2d at 661-62.)

11. Why is this jury instruction unclear? Does it accurately reflect New Hampshire law regarding design defects and inadequate warnings? Does the instruction reflect the holding in *Thibault v. Sears, Roebuck & Co.,* 395 A.2d 843, 846 (N.H. 1978)? Should it? What statement of law was given in the jury instruction that was the subject of the *Brochu* case? Is it reasonably clear that the jury could make a finding of fact based on this instruction?

12. What is the result if the jury instruction is unclear and confusing? What is the remedy? Under what standard could the New Hampshire Supreme Court decide that this jury instruction was, in fact, unclear and confusing? Does that change the result in the case on appeal? At what point in the trial is the jury instruction given?

Defective Warnings

A product may be rendered defective because it fails to contain a warning or instruction about the proper use of the product. The failure to include such a warning may take several forms, including the blatant absence of the warning, the misplacement of the warning, or the inadequacy of the warning that was provided with the product. In any one of these instances, the product itself is deemed to be defective.

Product sellers are expected to provide guidelines, instructions, and warnings on labels with the product at the time of sale. In some instances, product sellers are expected to have made such warnings and instructions available to subsequent product users. Ordinarily, these required warnings and instructions provide information about the proper use of the product. It is here that the absence, misplacement, or inadequacy of these materials directly affect the unreasonably unsafe or the inherent dangerousness of the product itself.

The *Restatement (Third)* defines an inadequate warning in § 2(c) as:

A product: (c) is defective because of inadequate instructions or warnings when the foreseeable risks of harm posed by the product could have been reduced or avoided by the provision of reasonable instructions or warnings by the seller or other distributor, or a predecessor in the commercial chain of distribution, and the omission of the instructions or warnings renders the product not reasonably safe.

 CASE LAW

◆ **distinguishing causes of action for failure to warn—negligence v. strict liability**

Carlin v. Superior Court of
Sutter County,
920 P.2d 1347 (Cal. 1996).

Plaintiff prescription drug user Carlin brought product liability action against Defendant drug manufacturer The Upjohn Company ("Upjohn") alleging Upjohn's failure to warn about the dangerous propensities and side affects of Halcion. Carlin claimed that Upjohn was strictly liable for its failure to warn about the drug. The trial court sustained Upjohn's motion to dismiss Carlin's failure to warn theory based on the argument that California law did not permit a cause of action in strict liability for failure to warn. The Court of Appeals disagreed and ordered the trial court to vacate its order granting Upjohn's motion to dismiss. The California Supreme Court granted review of this issue.

MOSK, Acting Chief Justice.

* * *

We recognized that the knowledge or knowability requirement for failure to warn infuses some negligence concepts into strict liability cases. [Citation omitted.] Indeed, in the failure-to-warn context, strict liability is to some extent a hybrid of traditional strict liability and negligence doctrine. As we explained, however, "the claim that a particular component 'rings of' or 'sounds in' negligence has not precluded its acceptance in the context of strict liability." Indeed, "the strict liability doctrine has incorporated some well-settled rules from the law of negligence and has survived judicial challenges asserting that such incorporation violates the fundamental principles of the doctrine." (*Anderson v. Owens-Corning Fiberglas Corp.*, 810 P.2d 549, Cal. 1991.) Thus, although *Anderson*, following *Brown*, incorporated certain negligence concepts into the standard of strict liability for failure to warn, it did not thereby adopt a simple negligence test. [Footnote omitted.]

"[F]ailure to warn in strict liability differs markedly from failure to warn in the negligence context. Negligence law in a failure-to-warn case requires a plaintiff to prove that a manufacturer or distributor did not warn of a particular risk for reasons which fell below the acceptable standard of care, i.e., what a reasonably prudent manufacturer would have known and warned about. Strict liability is not concerned with the standard of due care or the reasonableness of a manufacturer's conduct. The rules of strict liability require a plaintiff to prove only that the defendant did not adequately warn of a particular risk that was known or knowable in light of the generally recognized and prevailing best scientific and medical knowledge available at the time of manufacture and distribution. Thus, in strict liability, as opposed to negligence, the reasonableness of the defendant's failure to warn is immaterial.

Stated another way, a reasonably prudent manufacturer might reasonably decide that the risk of harm was such as not to require a warning as, for example, if the manufacturer's own testing showed a result contrary to that of others in the scientific community. Such a manufacturer might escape liability under negligence principles. In contrast, under strict liability principles the manufacturer has no such leeway; the manufacturer is liable if it failed to give warning of dangers that were known to the scientific community at the time it manufactured or distributed the product." (Anderson, 53 Cal.3d at pp. 1002-1003, 281 Cal.Rptr. 528, 810 P.2d 549, fn. omitted.) Similarly, a manufacturer could not escape liability under strict liability principles merely because its failure to warn of a known or reasonably scientifically knowable risk conformed to an industry-wide practice of failing to provide warnings that constituted the standard of reasonable care. [Footnote omitted.]

We explained the policy behind our strict liability standard for failure to warn as follows: " 'When, in a particular case, the risk qualitatively (e.g., of death or major disability) as well as quantitatively, on balance with the end sought to be achieved, is such as to call for a true choice judgment, *medical or personal*, the warning must be given. . . .' Thus, the fact that a manufacturer acted as a reasonably prudent manufacturer in deciding not to warn, while perhaps absolving the manufacturer of liability under the negligence theory, will not preclude liability under strict liability principles if the trier of fact concludes that, based on the information scientifically available to the manufacturer, the manufacturer's failure to warn rendered the product unsafe to its users." (*Anderson, supra*, 53 Cal.3d at p. 103, 281 Cal.Rptr. 528, 810 P.2d 549, italics added.) [Citation omitted.]

Upjohn and amici curiae argue that applying *Anderson* will place manufacturers of prescription drugs in an untenable position because they must comply with regulations set by the Food and Drug Administration (hereafter FDA), which may preclude them from labeling drugs with warnings of certain side effects. They also contend that *Anderson* would result in overlabeling of pharmaceuticals. Neither claim withstands scrutiny.

We are unpersuaded by Upjohn's argument that a strict liability standard for failure to warn about known or reasonably scientifically knowable risks from prescription drugs is inconsistent with federal regulatory policy. Upjohn concedes that FDA regulations do not expressly preempt common law tort remedies for failure to warn or occupy the entire field of regulation. As numerous courts have concluded, Congress evinced no intention of preempting state tort liability for injuries from prescription drugs. [Citations omitted.]

We disagree with Carlin's argument, however, that FDA regulations are essentially irrelevant in a common law action for failure to warn. We reiterate that strict liability for failure to warn *is not absolute liability*. Under *Anderson*, drug manufacturers are not strictly liable for a risk that was not known or reasonably scientifically knowable. In this context, it is significant that the FDA *precludes* drug manufacturers from warning about every conceivable adverse reaction; they may warn only if there exists significant medical evidence of a possible health hazard. They are also specifically precluded from warning of adverse reactions when differences of opinion exist within the medical community with regard to potential adverse reactions. [Citations omitted.] At the same time, however, they are required to "describe serious adverse reactions and potential safety hazards, limitations in use imposed by them, and steps that should be taken if they occur. The labeling shall be revised to include a warning as soon as there is reasonable evidence of an association of a serious hazard with a drug; a causal relationship need not have been proved." (*Id*, § 201.57(e).)

In appropriate cases, FDA action or inaction, though not dispositive, may be admissible under *Anderson* to show whether a risk was known or reasonably scientifically knowable. [Citations omitted.] Similarly, a drug manufacturer could present evidence to show that there was no "reasonably scientifically knowable risk" because, at the time of distribution, the cause of the alleged adverse effect was too speculative to have been reasonably attributable to the drug by a scientist conducting state-of-the-art research. Thus, when a plaintiff's claim is based on an allegation that a particular risk was "reasonably scientifically knowable," an inquiry may arise as to what a reasonable scientist operating in good faith should have known under the circumstances of the evidence. As we emphasized in *Anderson*, we do not altogether reject strict liability in the failure-to-warn context—for drugs or any other products—simply because some considerations of reasonableness sounding in negligence may be required. [Citation and footnote omitted.]

Moreover, in the case of an alleged "known" risk, if state-of-the-art scientific data concerning the alleged risk was fully disclosed to the FDA and it determined, after review, that the pharmaceutical manufacturer was *not permitted to warn*—e.g., because the data was inconclusive or the risk was too speculative to justify a warning—the manufacturer could present such evidence to show that strict liability cannot apply; the FDA's conclusion that there was, in effect, no "known risk" is controlling. [Citation omitted.]

We are also unpersuaded by Upjohn's assertion that applying strict liability to claims of injury for failure to warn will inevitably result in manufacturers inundating consumers with warnings of even speculative risks from prescription drugs. In *Finn v. G.D. Searle & Co.* (1984) 35 Cal.3d 691, 701, 200 Cal.Rptr. 870, 677 P.2d 1147, we addressed the potential problems of overlabeling: "[E]xperience suggest[s] that if every report of a possible risk, no matter how speculative, conjectural, or tentative, imposed an affirmative duty to give some warning, a manufacturer would be required to inundate physicians indiscriminately with notice of any and every hint of danger, thereby inevitably diluting the force of any specific warning given." (See *Anderson, supra*, 53 Cal.3d at p. 1002, 281 Cal.Rptr. 528, 810 P.2d 549, citing *Finn.*) The application of the failure-to-warn theory to pharmaceuticals requires determinations whether available evidence established a causal link between an alleged side effect and a prescription drug, whether any warning should have been given, and, if so, whether the warning was adequate. These are issues of fact involving, inter alia, questions concerning the state of the art, i.e., what was known or reasonably knowable by the application of scientific and medical knowledge available at the time of manufacture and distribution of the prescription drug. They also necessarily involve questions concerning whether the risk, in light of accepted scientific norms,

was more than merely speculative or conjectural, or so remote and insignificant as to be negligible. [Footnote omitted.]

Moreover, in the case of prescription drugs, the duty to warn runs *to the physician,* not to the patient. (See, e.g., *Brown, supra,* 44 Cal.3d at pp. 1061-1062, 245 Cal.Rptr. 412, 751 P.2d 470; *Stevens v. Parke, Davis & Co.* (1973) 9 Cal.3d 51, 65, 107 Cal.Rptr. 45, 507 P.2d 653 ["In the case of medical prescriptions, 'if adequate warning of potential dangers of a drug has been given to doctors, there is no duty by the drug manufacturer to insure that the warning reaches the doctor's patient for whom the drug is prescribed."]; but see *Davis v. Wyeth Laboratories, Inc., supra,* 399 F.2d at p. 131 [exception where prescription drug "was not dispensed as such," but administered in mass immunization program].) Thus, a pharmaceutical manufacturer may not be required to provide warning of a risk known to the medical community. (See *Plenger v. Alza Corp.* (1992) 11 Cal.App.4th 349, 362, 13 Cal.Rptr.2d 811 ["We are aware of no authority which requires a manufacturer to warn of a risk which is readily known and apparent to the consumer, in this case the physician."]; *Proctor v. Davis, supra,* 275 Ill.App.3d at pp. 605-606 [211 Ill.Dec. 831, 839, 656 N.E.2d 23, 31] [pharmaceutical manufacturer need not provide warning of risks known to the medical community].) [Footnote omitted.]

Nor does Upjohn offer any sound public policy rationale for departing from *Anderson* concerning the liability of manufacturers of prescription drugs for failure to warn of known or reasonably scientifically knowable risks. Thus, we are unpersuaded by the argument, purportedly derived from our reasoning in *Brown*, that manufacturers of prescription drugs should be exempt from the strict liability duty to warn because they might otherwise refrain from developing and marketing drugs, included "cutting-edge vaccines to combat human immunodeficiency virus (HIV)" and other diseases. Our rationale in *Brown*, which involved strict liability for *design defects*, is inapplicable: unlike strict liability for design defects, strict liability for failure to warn does not potentially subject drug manufacturers to liability for flaws in their products that they have not, and could not have, discovered. Drug manufacturers need only warn of risks that are *actually known or reasonably scientifically knowable*.

Upjohn offers no clear or sufficient basis for concluding that research and development will inevitably decrease as a result of imposing strict liability for failure to warn of *known or reasonably scientifically knowable* risks; indeed, requiring manufacturers to internalize the costs of failing to determine such risks may instead *increase* the level of research into safe and effective drugs. In any event, we see no reason to depart from our conclusion in *Anderson* that the manufacturer should bear the costs, in terms of preventable injury or death, of its own failure to provide adequate warnings of known or reasonably scientifically knowable risks. As we ob-

served: "Whatever may be reasonable from the point of view of the manufacturer, the user of the product must be given the option either to refrain from using the product at all or to use it in such a way as to minimize the degree of danger." (*Anderson, supra,* 53 Cal.3d at p. 1003, 281 Cal.Rptr. 528, 810 P.2d 549.) Although *Anderson* itself involved a nondrug, asbestos, our conclusion therein applies with equal force to prescription drugs. [Footnote omitted.]

Case Notes: Strict Liability Failure to Warn

1. The decision of the California Supreme Court in *Carlin* was the result of a long line of California cases that had considered the viability of a cause of action in strict liability for failure to warn. See *Canifax v. Hercules Powder Co.,* 237 Cal.App.2d 44, 46 Cal.Rptr. 552 (1965) (product may be defective under strict liability if it is unreasonably dangerous to place product in commerce without a suitable warning); *Cavers v. Cushman Motor Sales, Inc.,* 95 Cal.App.3d 338, 157 Cal.Rptr. 142 (1979) (product properly manufactured could be defective if absence of proper warning rendered product substantially dangerous to user); *Gonzales v. Carmenita Ford Truck Sales, Inc.,* 192 Cal.App.3d 1143, 238 Cal.Rptr. 18 (1987) (strict liability cause of action for failure to warn not limited to unavoidably dangerous or unsafe products); *Brown v. Superior Court,* 751 P.2d 470 (Cal. 1988) (manufacturer of prescription drugs is exempt from strict liability for injuries caused by scientifically unknowable dangerous propensities in product); *Anderson v. Owens-Corning Fiberglas Corp.,* 810 P.2d 549 (Cal. 1991) (defendant in strict liability case alleging failure to warn may present evidence that risk was scientifically knowable or unknowable at the time of manufacture or distribution of the product).

2. These courts, among others, have struggled with the separation of causes of action for failure to warn under negligence and strict liability theories. In *Cavers,* 95 Cal.App.3d at 347-348, the California Court of Appeals said the following:

> In assisting the jury's determination of whether the absence of a warning makes a product defective, the trial court should focus their attention on such relevant considerations as the normal expectations of the consumer as to how the product will perform, degrees of simplicity or complication in the operation or use of the product, the nature and magnitude of the danger to which the use is exposed, the likelihood of injury, and the feasibility and beneficial effect of including a warning.

3. Again, even in inadequate warning cases, the focus of the strict liability inquiry is the product itself. The court must determine whether the product is inherently or unreasonably dangerous in the absence of a warning. Thus, the inquiry is not the manufacturer's act or omission in providing or not providing a warning, but whether the product is made defective in the absence of a warning. One must not lose the focus of this inquiry, even if the inquiry includes certain concepts typically considered in negligence actions as one of many factors included in the strict liability analysis.

4. The cause of action in strict liability for inadequate warnings was contemplated by § 402A of the *Restatement (Second) of Torts* (1965) in Comment j.

Where warning is given, the seller may reasonably assume that it will be read and heeded; and a product bearing such a warning, which is safe for use if it is followed, is not in defective condition, nor is it unreasonably dangerous.

5. The strict liability action for inadequate warnings was furthered by § 2 *Restatement (Third)* (1988). It provided the following in Comment j:

   j. *Warnings: obvious and generally known risks.* In general a product seller is not subject to liability for failing to warn or instruct regarding risks and risk-avoidance measures that should be obvious to, or generally known by, foreseeable product users. When a risk is obvious or generally known, the prospective addressee of a warning will or should already know of its existence. Warning of an obvious or generally known risk in most instances will not provide an effective additional meas-ure of safety. Furthermore, warnings that deal with obvious or generally known risk may be ignored by users and consumers and may diminish the significance of warnings about non-obvious, not-generally-known risks. Thus, requiring warnings of obvious or generally-known risks could reduce the efficacy of warnings generally. When reasonable minds may differ as to whether the risk was obvious or generally known, the issue is to be decided by the trier of fact. The obviousness of risk may bear on the issue of design defect rather than failure to warn.

   An even more specific comment regarding inadequate warnings and adverse reactions to nonprescription drugs or cosmetics was provided in Comment k to § 2 *Restatement(Third)*.

   * * *

CASE PROBLEM

Strict-Liability Theories Regarding Industrial Equipment

Piggly Wiggly, LLC

Assume the facts described in Chapter Two, Negligence, for the Piggly Wiggly Squealer I. Assume further that pretrial discovery revealed that the design of the Piggly Wiggly Squealer I was a duplicate of a 1944 bacon press designed and manufactured by Piggly's corporate partner, MeatSlicer, Unlimited. However, MeatSlicer did not manufacture the Squealer I unit involved in Hoagge's accident; it was manufactured by Piggly.

1. Assume that you represent Sammy Hoagge. Draft a complaint on his behalf naming all potentially liable parties and identifying all viable liability theories. What strict liability theories are available to Hoagge? Which ones are not available? What facts support the essential elements of Hoagge's strict liability theories? How are these pleaded in the complaint?

2. Assume that the Squealer I did arrive at Lindy's with a warning properly attached to the metal guard. Assume further that Sammy Hoagge saw the warning when he first began operating the Squealer I on January 1, 1994, but disregarded the warning, and later did not use the guards when he was instructed by his supervisor, Lonnie Smith, to process more meat more quickly. How does this change Sammy Hoagge's potential liability claims against Piggly and others? What differences does it make to the facts pleaded in the complaint? What if the warning had been in place but Sammy Hoagge testifies that he never saw it? Based on these additional facts in this paragraph, draft a complaint on behalf of Sammy Hoagge.

3. Assume that you represent Lindy and that the law of the state of Columbia (where the lawsuits and the accident occurred) allows Lindy an indemnification against the manufacturer under the circumstances where Lindy has compensated its employee, Sammy Hoagge, for all personal injuries and damages associated with his accident, which occurred during the course and scope of Hoagge's employment. Draft a complaint on behalf of Lindy to claim indemnification from all proper parties. What theories are available to Lindy? What facts must be pleaded in Lindy's complaint in order to state a viable cause of action in strict liability against Piggly? Against MeatSlicer?

The Milair Air Scoop

Assume the same facts described in Chapter Two, Negligence, for the Milair Air Scoop.

1. Assume that you represent Milair. How would you evaluate potential liability for the company on all possible causes of action in strict liability? What report would you make to the company? Does Milair have liability exposure for defective manufacturing or defective design?

2. Assume that you continue to represent the Millers. Draft a complaint for the Millers alleging all possible causes of action in strict liability that exist under the facts as given. What facts are necessary to plead a cause of action for defective design? Can the Millers state a cause of action for defective manufacturing? Can the Millers also state an alternative cause of action in negligence?

3. Assume for this question only that an independent engineer retained by the National Board of Advocates for Safe Aviation (NBASA) also inspected the air crash and rendered an accident inspection report that concluded that "any installation of the M4880 or the M2213-5 Air Scoop would have been improper on the Rolls Royce engine because the specifications of these air scoops do not conform to Rolls Royce FAA-approved replacement specifications." Does this enhance the Millers' claims against Milair? Does this enhance the Millers' claims against National, Boeing, or Rolls Royce? What additional facts, if any, do you need to know?

4. Assume for this question only that all of the passenger wrongful death and personal injury suits have been completed. Assume also that the law of Columbia state (where the lawsuits have taken place) allows National, Boeing, and Rolls Royce to state a claim for indemnity against Milair, and that each has a claim for indemnity in the amount of $10,000,000. What causes of action are available for National, Boeing, or Rolls Royce against Milair? Draft a complaint for each entity that has a cause of action. What additional facts, if any, do you need? What strict-liability theories are available to National, Boeing, or Rolls Royce against Milair?

5. Assume that discovery has been complete and that you are preparing for trial to defend Milair against several passenger claims for wrongful death. What standard do you intend to endorse at court in your opening statement and through your expert engineer that the court should adopt to determine whether the Milair Air Scoop was defectively manufactured or defectively designed? Why should the court adopt the standard advocated by Milair? What authority can you identify in support of the standard adopted by Milair?

6. Assume that the warning was attached to each of the Rolls Royce engines on Flight 882. Assume further that the Milair Air Scoop was appropriately regarded as a safety device on each Rolls Royce engine. Does the availability of a warning change the Millers' proposed complaint? What additional causes of action are available to the Millers? To whom is the warning directed? What party(ies) are protected by the warning? How does the availability of the warning change the liability exposure of each party?

THEORIES OF DEFENSE

Chapter 5   Defenses and Responses

Defenses and Responses

INTRODUCTION

The defendant manufacturer's response to a plaintiff's lawsuit is built around affirmative defenses that require the defendant to prove that some aspect of plaintiff's conduct caused or contributed to cause plaintiff's injury. Many of a defendant's affirmative defenses are structured around the concept of plaintiff's own negligence, which can include improper conduct, misuse or alteration of the product, or assumption of the risk. Other defenses focus on the position of the product seller at the time the product was placed into the stream of commerce or the current status of industry technology when the product was placed into the stream of commerce. In each instance, the success or failure of the defense will depend on the particular facts and circumstances in each case.

Types of Defenses and Responses

This section is divided into defenses and responses. Defenses in a product liability case are typically comprised of affirmative defenses, which require that the defendant manufacturer or product seller carry the burden of pleading and proving such defenses against the plaintiff. These defenses are divided into common law and statutory defenses. The common law defenses have arisen through the development of a state's common law on negligence and, in some cases, product liability. These defenses are usually contributory negligence, comparative fault, misuse of the product, assumption of the risk, and application of the economic loss doctrine. Statutory defenses that specifically concern product liability have been codified in each state's statutes. These defenses are ordinarily seller in the stream of commerce, state-of-the-art, statutes of limitations, statutes of repose, and warranty disclaimers and limitations. Other defenses include the learned intermediary doctrine, government contractor defense, contribution and noncontractual indemnity, and alteration of the product. Responses to the product liability lawsuit—distinguished from defenses because they do not bar or reduce plaintiff's claim—include federal preemption and the compliance or noncompliance with safety statutes and regulations.

COMMON LAW DEFENSES

Contributory Negligence and Comparative Fault

Contributory negligence is the negligence of the plaintiff that contributed to her own injuries. Under common law negligence principles, plaintiff was held 100 percent responsible if she contributed any of her own negligence to her injuries and, for that reason, her negligence claim was completely barred. Section 463 *Restatement (Second) of Torts* defined contributory negligence as plaintiff's conduct that fell "below the standard to which [plaintiff] should conform for his own protection and which is a legally contributing cause co-operating with the negligence of the defendant in bringing about the plaintiff's harm."

Modern tort principles have relaxed contributory negligence as an absolute defense to plaintiff's claim. Now plaintiff's negligence, if any, is compared to that of the defendant's negligence and percentages of fault are assigned to each. This comparative principle is called comparative fault. In fact, many states have abolished contributory negligence in favor of comparative fault, particularly in the instance of product liability claims. Under either theory, the defendant must prove that plaintiff failed to exercise reasonable care in use of or knowledge about the product.

 CASE LAW

◆ **plaintiff's negligence as an affirmative defense**

McKinnie v. Lundell
Manufacturing Company,
825 F. Supp. 834
(W.D.Tenn. 1993).

Plaintiff brought product liability claims against defendant manufacturer for the wrongful death of her son who allegedly died as a result of defendant's allegedly defective and unreasonably dangerous shredder machine. Defendant Lundell raised affirmative defenses of plaintiff's own comparative fault and assumption of the risk.

TODD, Judge.

* * *

Plaintiff also moves to strike Defendant's second and fourth defenses—that Plaintiff's son assumed the risk of injury by the shredder and the son's death resulted from the negligence of a person or persons other than Defendant. Plaintiff does not assert Defendant's negligence as a basis for recovery. Rather, Plaintiff's sole theory of liability is the alleged defective and unreasonably dangerous condition of the slow-speed shredder manufactured

by Defendant. Defendant contends that, because it "raised the defenses of contributory negligence and assumption of risk simply to give the plaintiff fair notice that the issue of relevant [sic] fault would be raised at trial," the court should not strike the defense. (See Def.'s Response Pl.'s Mot.Strike at 2.) The court's inquiry is whether, under Tennessee law, the defenses of assumption of risk and comparative fault could, under any set of circumstances, succeed against a strict products liability claim.

Tennessee tort law has recently undergone substantial changes. In *McIntyre v. Balentine*, 833 S.W.2d 52 (Tenn.1992), the Tennessee Supreme Court abandoned the traditional contributory negligence doctrine and adopted comparative fault. [Footnote omitted.] Although the *McIntyre* court attempted to provide guidance to courts employing the new comparative fault standard, the court failed to resolve several issues concerning Tennessee tort law. [Citations omitted.] The Tennessee Supreme Court's adoption of comparative fault in negligence actions requires a determination of whether courts should extend comparative fault principles to strict liability cases. The Tennessee Supreme

Court has not addressed this issue. Therefore, this court must "make a considered 'educated guess' as to what decision the Supreme Court of Tennessee would reach." *Lee v. Crenshaw*, 562 F.2d 380, 381 (6th Cir.1977). [Footnote omitted.]

In cases decided prior to *McIntyre*, Tennessee courts had repeatedly held that the mere assertion of the plaintiff's negligence did not bar recovery in a strict products liability action brought in Tennessee. [Citations omitted.] The Tennessee Supreme Court recognized two justifications for this rule: (1) "allowing ordinary negligence to bar strict liability would defeat the purposes for which the theory of strict liability was created"; and (2) "Tennessee courts have never allowed contributory negligence as a defense . . . to conduct which is culpable regardless of the care exercised by the defendant." *Ellithorpe v. Ford Motor Co.*, 503 S.W.2d 516, 521 (Tenn. 1973). Comparative fault's abrogation of the harsh rule of contributory negligence, however, allows for a proportional allocation of liability while addressing the reasons for excluding a plaintiff's negligence as a defense to strict liability.

The Tennessee courts' concerns about the purposes of strict liability emphasize that, by adopting strict liability, the Tennessee Supreme Court intended such actions to differ from actions based on ordinary negligence. *Id.* [Citation omitted.] Proponents of the traditional rule against allowing a plaintiff's negligence to bar recovery under strict liability contend that allowing the plaintiff's simple negligence to defeat a strict liability claim would "reduce the action brought under [the strict liability] doctrine to one based on ordinary negligence." *Ellithorpe*, 503 S.W.2d at 521. [Citation omitted.] This argument emphasizes the basic societal policies underlying strict liability: (1) shifting the risk of loss caused by defective or unreasonably dangerous products to the parties most able to bear that loss—the manufacturers; and (2) encouraging manufacturers to take greater care in designing and manufacturing their products. *Ellithorpe*, 503 S.W.2d at 521. [Citation omitted.] Strict liability, however, is not intended to make the manufacturer the insurer of the product. [Citations omitted.]

Under a comparative fault system, a plaintiff's negligence does not preclude recovery, but merely reduces the manufacturer's liability. Although strict liability would operate similarly to ordinary negligence as to the reducing effect of a plaintiff's conduct, the two theories of liability would remain distinct in that strict liability actions would not require the plaintiff to prove that the manufacturer breached any duty of care. Unlike traditional contributory negligence, comparative fault would preserve the primary advantage that a plaintiff has in strict liability actions—imposition of liability against the manufacturer without any showing of the manufacturer's negligence. Extending comparative fault to strict liability actions would not defeat this policy underlying the strict liability doctrine. In addition, applying comparative fault to strict liability would not eliminate the deterrent effect of strict liability. Although the comparative fault system might yield smaller awards than traditional strict liability, manufacturers would remain liable for producing defective or unreasonably dangerous products. Incorporating comparative fault principles into products liability actions would also preserve strict liability's goal of shifting the risk of defective products to manufacturers without holding manufacturers liable for injuries resulting from plaintiffs' conduct.

The *McIntyre* court's definition of liability based on "fault" rather than "negligence" addresses the Tennessee Supreme Court's earlier concerns about interposing the plaintiff's negligence as a defense to "conduct which is culpable regardless of the care exercised by the defendant." See *Ellithorpe*, 503 S.W.2d at 521. Emphasizing "fault" rather than "negligence" appears to have been a conscious decision of the *McIntyre* court. Negligence implies a breach of a duty of care, while fault refers merely to an act imposing liability. [Citation omitted.] The comparative fault system's focus on the parties' relative "fault" avoids the "apples and oranges" argument, which contends that a plaintiff's negligence cannot be effectively compared to a manufacturer's conduct in producing a defective product because strict liability is not predicated on a breach of any duty of care. [Citations omitted.] Unlike a negligence-based system, which limits liability to the narrow basis of a party's breach of a duty of care, the fault-based system adopted by the *McIntyre* court allows the fact-finder to weigh the relative conduct of the parties. *See, e.g.*, Unif.Comparative Fault Act § 1(b) cmt., 12 U.L.A. 46 (West Supp.1993) ("Putting out a product that is dangerous to the user or the public . . . involves a measure of fault that can be weighed and compared, even though it is not characterized as negligence.").

The Tennessee Supreme Court has acknowledged that, in strict liability actions, the sufficiency of a defense based upon the plaintiff's conduct depends on the nature of that conduct, rather than the label applied to that conduct. [Citation omitted.] This focus on the substance of the defense rather than its form led the Tennessee Court of Appeals to conclude that,

> "when a plaintiff, with knowledge of the defect, uses the product in such a manner as to voluntarily and unreasonably encounter a known danger, that act may be plead [sic] as a defense to an action based on strict liability in tort. We do not deem it determinative of the availability of this defense whether it be called negligence, contributory negligence or assumption of risk. It is more a matter of the unreasonableness of permitting a plaintiff to deliberately put in motion a known danger and attempt to profit thereby."

Ellithorpe, 503 S.W.2d at 521. Thus, even under traditional strict liability standards, courts recognized that a plaintiff's conduct could preclude recovery. Given this background, this court must predict how the Tennessee Supreme Court would reconcile the policies underlying strict liability and the recent adoption of comparative fault.

Most courts that have addressed the issue have concluded that incorporating comparative fault principles in strict liability cases does not vitiate the policies underlying strict products liability. [Citations omitted.] In addition to judicial determinations that comparative fault principles should apply to strict liability, the Uniform Comparative Fault Act ("Uniform Act") defines "fault" as "acts or omissions that are in any measure negligent or reckless toward the person or property of the actor or others, or that subject a person to strict tort liability." Unif.Comparative Fault Act § 1(b), 12 U.L.A. 45 (West Supp.1993) (emphasis added). Several states have legislatively defined "fault," by adopting the Uniform Act's definition or a similarly broad definition, to include conduct that would render manufacturers liable under traditional strict liability doctrine. [Citations omitted.] As commentators have noted,

> [i]n the final analysis, most jurisdictions have decided that, regardless of semantics, it is fairer and more sensible to permit an allocation of a plaintiff's causal responsibility to reduce the liability of a products liability defendant. The policy objective of the strict lia-

bility doctrine for products is to compensate all those harmed by a defective and unreasonably dangerous product while using it in a reasonably foreseeable manner, but not to make the product supplier an insurer with respect to the product. The use of comparative fault as a defense is compatible with that policy. By transferring to consumers all the cost of the plaintiff's injury except that attributable to his own fault, the application of comparative faults helps to ensure that self-responsibility remains an appropriate factor in the apportionment process.

[Citations omitted.]

* * *

Given the Tennessee Supreme Court's focus on "fault" as the basis for liability and its reliance on the practices followed in other jurisdictions, this court concludes that the Tennessee Supreme Court would follow the numerous other jurisdictions that have extended comparative fault to strict liability. Accordingly, the court rules that, in light of the recent changes wrought by the Tennessee Supreme Court, the defense of comparative fault could succeed against the claim asserted—strict products liability—by means of reducing Defendant's liability by the proportion of fault attributable to Plaintiff or third parties. Therefore, the court DENIES Plaintiff's motion to strike Defendant's Fourth Defense.

Having concluded that comparative fault principles should be extended to strict liability cases, the court must now determine how the union of *McIntyre* and strict liability affects the defense of assumption of risk. Tennessee courts have traditionally recognized assumption of risk as a total bar to recovery in strict liability actions. [Citation omitted.] In order to establish the assumption of risk defense, a manufacturer must prove that the plaintiff voluntarily and unreasonably encountered a known danger. [Citation omitted.] To carry this burden, a manufacturer must demonstrate that the plaintiff: "(1) discover[ed] the defect, (2) fully [understood] the danger it present[ed] to her, then (3) disregard[ed] this known danger and voluntarily expose[d] herself to it." *Ellithorpe,* 503 S.W.2d at 522.

Plaintiff contends that, under comparative fault, assumption of risk no longer serves to preclude recovery in products liability actions, but merely reduces manufacturers' liability. (Mem.Supp.Pl.'s Mot.Strike at 2.) In support of her position that *McIntyre* removed assumption of risk as a total defense to products liability actions, Plaintiff relies upon *Perez v. McConkey,* No. 03A01-9209-CV-00331, 1993 WL 20147 (Tenn.Ct.App. Feb. 2, 1993), in which the Tennessee Court of Appeals for the Eastern Section held,

> first, express assumption of risk or consent, such as a contract between the parties, as qualified in *Olson v. Molzen,* 558 S.W.2d 429 [, 432] (Tenn.1977), remains an absolute bar to recovery by a plaintiff; second, primary assumption of risk, as when a plaintiff voluntarily assumes known risks inherent in an activity, retains its viability under comparative negligence as a complete bar to recovery; but third, under comparative fault, secondary implied assumption of risk, which is nothing more than an aspect of contributory negligence, may serve to reduce a plaintiff's damages, but not necessarily—depending on the degree of the plaintiff's negligence—preclude recovery. *Id.,* slip op. at 5. [Footnote omitted.]

The *Perez* courts' analysis of assumption of risk reflects the treatment of the doctrine by the Uniform Comparative Fault Act. As noted in the Comment to the Uniform Act, "[a]ssumption of risk is a term with a number of different meanings—only one of which is "fault" within the meaning of this Act." Unif.Comparative Fault Act § 1(b) cmt., 12 U.L.A. 46 (West Supp.1993); [Citations omitted.] The Uniform Act identifies the following "meanings" of assumption of risk: (1) valid and enforceable consent, such as a contractual waiver of liability; (2) a lack of violation of a duty by the defendant, such as a landowner's failure to warn a licensee of a patent danger on the premises; (3) a plaintiff's reasonable assumption of risk; [footnote omitted] and (4) a plaintiff's unreasonable assumption of risk, defined by the Uniform Act as "voluntary and with knowledge of the danger." [Footnote omitted.] Unif.Comparative Fault Act § 1(b) cmt., 12 U.L.A. 46 (West Supp.1993). The Uniform Act's definition of "fault" includes only the last meaning of assumption of risk. The first and second categories of assumption of risk are excluded by the Uniform Act because such cir-

cumstances—the plaintiff's consent or the defendant's lack of a duty—preclude any finding of liability of the defendant. The Uniform Act also excludes the third type of assumption of risk because a plaintiff's reasonable conduct cannot constitute "fault" of the plaintiff and should not affect recovery. Id. The fourth category, however, reflects the elements of the traditional assumption of risk defense, as defined by Tennessee courts, which requires a determination of the reasonableness of the plaintiff's conduct. [Citation omitted.] The reasonableness inquiry logically requires a comparison between the plaintiff's actions and the degree of risk presented by the defect or dangerous condition. [Citation omitted.] Such an inquiry readily comports with a comparative fault system under which each party bears the responsibility for any portion of the injuries resulting from his "fault"—whether fault arises from a manufacturer's production of a defective or unreasonably dangerous product or from a plaintiff's unreasonable conduct in voluntarily exposing himself to the risk presented by the product.

This court concludes that, rather than rely on obsolete labels, the Tennessee Supreme Court would adopt the "assumption of risk" structure embodied in the Uniform Act and employed by the Tennessee Court of Appeals in *Perez.* Under this standard, the extent to which a plaintiff's conduct affects his ability to recover against a manufacturer on the basis of strict liability is determined by focusing on the nature of the plaintiff's conduct. Whether a plaintiff's "assumption of the risk" would preclude or merely limit recovery depends on the specific conduct proven by the manufacturer. A plaintiff's conduct might still bar recovery in several situations, such as when the plaintiff assumes a risk by means of express contract, when the defendant has no duty to protect the plaintiff from a risk, or, under comparative fault, when the fault attributable to the plaintiff's conduct is equal to or greater than the fault attributable to the defendant. In other circumstances, the plaintiff's conduct might serve to merely reduce the plaintiff's recovery. Regardless of the effect of the plaintiff's conduct, this court predicts that assumption of risk will remain a valid defense in Tennessee, despite the supreme court's adoption of comparative fault. Accordingly, the court DENIES Plaintiff's motion to strike Defendant's Second Defense.

Case Notes: Contributory Negligence and Comparative Fault

1. Contributory negligence is "[t]he act or omission amounting to want of ordinary care on part of [the] complaining party, which, concurring with defendant's negligence, is [the] proximate cause of injury; [c]onduct by a plaintiff which is below the standard to which he is legally required to conform for his own protection and which is a contributing cause which cooperates with the negligence of the defendant in causing the plaintiff's harm." BLACK'S LAW DICTIONARY 931 (5th ed. 1979). Comparative negligence is "negligence measured in terms of percentage, and any damages allowed shall be diminished in proportion to [the] amount of negligence attributable to the person whose injury, damage, or death recovery is sought. Many states have replaced contributory negligence acts or doctrines with comparative negligence. Where negligence by both parties is concurrent and contributes to injury, recovery is not barred under such doctrine, but plaintiff's damages are diminished proportionately[]." *Id.*, at 255)[.]

2. The application of contributory negligence principles as a defense against a strict-liability action is ordinarily in the form of comparative fault. The Florida Supreme Court stated it this way in recognizing and applying the defense:

   Contributory negligence of the consumer or user by unreasonable use of a product after discovery of the defect and the danger is a valid defense. Prior to the adoption of the comparative negligence doctrine, a plaintiff's conduct as the sole proximate cause of his injuries would constitute a total defense. The defendant manufacturer may assert that the plaintiff was negligent in some specified manner other than failing to discover or guard against a defect, such as assuming the risk, or misusing a product, and that such negligence was a substantial proximate cause of the plaintiff's injuries or damages. The fact that plaintiff acts or fails to act as a reasonable prudent person, and such conduct proximately contributes to his injury, constitutes a valid defense. . . .

   We now have comparative negligence, so the defense of contributory negligence is available in determining the apportionment of the negligence by the manufacturer of the alleged defective product and the negligent use made thereof by the consumer. The ordinary rules of causation and the defenses applicable to negligence are available under our adoption of the Restatement rule. If this were not so, this Court would, in effect, abolish the adoption of comparative negligence. *West v. Caterpillar Tractor Company,* 336 So.2d 80 (Fla. 1976).

3. The concept of comparative fault and the specific defenses of misuse and assumption of the risk have a particular overlap in some jurisdictions. The federal district court in *Trust Corporation of Montana v. Piper Aircraft Corp.,* 506 F.Supp. 1093, 1096 (D.Mont. 1981) noted the following:

   The concepts of contributory negligence, assumption of risk, and misuse of the product overlap conceptually. [Citation omitted.] Common to all these concepts is the existence of some type of blameworthy conduct on the part of plaintiff. *Id.*

4. In negligence cases, the contributory negligence defense, as a complete bar to plaintiff's claim, is still available in some jurisdictions. Because strict liability claims do not involve the consideration of fault, most states have codified the comparative fault defense so that it is available to defendant manufacturers and product sellers in strict liability actions.

Apportionment of Fault

After a jury or court has found that plaintiff is comparatively negligent under the circumstances of the case, a percentage of fault must be assigned to plaintiff's negligence. If more than one defendant is responsible for the product defect, percentages of fault must also be assigned to each of these defendants. Some states have adopted *pure* comparative fault, which assigns responsibility to each liable party so that the cumulatively assigned fault is 100 percent. Other jurisdictions follow a *modified* comparative fault rule that assigns predetermined percentages of responsibility to each liable party. In some states, plaintiff's product claim is totally barred if plaintiff is found to be more than 50 percent at fault. Generally, a plaintiff's damages may be reduced if the plaintiff's own conduct contributed to his injury. The *Restatement (Third)* has adopted a statement regarding apportionment of fault, which is found at § 17.

 CASE LAW

◆ **apportionment of fault in a wrongful death case**

*Poliseno v. General Motors
Corporation,* 744 A.2d 679
(N.J. Super. Ct. 2000).

Wife brought wrongful death suit against defendant automobile manufacturer alleging that driver's side door was defectively manufactured. On appeal, court considered proper apportionment of fault.

KEEFE, J.A.D.

* * *

The trial judge, in her written opinion denying post-trial motions, held that while "death is indivisible as [to] result," it is capable of apportionment in terms of causation. We agree. As the judge noted, general tort law endorses the principle that "[d]amages for harm are to be apportioned among two or more causes where . . . there is a reasonable basis for determining the contribution of each cause to a single harm." Restatement (Second) of Torts § 433A(1)(b)(1964). Apportionment of damages based on causation has been favored in our case law. [Citations omitted.] The same principle applies to crashworthy cases. Section 16 of the Restatement (Third) of Torts: Products Liability, supra, provides:

    (b) If proof supports a determination of the harm that would have resulted from other causes in the absence of the product defect, the product seller's liability is limited to the increased harm attributable solely to the product defect.

    (c) If proof does not support a determination under Subsection (b) of the harm that would have resulted in the absence of the product defect, the product seller is liable for all of the plaintiff's harm attributable to the defect and other causes.

The Green court adopted these principles for use in New Jersey crashworthy cases, as do we. Green, supra, 310 N.J.Super. at 528, 709 A.2d 205.

There is no impediment to apportioning damages in this case as to causation simply because the alleged "other cause" results from Kuhlbars' conduct. While the Restatement Reporters observed that use of plaintiff's conduct in this setting is a "difficult issue" in terms of comparative fault, it is clear that a majority of jurisdictions allow plaintiff's conduct to be considered in the context of causation. Restatement (Third) of Torts: Products Liability, supra, § 16, Reporters' Note, comment f; see also Dafler, supra, 259 N.J.Super. at 28, 611 A.2d 136 (noting that apportionment rules apply "where one of the causes in question is the conduct of the plaintiff himself, whether it be negligent or innocent") (quoting Restatement (Second) of Torts § 433A comment (a) (1964)).

We recognize that in the typical product setting, New Jersey case law indicates that plaintiff's conduct is irrelevant in terms of comparative fault where it amounts to little more than negligent failure to observe the very danger that a properly manufactured or designed product would have rendered safe. [Citation and footnote omitted.] The rule is grounded in policy reasons that undergird strict products liability law. Those same policy reasons do not exist, however, where the plaintiff's conduct was a factor in the happening of the accident but not because of his or her use of the product in the traditional product liability context. In such cases, plaintiff's conduct is at least relevant on the issue of proximate cause. [Citation omitted.] This concept was recognized in *Green*. Judge Dreier wrote: "If the speed [of plaintiff's vehicle] was beyond the design limits [for making a crashworthy vehicle], speed would have been a proper factor to determine proximate cause and a later apportionment of liability." Green, supra, 310 N.J.Super. at 521, 709 A.2d 205. Thus, in this case, Kuhlbars' conduct in losing control of his vehicle and leaving the roadway, irrespective of fault, was relevant on the issue of the cause of the death producing injuries because, under the defense theory, it was that conduct which caused Kuhlbars' death producing head injuries. As will be discussed more fully later, the evidence was sufficient for a jury to conclude that the first and second collisions were concurrent causes of Kuhlbars' death.

Our discussion here of causation and apportionment should not be confused with the question of whether plaintiff's fault in causing the first collision is admissible to diminish plaintiff's recovery on comparative fault grounds where the first collision results in a defect-related enhanced injury solely caused by the second collision. The Restatement (Third) of Torts: Products Liability, supra, § 16 comment f states that such "fault is relevant in apportioning responsibility between or among the parties[.]" The Restatement's justification for the rule is that requiring a manufacturer to design a product "reasonably to prevent increased harm aims to protect persons in circumstances in which they are unable to protect themselves." *Id.*

* * *

Rather, in this case, defendant addressed driver conduct, irrespective of fault, that a jury could find to be a concurrent cause of a single injury. The focus was on driver conduct as it related to apportionment of damages based on causation, not comparative fault. Plaintiff confuses the two interrelated but distinct concepts in her appellate brief.

III.

Having decided that death is capable of apportionment as to cause, we now decide whether there was sufficient evidence to permit such apportionment. As can clearly be seen from the earlier recitation of the facts, plaintiff's expert attributed Kuhlbars' death solely to the intrusion of the tree into the vehicle because of the defective welds, while the defendant's expert opined that Kuhlbars' head struck the tree and received the death-producing blow before the welds on the door gave way. Neither expert suggested that trauma from the first collision combined with trauma from the second collision produced Kuhlbars' death. Thus, if the jury accepted either expert's opinion fully, there would be no basis for apportionment.

It appears from the verdict that the jury found some basis to apportion damages. Plaintiff argues that the jury's conclusion was against the weight of the evidence and that plaintiff is entitled to 100 percent of the verdict. Defendant, on the other hand, argues that there was a sufficient basis in the evidence to permit the jury to consider the question irrespective of each expert's opinion. We agree with defendant.

The jury was correctly instructed that it was free to accept that part of each expert's testimony that it found logical and credible, while rejecting such testimony that it found to be illogical or incredible. As our Supreme Court has noted:

"A jury has no duty to give controlling effect to any or all of the testimony provided by the parties' experts, even in the absence of evidence to the contrary. 'The jury may adopt so much of it as appears sound, reject all of it, or adopt all of it.' " [*Waterson v. General Motors Corp.*, 111 N.J. 238, 248, 544 A.2d 357 (1988)(*quoting Amaru v. Stratton*, 209 N.J.Super. 1, 20, 506 A.2d 1225 (App.Div.1985).]

When viewed from that perspective, it is clear that there was sufficient evidence in the record from which the jury could have accepted part of Mackay's testimony concerning the dynamics of the first collision and the movement of Kuhlbars' body within the vehicle. From that testimony, the jury could have found that Kuhlbars received substantial head trauma from contact with the tree before the defective welds in the door permitted incursion of the tree into the passenger compartment. The jury, however, did not have to accept Mackay's testimony that the trauma from the first collision was sufficient alone to have produced Kuhlbars' death. It could have found that the defective welds permitted the door beam to separate from the door frame and permitted incursion of the tree into the passenger compartment producing additional head trauma that would not have occurred had there been no manufacturing defect. That is, the jury could have found concurrent causation of the death-producing injuries.

Though the trial judge did not make the same analysis of the evidence as we have made, she found that there was sufficient evidence in the record for the jury to have made an apportionment as to the cause of Kuhlbars' death. We agree with the trial judge. Irrespective of what party had the burden of producing the evidence to enable apportionment, sufficient evidence was produced in this case to permit it. The defendant was not required to produce evidence amounting to scientific or mathematical precision as to how much each colli-

sion contributed in percentage points to Kuhlbars' ultimate death. As this court noted in Dafler, supra:

> "Where a factual basis can be found for some rough practical apportionment, which limits a defendant's liability to that part of the harm of which that defendant's conduct has been a cause in fact, it is likely that the apportionment will be made." [259 N.J.Super. at 28, 611 A.2d 136 (quoting Prosser and Keeton on Torts § 52 at 345 (5th ed. 1984)).]

While "outright guesswork" should not be permitted, when expert testimony provides "a rational explanation derived from a causal analysis, the testimony should, subject to the normal discretion of the trial court, be admitted for consideration by the trier of fact." Restatement (Third) of Torts: Products Liability, supra, § 16 comment c. "[I]t is preferable in the interest of fairness to permit some rough apportionment of damages, rather than to hold the defendant entirely liable for a harm that was inflicted by separate causes." Dafler, supra, 259 N.J.Super. at 31, 611 A.2d 136. Applying these principles to this case, we conclude that the evidence was sufficient to have the jury determine the issue. Therefore, the trial judge did not err in doing so.

Case Notes: Apportionment of Fault

1. Depending on the jurisdiction, some forms of plaintiff's comparative fault may be a total bar to plaintiff's claims. These forms may be plaintiff's misuse or alteration of the product or plaintiff's assumption of the risk. In those jurisdictions, plaintiff would be assigned 100 percent of the fault. Otherwise, the assigned percentage would be a fact question for the jury at trial. See Fischer, *Products Liability—Applicability of Comparative Negligence*, 43 Mo.L.Rev. 431, 450 (1978); Plant, *Comparative Negligence and Strict Tort Liability*, 40 La.L.Rev. 403 (1980); Phillips, *The Case for Judicial Adoption of Comparative Negligence in South Carolina*, 32 S.C.L.Rev. 295 (1980); 1 Comparative Negligence: Law and Practice § 9.30 (Matthew Bender 1993); Prosser and Keeton on the Law of Torts §§ 67, 60 (5th ed. 1984 & Supp. 1988); Unif. Comparative Fault Act § 1, 12 U.L.A. 45 (West Supp. 1993).

2. The *Restatement (Third)* noted that evidence of plaintiff's comparative fault is essential before fault can actually be assigned. See comment d, *Particular forms or categories of plaintiff's conduct*, § 17 of the *Restatement (Third)*.

Misuse and Assumption of the Risk

Misuse of a product occurs when the plaintiff used the product in a manner that was not foreseeable by the manufacturer, and that particular use was a proximate cause of plaintiff's own injuries. Assumption of the risk occurs when the plaintiff voluntarily and knowingly proceeds in using a product after having already encountered a known risk. In some jurisdictions, these defenses are a total bar to plaintiff's product liability claim. In other states, these defenses are merely types of plaintiff's own negligence, and percentages of fault are assigned that reduce plaintiff's overall recovery.

 CASE LAW

◆ **misuse and assumption of risk as affirmative defenses**

Campbell v. Robert Bosch Power Tool Corporation, 795 F. Supp. 1093 (M.D. Ala. 1992).

Plaintiff brought strict liability failure to warn claim against defendant manufacturer Robert Bosch of grinder disc that allegedly shattered and injured Campbell's eye when he was not wearing eye protection. Warning on grinding tool specifically stated: "use guards and goggles." Campbell sought summary judgment on Robert Bosch's two affirmative defenses of misuse and assumption of the risk, alleging that the defendant manufacturer had no facts upon which to base either defense.

MYRON H. THOMPSON, Chief Judge.

* * *

I. Background

Mr. Campbell was injured when the Bosch disc, which was affixed to the electrically powered sanding and grinding tool he was using, fractured into several pieces, one of which struck him in the eye. Although the disc bore a label instructing operators to "use guards and goggles," Campbell had removed the wheel guard with which the tool was equipped, and he was not wearing eye protection at the time of his injury. Campbell charges Bosch with failure to warn based upon the Alabama Extended Manufacturer's Liability Doctrine ("AEMLD"), claiming that the disc's label did not pro-

vide an adequate warning of the dangers of not using guards and goggles while operating the sanding and grinding tool.

* * *

III. The Campbells' Failure-To-Warn Claim

The Campbells' failure-to-warn claim is predicated on the AEMLD. In order to recover, a plaintiff must demonstrate that the defendant manufactured, designed, or sold a defective product which, because of its unreasonably unsafe condition, injured the plaintiff or damaged the plaintiff's property when the product was put to its intended or customary use without substantial alteration. [Citation omitted.] This doctrine, although similar to the concept of strict liability under § 402A, Restatement (Second) of Torts, rejects the no-fault aspect of § 402A. Under the doctrine, the manufacturer or seller is negligent, and thus at fault, as a matter of law in placing an unreasonably unsafe product on the market. [Citations omitted.]

A plaintiff may bring an AEMLD action by alleging that a product was either inadequately designed or defectively manufactured. Furthermore, as the Campbells assert in this case, a product may be inherently dangerous when used in its customary manner even though it is not "defective" in the usual sense of the word. In such cases, the AEMLD imposes on the manufacturer and seller a duty to warn of such dangers. As the Alabama Supreme Court has explained,

> "if a manufacturer or seller places goods on
> the market that are imminently dangerous

when put to their intended purpose and the defendant knows or should know that the goods can create danger when used in their customary manner, the defendant must exercise reasonable diligence to make such danger known to the person likely to be injured by the product." *King v. S.R. Smith, Inc.,* 578 So.2d 1285, 1287 (Ala.1991). [Citations omitted.]

Therefore, under the AEMLD, when the manufacturer or seller has a duty to warn adequately, a product sold without such warning is in a defective condition just as if the product were defectively designed or manufactured; this duty to warn applies, however, only to the extent the product is dangerous when put to its intended or customary use without substantial alteration.

In conclusion, to establish a failure-to-warn claim, a plaintiff must demonstrate at trial that: (1) the defendant was under a duty to warn the plaintiff regarding the product-in-question's danger when used in its intended or customary manner, (2) the warning the defendant provided breached that duty because it was inadequate, and (3) the breach proximately caused the plaintiff's injuries. Here, the Campbells must therefore show that: Bosch was under a duty to warn Mr. Campbell to use eye protection and a guard, the warning Bosch provided breached that duty because it was inadequate, and the breach proximately caused Mr. Campbell's injuries.

* * *

IV. Bosch's Affirmative Defenses

In defending this AEMLD action, Bosch not only denies that the elements necessary to establish a failure-to-warn claim are present, the company also asserts certain affirmative defenses for which, of course, it bears the burden of establishing at trial. [Citation omitted.] As stated, the Campbells contend that they are entitled to summary judgment on two of these defenses: misuse of the product and assumption of the risk.

A. Product Misuse

Alabama case law on the affirmative defense of product misuse is not only recent and scarce, it is also confusing if not conflicting. Nevertheless, it is comfortably apparent from this case law that the Campbells are entitled to summary judgment on the defense.

* * *

This court need not attempt to resolve how the Alabama Supreme Court will define the misuse defense. Under either definition, Bosch's invocation of the defense is not supported by the evidence. If "misuse" means the plaintiff used the product in an unforeseeable manner, then Bosch has no grounds to raise this defense. Bosch has admitted that it foresaw that consumers might use its product without guards and goggles; indeed, this foreseeability was the very reason why Bosch placed the warning label on its discs. Alternatively, if Bosch's defense is understood to mean that Mr. Campbell was negligent in his use of the disc, then Bosch's evidence in this regard is also insufficient. Bosch does not contend and has not offered any evidence that Mr. Campbell was inattentive or careless in his operation of the grinding tool. Instead, Bosch's argument is that the warning label indicated to Mr. Campbell that the Bosch disc was "intended" to be used only with the safety devices in question, and Campbell misused the tool by ignoring the warnings and operating the tool without these protections. In effect, therefore, Bosch's misuse defense is premised on the warning label itself, the very warning that the Campbells argue was inadequate. When viewed within the parameters of an AEMLD failure-to-warn claim, Bosch's misuse defense is no more than an argument, in another guise, that the warning on its disc was adequate. The adequacy of the warning is usually a question for the jury [citation omitted], which is guided by the principle that an adequate warning is "one that is reasonable under the circumstances and it need not be the best possible warning." *Gurley v. American Honda Motor Co.,* 505 So.2d 358, 361 (Ala. 1987).

* * *

Bosch argues that *Gurley v. American Honda Motor Co.,* 505 So.2d 358 (Ala. 1987), commands a different conclusion. There, the plaintiff was injured while riding with a passenger on a motorcycle manufactured by the defendant. The court held that the defendant had no duty to warn of the dangers of riding with a passenger because the combination of the motorcycle's small size, lack of rear foot pegs, instructions in the owner's manual, and gas tank label stating "WARNING—OPERATOR ONLY—NO PASSENGER," made it clear that the practice of riding double was an unintended use of the vehicle. 505 So.2d at 361. Bosch's reliance on Gurley is misplaced. First, Gurley was tried under a negligent failure-to-warn theory, not the AEMLD. Under the former, there is no duty to warn of dangers which are open and obvious, while under the AEMLD this concept is addressed in a somewhat altered manner by the affirmative defense of assumption of the risk, not by the defense of product misuse. *King v. S.R. Smith, Inc.,* 578 So.2d 1285, 1287 (Ala. 1991); *Nettles v. Electrolux Motor,* 784 F.2d 1574, 1578-79 (11th Cir. 1986); *Ford Motor Co. v. Rodgers,* 337 So.2d 736, 740-41 (Ala.1976). Therefore, the *Gurley* court's determination that the motorcycle's design, combined with its warning label, made the danger of double riding an "open and obvious danger," is not applicable to the Campbells' misuse claim. Second, Bosch, unlike the defendant in *Gurley,* has not offered any evidence that the disc was specifically designed to be used with guards and goggles and that this design would be apparent to a user. Instead, Bosch relies solely on its label as notice that the disc was "intended" to be used only with goggles and guards. Finally, the court in *Gurley* found that warnings provided by the defendant were adequate as a matter of law, while Bosch has made no such showing with regard to its own warning label.

B. Assumption of the Risk

Assumption of the risk is a contention by the defendant that, regardless of the reasonableness of the warning, the plaintiff understood the danger involved and chose to accept the risk of harm. The essential elements that a defendant must show to establish a defense of assumption of the risk are: (1) knowledge by the plaintiff of the dangerous condition, (2) appreciation of the danger under the surrounding conditions and circumstances, and (3) that the plaintiff acted unreasonably by placing himself into the way of the known danger. [Citations omitted.]

In this regard, Bosch has offered evidence that Mr. Campbell had extensive experience and training with power tools such as electric drills, bench grinders, sanders, buffing machines, power saws, and lathes. The evidence further indicates that Campbell was aware of the potential of many of these devices to cause eye injury, and he owned a welding hood which he would wear to protect his eyes when he thought it necessary. Mr. Campbell admits that he was aware that swarf or grit kicked up by many of these tools, including the grinding and sanding tool in question, could cause eye injury, and he admits that he assumed that particular risk by not us-

ing a guard or goggles on many occasions, including the occasion of his injury.

One of the tools Mr. Campbell owned, a Dremel "Moto-Tool" which serves as a sander and grinder, came with an owner's manual which Mr. Campbell admits to having read. The manual contained a number of admonishments for users to wear safety glasses, such as: "The operation of any power tool can result in foreign objects being thrown onto the eyes, which can result in severe eye damage. Always wear safety glasses or eye shields before commencing power tool operation." On the same page as two eye protection notices, the manual bore a passage which read:

> "!WARNING When using the steel saw wheels . . . or cutoff wheels . . . always have the work securely clamped. Never attempt to hold the work with one hand while using either of these accessories. The reason is that these wheels will grab if they become slightly canted in the groove, and can kick-back causing loss of control resulting in serious injury. . . . When a cutoff wheel grabs, the wheel itself usually breaks. When the steel saw wheel grabs, it may jump from the groove and you could lose control of the tool."

Finally, Bosch offers evidence that Campbell has sustained four eye injuries prior to the date of the accident in question.

As the Campbells correctly point out, to bar recovery it is not enough that the plaintiff knew of a general danger connected with the use of the product. Instead, to prevail with an assumption-of-the-risk defense, the defendant must show that the plaintiff actually appreciated the specific danger which caused his injuries. "The fact that the plaintiff is fully aware of one risk . . . does not mean that he assumes another of which he is unaware." *Davis v. Liberty Mut. Ins. Co.,* 525 F.2d 1204, 1206-07 (5th Cir. 1976) (applying Alabama law) (quoting W. Prosser, Law of Torts, § 68, at 449 (4th ed. 1971)). [Citations omitted.] Therefore, evidence which at most demonstrates that Mr. Campbell was aware of a generalized danger of eye injury when using power tools, or evidence that he assumed the risk of having small particles of wood or metal striking his eye, is insufficient to raise an issue of material fact concerning assumption of the risk of harm from a shattering grinding disc. The danger presented by swarf or grit is different in kind and magnitude from the danger presented by a shattering disc, and Mr. Campbell's assumption of the risk of the former does not evidence his intent to assume the latter. [Citations omitted.]

On the other hand, the owner's manual which accompanied the Dremel Moto-Tool warned specifically that cutoff wheels "usually" break when they grab. Both this tool and the one Mr. Campbell was using when he was injured appear to utilize high-speed rotating wheels, discs, or cutters to cut, grind, sand, or polish materials such as wood or metal. Viewing the evidence in the light most favorable to Bosch and on the very limited record presented so far by the parties, the court cannot rule out the possibility that these tools are relatively similar, and knowledge of the specific dangerous propensities of one tool could translate into specific knowledge regarding the other.

Accordingly, for the above reasons, it is ORDERED that the plaintiffs' renewed motion for partial summary judgment, filed on November 15, 1991, with regard to defendant Robert Bosch Power Tool Corporation's affirmative defenses to the plaintiffs' failure-to-warn claim, be and it is hereby granted with regard to the defense of product misuse, and denied with regard to the defense of assumption of the risk.

Case Notes: Misuse and Assumption of the Risk

1. Typically, a plaintiff's misuse will manifest itself in one of two types of acts: (1) plaintiff's use of a product for an improper purpose, or (2) plaintiff's use of a product for a proper purpose but in an improper manner. Although this distinction recognizes two separate types of acts in which a plaintiff may engage, either one of these acts will result in plaintiff's own liability in the matter. See *Port Authority of New York and New Jersey v. Arcadian Corporation*, 991 F.Supp. 390, 400 (D. N.J. 1997).

2. In *Campbell*, the Court defined misuse as a plaintiff's act that "refers not to one's carelessness or inadvertence in the use of the product, but rather to the use of a product in a manner not reasonably foreseen by the defendant." Other courts have used the term misuse to refer to any unintended or abnormal use of a product, but recognize only an unforeseeable misuse as a bar to recovery. *Campbell*, 795 F.Supp. at 1097-98.

3. The foreseeability of plaintiff's misuse of defendant's product is key. In *Port Authority of New York and New Jersey v. Arcadian Corporation*, the plaintiff argued that the defendant manufacturer of fertilizer, subsequently used in terrorists' fertilizer bomb at the New York World Trade Center, could have objectively foreseen the terrorists' misuse of fertilizer. In evaluating the defendant manufacturer's foreseeability that terrorists would use fertilizer in a bomb, the Court held as follows:

> Defendants are still entitled to dismissal because the alterations and misuse of Defendants' fertilizer products were not objectively foreseeable. Objective foreseeability means reasonable foreseeability. *The standard "does not affix responsibility for future events that are only theoretically, remotely, or just possibly foreseeable, or even simply subjectively foreseen by a particular manufacturer.."* *Brown v. United States Stove Co.*, 484 A.2d 1234 (N.J. 1984) (emphasis in original). Rather it "applies to those future occurrences that, in light of the general experiences within the industry when the product was manufactured, objectively and reasonably could have been anticipated." *Id.*; [Citations omitted.]

4. Misuse and assumption of the risk are often confused with one another. Misuse is characterized by plaintiff's use of a product that was not foreseen by the product's manufacturer. Assumption of risk is characterized by plaintiff knowing of the hazardous risk posed by the product but using it anyway.

An Indiana appellate court succinctly delineated this difference in *Perfection Paint & Color Co. v. Konduris*, 258 N.E.2d 681 (Ind. Ct. App. 1970):

> A legal description of those acts which constitute a "misuse" of a product has proven to be difficult to achieve. The problem appears to us to be one of failing to differentiate between misuse of a product which does not exhibit any defective condition until misused, or which does not appear to be defective and unreasonably dangerous, and misuse of a product when the defective and unreasonably dangerous condition is either discovered by the consumer or brought to his attention by a legally sufficient warning. While in either situation a product is being misused, the former constitutes the true category of misuse while the latter form of misuse is tantamount to the traditional concepts of incurred or assumed risk. The former . . . will apply in a situation in which a product is used for a purpose which is unforeseeable with that for which it was manufactured, or when used for a foreseeable purpose, is subject to an unforeseeable or overly harsh use. . . . The latter form of misuse, that which is analogous to the defenses of incurred or assumed risk, occurs when a product, being used in the manner intended by the manufacturer and for the purpose intended by the manufacturer, proves to be defective and the defect is discovered, or when a defect and unreasonably dangerous product, acknowledged to be such by a manufacturer's warnings or instructions on proper use, is used in contravention of the instructions or warnings.

Economic Loss Doctrine

The Economic Loss Doctrine does not allow a purchaser of a defective product to recover in negligence or strict liability for damage to only the product itself. Under such circumstances, the product purchaser must recover under a contract theory, if at all. The *Restatement (Third)* defines recovery for economic loss. See § 21 of the *Restatement (Third)*.

 CASE LAW

◆ **economic loss doctrine as bar to damages to product itself**

*East River Steamship
Corporation v.
Transamerica Delaval, Inc.,*
476 U.S. 858 (1986).

All four of respondent Transamerica's turbine engines malfunctioned due to design and manufacturing defects in each engine. Only the engines themselves were damaged. Issue before the United States Supreme Court was whether the plaintiff pur- *chaser of the turbine engines could state a cause of action in negligence or strict liability for damages caused to only the product itself.*

BLACKMUN, Justice.

* * *

Products liability grew out of a public policy judgment that people need more protection from dangerous products than is afforded by the law of warranty. [Citation omitted.] It is clear, however, that if this development were allowed to progress too far, contract law would drown in a sea of tort. [Citation omitted.] We must determine whether a commercial product injuring itself is the kind of harm against which public policy requires manufacturers to protect, independent of any contractual obligation.

A

The paradigmatic products-liability action is one where a product "reasonably certain to place life and limb in peril," distributed without reinspection, causes bodily injury. *See, e.g., MacPherson v. Buick Motor Co.,* 217 N.Y. 382, 389, 111 N.E. 1050, 1051, 1053 (1916). The manufacturer is liable whether or not it is negligent because "public policy demands that responsibility be fixed wherever it will most effectively reduce the hazards to life and health inherent in defective products that reach the market." *Escola v. Coca Cola Bottling Co. of Fresno,* 24 Cal.2d, at 462, 150 P.2d, at 441 (opinion concurring in judgment).

* * *

B

The intriguing question whether injury to a product itself may be brought in tort has spawned a variety of answers. [Footnote omitted.] At one end of the spectrum, the case that created the majority land-based approach, *Seely v. White Motor Co.,* 63 Cal.2d 9, 45 Cal.Rptr. 17, 403 P.2d 145 (1965) (defective truck), held that preserving a proper role for the law of warranty precludes imposing tort liability if a defective product causes purely monetary harm. [Citation omitted.]

At the other end of the spectrum is the minority land-based approach, whose pro-genitor, *Santor v. A & M Karagheusian, Inc.,* 44 N.J. 52, 66-67, 207 A.2d 305, 312-313 (1965) (marred carpeting), held that a manufacturer's duty to make nondefective products encompassed injury to the product itself, whether or not the defect created an unreasonable risk of harm. [Footnote and citation omitted.] The courts adopting this approach, including the majority of the Courts of Appeals sitting in admiralty that have considered the issue [footnote and citation omitted], find that the safety and insurance rationales behind strict liability apply equally where the losses are purely economic. These courts reject the *Seely* approach because they find it arbitrary that economic losses are recoverable if a plaintiff suffers bodily injury or property damage, but not

if a product injures itself. They also find no inherent difference between economic loss and personal injury or property damage, because all are proximately caused by the defendant's conduct. Further, they believe recovery for economic loss would not lead to unlimited liability because they think a manufacturer can predict and insure against product failure. [Citation omitted.]

Between the two poles fall a number of cases that would permit a products-liability action under certain circumstances when a product injures only itself. These cases attempt to differentiate between "the disappointed users . . . and the endangered ones," *Russell v. Ford Motor Co.,* 281 Or. 587, 595, 575 P.2d 1383, 1387 (1978), and permit only the latter to sue in tort. The determination has been said to turn on the nature of the defect, the type of risk, and the manner in which the injury arose.

* * *3

We find the intermediate and minority land-based positions unsatisfactory. The intermediate positions, which essentially turn on the degree of risk, are too indeterminate to enable manufacturers easily to structure their business behavior. Nor do we find persuasive a distinction that rests on the manner in which the product is injured. We realize that the damage may be qualitative, occurring through gradual deterioration or internal breakage. Or it may be calamitous. [Citation omitted.] But either way, since by definition no person or other property is damaged, the resulting loss is purely economic. Even when the harm to the product itself occurs through an abrupt, accident-like event, the resulting loss due to repair costs, decreased value, and lost profits is essentially the failure of the purchaser to receive the benefit of its bargain—traditionally the core concern of contract law. See E. Farnsworth, Contracts § 12.8, pp. 839–840 (1982).

* * *

C

Exercising traditional discretion in admiralty [citation omitted], we adopt an approach similar to *Seely* and hold that a manufacturer in a commercial relationship has no duty under either a negligence or strict products-liability theory to prevent a product from injuring itself. [Footnote omitted.]

"The distinction that the law has drawn between tort recovery for physical injuries and warranty recovery for economic loss is not arbitrary and does not rest on the 'luck' of one plaintiff in having an accident causing physical injury. The distinction rests, rather, on an understanding of the nature of the responsibility a manufacturer must undertake in distributing his products." *Seely v. White Motor Co.*, 63 Cal.2d, at 18, 45 Cal.Rptr., at 23, 403 P.2d, at 151. When a product injures only itself the reasons for imposing a tort duty are weak and those for leaving the party to its contractual remedies are strong.

The tort concern with safety is reduced when an injury is only to the product itself. When a person is injured, the "cost of an injury and the loss of time or health may be an overwhelming misfortune," and one the person is not prepared to meet. *Escola v. Coca Cola Bottling Co.*, 24 Cal.2d, at 462, 150 P.2d, at 441 (opinion concurring in judgment). In contrast, when a product injures itself, the commercial user stands to lose the value of the product, risks the displeasure of its customers who find that the product does not meet their needs, or, as in this case, experiences increased costs in performing a service. Losses like these can be insured. [Citations omitted.] Society need not presume that a customer needs special protection. The increased cost to the public that would result from holding a manufacturer liable in tort for injury to the product itself is not justified. [Citation omitted.]

Damage to a product itself is most naturally understood as a warranty claim. Such damage means simply that the product has not met the customer's expectations, or, in other words, that the customer has received "insufficient product value."

* * *

Contract law, and the law of warranty in particular, is well suited to commercial controversies of the sort involved in this case because the parties may set the terms of their own agreements. [Footnote omitted.] The manufacturer can restrict its liability, within limits, by disclaiming warranties or limiting remedies.

* * *

A warranty action also has a built-in limitation on liability, whereas a tort action could subject the manufacturer to damages of an indefinite amount. The limitation in a contract action comes from the agreement of the parties and the requirement that consequential damages, such as lost profits, be a foreseeable result of the breach. See *Hadley v. Baxendale*, 9 Ex. 341, 156 Eng.Rep. 145 (1854). In a warranty action where the loss is purely economic, the limitation derives from the requirements of foreseeability and of privity, which is still generally enforced for such claims in a commercial setting. See UCC § 2-715; White & Summers, *supra*, at 389, 396, 406-410.

In products-liability law, where there is a duty to the public generally, foreseeability is an inadequate brake. Cf. *Kinsman Transit Co. v. City of Buffalo*, 388 F.2d 821 (CA2 1968). See also Perlman, Interference with Contract and other Economic Expectancies: A Clash of Tort and Contract Doctrine, 49 U.Chi.L.Rev. 61, 71-72 (1982). Permitting recovery for all foreseeable claims for purely economic loss could make a manufacturer liable for vast sums. It would be difficult for a manufacturer to take into account the expectations of persons downstream who may encounter its product. In this case, for example, if the charterers—already one step removed from the transaction—were permitted to recover their economic losses, then the companies that subchartered the ships might claim their economic losses from the delays, and the charterers' customers also might claim their economic losses, and so on. "The law does not spread its protection so far." *Robins Dry Dock & Repair Co. v. Flint*, 275 U.S. 303, 309, 48 S.Ct. 134, 135, 72 L.Ed. 290 (1927).

And to the extent that courts try to limit purely economic damages in tort, they do so by relying on a far murkier line, one that negates the charterers' contention that permitting such recovery under a products-liability theory enables admiralty courts to avoid difficult line drawing. [Citations omitted.]

* * *

Case Notes: Economic Loss Doctrine

1. The doctrine does *not* apply to the economic damages sustained by an individual, such as lost wages, as a result of personal injuries sustained by that individual. See Comment b, c. to § 21 of *Restatement (Third)*. The rule applies only when property damage to the product itself is the alleged loss. See *Budgetel Inns, Inc. v. Micros Systems, Inc.*, 8 F.Supp.2d 1137 (E.D.Wis. 1998).

2. The doctrine applies equally to all consumer purchasers of defective products. See *Koss Construction v. Caterpillar, Inc.*, 960 P.2d 255, Syl. 2 (1998) ("consumer purchasers"); *State Farm Mutual Automobile Ins. Co. v. Ford Motor Co.*, 572 N.W.2d 321, 324 (Minn. Ct. App. 1997) (doctrine applies to consumers and businesses); *Danforth v. Acorn Structures, Inc.*, 608 A.2d 1194, 1200 (Del. 1992) (doctrine applies to individual consumers); *Waggoner v. Town & Country Mobile Homes, Inc.*, 808 P.2d 649, 653 (Okla. 1990) (doctrine barred claim for defective mobile home); *Wellcraft Marine v. Zarzour*, 577 So.2d 414, 418 (Ala. 1990) (doctrine remains the same regardless of the type of consumer).

3. Damage to the product itself may manifest in one of two different forms: (1) harm that renders the product ineffective and requires repair or replacement; or (2) harm that renders the product inherently dangerous, but does not cause harm to persons or property. See Comment d, *Harm to the defective product itself*, at § 21 to the *Restatement (Third)*. The *Restatement (Third)* noted that the remedies provided in the Uniform Commercial Code were sufficiently equipped to redress these losses.

STATUTORY DEFENSES

Seller in the Stream of Commerce

Sellers in the stream of commerce include any individual or entity that participated in the distribution of the product after it left the manufacturer and before it reached the ultimate consumer. Typically, these sellers are distributors, wholesalers, and retailers, but others may have participated in the chain of distributing the product. Many states have statutes that dismiss an innocent seller in the stream of commerce if (1) the manufacturer or some seller higher in the chain of distribution is before the court, and (2) the seller seeking dismissal is, in fact, without liability for the allegedly defective product.

The Model Uniform Product Liability Act provides typical language from which state legislatures have formed their respective innocent seller in the stream of commerce statutory defenses. Section 105 of the Model Act provides:

Sec. 105. Basic Standards of Responsibility for Product Sellers Other Than Manufacturers.

(A) A product seller, other than a manufacturer, is subject to liability to a claimant who proves by a preponderance of the evidence that claimant's harm was proximately caused by such product seller's failure to use reasonable care with respect to the product.

* * *

Unless Subsection (B) or (C) is applicable, product sellers shall not be subject to liability in circumstances in which they did not have a reasonable opportunity to inspect the product in a manner which would or should, in the exercise of reasonable care, reveal the existence of the defective condition.

(B) A product seller, other than a manufacturer, who makes an express warranty about a material fact or facts concerning a product is subject to the standards of liability set forth in Subsection 104(D).

(C) A product seller, other than a manufacturer, is also subject to the liability of manufacturer under Section 104 if:

(1) The manufacturer is not subject to service of process under the laws of the claimant's domicile; or

(2) The manufacturer has been judicially declared insolvent in that the manufacturer is unable to pay its debts as they become due in the ordinary course of business; or

(3) The court determines that it is highly probable that the claimant would be unable to enforce a judgment against the product manufacturer.

* * *

 CASE LAW

◆ **innocent seller in the stream of commerce must have manufacturer properly before the court**

Malone v. Schapun, Inc.,
965 S.W.2d 177 (Mo. Ct.
App. 1997).

Plaintiff purchaser of a rubber tarp strap was injured when strap broke and struck Malone in the head in eye rendering him without vision in his left eye. Malone had purchased the strap from defendant Schapun d/b/a True Value hardware. The manufacturer and supplier of the strap had already been dismissed from the lawsuit.

RHODES RUSSELL, Judge.

* * *

In their first point, the Malones contend that the trial court erred in granting retailer's motion to dismiss their strict liability claims. The Malones maintain that no other defendant was "properly before the court from whom total recovery may have been had for their claim" because 1) they had settled with the other defendants who had consistently denied their status as upline suppliers of the tarp strap; 2) they had given the settling defendants partial releases which expressly reserved the

Malones' strict liability claims against retailer under the terms of the settlement agreement; 3) section 537.060 provides that retailer should not stand discharged as a result of the settlement with the other defendants; and, 4) the settlement agreement preserved retailer's potential claim of indemnity against the defendants. The Malones insist that neither supplier nor manufacturer were "properly before the court" when the trial court sustained retailer's motion to dismiss because those parties had been dismissed from the lawsuit less than a month before.

Section 537.762 provides that a defendant, whose liability is based solely on his status as a seller in the stream of commerce, may be dismissed from a product liability claim "if another defendant, including the manufacturer, is properly before the court and from whom total recovery may be had for plaintiff's claim." Section 537.762.3 states that a defendant may move for dismissal by filing a motion accompanied by an affidavit stating that "the defendant is aware of no facts or circumstances upon which a verdict might be reached against him, other than his status as a seller in the stream of commerce." Once another defendant is properly before the court from whom total recovery may be had, and the party moving for dismissal avers that he is merely a seller in the stream of commerce, the other party should come forward with evidence that the defendant seeking dismissal is liable on some basis other than his status as a seller in the stream of commerce. Section 537.762.5. Otherwise, the court shall dismiss without prejudice the claim as to that defendant. *Id.* However, the party moving for dismissal must meet the threshold requirements of subsections 2 and 3 before dismissal is granted. *Id.*

Section 537.762 has been described as the "innocent seller statute." *Revisited: A Look at Missouri Strict Products Liability Law Before and After the Tort Reform Act,* 53 Mo.L.Rev. 227, 326 (1988). Other states have adopted "innocent seller" statutes, but none are substantially similar to section 537.762. Some statutory schemes completely exempt a non-manufacturer of a product from strict product liability regardless whether the manufacturer is unavailable or insolvent. *See,* Neb.Rev.St. section 25-21, 181 (1985); S.D. Codified Laws Ann. Section 20-9-9 (1979). Other statutory schemes, however, only exempt the non-manufacturer seller from strict product liability if the manufacturer is subject to service of process within the state and is able to satisfy the plaintiff's judgment. *See,* ILL. ANN.STAT. Ch 110, para 2-621 (Smith-Hurd 1987); MINN.STAT.ANN. Section 544.41 (West 1990).

Many of the statutory schemes dealing with the liability of non-manufacturers are loosely patterned after the Model Uniform Product Liability Act (Model Act). [Footnote and citation omitted.] Section 105(A) of the Model Act provides that a non-manufacturer is subject to liability for its failure to use reasonable care with respect to a product. Section 105(B) also holds a non-manufacturer strictly liable for any express warranties given. Thus, under the Model Act, a non-manufacturer will not be held liable for a product liability claim unless it is somehow negligent with respect to the product or has made an express warranty about the product. However, a non-manufacturer seller will be held to the same standards as a manufacturer under section 105(c) if: 1) the manufacturer is not subject to service of process in the plaintiff's domicile; or 2) the manufacturer has been declared insolvent; or 3) the court determines it is highly probable that the plaintiff would not be able to enforce a judgment against the manufacturer.

Section 105 attempts to achieve a balance between protecting non-manufacturers, except from their own negligence or specific guarantees, and protecting an innocent consumer's right to recover. [Citation omitted.] Although the Model Act recognizes that the manufacturer should be ultimately held liable for its defective product, section 105(c) also recognizes that "[i]n some cases the retailer may be the only member of that enterprise reasonably available to the injured plaintiff." *Id.,* (quoting *Vandermark v. Ford Motor Co.,* 61 Cal.2d 256, 37 Cal.Rptr. 896, 899-900, 391 P.2d 168, 171-72 (1964)). Section 105(c) ensures that the negligence standard will protect the non-manufacturer if the manufacturer is available and solvent. [Citation omitted.]

Although section 537.762 does not use the terminology of the Model Act or other state statutes, it does address similar concerns. First, like the Model Act, a seller is still liable for its own negligence or other conduct other than its status as a seller in the stream of commerce. Under section 537.762, dismissal is only proper where the defendant's liability is based solely on its status as a seller in the stream of commerce. Further, a defendant who is a mere seller in the stream of commerce may not be dismissed unless "another defendant, including the manufacturer, is properly before the court and from whom total recovery may be had for plaintiff's claim." Section 537.762.2. As with the Model Act, section 537.762 addresses both the availability and solvency of the manufacturer of the defective product. Although one of the apparent purposes of section 537.762 is to protect a seller from becoming principally liable when there is a culpable manufacturer or other culpable upline supplier, the statutory requirement that there must be another defendant properly before the court and from whom total recovery may be had, ensures that the plaintiff will not be prejudiced by the dismissal. An innocent seller under section 537.762 should not be dismissed unless the injured party is ensured that another defendant, who is not an innocent seller, is properly before the court and can satisfy the injured party's claim. Thus, similar to the Model Act, dismissal of a non-manufacturer (i.e., seller in the stream of commerce) should not be granted where the product manufacturer is not subject to process under Missouri law or is insolvent. [Citation omitted.]

Section 537.762, by its very terms, does not change the substantive law relating to an innocent seller's liability; as its effect is only procedural. [Citation omitted.] A seller in the stream of commerce is still subject to liability under the doctrine of strict product liability. [Citation omitted.] The purported purpose of section 537.762 is to allow a seller in the stream of commerce "to be released at an early stage of the litigation, rather than wait until the completion of litigation to obtain indemnity."

Retailer argues that manufacturer and supplier "were properly before the court" on January 7, 1997, because the court retained jurisdiction over these parties after their voluntary dismissal from the suit under Rule 75.01. Pursuant to Rule 75.01, the trial court has power to vacate, reopen, correct, amend or modify a judgment during the 30 days immediately following entry of the judgment. Retailer contends that the trial court exercised its jurisdiction over manufacturer and supplier when the court sustained their motion to disclose the settlement terms on January 7, 1997. We disagree.

Rule 75.01 provides that the trial court retains control over judgments during the 30-day period after entry of judgment. However, a voluntary dismissal under Rule 67.01 is not a judgment of the court within the meaning of Rule 75.01. [Citation omitted.] Once a plaintiff voluntarily dismisses a claim prior to the introduction of evidence, it is as if the suit were never brought. [Citation omitted.] No action can be taken by the trial court, and any action attempted in the dismissed suit is a nullity. Further, the trial court has no power to reinstate a voluntarily dismissed case.

The claims against supplier and manufacturer had been voluntarily dismissed on December 20, 1996. After that date, the trial court was without jurisdiction as to matters relating to the dismissed suits against supplier and manufacturer. The trial court would not have had the power to reinstate the causes of action against manufacturer and supplier. Furthermore, defendants mischaracterize the January 7, 1997 order in which the trial court ordered the terms of the settlement agreement to be disclosed. When the trial court ordered the terms of the settlement agreement to be disclosed, it was not exercising jurisdiction over the dismissed manufacturer or supplier. The motion to disclose the terms of the settlement agreement filed by retailer and owners/managers requested that the Malones be required to disclose the terms. Thus, the trial court exercised jurisdiction over the Malones and not manufacturer or supplier. We find retailer's argument that manufacturer and supplier were properly before the court because the trial court retained jurisdiction over them to be without merit.

Even if we were to assume *arguendo* that supplier and manufacturer were properly before the court when retailer was dismissed, it was disputed whether they were the actual supplier and manufacturer of the tarp strap in question. Throughout the entire course of the litigation, and concluding with the settlement, both supplier and manufacturer continued to deny that they manufactured, distributed, sold, or in any manner supplied the tarp strap which injured Malone. No admissions were made by supplier and manufacturer in the settlement agreement, and the fact that they settled with the Malones does not establish that they were the manufacturer and/or supplier of the tarp strap. [Citation omitted.] As there was a material issue of fact as to whether supplier and manufacturer were upline suppliers of the tarp strap, and because there were no other defendants properly before the court, the trial court erred in dismissing retailer in that the requirements of section 537.762.2 were not met. [Footnote omitted.]

Retailer argues that the Malones' settlement with supplier and manufacturer bars the Malones from pursuing their strict liability claims against retailer. Retailer contends section 537.762 recognizes that retailers of defective products are only secondarily liable to injured plaintiffs, and therefore, when a plaintiff settles with an upstream defendant, the settlement agreement serves to bar any subsequent strict liability action against the retailer. Retailer essentially argues that since its liability is secondary or derivative, the release of both supplier and manufacturer served to discharge their liability. We disagree.

Section 537.060 states that "[w]hen an agreement by release, covenant not to sue or not to enforce a judgment is given in good faith to one of two or more persons liable in tort for the same injury or wrongful death, such agreement shall not discharge any of the other tort-feasors for the damage unless the terms of the agreement so provide. . . ." In *Manar v. Park Lane Medical Center*, 753 S.W.2d 310 (Mo.App.1988), the Western District of this court held that the release of medical malpractice claims against medical practitioners did not operate to release the plaintiff's derivative claims against the hospital. Basing its decision on section 537.060 and Judge Robertson's majority opinion in *Aherron v. St. John's Mercy Medical Center*, [citation omitted] the Court stated that section 537.060 preserved claims of vicarious liability against tort-feasors not included in the partial release. *Id.* at 313-14.

We have not discovered any Missouri case which holds that when a plaintiff releases a manufacturer of a defective product, the retailer is also released. Other jurisdictions, however, have held that a release of the manufacturer does not release the retailer from the plaintiff's product liability claims.

* * *

Here, the partial releases given to supplier and manufacturer provided:

This partial release is given by the undersigned with the express understanding that the undersigned does not hearby release [retailer] and [owners/managers], but instead the undersigned expressly reserve the right to proceed and shall continue in their suit, action, claims, and causes of action, against [retailer] and [owners/managers], including but not limited to any claims under a theory of strict liability in tort.

Since the express terms of the release expressly reserved the Malones' cause of action against retailer, by operation of section 537.060, the release of supplier and manufacturer did not discharge retailer from liability.

We find that the trial court erred in dismissing retailer under section 537.762 in that there was no defendant properly before the court from whom total recovery may be had for the Malones' product liability claims. We reverse and remand this cause to the trial court for further proceedings.

* * *

Case Notes: Innocent Seller in the Stream of Commerce

1. Should the Court in *Malone* have affirmed the lower court's dismissal of the retailer? What action did the retailer take to manufacture, design, or warn about the defective strap? Was there any evidence that the retailer even knew that the strap purchased by Malone was defective? If not, how can the Court's decision be the correct result? Why should it matter whether the manufacturer or supplier, distributor, or wholesaler is properly before the Court in order for the Court to dismiss the retailer? Can other state statutes differ? Was the Missouri statute unique in this regard? Did plaintiff have evidence that Schapun might be liable to plaintiff in some way other than as a retailer in the stream of commerce? Would this evidence make a difference?

2. The Missouri seller in the stream of commerce statute provides the following:

   (1) A defendant whose liability is based solely on his status as a seller in the stream of commerce may be dismissed from a products liability claim as provided in this section.

   (2) This section shall apply to any products liability claim in which another defendant, including the manufacturer, is properly before the court and from whom total recovery may be had for plaintiff's claim.

   (3) A defendant may move for dismissal under this section within the time for filing an answer or other responsive pleading unless permitted by the court at a later time for good cause shown. The motion shall be accompanied by an affidavit which shall be made under oath and shall state that the defendant is aware of no facts or circumstances upon which a verdict might be reached against him, other than his status as a seller in the stream of commerce.

   (4) The parties shall have sixty days in which to conduct discovery on the issues raised in the motion and affidavit. The court for good cause shown, may extend the time for discovery, and may enter a protective order pursuant to the rules of civil procedure regarding the scope of discovery on other issues.

(5) Any party may move for a hearing on a motion to dismiss under this section. If the requirements of subsections 2 and 3 of this section are met, and no party comes forward at such a hearing with evidence of facts which would render the defendant seeking dismissal under this section liable on some basis other than his status as a seller in the stream of commerce, the court shall dismiss without prejudice the claim as to that defendant.

(6) No order of dismissal under this section shall operate to divest a court of venue or jurisdiction otherwise proper at the time the action was commenced. A defendant dismissed pursuant to this section shall be considered to remain a party to such action only for such purposes.

(7) An order of dismissal under this section shall be interlocutory until final disposition of plaintiff's claim by settlement or judgment and may be set aside for good cause shown at anytime prior to such disposition. (Mo. Rev. Stat. 537.762 (1987).)

3. In what ways could the Missouri statute be improved? Does the Missouri statute accomplish the purpose of dismissing an innocent seller in the stream of commerce that had no connection with the defective product that injured plaintiff? Was this, in fact, the purpose of the statute? What purpose was enunciated by the appellate court in *Malone v. Schapun, Inc.?* See Cavico, Jr., *The Strict Tort Liability of Retailers, Wholesalers, and Distribu-*

tors of Defective Products, 12 Nova.L.Rev. 213 (1987).

4. The *Restatement (Third)* defines "One Who Sells or Otherwise Distributes" in § 20 as follows:

For purposes of this *Restatement:*

(a) One sells a product when, in a commercial context, one transfers ownership thereto either for use or consumption or for resale leading to ultimate use or consumption. Commercial product sellers include, but are not limited to, manufacturers, wholesalers, and retailers.

(b) One otherwise distributes a product when, in a commercial transaction other than a sale, one provides the product to another either for use or consumption or as a preliminary step leading to ultimate use or consumption. Commercial non-sale product distributors include, but are not limited to, lessors, bailors, and those who provide products to others as a means of promoting either the use or consumption of such products or some other commercial activity.

(c) One also sells or otherwise distributes a product when, in a commercial transaction, one provides a combination of products and services and either the transaction taken as a whole, or the product component thereof, satisfies the criteria in Subsection (a) or (b). *Restatement (Third)* at § 20 (a-c).

Other Participants in the Stream of Commerce

 CASE LAW ────────────────────────────────◆

◆ **lessor in the stream of commerce**

Samuel Friedland Family Enterprises, et al. v. Amoroso, 630 So.2d 1067 (Fla. 1994).

Mrs. Amoroso sued a sailboat rental entity and affiliated hotel for injuries she received when the crossbar of the sailboat broke and struck Mrs. Amoroso.

GRIMES, Justice.

* * *

The underlying basis for the doctrine of strict liability is that those entities within a product's distributive chain "who profit from the sale or distribution of [the product] to the public, rather than an innocent person injured by it, should bear the financial burden of even an undetectable product defect." *North Miami General Hosp., Inc. v. Goldberg*, 520 So.2d 650, 651 (Fla. 3d DCA 1988). Those entities are in a better position to ensure the safety of the products they market, to insure against defects in those products, and to spread the cost of any injuries resulting from a defect.

This Court adopted the doctrine of strict liability, as stated by the A.L.I. Restatement (Second) of Torts section 402A (1965), in *West v. Caterpillar Tractor Co.*, 336 So.2d 80, 87 (Fla. 1976). [Footnote omitted.] In *West*, an individual who was injured by a negligently designed grader brought a strict liability action against the manufacturer of the grader. *Id.* at 82. In adopting strict liability, we recognized that a manufacturer, who places a potentially dangerous product on the market and encourages its use, undertakes a special responsibility toward members of the public who may be injured by the product. *Id.* at 86. Since *West*, Florida courts have expanded the doctrine of strict liability to others in the distributive chain including retailers, wholesalers, and distributors. [Citations omitted.]

In addition to the court below, several other district courts of appeal have already applied the doctrine to commercial lessors. [Citations omitted.] The courts of many other states have also held that commercial lessors can be held strictly liable for defective products they lease.

In *Cintrone v. Hertz Truck Leasing & Rental Service*, 45 N.J. 434, 212 A.2d 769, 778-79 (1965), the New Jersey Supreme Court held that a truck rental company could be held strictly liable for injuries caused by a defective condition in one of the trucks it leased. In reaching this conclusion, the court found little difference between sales and lease transactions, and recognized that, like a purchaser of new goods, a lessee is entitled to expect that a product is being delivered in a nondefective condition. *Id.*, 212 A.2d at 776-77. In fact, after taking note of the growth of the car and truck rental business, the court suggested that the rationale for imposing strict liability on manufacturers and sellers may even be greater in the context of leased goods as a lessee usually has less opportunity to inspect items and lessors, by repeatedly introducing and reintroducing products into the stream of commerce, are exposing the public to a proportionately greater risk of injury. *Id.*

In *Price v. Shell Oil Co.*, 2 Cal.3d 245, 85 Cal.Rptr. 178, 179, 466 P.2d 722, 723 (1970), the Supreme Court of California also addressed the application of strict liability to commercial lease transactions. Price involved an aircraft mechanic who was injured when a ladder, which was attached to a gasoline truck, broke. *Id.*, 85 Cal.Rptr. at 179-80, 466 P.2d at 723-24. The truck was leased by the mechanic's employer from Shell Oil Company. *Id.* at 182, 466 P.2d at 726.

Prior to *Price*, California courts had applied the doctrine of strict tort liability to manufacturers, retailers, suppliers of personal property, and residential builders. *Id.* at 181-82, 466 P.2d at 725-26. In determining whether to further expand the strict liability cause of action, the court reasoned:

> Such a broad philosophy evolves naturally from the purpose of imposing strict liability which "is to insure that the costs of injuries resulting from defective products are borne by the manufacturers that put such products on the market rather than by the injured persons who are powerless to protect themselves." [*Greenman v. Yuba Power Products, Inc.*, 59 Cal.2d 57, 27 Cal.Rptr. 697, 701, 377 P.2d 897, 901 (1963).] Essentially the paramount policy to be promoted by the rule is the protection of otherwise defenseless victims of manufacturing defects and the spreading throughout society of the cost of compensating them. . . .

> . . . [W]e can perceive no substantial difference between sellers of personal property and non-sellers, such as bailors and lessors. In each instance, the seller or non-seller "places [an article] on the market, knowing that it is to be used without inspection for defects, . . ." [*Greenman*, 27 Cal.Rptr. at 700, 377 P.2d at 900.] In light of the policy to be subserved, it should make no difference that the party distributing the article has retained title to it. Nor can we see how the risk of harm associated with the use of the chattel can vary with the legal form under which it is held. Having in mind the market realities and the

widespread use of the lease of personality in today's business world, we think it makes good sense to impose on the lessors of chattels the same liability for physical harm which has been imposed on the manufacturers and retailers. The former, like the latter, are able to bear the cost of compensating for injuries resulting from defects by spreading the loss through an adjustment of the rental. [Citation omitted.]

The court concluded that lessors can be held strictly liable. [Citation omitted.] However, this holding was limited to those lessors "found to be in the business of leasing, in the same general sense as the seller of personality is found to be in the business of manufacturing or retailing." *Id.* at 184, 466 P.2d at 728. To do otherwise would work an injustice on those lessors who cannot adjust the costs associated with strict liability in an economically viable manner, such as where the lease is an isolated transaction. [Citation omitted.]

The Diplomat argues that the district court opinion in the instant case "casts too wide a net." They contend that applying the doctrine of strict liability to all commercial lease transactions is unfair. It would cause a vast increase in potential liability which small businesses in Florida would be unable to bear. Thus, if we were to apply the doctrine of strict liability to commercial lease transactions, the Diplomat urges us to limit our holding to those lessors who are "mass dealers in chattel."

However, we note that no state which has applied strict liability to lessors has retreated from this view because of its economic consequences on commercial leasing. Also, we can find no express authority for the proposition that the doctrine of strict liability should be limited to those lessors who can be called "mass dealers in chattel," and, if such authority does exist, it is certainly a minority view. For purposes of applying strict liability, we can discern no reason to differentiate between a business which is a mass dealer in a product and one which is not, provided each is actually engaged in the business of leasing the defective product.

* * *

Case Notes: Other Sellers in the Stream of Commerce

1. Should a seller or lessor of used products be excused from liability as a retailer in the stream of commerce? In *Amoroso*, the Florida Supreme Court was careful to distinguish the lessor of products from the sellers of used products. The Court said

> Lessors and sellers of used goods are not necessarily analogous in light of the policies underlying strict tort liability. The Supreme Court of Wisconsin rejected a similar argument in holding that the doctrine of strict liability applied to commercial lessors. *Kemp v. Miller*, 453 N.W.2d 872, 879 (Wis. 1990). * * *

Discussing the unique position of sellers of used products, the Court stated:

> This court's decision in Burrows is based on the realization that the imposition of strict liability on a seller of used products, for defects that arise after manufacture and before the product reaches the seller, places the risk of loss associated with the use of defective products on one who has neither created nor assumed the risk and on one who is not in a position to implement procedures to avoid the distribution of defective products in the future. Defects in a used product typically arise before the product reaches the seller and while the product was in the hands of an unknown previous owner. The used product seller is rarely familiar with the prior history of the products he or she sells and can discover and correct latent defects in those products only at great cost by means of individual inspection. [Citation omitted.]

* * *

The court then explained that commercial lessors are in a different position regarding the products they lease.

The imposition of strict liability on a commercial lessor, for defects that arise after manufacture and while the product is under the ownership and control of the lessor, places the risk of loss associated with the use of defective products on one who created and assumed the risk and on one who can implement procedures to avoid the distribution of defective products in the future. Defects in a leased product may surface or be discovered after a product reaches the lessor. The commercial lessor is familiar with the characteristics and prior history of the products he or she leases and is in a position to discover and correct defects in those products by means of routine inspection, servicing, and repair. Further, by placing products on the market, the commercial lessor impliedly represents that those products will be fit for use throughout the term of the lease and, consequently, assumes the risk of damages resulting from a defective product.

Amoroso, 630 So.2d 1067, 1070 (Fla. 1994) *citing Kemp v. Miller,* 453 N.W.2d at 879; *see also Restatement (Third)* at § 8, *Liability of Commercial Seller or Distributor of Defective Used Products.*

2. As an underlying policy justification, the Court in *Amoroso* pointed to "the recent growth of the commercial leasing business in recent years" as a rationale for imposing strict liability on commercial lessors. *Amoroso,* 630 So.2d at 1070-71; see also Annotation, *Application of Strict Liability in Tort Doctrine to Lessor of Personal Property,* 52 A.L.R.3d 121 (1973).

3. The *Restatement (Third)* provides, in its section 20 defining "One Who Sells or Otherwise Distributes," that lessors are generally subject to the same liability rules as product sellers. See Comment c to § 20 of the *Restatement (Third).*

4. Other participants who do not directly participate in the stream of commerce but are essential in the marketing of a defective product or otherwise providing it in or through the stream of commerce may also be held strictly liable for the product's defect. In *Bittler v. White and Company, Inc.,* 560 N.E.2d 979, 981-82 (Ill. App. 5 Dist. 1990), the Fifth District Court of Appeals in Illinois held that the executive sales representative of an Ultravac machine (a truck-mounted vacuum loader and cleaner) had a significant "participatory connection" to the stream of commerce, which allowed the Court to impose strict liability against it. There, the Court said

The public policy rationale which justifies imposing strict liability on manufacturers as well as sellers, suppliers, wholesalers, distributors, and even lessors, is based on the fact that these entities, as part of the chain of distribution, are involved in and reap a profit from the placement of the allegedly defective product into the stream of commerce. Even parties who are not within the actual chain of distribution, but who play an integral role in the marketing enterprise of an allegedly defective product and participate in the profits derived from placing the product into the stream of commerce, are held liable under the doctrine of strict liability applied to Uniroyal despite the fact that its only link to the chain of distribution was its authorization of the use of its trademark, which appeared on the allegedly defective tire that was admittedly manufactured by a Belgian company and sold by that company to General Motors, who then installed the tire on their automobile, which was eventually sold to plaintiff.

Consequently, it appears that the imposition of strict liability hinges on whether the party in question has any "participatory connection, for personal profit or other benefit, with the injury-causing product and with the enterprise that created consumer demand for and reliance upon the product." *Kasel v. Remington Arms, Inc.,* (1972), 24 Cal.App.3d 711, 725, 101 Cal.Rptr. 314, 323, quoted in *Hebel v. Sherman Equipment,*

92 Ill.2d at 379, 65 Ill.Dec. at 894, 442 N.E.2d at 205. [Citation omitted.]

In the present case White, the exclusive sales representative for D.P. Way, contends that it merely acted as a liaison between the manufacturer/seller (D.P. Way) and the purchaser (Commonwealth Edison) and that its role in the sales transaction was tangential, placing it outside the chain of distribution. However, this characterization belies the truth, which is that White was bound by its exclusive sales representative contract with D.P. Way to promote the sale of D.P. Way products and, through this relationship, derived an economic benefit in the form of a commission from all D.P. Way sales made within its territory, including, apparently, the one involved here. For this reason we find that White's "participatory connection" with the allegedly defective product was sufficient to make it subject to the application of the strict liability doctrine and so we reverse the trial court's grant of summary judgment in favor of White on the strict liability counts. *Id.*

State of the Art

A defendant manufacturer invoking a state-of-the-art defense seeks to convince the finder of fact that no one in the industry knew about the defects in the product or the affects from it at the time the product was made. Some jurisdictions recognize the defense as simply the customary practice in the industry. Other jurisdictions require that the evidentiary support of the defense reveal that the product used the safest and most advanced technology available at the time the product was made. See Comment d. *Design defects: general considerations, § 2 Restatement (Third) of Torts: Product Liability.*

 CASE LAW

♦ **state-of-the-art as an affirmative defense**

*O'Brien v. Muskin
Corporation,* 463 A.2d 298
(N.J. 1983).

Plaintiff sued defendant pool manufacturing company after plaintiff dove into 3½ feet of water in above-ground pool and sustained head and neck injuries. Defendant Muskin attempted to defend its pool based on a state-of-the-art defense.

POLLOCK, J.

* * *

The "state-of-the-art" refers to the existing level of technological expertise and scientific knowledge relevant to a particular industry at the time a product is designed. [Citation omitted.] Although customs of an industry may be relevant [citation omitted], because those customs may lag behind technological development, they are not identical with the state-of-the-art. [Citations omitted.] A manufacturer may have a duty to make products pursuant to a safer design even if the custom of the industry is not to use that alternative.

State-of-the-art relates to both components of the risk-utility equation. [Citation omitted.] Although the focus is on the product, our attention is drawn to the reasonableness of the manufacturer's conduct in placing the product on the market. In that regard, the risk side of the equation may involve, among other factors, risks that the manufacturer knew or should have known would be posed by the product, as well as the adequacy of any warnings. The utility side generally will include an appraisal of the need for the product and available design alternatives. Furthermore, some products are unavoidably unsafe; the need for a product may be great, but the existing state of human knowledge may not make it safe. *Restatement* § 402A, comment k. With those products, the determination of liability may be achieved more appropriately through an evaluation of the adequacy of the warnings. In brief, risk-utility analysis is not a petrified, but a dynamic process. Where a particular product falls on the risk-utility continuum will depend on the facts of each case. A toy that poses undue risks to infants may be viewed differently from a therapeutic device that protects or prolongs life. As we proceed, as we must, on a case-by-case basis, risk-utility analysis provides the flexibility necessary for an appropriate adjustment of the interests of manufacturers, consumers, and the public.

Although state-of-the-art evidence may be dispositive on the facts of a particular case, it does not constitute an absolute defense apart from risk-utility analysis. [Citation omitted.] The ultimate burden of proving a defect is on the plaintiff, but the burden is on the defendant to prove that compliance with state-of-the-art, in conjunction with other relevant evidence, justifies placing a product on the market. Compliance with proof of state-of-the-art need not, as a matter of law, compel a judgment for a defendant. State-of-the-art evidence, together with other evidence relevant to risk-utility analysis, however, may support a judgment for a defendant. In brief, state-of-the-art evidence is relevant to, but not necessarily dispositive of, risk-utility analysis. That is, a product may embody the state-of-the-art and still fail to satisfy the risk-utility equation.

The assessment of the utility of a design involves the consideration of available alternatives. If no alternatives are available, recourse to a unique design is more defensible. The existence of a safer and equally efficacious design, however, diminishes the justification for using a challenged design.

The evaluation of the utility of product also involves the relative need for that product; some products are essentials, while others are luxuries. A product that fills a critical need and can be designed in only one way should be viewed differently from a luxury item. Still other products, including some for which no alternative exists, are so dangerous and of such little use that under the risk-utility analysis, a manufacturer would bear the cost of liability of harm to others. That cost might dissuade a manufacturer from placing the product on the market, even if the product has been made as safely as possible. Indeed, plaintiff contends that above-ground pools with vinyl liners are such products and that manufacturers who market those pools should bear the cost of injuries they cause to foreseeable users.

A critical issue at trial was whether the design of the pool, calling for a vinyl bottom in a pool four feet deep, was defective. The trial court should have permitted the jury to consider whether, because of the dimensions of the pool and slipperiness of the bottom, the risks of injury so outweighed the utility of the product as to constitute a defect. In removing that issue from consideration by the jury, the trial court erred. To establish sufficient proof to compel submission of the issue to the jury for appropriate fact-finding under risk-utility analysis, it was not necessary for plaintiff to prove the existence of alternative, safer designs. Viewing the evidence in the light most favorable to plaintiff, even if there are no alternative methods of making bottoms for above-ground pools, the jury might have found that the risk posed by the pool outweighed its utility.

In a design-defect case, the plaintiff bears the burden of both going forward with the evidence and of persuasion that the product contained a defect. To establish a *prima facie* case, the plaintiff should adduce sufficient evidence on the risk-utility factors to establish a defect. With respect to above-ground swimming pools, for example, the plaintiff might seek to establish that pools are marketed primarily for recreational, not therapeutic purposes; that because of their design, including their configuration, inadequate warnings, and the use of vinyl liners, injury is likely; that, without impairing the usefulness of the pool or pricing it out of the market, warnings against diving could be made more prominent and a liner less dangerous. It may not be necessary for the plaintiff to introduce evidence on all those alternatives. Conversely, the plaintiff may wish to offer proof on other matters relevant to the risk-utility analysis. It is not a foregone conclusion that plaintiff ultimately will prevail on a risk-utility analysis, but he should have an opportunity to prove his case.

Case Notes: State-of-the-Art Defense

1. State-of-the-art is generally referred to as "facts which were either known or discoverable in light of the scientific and technological knowledge available to the defendants at the time the products were produced and distributed." *In Re: Hawaii Asbestos Cases,* 699 F.Supp. 233, 234 (D.Hi. 1988). Some jurisdictions regard the defense as one that "reflects technology at the cutting edge of scientific knowledge." See Comment d, § 2 *Restatement (Third)*; see also *Phillips v. Cameron Tool Corporation,* 950 F.2d 488 (1991) (noting confusion in the definition of state-of-the-art). The Model Uniform Product Liability Act considered state-of-the-art in terms of "practical technological feasibility," which the UPLA defined as the "technology, mechanical, and scientific knowledge relating to product safety that was reasonably feasible for use, in light of economic practicality, at the time of manufacture" (UPLA at § 107 (D)). See also Karazck, *State of the Art or Science, Is it a Defense in Products Liability?,* 60 Ill.B.J. 348 (1972); Robb, *A Practical Approach to Use of State of the Art Evidence in Strict Products Liability Cases,* 77 Nw.U.L.Rev. 1 (1977).

2. The Model Uniform Product Liability Act provided suggested defense language from which various state-of-the-art statutes have been drafted. Section 107 (E) provides the following:

   (E) If the product seller proves, by a preponderance of the evidence, that it was not within practical technological feasibility for it to make the product safer with respect to design and warnings or instructions at the time of manufacture so as to have prevented claimant's harm, the product seller shall not be subject to liability for harm caused by the product unless the trier of fact determines that:

   (1) The product seller knew or had reason to know of the danger and, with that knowledge, acted unreasonably in selling the product at all;

   (2) The product was defective in construction under Subsection 104(A);

   (3) The product seller failed to meet the post-manufacture duty to warn or instruct under Subsection 104 (C)(6); or

   (4) The product seller was subject to liability for express warranty under Subsection 104 (D) or 105 (B).

3. The risk-utility test is relevant to determine sufficient evidence of the state-of-the-art defense. *O'Brien,* 463 A.2d at 304. Conversely, evidence of the state-of-the-art at the time when defendant's product was manufactured is relevant to determine the appropriate application of the risk-utility test. *Id.* at 305.

4. A risk-utility analysis includes some of the following factors:

   (1) The usefulness and desirability of the product—its utility to the user and to the public as a whole;

   (2) The safety aspects of the product—the likelihood that it will cause injury, and the probable seriousness of the injury;

   (3) The availability of a substitute product which would meet the same need and not be as unsafe;

   (4) The manufacturer's ability to eliminate the unsafe character of the product without impairing its usefulness or making it too expensive to maintain its utility;

   (5) The user's ability to avoid danger by the exercise of care in the use of the product;

   (6) The user's anticipated awareness of the dangers inherent in the product and their avoidability, because of general public knowledge of the obvious condition of the product, or of the existence of suitable warnings or instructions;

   (7) The feasibility, on the part of the manufacturer, of spreading the loss by setting the price of the product or carrying liability insurance. *O'Brien,* 463 A.2d at 304-05, *citing Cepeda v. Cumberland Engineering Co., Inc.,* 386 A.2d 816 (N.J. 1978).

5. The defense does not insulate the manufacturer from its post-sale duty to warn its product users about dangers in the use of the product that come to its attention after the

product was made. See *George v. Celotex Corporation*, 914 F.2d 26 (2d Cir. 1990); *Rozier v. Ford Motor Company*, 573 F.2d 1332 (5th Cir. 1978).

6. State-of-the-art defenses are typically seen in asbestos cases. See *In Re: Hawaii Asbestos Cases*, 699 F.Supp. 233, 234 (D.Hi. 1988); *Gogol v. Johns-Manville Sales Corporation et al.*, 595 F.Supp. 971 (D.N.J. 1984). The defense is also noted in silicone implant litigation and other mass torts.

Statutes of Limitation and Repose

The statutes of limitation and repose impose limitations upon plaintiff to file her or his product liability suit within a prescribed time period. Each serves a different purpose. The statute of limitations requires that a products suit be filed within a particular time, such as five years in some states. The UCC requires that breach of warranty cases be filed within four years. Its purpose is to require plaintiff to file her or his product liability lawsuit within a particular time *after* injuries occurred or cause of action otherwise accrued.

The statute of repose prescribes an outside time period on plaintiff's right to pursue a products liability claim based upon various factors, such as date of delivery or date of sale, without regard to when the product may have injured the plaintiff. It requires that all claims regarding a manufacturer's products be filed within a particular time. If they are not, plaintiff is forever barred in bringing the lawsuit, regardless of when plaintiff's injury occurred or cause of action accrued.

 CASE LAW

◆ **statutes of limitation and repose as affirmative defenses**

Anabaldi v. Sunbeam Corporation, 651 F.Supp. 1343 (N.D.Ill. 1987).

Plaintiff alleged strict liability, negligence, and breach of express and implied Warranty counts against defendant manufacturer. Sunbeam defended by alleging the affirmative defenses of the Illinois statutes of limitation and repose.

BRIAN BARNETT DUFF, Judge.

* * *

Defendant Sunbeam Corp. is a Delaware corporation with its principal place of business in Illinois. Sunbeam manufactured home cooker/fryers at its plant in Illinois and distributed them in Pennsylvania where, in October, 1980, a cooker/fryer filled with hot oil tipped over and severely burned the two plaintiff children, both Pennsylvania residents.

Plaintiffs filed this action in May, 1982, and Sunbeam answered the complaint soon afterwards. In November, 1984, Sunbeam amended its answer to assert two affirmative defenses: first, that because it initially sold the cooker/fryer no later than May, 1968, the 12-year statute of repose for products liability actions in Illinois, Ill. Rev. Stat. Ch. 110, para. 13-213, bars plaintiffs' strict liability claim; and second, that for the same reason, the four-year statute of limitations for breach of warranty actions in Illinois, Ill. Rev. Stat. Ch. 26, § 2-725, bars plaintiffs' breach of warranty claims.

* * *

A determination that the substantive law of Pennsylvania governs this case does not settle the adequacy [**4] of Sunbeam's affirmative defenses, however, because it leaves open the question of whether an Illinois court would apply Illinois or Pennsylvania statutes of limitation to plaintiffs' claims. As a general rule Illinois courts apply Illinois statutes of limitation to common law causes of action arising in other states, even when those causes of action are governed by foreign law. [Citations omitted.] Because both strict liability and breach of warranty are common law causes of action in Pennsylvania, Illinois statutes of limitation govern this suit.

Sunbeam's first affirmative defense invokes the 12-year statute of repose for strict liability actions in Illinois, Ill. Rev. Stat. Ch. 110, para. 13-213. But not all statutes of "repose" are statutes of "limitations"; a statute of limitations is a procedural rule requiring a plaintiff to bring suit within a certain time after her cause of action has accrued. [Citation omitted.] The Illinois statute of repose for strict liability claims is not a true statute of limitations because it is a substantive rule extinguishing a cause of action upon the lapse of a given period of time—regardless of whether the cause of action ever accrued. *Id.*

Because the Illinois statute of repose for strict liability claims is substantive and the substantive law of Pennsylvania governs this case, Sunbeam cannot assert the Illinois statute of repose. Illinois applies its general statute of limitations for personal injury actions to product liability claims [citation omitted], and that limitations period is two years, Ill. Rev. Stat. Ch. 110 para. 13-202. Plaintiffs complied with para. 13-202 by bringing suit within two years from the date of the accident. Sunbeam's first affirmative defense therefore must be stricken.

Sunbeam's second affirmative defense asserts Illinois' four-year statute of limitations for actions on contracts for sale, Ill. Rev. Stat. Ch. 26, para. 2-725, which governs actions for breach of warranty. [Citation omitted.] Section 2-275 is a true statute of limitations, providing that an action for breach of warranty must be initiated within four years of its accrual, which the section defines as occurring upon tender of deliver, "except that where a warranty explicitly extends to future performance of the goods and discovery of the breach must await the time of such performance the cause of action accrues when the breach is or should have been discovered." Because § 2-725 is the applicable statute of limitations for plaintiffs' breach of warranty claims, and Sunbeam may be able to show that plaintiffs failed to comply with the statute, Sunbeam's second affirmative defense is proper.

There is no merit to plaintiffs' argument that it is unfair for Sunbeam to assert its statute of limitations defense so late in the litigation. Pennsylvania's statute of limitations for breach of warranty actions is identical to the Illinois statute [citation omitted], so Sunbeam's late assertion of the defense has not deprived plaintiffs of the ability to pursue their claims in a more generous forum.

Accordingly, the court finds that Pennsylvania substantive law governs this case, and strikes Sunbeam's first affirmative defense. Sunbeam's second affirmative defense stands.

IT IS SO ORDERED.

Case Notes: Statute of Limitation.

1. The distinguishing feature between the statute of limitations and a statute of repose is whether the prescribed time period begins to run when plaintiff was injured. If so, it is a statute of limitations period. If not, it is a statute of repose period. A secondary feature is that the statute of limitations protects against the aging of plaintiff's case after plaintiff's incident with the product has already occurred. The statute of repose protects against the aging of plaintiff's product long after the product was placed in the marketplace by the manufacturer. See HEAFY & KENNEDY, PRODUCT LIABILITY: WINNING STRATEGIES AND TECHNIQUES § 5.03 (1996).

2. The United States District Court for the District of Kansas noted the difference between the two statutes in *Menne v. The Celotex Corporation, et al.,* 722 F.Supp. 662, 665 (D.Kan. 1989):

   Statutes of limitation and repose may be distinguished both by their method of operation and their underlying purpose. Although the two terms have traditionally been used interchangeably, in recent years the term "statute of repose" has been used to distinguish ordinary statutes of limitation from those statutes which begin to run "at a time unrelated to the traditional accrual of the cause of action. F.McGovern, *The Variety, Policy and Constitutionality of Product Liability Statutes of Repose,* 30 Am.U.L.Rev. 579, 584 (1981). Statutes of repose run from an arbitrary event such as the date of a product's purchase, and do not use the date of injury as a factor in computing the limitation pe-

riod. Statutes of limitation, on the other had, generally "set much shorter time periods which run from the time the cause of action accrues." *Wayne v. Tennessee Valley Authority,* 730 F.2d 392, 401-402 (5th Cir. 1984), *cert. denied,* 469 U.S. 1159, 83 L.Ed.2d 922, 105 S.Ct. 908 (1985) (*citing* McGovern). *Id.*

Warranty Limitations, Disclaimers, and Exclusions

The UCC restricts the manner and extent to which express and implied warranties may be excluded, modified, or otherwise limited.

UCC 2-316. Exclusion or modification of warranties.

(1) Words or conduct relevant to the creation of an express warranty and words or conduct tending to negate or limit warranty shall be construed wherever reasonable as consistent with each other; but subject to the provisions of this article on parol or extrinsic evidence, negation or limitation is inoperative to the extent that such construction is unreasonable.

(2) Subject to subsection (3) of this section, to exclude or modify the implied warranty of merchantability or any part of it, the language must mention merchantability and in case of a writing must be conspicuous, and to exclude or modify any implied warranty of fitness the exclusion must be by a writing and conspicuous. Language to exclude all implied warranties of fitness is sufficient if it states, for example, that "There are no warranties which extend beyond the description on the face hereof."

(3) Notwithstanding subsection (2) of this section:

  (A) Unless the circumstances indicate otherwise, all implied warranties are excluded by expressions like "as is", "with all faults" or other language which in common understanding calls the buyer's attention to the exclusion of warranties and makes plain that there is no implied warranty; and

  (B) When the buyer before entering into the contract has examined the goods or the sample or model as fully as he desired or has refused to examine the goods, there is no implied warranty with regard to defects which an examination ought in the circumstances to have revealed to him; and

  (C) An implied warranty can also be excluded or modified by course of dealing or course of performance or usage of trade.

(4) Remedies for breach of warranty can be limited in accordance with the provisions of this article on liquidation of damages and on contractual modification of remedy.

The *Restatement (Third)* also restricts the use of warranty disclaimers and waivers and specifically notes that such contractual exculpations do not preclude a valid product liability claim. See § 18, *Disclaimers, Limitations, Waivers, and Other Contractual Exculpations as Defenses to Products Liability Claims for Harm to Persons, Restatement (Third).*

CASE LAW

◆ **waiver and disclaimer of implied warranties**

Testo v. Russ Dunmire
Oldsmobile, Inc., 554 P.2d
349 (Wash. Ct. App. 1976).

Plaintiff purchaser of used automobile sued defendant seller Dunmire Oldsmobile seeking return of purchase price because the car was equipped with racing modifications and, therefore, not merchantable. The Washington Court of Appeals affirmed a judgment for plaintiff that was based, in part, on Dunmire's inability to effectively disclaim its warranty of merchantability.

PETRIE, Chief Judge.

* * *

We turn now to defendant's secondary argument—that if an implied warranty of merchantability did arise in the sale of this automobile, as we have declared it did, then that warranty was excluded by (1) plaintiff's inspection of the vehicle, and (b) certain contract disclaimers.

RCW 62A.2-316(3)(b) provides that:

> when the buyer before entering into the contract has examined the goods
>
> . . . as fully as he desired . . . *there is no implied warranty with regard to defects which an examination ought in the circumstances to have revealed to him; . . .* (Emphasis added.)

Although the evidence shows the plaintiff test drove the automobile and looked it over before making the purchase, nothing in the evidence would compel a finding that the defects which soon rendered the vehicle inoperable and unacceptable should have been discovered by him through normal test driving and inspection. Plaintiff was aware of the factory-installed high performance qualities of a Camaro Z-28, but it is unreasonable to require of a used-car buyer, even one with Mr. Testo's mechanical aptitude, that he be held to knowledge of substantial mechanical adaptations and modifications to accommodate extensive racing activity. We hold that the plaintiff did not waive any implied warranty of merchantability.

Defendant attempts to bring itself within the provisions of RCW 62A.2-316(2) and (3)(a), which respectively state:

(2)   Subject to subsection (3), to exclude or modify the implied warranty of merchantability or any part of it the language must mention merchantability and in case of a writing must be conspicuous,

(3)   Notwithstanding subsection (2)

(a)   unless the circumstances indicate otherwise, all implied warranties are excluded by expressions like "as is", "with all faults" or other language which in common understanding calls the buyer's attention to the exclusion of warranties and makes plain that there is no implied warranty:

* * *

The evidence establishes that before taking actual delivery, plaintiff signed 2 documents. The first, denominated "purchase order," was signed contemporaneously with payment. It contained the following provision:

> 9. ANY USED VEHICLE SOLD TO PURCHASER BY DEALER UNDER THIS ORDER IS SOLD AT THE TIME OF DELIVERY BY SELLER WITHOUT ANY GUARANTY OR WARRANTY, EXPRESSED OR IMPLIED, INCLUDING BUT NOT LIMITED TO, ANY IMPLIED WARRANTY OF MERCHANTABILITY
> . . .

After plaintiff paid his money and the used-car sales manager approved the terms of purchase, plaintiff was handed a card entitled "G W Agreement" (General Warranty Agreement). It provided for a 15 percent discount on necessary parts and labor for a period of 2 years, but otherwise the vehicle was sold "as is."

At trial, the used-car salesman who negotiated the sale was asked: "Prior to the time that the papers were signed, . . . was there a discussion . . . regarding what warrant*ee,* if any, was to be carried on this car?" He responded: "Not until actually the sale was closed." Plaintiff and his wife both testified that defendant's used-car salesman did not mention warranties until after they had paid the purchase price and then there was only a momentary reference to the 15 percent discount.

In disposing of this issue of the effectiveness of defendant's attempted disclaimer, we start with the established rule that printed disclaimers of warranties in form contracts are not favored by the courts and should be strictly construed against the seller. [Citation omitted.] Although a general disclaimer clause may negate implied warranties if there is a negotiated contract between a commercial seller and a commercial buyer, it is not appropriate to a consumer sale. This is so unless it is shown that the so-called disclaimer was *"explicitly negotiated between buyer and seller and set forth with particularity showing the particular qualities and characteristics of fitness which are being waived."* (Emphasis added.)

There is no evidence that prior to sale the parties discussed, let alone negotiated, the issue of disclaimers. The only reference to the subject was limited to the provision of the G W Agreement which *granted* a 15 percent discount. The purported effect of the disclaimer—to *take away* all warranties and limit any potential remedies—was never brought to the plaintiff's attention. We cannot say, therefore, that plaintiff and defendant "explicitly negotiated" the terms of the disclaimer clauses.

Likewise, it cannot be said that the buyer understood "with particularity" what defects and conditions he was supposedly waiving when it is clear that he did not even know the true character of the commodity he was purchasing.

The rule enunciated in *Berg* has not been altered by adoption of the Code, *see Dobias v. Western Farmers Ass'n,* 6 Wash.App. 194, 491 P.2d 1346 (1971); *Schroeder v. Fageol Motors Inc.,* 86 Wash.2d 256, 544 P.2d 20 (1975), and it applies with equal force to the sale of used as well as new automobiles.

Therefore, we hold that the attempted disclaimers were insufficient to relieve Russ Dunmire Oldsmobile, Inc., of liability for breach of implied warranty of merchantability.

Case Notes: Limitations and Disclaimers on Warranties

1. Generally, courts will not allow the exclusion of express or implied warranties to be unconscionable. In *Anderson v. Chrysler Corp.,* 403 S.E.2d 189, 195-96 (W.Va. 1991), Chrysler argued that its automobile purchaser, Anderson, could not recover for breach of an express warranty because damage caused by the fire at issue in the case was expressly excluded. The warranty provided that "[r]epairs required as a result of failure to properly care or maintain this vehicle, fire, accident, abuse or negligence" were not covered. The West Virginia Supreme Court rejected Chrysler's argument and held that "the warranty could not be so easily eviscerated." *Id.* at 196. In so holding, the Court cited the following similar Missouri decision:

   Laws governing warranties, express and implied, should be so administered as to be fair to all parties concerned. Such warranties should be meaningful. To rule in this case as defendants wish us to do, would be to leave the buyers of new automobiles subject to the delusion of warranties and yet without real protection. Consumers keep the automobile industry solvent and prosperous. To rule as defendants ask would not promote the welfare of buyers, dealers, or manufacturers. *Id., citing Jacobson v. Broadway Motors, Inc.,* 430 S.W.2d 602, 607 (Mo. Ct. App. 1968).

2. Individual states are responsible for their own adoption of the U.C.C. In some states, certain provisions of the UCC may vary, including the sections that limit and disclaim express and implied warranties. In Missouri, for example, the state legislature added subsection 5 to its § 2-316 regarding the merchantability or fitness of livestock. This subsection disclaims warranty liability as follows:

   A seller is not liable for damages resulting from the lack of merchantability or fitness for a particular purpose of livestock he sells if the contract for the sale of the livestock does not contain a written statement as to a warranty of merchantability or fitness for a particular purpose of livestock. Mo. Rev. Stat. § 400.2-316.

3. The *Restatement (Third)* also addresses the effect of contractual defenses on a product liability claim under either tort or warranty principles, stating that similar limiting terms in a contract would not allow a defendant to avoid liability in a product liability claim. See Comment a to § 18 *Restatement (Third)*.

RESPONSES

Compliance with Safety Regulations

§ 4 Noncompliance and Compliance with Product Safety Statutes or Regulations.

In connection with liability for defective design or inadequate instructions or warnings;

(a) a product's noncompliance with an applicable product safety statute or administrative regulation renders the product defective with respect to the risks sought to be reduced by the statute or regulation; and

(b) a product's compliance with an applicable product safety statute or administrative regulation is properly considered in determining whether the product is defective with respect to the risks sought to be reduced by the statute or regulation, but such compliance does not preclude as a matter of law a finding of product defect. *Restatement (Third) of Torts: Product Liability* at § 4.

 CASE LAW

◆ **statutory violation as evidence of defendant's negligence per se**

Lowe v. General Motors Corp., 624 F.2d 1373 (5th Cir. 1980).

Lowe and Fulford (in a companion case) brought wrongful death suits against automobile manufacturer alleging that the steering mechanism in the 1971 Chevrolet Impala unexpectedly locked causing the decedents' accident. Plaintiffs also alleged that defendant General Motors had violated the Motor Vehicle Safety Act of 1966, 15 U.S.C. § 1402 (1974), which established negligence per se against General Motors.

BROWN, Circuit Judge.

* * *

III. The Motor Vehicle Safety Act—A Private Right Of Action Or Evidence Of Negligence Or Negligence Per Se?

We conclude the District Court misinterpreted or misapplied the Supreme Court decision in *Cort v. Ash* when it used that decision as the basis for granting defendant's motion for a new trial. In *Cort v. Ash,* jurisdiction over the plaintiff's claim was founded on 28 U.S.C.A. § 1331 as a claim arising under a Federal statute. The Federal statute under which the plaintiff alleged his claim arose was 18 U.S.C.A. § 610, a criminal statute which provided no civil remedy. The second count of the complaint presented a state law claim, but this was independent of the claim under § 610. Jurisdiction over this state claim was pendent to that of the Federal claim but was not based on § 610 directly. Thus, the very existence of the case in Federal Court depended on the theory of a private right of action which, the plaintiff asserted, arose under § 610.

The case before us today presents quite a different situation, procedurally and substantively. It was brought in Alabama State Court as an action based on the Alabama Wrongful Death Statute. It was removed to Federal Court because diversity jurisdiction existed. 28 U.S.C.A. § 1332 (West 1966 and West Supp. 1980). Fulford and Lowe never asserted Federal jurisdiction based on § 1331, arising under any Federal statute. Although the MVSA and its application might have significance or bearing on the case, the suit was not to enforce the MVSA, nor would an application one way or the other necessarily have had decisive consequences.

Fulford and Lowe made it quite clear that the only relationship the alleged violation of the MVSA had to this case was simply as evidence of GM's negligence. The concept that violation of a criminal or penal statute can be evidence of negligence in a civil action is not new to tort law. "[I]t is said that the reasonable man would obey the criminal law, and that one who does not is not acting as a reasonable man, and therefore must be negligent." W. Prosser, Law of Torts 191 (4th ed. 1971) (Footnote omitted.)

> "Motor vehicle safety" is defined in the MVSA as
>
> the performance of motor vehicles or motor vehicle equipment in such a manner that the public is protected against *unreasonable* risk of accidents occurring as a result of the design, construction or performance of motor vehicles and is also protected against *unreasonable* risk of death or injury to persons in the event accidents do occur, and includes nonoperational safety of such vehicles.

15 U.S.C.A. § 1391(1) (1974) (emphasis added.) Thus, the Act creates a duty upon the automobile manufacturer to construct his product to be "reasonably" safe. Under § 1402, it was also "reasonable" for the manufacturer promptly to notify the owners of his product of any safety-related defect and how to remedy it.

This Court has often held that violation of a Federal law or regulation can be evidence of negligence, and even evidence of negligence per se. [Citations omitted.]

The mere fact that the law which evidences negligence is Federal while the negligence action itself is brought under State common law does not mean that the state law claim metamorphoses into a private right of action under Federal regulatory law. In *Nevels v. Ford Motor Company,* 439 F.2d 251 (5th Cir. 1971), a negligence action under Georgia law, we held that violation of § 1402 "was relevant [evidence] not only with respect to the statutory duty of Ford, but also in regard to plaintiff's contention of negligent assembly in the manufacturing process." *Id.* at 258. Once this evidence was submitted to support the plaintiff's assertion of negligence, the issue should go to the jury. *Id.* [Citation omitted.]

Nevels, supra, held that violation of the MVSA was evidence of negligence, but did not specifically hold that it was evidence of negligence per se. However, that case relied on Georgia law to determine negligence. "In this diversity action, we are bound by Georgia law with respect to the measure of care owed by the manufacturer to a third person." 439 F.2d at 255.

Turning to Alabama law in the diversity case before us, we find that it states that violation of a statute is negligence per se if the following criteria are met:

(1) The trial judge must determine as a matter of law that the statute was enacted to protect a class of persons which includes the litigant seeking to assert the statute.

* * *

(2) The trial judge must find the injury was of a type contemplated by the statute.

* * *

(3) The party charged with negligent conduct must have violated the statute.

* * *

(4) The jury must find the statutory violation proximately caused the injury. *Fox v. Bartholf,* 374 So.2d 294, 295-96 (Ala. 1979) (Citations omitted).

We conclude that under *Fox* violation of the MVSA is evidence of negligence per se in Alabama. The purpose of the MVSA "is to reduce traffic accidents and deaths and injuries to persons resulting from traffic accidents," by "establish[ing] motor vehicle safety standards for motor vehicles. . . ." 15 U.S.C.A. § 1381. Thus, it is clear that Mrs. Fulford, as the driver, and Mrs. Lowe, as the passenger, of the automobile whose manufacturer was subject to the Act, were, as a matter of law, within the class of persons protected. And the trial judge so held in his order granting a new trial, even if it was with respect to the first criterion of *Cort v. Ash.* See note 2, *supra.* The trial judge also stated that "[t]he Act was clearly designed to reduce traffic accidents and the resulting deaths and injuries." Therefore, the danger which caused their deaths was allegedly the type the Act guards against.

Whether the statute was violated and whether that violation proximately caused the injury were questions of fact for the jury. After the first trial, the District Court judge gave proper instructions to the jury on these two issues and in their general verdict the jury implicitly answered both questions in the affirmative. Thus, all four of the *Fox* criteria for finding negligence per se were satisfied.

We find another indication, within the Act itself, that its violation is evidence of negligence per se in a tort action. 15 U.S.C.A. § 1391(2) states:

> "Motor vehicle safety standards" means a minimum standard for motor vehicle performance, or motor vehicle equipment performance, which is practicable, which meets the need for motor vehicle safety and which provides objective criteria.

To say that violation of a statute is negligence per se is to say that "an unexcused violation is conclusive on the issue of negligence." *Prosser, supra* at 200. If the statute in question creates a minimum standard of care, as it does here, then an unexcused violation, an act done with less than minimum care, would have to be negligence.

We conclude that the jury charges in the first trial on violation of the MVSA as evidence of negligence per se were correct, and that *Cort v. Ash* is not at all at issue in this case. Since evidence of GM's violation of the MVSA was relevant and properly admissible, the verdict of the second trial, in which no evidence of this violation was admitted, cannot stand. We believe the proper action to take is to reverse the order granting a new trial and remand to reinstate the jury verdict of the first trial, at least to the issue of negligence.

Case Notes: Compliance with Statutes and Safety Regulations

1. The *Restatement (Third)* has taken the controversial position that evidence of a defendant manufacturer's noncompliance with safety statutes or regulations is evidence of the defect in the product. In fact, the *Restatement (Third)*'s statement on the issue is conclusory in that such noncompliance "renders the product defective." § 4 (a) *Restatement (Third).* In some circumstances, however, the general rule does not apply, such as after repeal of a regulation or when a regulation makes suggestions and not requirements. See Comment d to § 4 *Restatement (Third).*

2. Compliance with safety statutes and administrative regulations are distinct from the decision that a matter is preempted by federal law. The *Restatement (Third)* made clear this difference in Comment e:

> Comment e. Compliance with Product Safety Statute or Administrative Regulation. * * * When a court concludes that a defendant is not liable by reason of having complied with a safety design or warnings statute or regulation, it is deciding that the product in question is not defective as a matter of the law of that state. The safety statute or regulation may be a federal provision, but the decision to give it determinative effect is a state-law determination. In contrast, in federal preemption, the court decides as a matter of federal law that the relevant federal statute or regulation reflects, expressly or impliedly, the intent of Congress to displace state law, include state tort law, with the federal statute or regulation. The question of preemption is thus a question of federal law, and a determination that there is preemption nullifies otherwise operational state law. Comment e to § 4 of the *Restatement (Third).*

3. Not all agree that with the *Restatement (Third)* regulatory noncompliance is conclusive as to the defective nature of a product. See Green, *Statutory Compliance and Tort Liability: Examining The Strongest Case*, 30 Univ. of Michigan J. of L.Ref. 461 (1997); Schwartz, *Regulatory Standards and Products Liability: Striking the Right Balance Between the Two*, 30 Univ. of Michigan J. of L.Ref. 431 (1997); D'Angelo, *Effect of Compliance or Noncompliance with Applicable Governmental Product Safety Regulations on a Determination of Product Defect*, 36 So.Tex.L.Rev. 453 (1995); Kahn, *Regulation and Simple Arithmetic: Shifting the Perspective on Tort Reform*, 72 N.C.L. Rev. 1129 (1994).

4. Does compliance with a safety statute or regulation conversely prove the absence of fault or liability on the part of the defendant manufacturer? Is a defendant manufacturer's noncompliance conclusive on the issue of fault or liability? What standards govern compliance?

Federal Preemption

A plaintiff's product liability claim in state court may be preempted by federal law if the federal statute expressly or impliedly provides that it applies exclusively to the product at issue. The federal statute or its legislative history may state verbatim that it is intended to apply in place of any other laws, including any conflicting laws from state legislatures. Alternatively, the federal statute will be given application in place of any conflicting state laws from state legislatures. In such instances, a plaintiff's state law product liability claim is governed by the applicable federal statute and plaintiff's claim, if any, must be brought in federal court.

 CASE LAW

♦ **principles of federal preemption**

Medtronic, Inc. v. Lora Lohr,
et al., 518 U.S. 470 (1996).

Plaintiff recipient of pacemaker brought product liability claims in state court asserting negligence and strict liability against the defendant manufacturer. Medtronic removed to federal court and thereafter subsequently moved for summary judgment asserting federal preemption based upon 21 U.S.C. § 510(k), the Medical Device Amendment under the Food, Drug & Cosmetic Act.

STEVENS, Justice.

* * *

As in *Cipollone v. Liggett Group, Inc.*, 505 U.S. 504, 112 S.Ct. 2608, 120 L.Ed.2d 407 (1992), we are presented with the task of interpreting a statutory provision that expressly preempts state law. While the preemptive language of § 360k(a) means that we need not go beyond that language to determine whether Congress intended the MDA to preempt at least some state law [citation omitted], we must nonetheless "identify the domain expressly preempted" by that language. Although our analysis of the scope of the preemption statute must begin with its text [citation omitted], our interpretation of that language does not occur in a contextual vacuum. Rather, that interpretation is informed by two presumptions about the nature of preemption.

First, because the States are independent sovereigns in our federal system, we have long presumed that Congress does not cavalierly preempt state-law causes of action. In all preemption cases, and particularly in those in which Congress has "legislated . . . in a field which the States have traditionally occupied," *Rice v. Santa Fe Elevator Corp.*, 331 U.S. 218, 230, 67 S.Ct. 1146, 1152, 91 L.Ed. 1447 (1947), we "start with the assumption that the historic police powers of the States were not to be superseded by the Federal Act unless that was the clear and manifest purpose of Congress." Id. [Citations omitted.] Although dissenting Justices have argued that this assumption should apply only to the question whether Congress intended any preemption at all, as opposed to questions concerning the scope of its intended invalidation of state law, we used a "presumption against the preemption of state police power regulations" to support a narrow interpretation of such an express command in *Cipollone*. [Citation omitted.] That approach is consistent with both federalism concerns and the historic primacy of state regulation of matters of health and safety.

Second, our analysis of the scope of the statute's preemption is guided by our oft-repeated comment [citation omitted], that "[t]he purpose of Congress is the ultimate touchstone" in every preemption case. See, e.g., *Cipollone*, 505 U.S., at 516, 112 S.Ct., at 2617; *Gade*, 505 U.S., at 96, 112 S.Ct., at 2381-2382; *Malone v. White Motor Corp.*, 435 U.S. 497, 504, 98 S.Ct. 1185, 1190, 55 L.Ed.2d 443 (1978). As a result, any understanding of the scope of a preemption statute must rest primarily on "a fair understanding of congressional purpose." *Cipollone*, 505 U.S., at 530, n. 27, 112 S.Ct., at 2624, n. 27. Congress' intent, of course, primarily is discerned from the language of the preemption statute and the "statutory framework" surrounding it. [Citation omitted.] Also relevant, however, is the "structure and purpose of the statute as a whole," [citation omitted] as revealed not only in the text, but through the reviewing court's reasoned understanding of the way in which Congress intended the statute and its surrounding regulatory scheme to affect business, consumers, and the law.

With these considerations in mind, we turn first to a consideration of petitioner Medtronic's claim that the Court of Appeals should have found the entire action preempted and then to the merits of the Lohrs' cross-petition.

IV

In its petition, Medtronic argues that the Court of Appeals erred by concluding that the Lohrs' claims alleging negligent design were not preempted by 21 U.S.C. § 360k(a). That section provides that "no State or political subdivision of a State may establish or continue in effect with respect to a device intended for human use any requirement (1) which is different from, or in addition to, any requirement applicable under this chapter to the de-

vice, and (2) which relates to the safety or effectiveness of the device or to any other matter included in a requirement applicable to the device under this chapter." Medtronic suggests that any common-law cause of action is a "requirement" which alters incentives and imposes duties "different from, or in addition to," the generic federal standards that the FDA has promulgated in response to mandates under the MDA. In essence, the company argues that the plain language of the statute preempts any and all common-law claims brought by an injured plaintiff against a manufacturer of medical devices.

Medtronic's argument is not only unpersuasive, it is implausible. Under Medtronic's view of the statute, Congress effectively precluded state courts from affording state consumers any protection from injuries resulting from a defective medical device. Moreover, because there is no explicit private cause of action against manufacturers contained in the MDA, and no suggestion that the Act created an implied private right of action, Congress would have barred most, if not all, relief for persons injured by defective medical devices. [Footnote omitted.] Medtronic's construction of § 360k would therefore have the perverse effect of granting complete immunity from design defect liability to an entire industry that, in the judgment of Congress, needed more stringent regulation in order "to provide for the safety and effectiveness of medical devices intended for human use," 90 Stat. 539 (preamble to Act). It is, to say the least, "difficult to believe that Congress would, without comment, remove all means of judicial recourse for those injured by illegal conduct," *Silkwood v. Kerr-McGee Corp.*, 464 U.S. 238, 251, 104 S.Ct. 615, 623, 78 L.Ed.2d 443 (1984), and it would take language much plainer than the text of § 360k to convince us that Congress intended that result.

Furthermore, if Congress intended to preclude all common-law causes of action, it chose a singularly odd word with which to do it. The statute would have achieved an identical result, for instance, if it had precluded any "remedy" under state law relating to medical devices. "Requirement" appears to presume that the State is imposing a specific duty upon the manufacturer, and although we have on prior occasions concluded that a statute preempting certain state "requirements" could also preempt common-law damages claims [citation omitted], that statute did not sweep nearly as broadly as Medtronic would have us believe that this statute does.

The preemptive statute in *Cipollone* [footnote omitted] was targeted at a limited set of state requirements—those "based on smoking and health"—and then only at a limited subset of the possible applications of those requirements—those involving the "advertising or promotion of any cigarettes the packages of which are labeled in conformity with the provisions of" the federal statute. [Citation omitted.] In that context, giving the term "requirement" its widest reasonable meaning did not have nearly the preemptive scope nor the effect on potential remedies that Medtronic's broad reading of the term would have in this suit. The Court in *Cipollone* held that the petitioner in that case was able to maintain some common-law actions using theories of the case that did not run afoul of the preemption statute. [Citation omitted.] Here, however, Medtronic's sweeping interpretation of the statute would require far greater interference with state legal remedies, producing a serious intrusion into state sovereignty while simultaneously wiping out the possibility of remedy for the Lohrs' alleged injuries. [Footnote omitted.] Given the ambiguities in the statute and the scope of the preclusion that would occur otherwise, we cannot accept Medtronic's argument that by using the term "requirement," Congress clearly signaled its intent to deprive States of any role in protecting consumers from the dangers inherent in many medical devices.

* * *

An examination of the basic purpose of the legislation as well as its history entirely supports our rejection of Medtronic's extreme position. The MDA was enacted "to provide for the safety and effectiveness of medical devices intended for human use." 90 Stat. 539. Medtronic asserts that the Act was also intended, however, to "protect innovations in device technology from being 'stifled by unnecessary restrictions,'" Brief for Petitioner in No. 95-754, p. 3 (citing H.R. Rep. No. 94-853, at 12), and that this interest extended to the preemption of common-law claims. While the Act certainly reflects some of these concerns, [footnote omitted] the legislative history indicates that any fears regarding regulatory burdens were related more to the risk of additional federal and state regulation rather than the danger of pre-existing duties under common law. [Citation omitted.] Indeed, nowhere in the materials relating to the Act's history have we discovered a reference to a fear that product liability actions would hamper the development of medical devices. To the extent that Congress was concerned about protecting the industry, that intent was manifested primarily

through fewer substantive requirements under the Act, not the preemption provision; furthermore, any such concern was far outweighed by concerns about the primary issue motivating the MDA's enactment: the safety of those who use medical devices.

The legislative history also confirms our understanding that § 360(k) simply was not intended to preempt most, let alone all, general common-law duties enforced by damages actions. There is, to the best of our knowledge, nothing in the hearings, the Committee Reports, or the debates suggesting that any proponent of the legislation intended a sweeping preemption of traditional common-law remedies against manufacturers and distributors of defective devices. If Congress intended such a result, its failure even to hint at it is spectacularly odd, particularly since Members of both Houses were acutely aware of ongoing product liability litigation. [Footnote omitted.] Along with the less-than-precise language of § 360k(a), that silence surely indicates that at least some common-law claims against medical device manufacturers may be maintained after the enactment of the MDA.

V

Medtronic asserts several specific reasons why, even if § 360k does not preempt all common-law claims, it at least preempts the Lohrs' claims in this suit. In contrast, the Lohrs argue that their entire complaint should survive a reasonable evaluation of the preemptive scope of § 360k(a). First, the Lohrs claim that the Court of Appeals correctly held that their negligent design claims were not preempted because the § 510(k) premarket notification process imposes no "requirement" on the design of Medtronic's pacemaker. Second, they suggest that even if the FDA's general rules regulating manufacturing practices and labeling are "requirements" that preempt different state requirements, § 360k(a) does not preempt state rules that merely duplicate some or all of those federal requirements. Finally, they argue that because the State's general rules imposing common-law duties upon Medtronic do not impose a requirement "with respect to a device," they do not conflict with the FDA's general rules relating to manufacturing and labeling and are therefore not preempted.

Design Claim

The Court of Appeals concluded that the Lohrs' defective design claims were not preempted because the requirements with which the company had to comply were not sufficiently concrete to constitute a preempting federal requirement. Medtronic counters by pointing to the FDA's determination that Model 4011 is "substantially equivalent" to an earlier device as well as the agency's continuing authority to exclude the device from the market if its design is changed. These factors, Medtronic argues, amount to a specific, federally enforceable design requirement that cannot be affected by state-law pressures such as those imposed on manufacturers subject to product liability suits.

The company's defense exaggerates the importance of the § 510(k) process and the FDA letter to the company regarding the pacemaker's substantial equivalence to a grandfathered device. As the court below noted, "[t]he 510(k) process is focused on equivalence, not safety." 56 F.3d, at 1348. As a result, "substantial equivalence determinations provide little protection to the public. These determinations simply compare a post-1976 device to a pre-1976 device to ascertain whether the later device is no more dangerous and no less effective than the earlier device. If the earlier device poses a severe risk or is ineffective, then the later device may also be risky or ineffective." *Adler*, 43 Food Drug Cosm. L. J., at 516. The design of the Model 4011, as with the design of pre-1976 and other "substantially equivalent" devices, has never been formally reviewed under the MDA for safety or efficacy.

* * *

Thus, even though the FDA may well examine § 510(k) applications for Class III devices (as it examines the entire medical device industry) with a concern for the safety and effectiveness of the device, see Brief for Petitioner in No. 95-754, at 22-26, it did not "require" Medtronics' pacemaker to take any particular form for any particular reason; the agency simply allowed the pacemaker, as a device substantially equivalent to one that existed before 1976, to be marketed without running the gauntlet of the PMA process. In providing for this exemption to PMA review, Congress intended merely to give manufacturers the freedom to compete, to a limited degree, with and on the same terms as manufacturers of medical devices that existed prior to 1976. [Footnote omitted.] There is no suggestion in either the statutory scheme or the legislative history that the § 510(k) exemption process was intended to do anything other than maintain the status quo with re-

spect to the marketing of existing medical devices and their substantial equivalents. That status quo included the possibility that the manufacturer of the device would have to defend itself against state-law claims of negligent design. Given this background behind the "substantial equivalence" exemption, the fact that "[t]he purpose of Congress is the ultimate touchstone" in every preemption case, 505 U.S., at 516, 112 S.Ct., at 2617 (internal quotation marks and citations omitted), and the presumption against preemption, the Court of Appeals properly concluded that the "substantial equivalence" provision did not preempt the Lohrs' design claims.

Identity of Requirements Claims

The Lohrs next suggest that even if "requirements" exist with respect to the manufacturing and labeling of the pacemaker, and even if we can also consider state law to impose a "requirement" under the Act, the state requirement is not preempted unless it is "different from, or in addition to," the federal requirement. § 360k(a)(1). Although the precise contours of their theory of recovery have not yet been defined (the preemption issue was decided on the basis of the pleadings), it is clear that the Lohrs' allegations may include claims that Medtronic has, to the extent that they exist, violated FDA regulations. At least these claims, they suggest, can be maintained without being preempted by § 360k, and we agree.

Nothing in § 360k denies Florida the right to provide a traditional damages remedy for violations of common-law duties when those duties parallel federal requirements. Even if it may be necessary as a matter of Florida law to prove that those violations were the result of negligent conduct, or that they created an unreasonable hazard for users of the product, such additional elements of the state-law cause of action would make the state requirements narrower, not broader, than the federal requirement. While such a narrower requirement might be "different from" the federal rules in a literal sense, such a difference would surely provide a strange reason for finding preemption of a state rule insofar as it duplicates the federal rule. The presence of a damages remedy does not amount to the additional or different "requirement" that is necessary under the statute; rather, it merely provides another reason for manufacturers to comply with identical existing "requirements" under federal law.

The FDA regulations interpreting the scope of § 360k's preemptive effect support the Lohrs' view, and our interpretation of the preemption statute is substantially informed by those regulations. The different views expressed by the Courts of Appeals regarding the appropriate scope of federal preemption under § 360k demonstrate that the language of that section is not entirely clear. In addition, Congress has given the FDA a unique role in determining the scope of § 360k's preemptive effect. Unlike the statute construed in *Cipollone* for instance, preemption under the MDA does not arise directly as a result of the enactment of the statute; rather, in most cases a state law will be preempted only to the extent that the FDA has promulgated a relevant federal "requirement." Because the FDA is the federal agency to which Congress has delegated its authority to implement the provisions of the Act [footnote omitted], the agency is uniquely qualified to determine whether a particular form of state law "stands as an obstacle to the accomplishment and execution of the full purposes and objectives of Congress," *Hines v. Davidowitz*, 312 U.S. 52, 67, 61 S.Ct. 399, 404, 85 L.Ed. 581 (1941), and, therefore, whether it should be preempted.

The regulations promulgated by the FDA expressly support the conclusion that § 360k "does not preempt State or local requirements that are equal to, or substantially identical to, requirements imposed by or under the act." 21 CFR § 808.1(d)(2) (1995); see also § 808.5(b)(1)(i). [Footnote omitted.] At this early stage in the litigation, there was no reason for the Court of Appeals to preclude altogether the Lohrs' manufacturing and labeling claims to the extent that they rest on claims that Medtronic negligently failed to comply with duties "equal to, or substantially identical to, requirements imposed" under federal law.

Manufacturing and Labeling Claims

Finally, the Lohrs suggest that with respect to the manufacturing and labeling claims, the Court of Appeals should have rejected Medtronic's preemption defense in full. The Court of Appeals believed that these claims would interfere with the consistent application of general federal regulations governing the labeling and manufacture of all medical devices, and therefore concluded that the claims were preempted altogether.

The requirements identified by the Court of Appeals include labeling regulations that require manufacturers of every medical device, with a few limited exceptions, to include with the device a label containing "information for use, . . . and any relevant hazards, contraindications, side effects, and precautions." 21 CFR §§ 801.109(b) and (c) (1995). Similarly, manufacturers are required to comply with "Good Manufacturing Practices," or "GMP's," which are set forth in 32 sections and less than 10 pages in the Code of Federal Regulations. [Footnote omitted.] In certain circumstances, the Court of Appeals recognized, the FDA will enforce these general requirements against manufacturers that violate them. See 56 F.3d, at 1350-1351.

While admitting that these requirements exist, the Lohrs suggest that their general nature simply does not preempt claims alleging that the manufacturer failed to comply with other duties under state common law. In support of their claim, they note that § 360k(a)(1) expressly states that a federal requirement must be "applicable to the device" in question before it has any preemptive effect. Because the labeling and manufacturing requirements are applicable to a host of different devices, they argue that they do not satisfy this condition. They further argue that because only state requirements "with respect to a device" may be preempted, and then only if the requirement "relates to the safety or effectiveness of the device or to any other matter included in a requirement applicable to the device," § 360k(a) mandates pre-emption only where there is a conflict between a specific state requirement and a federal requirement "applicable to" the same device.

The Lohrs' theory is supported by the FDA regulations, which provide that state requirements are preempted "only" when the FDA has established "specific counterpart regulations or . . . other specific requirements applicable to a particular device." 21 CFR § 808.1(d) (1995). They further note that the statute is not intended to preempt "State or local requirements of general applicability where the purpose of the requirement relates either to other products in addition to devices . . . or to unfair trade practices in which the requirements are not limited to devices." § 808.1(d)(1). The regulations specifically provide, as examples of permissible general requirements, that general electrical codes and the Uniform Commercial Code warranty of fitness would not be preempted. See ibid. The regulations even go so far as to state that § 360k(a) generally "does not preempt a state or local requirement prohibiting the manufacture of adulterated or misbranded devices" unless "such a prohibition has the effect of establishing a substantive requirement for a specific device." § 808.1(d) (6)(ii). Furthermore, under its authority to grant exemptions to the preemptive effect of § 360k(a), the FDA has never granted, nor, to the best of our knowledge, even been asked to consider granting, an exemption for a state law of general applicability; all 22 existing exemptions apply to excruciatingly specific state requirements regarding the sale of hearing aids. See §§ 808.53-808.101.

Although we do not believe that this statutory and regulatory language necessarily precludes "general" federal requirements from ever preempting state requirements, or "general" state requirements from ever being preempted, . . . it is impossible to ignore its overarching concern that preemption occur only where a particular state requirement threatens to interfere with a specific federal interest. State requirements must be "with respect to" medical devices and "different from, or in addition to," federal requirements. State requirements must also relate "to the safety or effectiveness of the device or to any other matter included in a requirement applicable to the device," and the regulations provide that state requirements of "general applicability" are not preempted except where they have "the effect of establishing a substantive requirement for a specific device." Moreover, federal requirements must be "applicable to the device" in question, and, according to the regulations, preempt state law only if they are "specific counterpart regulations" or "specific" to a "particular device." The statute and regulations, therefore, require a careful comparison between the allegedly preempting federal requirement and the allegedly preempted state requirement to determine whether they fall within the intended preemptive scope of the statute and regulations. [Footnote omitted.]

Such a comparison mandates a conclusion that the Lohrs' common-law claims are not preempted by the federal labeling and manufacturing requirements. The generality of those requirements make this quite un-

like a case in which the Federal Government has weighed the competing interests relevant to the particular requirement in question, reached an unambiguous conclusion about how those competing considerations should be resolved in a particular case or set of cases, and implemented that conclusion via a specific mandate on manufacturers or producers. Rather, the federal requirements reflect important but entirely generic concerns about device regulation generally, not the sort of concerns regarding a specific device or field of device regulation that the statute or regulations were designed to protect from potentially contradictory state requirements.

Similarly, the general state common-law requirements in this suit were not specifically developed "with respect to" medical devices. Accordingly, they are not the kinds of requirements that Congress and the FDA feared would impede the ability of federal regulators to implement and enforce specific federal requirements. The legal duty that is the predicate for the Lohrs' negligent manufacturing claim is the general duty of every manufacturer to use due care to avoid foreseeable dangers in its products. Similarly, the predicate for the failure to warn claim is the general duty to inform users and purchasers of potentially dangerous items of the risks involved in their use. These general obligations are no more a threat to federal requirements than would be a state-law duty to comply with local fire prevention regulations and zoning codes, or to use due care in the training and supervision of a work force. These state requirements therefore escape preemption, not because the source of the duty is a judge-made common-law rule, but rather because their generality leaves them outside the category of requirements that § 360k envisioned to be "with respect to" specific devices such as pacemakers. As a result, none of the Lohrs' claims based on allegedly defective manufacturing or labeling are preempted by the MDA.

Case Notes: Federal Preemption

1. Preemption is a "[d]octrine adopted by U.S. Supreme Court holding that certain matters are of such a national, as opposed to local, character that federal laws pre-empt or take precedence over state laws. As such, a state may not pass a law inconsistent with the federal law" BLACK'S LAW DICTIONARY, 1060 5th Ed. [1979]).

2. Five federal statutes currently preempt specific product liability claims that plaintiffs may pursue in state court. These five federal statutes include the following:
   - National Traffic & Motor Vehicle Safety Act, 15 U.S.C. § 1392(d) (motor vehicle safety, particularly airbags and restraint systems);
   - Federal Boat Safety Act, 46 U.S.C. § 4306 (boat safety);
   - Federal Insecticide, Fungicide & Rodenticide (FIFRA), 7 U.S.C. § 136v(b) (environmental pesticide control);
   - 1976 Medical Device Amendment to the Federal Food, Drug & Cosmetic Act, 21 U.S.C. § 360k(a) (medical devices);
   - Cigarette Labelling and Advertising Act, 15 U.S.C. § 1334 (cigarette labelling).

3. Federal circuit courts continue to wrestle with preemption issues regarding each of the five previously named federal statutes. Each circuit has its own prevailing view as to whether these federal statutes preempt a plaintiff's product liability claim in state court. See *e.g., Gracia v. Volvo Europa Truck, N.V.,* 112 F.2d 291 (7th Cir. 1997) (express preemption found under National Traffic & Motor Vehicle Safety Act); *Geier v. American Honda Motor Company, Inc.,* 166 F.3d 1236 (D.C.Cir. 1999) (implied preemption under same); *Buzzard v. Roadrunner Trucking, Inc.,* 966 F.21d 777 (3rd Cir. 1992) (no preemption under same); *Carstensen v. Brunswick Corp.,* 49 F.3d 430 (8th Cir. 1995) (preemption found regarding propeller guard under Federal Boat Safety Act); *MacDonald v. Monsanto Company,* 27 F.3d 1021 (5th Cir. 1994) (preemption found under FIFRA); *Worm v. American Cyanamid Company,* 5 F.3d 744 (4th Cir. 1993) (preemption found under same); *Ferebee v. Chevron Chemical Company,* 736 F.2d 1529 (D.C.Cir. 1984) (no preemption found under FIFRA).

4. The two leading U.S. Supreme Court cases on the preemption issue as it applies to product liability cases are *Cipollone v. Liggett Group, Inc.,* 505 U.S. 504 (1992); *Medtronic, Inc. v. Lohr,* 518 U.S. 470 (1996). See also Comment, *The Impact of Cipollone and Federal Preemption on State Common-Law Tort Actions in Missouri's State and Federal Courts,* 64 UMKC L. Rev. 357 (Winter 1995); Comment, *Cipollone & Myrick: Deflating The Airbag Preemption Defense,* 30 Indiana L. Rev. 827 (1997); Lichtenstein & Ferrera, *Airbag Products Liability Litigation: State Common Law Tort Claims Are Not Automatically Preempted By Federal Legislation,* 45 Cleveland State L. Rev. 1 (1997); Lebow, *Federalism and Federal Product Liability Reform: A Warning Not Heeded,* 64 Tennessee L. Rev. 665 (1997).

5. Why should a plaintiff's strict liability claims be excluded in favor of the federal statute? What purpose does policy serve? Are plaintiffs whose claims are prone to preemption prejudiced by such a policy? Are their recoveries limited or enhanced?

 CASE PROBLEM

Piggly Wiggly, LLC

Assume the same facts described in Chapter 2, Negligence, for Piggly Wiggly, L.L.C.

1. Assume you represent Piggly Wiggly, L.L.C. ("Piggly") in defense of the product liability suit brought by Sammy Hoagge. Mr. Hoagge has alleged a strict liability theory, all express and implied warranty theories, and negligence against Piggly in his personal injury lawsuit. As damages, he claims personal injury and lost wages. What defenses are available to Piggly? Which of these are affirmative defenses? What additional facts do you need to determine whether other affirmative defenses are applicable? Draft an answer on behalf of Piggly and include all affirmative defenses that are applicable based upon the facts given in Chapter 2, Negligence.

2. Prepare 15 interrogatories, 15 requests for production, and 15 requests for admissions on behalf of defendant Piggly. What information do you need to assist in your liability analysis? What information do you need to prepare an analysis of Mr. Hoagge's damages? What is the best information that can be obtained from this written discovery? Why would you submit it now? What information is best obtained later during depositions, from third parties, or from expert witnesses? Who should you depose? Who should you interview?

3. Based upon the facts described in Chapter 2, Negligence, what information distinguishes Mr. Hoagge's misuse from his assumption of the risk? Which affirmative defense is applicable here? What additional information do you need to make this decision? Do either of these theories provide a viable defense? Which affirmative defense should be pleaded in Piggly's Answer?

4. In what way does the affirmative defense "state of the art" assist Piggly in its defense strategy? Why is this important? What additional information do you need to make this a viable defense for Piggly? Should it be pleaded as an affirmative defense in Piggly's Answer?

5. What facts distinguish the statute of limitations defense from the statute of repose? Are either applicable here? Can either or both of these affirmative defenses be pleaded in Piggly's Answer? What additional information do you need to make these theories viable defenses from Piggly?

6. Assume that applicable Occupational Safety Hazard ("OSHA") regulations required that the Squealer I be operated only when the metal guards were functional and in place. Based upon the facts described in Chapter 2, Negligence, what defense strategy is available for Piggly? What facts make this a viable defense for Piggly? What additional information do you need?

7. Review the section in Chapter 7 regarding Defendant Employers. What role does Lindy have in Mr. Hoagge's lawsuit? Is Lindy a proper party defendant or third-party defendant in this lawsuit? In what way is Lindy liable for Mr. Hoagge's damages? How is that liability assessed in Mr. Hoagge's lawsuit against Piggly?

The Milair Air Scoop.

Assume the same facts described in Chapter Two, Negligence, for the Milair Air Scoop.

1. Assume that you represent Milair in a lawsuit brought by the passengers. The passengers have alleged wrongful death and personal injuries and have pleaded all strict liability theories, all express and implied warranty theories, and a negligence theory against Milair in their complaint. What are all of the available defenses that can be pleaded on behalf of Milair in their answer? Which of these are affirmative defenses? Why do certain defenses not apply? What additional facts, if any, do you need to determine the applicability of certain defenses? Draft an answer on behalf of Milair.

2. Assume that you represent Rolls Royce in a lawsuit brought by the passengers. The passengers have alleged wrongful death and personal injuries and have pleaded all strict liability theories, all express and implied warranty theories, and a negligence theory against Rolls Royce in their complaint. What are all of the available defenses that can be pleaded on behalf of Milair in their answer? Which of these are affirmative defenses? Why do certain defenses not apply? What additional facts, if any, do you need in order to determine the applicability of certain defenses? Draft an answer on behalf of Milair.

3. Assume for this question only that all of the passenger wrongful death and personal injury suits have been completed. Assume also that the law of Columbia state (where the lawsuits have taken place) allows National, Boeing, and Rolls Royce to state a claim for indemnity against Milair, and that each has a claim for indemnity in the amount of $10,000,000. Assume further that you represent Milair. Based upon the complaint that you drafted in response to Question 4 in Chapter Four, Strict Liability, what answer must you file on behalf of Milair. What additional facts, if any, do you need?

4. Assume you represent all potential defendants. Answer the complaint that you prepared in response to Question 3 in Chapter Two, Negligence, and an answer to the complaint you prepared in response to Question 2 in Chapter Three, Warranties.

5. Assume that you have filed an answer on behalf of Milair in a lawsuit, brought by all passengers, that

identifies all available theories in strict liability, warranty, and negligence. Assume further that National, Boeing, and Rolls Royce are named as co-defendants. What key facts do you want to learn during discovery? What should you seek through interrogatories? Through request for productions? Through requests for admissions? Draft 15 interrogatories requesting information from each of the co-defendants that is pertinent to the Milair Air Scoops, their design and installation, and any applicable warnings that should have accompanied the product.

6. Assume that the NTSB engineer obtained files from the Federal Aviation Administration (FAA) that revealed neither the M4880 "or the M2213-5 Milair Air Scoop complied with Federal Aviation Regulations (FARs) regarding the weight, form, and fit of the component part on Rolls Royce turbine engines. What defenses are available to Rolls Royce? What liability theories against Milair are available to plaintiffs? Against National, Rolls Royce, or Boeing?

7. Draft 15 interrogatories, 15 requests for production, and 15 requests for admissions on behalf of Milair. To whom should you direct this written discovery? What essential information should you obtain from these defendants during written discovery? Who should you depose? Who should you interview? Who can you interview?

SECTION THREE

PARTICULAR PRODUCT PROBLEMS

Chapter 6   Particular Product Problems

Particular Product Problems

INTRODUCTION

Product cases are similar to one another. The very heart of product liability law is the development of strict liability, no-fault principles that seek to protect unknowing product users and impose obligations on manufacturers and sellers to provide safe products. The key to understanding strict liability as it applies to allegedly defective products is to focus on the product itself. That focus will determine the existence of manufacturing, design, or warning defects and, thus, the basis for liability. That focus will also determine whether the particular product at issue in the case includes any additional liability or defense theories that are unique to the product. It is there that product cases become dissimilar from one another. For example, consider the practical steps of how the product is expected to be used, who uses the product, who distributes the product, to whom the product is intended to be provided, how long the product has been in use, and whether the product manufacturer or seller has learned more about the safe use of the product since it was sold. These considerations are at the heart of most liability problems that are unique to individual products.

Types of Product Problems

This chapter explores a range of liability problems that may be encountered depending on the category of allegedly defective products. Unlike previous chapters that focused on the applicable theories that provided a basis for liability or defense, this chapter is specifically about problems that are unique to the product itself. Each problem changes with each product. For example, component part manufacturers may not be liable under any strict liability, negligence, or warranty theory if they did not participate in the integration of the product into the final, completed product. Prescription drugs and medical devices are not inherently defective if their foreseeable therapeutic benefit is greater than the foreseeable risks of harm posed by the product. Pharmaceutical and medical device manufacturers may not be liable under a plaintiff's failure to warn theory if the manufacturer provided adequate warnings and instructions to a learned intermediary, such as a physician, who prescribed the drug or product for a patient's use. Food manufacturers are liable for defective foodstuffs that contain foreign ingredients that a consumer would not reasonably expect it to contain. These examples are not difficult to learn and remember, because they are the subject of several sections of the *Restatement (Third)*. See §§ 5-7 *Restatement (Third): Product Liability*. Other categories of products also have rules that are unique to that particular product and many continue to be developed without much more recognition than through common case law.

This chapter provides examples of a few particular product problems, including component parts, pharmaceuticals, medical devices, food, used products, handguns, and the post-sale duties of product manufacturers. The list is not exhaustive. It is likely that there are as many particular product problems as there are products. Many of these will be evidentiary and regulatory considerations. But the common element among these product problems is that the use of the product modified existing liability theories into broadly recognized exceptions or defenses or, in some cases, imposed additional liability burdens on the product provider. This common element is the key to discovering problems that are unique to other products not mentioned here, including products that have not yet been manufactured.

Component Parts

A manufacturer of component parts is a seller in the stream of commerce and for that reason is subject to liability for any product that he or she may place in the stream of commerce that is inherently dangerous. Ordinarily, the component part manufacturer must have substantially participated in the integration of the component into the final assembly and, of course, it must be the component itself that is defective and that produced the injured plaintiff's harm. If the component manufacturer produced the subject component according to the specifications of the final manufacturer or assembler, the component manufacturer bears little responsibility for the defective nature of the final product. If the component manufacturer made the product under its own specifications, the reverse is true. In either instance, the integration of the component into the final assembled product is key to determining whether the component manufacturer bears any liability in the case.

See § 5 *Restatement (Third), Liability of Commercial Seller or Distributor of Product Components for Harm Caused by Products Into Which Components are Integrated.*

 CASE LAW

◆ **liability of the component part manufacturer**

Jacobs v. E.I. Du Pont De Nemours & Co., 57 F.3d 1219 (6th Cir. 1995).

Trial court dismissed component part manufacturer, Du Pont, on the basis that it had no obligation to warn end-users of the finished product about the potentially dangerous nature of its components in the finished product. Du Pont manufactured Proplast, a composite consisting of polytetrafluoroethylene (PTFE), and a fluorinated ethylene propylene film (FEP), that were used as components in a temporomandibular joint Inter-

positional Implant (IPI) manufactured and distributed by the now-bankrupt Vitek, Inc. Plaintiff appealed complaining that the component parts manufacturer was liable in strict liability for failure to warn and for defective design.

ROSEN, District Judge.

* * *

1. **The district court properly granted summary judgment under the "component parts" doctrine.**

Ohio law is settled that a component part manufacturer has no duty to warn end-users of the finished product of the potentially dangerous nature of its parts in that product. In *Temple v. Wean United, Inc.*, 50 Ohio St.2d 317, 364 N.E.2d 267 (1977), the Ohio Supreme Court held that the supplier of operating buttons in a power press, which when assembled and modified by third parties caused serious injuries to the plaintiff, did not have a duty to warn end-users of the dangers posed by the inclusion of those buttons in the final power press. In the court's words:

> In our opinion, the obligation that generates the duty to warn does not extend to the speculative anticipation of how manufactured components, not in and of themselves dangerous or defective, can become potentially dangerous dependent on the integration into a unit designed and assembled by another. Because of the limited contact [with the power press manufacturer] there is no indication that [the operating button supplier] could have known that its components were to be fashioned or fabricated into the power press in the particular manner that they were.

See 364 N.E.2d at 272. *See also Searls v. Doe,* 29 Ohio App.3d 309, 505 N.E.2d 287, 290 (1986) ("[D]efendants, as manufacturers of component parts, had no duty to warn plaintiff of a potentially dangerous or defective design of a [beer can ejection system] where defendants were not responsible for the design and manufacture of the entire system and where the component parts, not in and of themselves dangerous or defective, were manufactured in accordance with [the purchaser/manufacturer's] specifications."). *Cf. Childress v. Gresen Mfg. Co.,* 888 F.2d 45, 49 (6th Cir.1989) ("[A] component supplier has no duty, independent of the completed product manufacturer, to analyze the design of the completed product which incorporates its non-defective component part.")

In response to the rule announced in these cases, Appellants rely principally upon *Miles v. Kholi & Kaliher Assocs., Ltd.,* 917 F.2d 235 (6th Cir. 1990). We believe that this case is distinguishable. In *Miles,* the component part supplier of bridge materials also drafted the design of the finished product—the bridge. Thus, it was appropriate in that case to hold that the supplier had a duty to warn end-users of the dangers of that product, since it had superior knowledge of those dangers. *See* 917 F.2d at 245.

Here, Du Pont had no role in the development of the IPI, and, despite its increased knowledge of the device after Mr. Bernhardt's investigation, it is clear that Vitek was always in a better position than Du Pont to assess the risks of the IPI.

None of the other cases on which Appellants rely to show that Du Pont breached the duty to warn attributable to component part manufacturers alters our conclusion. In *Fleck v. KDI Sylvan Pools, Inc.* 981 F.2d 107 (3d Cir.1992), *cert. denied sub nom. Doughboy Recreational Inc., Div. of Hoffinger Indus., Inc. v. Fleck,* —U.S.—, 113 S.Ct. 1645, 123 L.Ed.2d 267 (1993), the Third Circuit, applying Pennsylvania law, found that the manufacturer of a replacement pool liner was strictly liable for a failure to attach warning labels stressing the dangers of diving into a shallow pool. The pool liner manufacturer argued that he was only the supplier of a component part and should not be expected to foresee the dangers of diving into a shallow pool. The Third Circuit rejected this argument on the basis that a pool liner has but one use—to line a pool—and that the manufacturer, therefore, could easily foresee the dangers of failing to affix warning labels., *See* 981 F.2d at 117-19. The *Fleck* court specifically distinguished the situation before it from the one presented here; namely, where plaintiffs seek to impose a duty to warn about a specific application of a product, like Teflon, which has many different uses. *See* 981 F.2d at 118.

In another case cited by Appellants, *Beauchamp v. Russell,* 547 F.Supp. 1191 (N.D.Ga. 1982), the district court denied summary judgment to a component part manufacturer of an air valve used in a food can casemaking device. The record at that point in the case indicated that the air valve manufacturer did not supply instructions or warnings to the can casemaker manufacturer about the use of its air valve and of the need to ensure an air-pressure release mechanism. Such instructions and warnings were common in the air-valve industry. *See* 547 F.Supp. at 1197-98. *See also Suchomajcz v. Hummell Chem. Co.,* 524 F.2d 19, 27 (3d Cir.1975) (denying summary judgment to a component part supplier of chemicals used to make fireworks in part because the supplier did not provide any warnings to the fireworks manufacturer). Here, of course, Du Pont did bring to Dr. Homsy's attention Dr. Charnley's adverse study of the use of PTFE in a load-bearing joint, and it also repeatedly stated to Vitek that it was up to the medical community to determine the extent of safe prosthetic applications of Teflon.

Appellants also cite two Illinois asbestos cases in support of their contention that a component part supplier has a duty to warn end-users of the dangers of its products. The first, *Hammond v. North Am. Asbestos Corp.*, 97 Ill.2d 195, 73 Ill. Dec. 350, 454 N.E.2d 210 (1983), affirmed a jury verdict for a plaintiff who had suffered injury as a result of handling raw asbestos manufactured by defendant. Crucially, the raw asbestos was sold to plaintiff's employer without warnings of dangers known to defendant. *See* 73 Ill. Dec. at 357, 454 N.E.2d at 217. Thus, *Hammond* is not instructive in the instant case when one considers that Du Pont warned Vitek of all of the hazards that it knew of concerning the medical applications of its product.

The second Illinois case, *Board of Educ. of City of Chicago v. A, C & S, Inc.*, 131 Ill.2d 428, 137 Ill. Dec. 635, 546 N.E.2d 580 (1989), is also distinguishable. The procedural posture in that decision was quite different from this one in that defendants, a number of asbestos manufacturers and suppliers, sought a dismissal of the complaints for failure to state a claim. In addition, the issue in *A, C & S* was simply whether asbestos placed in school buildings was a "product" for purposes of application of strict products liability law. The Illinois Supreme Court found that asbestos was indeed a product because that finding "will effectuate the policy basis for imposing strict liability in tort." *See* 137 Ill. Dec. at 646, 546 N.E.2d at 591. That court went on to deny defendants' motion to dismiss because plaintiffs had on the face of their complaints stated an actionable claim. 137 Ill. Dec. at 646, 546 N.E.2d at 591. Here, it is undisputed that Du Pont's Teflon products are items subject to product liability analysis. Moreover, the summary judgment record in this case is far more developed than the pleadings before the *A, C & S* court, and that record indicates that a reasonable jury could only find for Du Pont. *A, C & S*, then, adds nothing to the present inquiry.

Consequently, we hold that the district court properly applied Ohio's "component parts" doctrine in reaching its conclusion that Du Pont had no duty to warn end-users of the potential problems arising from the use of Teflon products in the IPI.

2. Even assuming that Du Pont had a duty to warn end-users, this duty was fulfilled by application of the "bulk-supplier/sophisticated intermediary" rule.

Similarly, we believe that the district court properly held that Du Pont discharged any potential duty to warn by informing Dr. Homsy and Vitek of the known dangers of using Teflon in medical applications.

Section 388 of the Restatement (2d) of Torts, which both parties agree controls the inquiry into Du Pont's fulfillment of any duty to warn, states:

> One who supplies directly or through a third person a chattel for another to use is subject to liability to those whom the supplier should expect to use the chattel with the consent of the other or to be endangered by its probable use, for physical harm caused by the use of the chattel in the manner for which and by a person for whose use it was supplied, if the supplier
>
> (a) knows or has reason to know that the chattel is or is likely to be dangerous for the use for which it is supplied, and
>
> (b) has no reason to believe that those for whose use the chattel is supplied will realize its dangerous condition, and
>
> (c) fails to exercise reasonable care to inform them of its dangerous condition or of the facts which make it likely to be dangerous.

Comment n to this section explains in detail the scope of the above duty when there is an intermediary between the supplier of chattels and their end-users. This comment reads as follows:

> *Warnings given to third persons.* Chattels are often supplied for the use of others, although the chattels or the permission to use them are not given directly to those for whose use they are supplied. . . . In all such cases the question may arise as to whether the person supplying the chattel is exercising that reasonable care, which he owes to those who are to use it, by informing the third person through whom the chattel is supplied of its actual character.

Giving to the third person through whom the chattel is supplied all the information necessary to its safe use is not in all cases sufficient to relieve the supplier from liability. It is merely a means by which this information is to be conveyed to those who are to use the chattel. The question remains whether this method gives a reasonable assurance that the information will reach those whose safety depends upon their having it.

The comment then goes on to describe some of the factors that courts should consider in determining if a product supplier can reasonably rely on a third party to pass on warnings:

> These circumstances include the known or knowable character of the third person and may also include the purpose for which the chattel is given. Modern life would be intolerable unless one were permitted to rely to a certain extent on others doing what they normally do, particularly if it is their duty to do so. If the chattel is one which if ignorantly used contains no great chance of causing anything more than some comparatively trivial harm, it is reasonable to permit the one who supplies the chattel through a third person to rely upon the fact that the third person is an ordinary normal man to whose discredit the supplier knows nothing, as a sufficient assurance that information given to him will be passed on to those who are to use the chattel.

If, however, the third person is known to be careless or inconsiderate, or if the purpose for which the chattel is to be used is to his advantage and knowledge of the true character of the chattel is likely to prevent its being used and so to deprive him of this advantage—as when the goods are so defective as to be unsalable are sold by a wholesaler to a retailer—the supplier of the chattel has reason to expect, or at least suspect, that the information will fail to reach those who are to use the chattel and whose safety depends upon their knowledge of its true character. In such a case, the supplier may well be required to go further than to tell such a third person of the dangerous character of the article, or, if he fails to do so, to take the risk of being subjected to liability if the information is not brought home to those whom the supplier should expect to use the chattel. . . . Even though the supplier has no practicable opportunity to give this information directly and in person to those who are to use the chattel or share in its use, it is not unreasonable to require him to make good any harm which is caused by his using so unreliable a method of giving the information which is obviously necessary to make the chattel safe for those who use it and those in the vicinity of its use.

The comment continues by stating:

> [I]f the danger involved in the ignorant use of a particular chattel is very great, it may be that the supplier does not exercise reasonable care in entrusting the communication of the necessary information even to a person whom he has good reason to believe to be careful. Many such articles can be made to carry their own message to the understanding of those who are likely to use them by the form in which they are put out, by the container in which they are supplied, or by a label or other device, indicating with a substantial sufficiency their dangerous character. Where the danger involved in the ignorant use of their true quality is great and such means of disclosure are practicable and not unduly burdensome, it may well be that the supplier should be required to adopt them. . . .

In applying § 388 and its commentary to this case, we must decide as an initial matter whether Appellants correctly contend that Du Pont's duty to warn end-users was non-delegable. We believe that this argument misreads comment n, which clearly permits a supplier of chattels to rely upon a learned intermediary in certain circumstances. *See also Adkins v. GAF Corp.*, 923 F.2d 1225, 1230 (6th Cir. 1991) (applying Ohio law) ("Comment n to section 388 states that the supplier's duty to warn may be discharged by providing information about the product's dangerous propensities to a third person upon whom it can reasonably rely to communicate the information to the ultimate users of the product or those who may be exposed to its hazardous effects.") We therefore hold that, in certain circumstances, a supplier of chattels can effectively delegate the duty to warn end-users to a third-party intermediary.

We also believe that Du Pont reasonably relied upon Vitek to pass on warnings of PTFE and FEP's possible unsuitability for use in load-bearing joints—a warning which Du Pont gave to Dr. Homsy as early as 1967 by citing Charnley's study to him and by stating that the medical efficacy of Du Pont's Teflon products remained highly uncertain. It is indisputable that Vitek, as the manufacturer of the finished product, had both a statutory and common law duty to warn end-users of the pitfalls of its finished medical device. [Citation omitted.] Equally irrefutable is the fact that Vitek had superior access to the oral surgeons and patients who used its IPIs. Moreover, although it is unclear if Du Pont knew all about Dr. Homsy that is currently known, it is manifest from his time with Du Pont, his correspondence with Du Pont after he left, and Mr. Bernhardt's notes, that Du Pont recognized Dr. Homsy as a leader in the field of using plastics in medical applications.

This case, then, is legally indistinguishable from *Adams v. Union Carbide Corp.,* 737 F.2d 1453 (6th Cir.) (applying Ohio law), *cert. denied,* 469 U.S. 1062, 105 S.Ct. 545, 83 L.Ed.2d 432 (1984). In that case, plaintiff, a General Motors employee, sued Union Carbide, a chemical manufacturer which sold a dangerous chemical (TDI) to GM, for failure to warn her and other GM employees of the hazards of that chemical. We held in *Adams* that the district court properly granted Union Carbide summary judgment because it discharged its duty to warn, pursuant to § 388 of the Restatement, by providing GM with detailed warnings of TDI's effects and suggestions on how to avoid them. Specifically, we stated:

> The fact that GMC repeatedly updated its information about TDI from Union Carbide, coupled with the fact that GM itself had a duty to its employees to provide them with a safe place to work, supports the inescapable conclusion that it was reasonable for Union Carbide to rely upon GMC to convey the information about the hazardous propensities of TDI to its employees within the context of comment n of the Restatement. *See* 737 F.2d at 1457.

The same kind of facts are present in this case. Du Pont warned Dr. Homsy and Vitek of what it knew regarding the dangers of using Teflon products in load-bearing joints, and Vitek had a clear duty under law to provide all necessary warnings applicable to its IPI. As in *Adams,* then, the relevant product manufacturer in this case, Du Pont, fulfilled its duties under § 388. [Footnote omitted.]

Appellants contend that Dr. Homsy demonstrated a complete inability to heed the dangers that the Vitek IPI posed and that, therefore, Du Pont unreasonably relied upon him to warn end-users of Teflon's inefficacy in load-bearing situations. Appellants rely primarily upon Dr. Homsy's attempts in various writings to rebut the findings in the Charnley and Liedholt studies in making this argument.

The record, however, demonstrates that Dr. Homsy's writings were an effort to *distinguish* these studies, not disregard them. His correspondence to Du Pont and professional writings explicitly noted the experimental contrasts between his work and that of Drs. Charnley and Leidholt. Furthermore, Dr. Homsy carefully developed means and methods to address the concerns raised in those studies in creating Vitek's prostheses. For example, he did not use raw PTFE in any of his applications, but, rather, manufactured Proplast with PTFE combined with salt and carbon or aluminum oxide fibers. Similarly, Dr. Homsy added a lamination of FEP film to the Proplast so that it would not come in direct contact with adjoining surfaces. Du Pont was aware of these changes by 1984, and it also knew at that time that the IPI was a widely used medical device which had been approved, at least for marketing, by the FDA.

Du Pont, then, had substantial grounds on which to reasonably rely on Dr. Homsy and Vitek to pass on to end-users any known dangers of the IPI because of: (1) their legally established and clear duty to warn end-users; (2) their undisputed leadership in the plastic prosthesis field; and (3) their superior access to oral surgeons and patients. Such a finding of reasonable reliance is not rebutted by any evidence that Vitek passed on to patients and oral surgeons inadequate warnings or that, even if they did, Du Pont had or should have had actual or constructive knowledge of this fact. Since there is significant evidence of the reasonableness of Du Pont's reliance on Dr. Homsy and Vitek to pass on the warnings Du Pont gave to them, and no proof that Du Pont actually knew that they were issuing inadequate warnings, we hold that Du Pont discharged its duty to warn in accordance with § 388 comment n. [Footnote omitted.]

As a final note, we believe that the common law cannot countenance what Appellants insist we do, which is to make raw material suppliers guarantors of finished products over which they have little control. Under such a reading of the law, companies like Du Pont would have no choice but to take their products off the market entirely or to double-check their suitability in many new applications before making any sales. *See Childress,* 888 F.2d at 49 (citing with favor the district court's reasoning that imposing responsibility for a completed product on a component part supplier "would be contrary to public policy, as it would encourage ignorance on the part of component part manufacturers [of the ultimate use of the component part] or alternatively require them to 'retain an expert in the client's field of business to determine whether the client intends to develop a safe product.' " (Citation omitted)).

If we adhered to Appellants' theory, access to raw materials like Teflon for entrepreneurs seeking new applications would either disappear or be undermined by an inevitable increase in price. This, of course, would stymie the kind of beneficial scientific innovation which, sadly, did not take place here, but which has occurred in many other areas of human endeavor. We believe, for the reasons stated above, that the law has developed so as to preclude this result.

3. The district court properly held that PTFE and FEP were not defective products in and of themselves.

We also believe that the district court ruled properly that PTFE and FEP were not defective in and of themselves. Appellants contend that Du Pont is strictly liable for the defective design and manufacture of PTFE and FEP pursuant to Restatement 2d of Torts § 402A and Ohio statutory law.

* * *

Without question, this section does not apply since there is no evidence that Du Pont's Teflon products, in and of themselves, were defective or that they were unreasonably dangerous independent of, and *prior to*, their incorporation into the IPI. [Footnote omitted.] Indeed, the record reveals that PTFE and FEP have many useful industrial and medical applications for which its design is perfectly suited.

* * *

In similar situations, where a component part is not dangerous until incorporated into a finished product, courts have held that the component part supplier cannot be held liable on a common law design or manufacturing defect theory, unless the supplier exercised some control over the *final* product's design. *Compare Sperry v. Bauermeister,* 4 F.3d 596, 598 (8th Cir. 1993) (applying Missouri law) ("suppliers of non-defective component parts are not responsible for accidents that result when the parts are integrated into a larger system that the component part supplier did not design or build"); *and Childress v. Gresen Mfg. Co.,* 888 F.2d 45, 48-49 (6th Cir. 1989) (applying Michigan law) (component part manufacturer is not liable for defective design of a final product when component part is not in and of itself defectively designed); *with DeSantis v. Parker Feeders, Inc.,* 547 F.2d 357, 361 (7th Cir. 1976) (affirming jury verdict against component part manufacturer for the design defect of a finished product because every single part of that product was made by the component part manufacturer, and each part was dependent upon all the others for the product to work); *and Estate of Carey v. Hy-Temp Mfg., Inc.,* 702 F.Supp. 666, 670-71 (N.D.Ill. 1988) (denying summary judgment to component part manufacturer where evidence showed that it influenced the design of the final product). Here, it cannot be disputed that Vitek, and Vitek alone, developed the IPI. Therefore, Appellants' failure to demonstrate that PTFE and FEP were defective and/or unreasonably dangerous in and of themselves, or that Du Pont influenced the design of the IPI, warrants entry of summary judgment on the § 402A design/manufacturing defect claim.

Case Notes: Component Parts.

1. The phrase "component parts" typically describes a broad spectrum of products. Generally, components include the smaller product components that are intended for integration into the larger, final and completed products, as well as raw materials and bulk products. The eventual integration of components into larger assemblies or final, completed products defines a product as a component. *The Restatement (Third)* recognizes "components" as, for example, "raw materials, valves, or switches, [that] have no functional capabilities unless integrated into other products. Other components, such as a truck chassis or a multifunctional machine, function on their own but still may be utilized in a variety of ways by assemblers of other products." *See Restatement (Third):* Product Liability at Comment a, § 5; *Americo C. Buonanno, III v. Colmar Belting, Co., Inc.,* 733 A.2d 712, 716 (R.I. 1999) (component manufacturer should not be liable under § 5 of the *Restatement* "unless the component part itself was defective when it left the manufacturer"); *see also* Mansfield, *Reflections on Current Limits on Component and Raw Material Supplier Liability and The Proposed* (Third) Restatement, 84 Ky. L. J. 221 (1995-96).

2. The general rule is that manufacturers of component parts are not liable for defects in the final, completed product unless the component part itself is defective. The rationale for the

general rule is a practical one: component manufacturers cannot realistically exercise any control over the quality, manufacturing, or assembly of the final product. Even if these manufacturers could exercise such control, that process would require second guessing the manufacturer/assembler of the final, completed product. It is impractical, if not impossible, to charge the component supplier with knowledge that is superior to that of the completed product manufacturer. These practical reasons dictate that the component manufacturer not be charged with any liability in connection with a defect in the final product unless the component part itself was defective. *See Loos v. American Energy Savers Corp.*, 522 N.E.2d 841, 845 (Ill. App. Ct. 1988) (component manufacturer need not anticipate how non-dangerous part may become dangerous in final assembly); *Ruegger v. International Harvester Co.*, 576 N.E.2d 288, 292 (Ill. App. Ct. 1991) (component manufacturer not liable because it had no control over final assembly or usage); *Crossfield v. Quality Control Equipment Co., Inc.*, 1 F.3d 701, 703-06 (8th Cir. 1993) (Missouri law) (component manufacturer was not liable for hazard arising in larger, integrated product); Comment a to § 5, *Restatement (Third): Product Liability.*

3. Some jurisdictions refer to the general rule as the "sophisticated purchaser" or "sophisticated intermediary" rule because it expresses the knowledge and position of the final, completed product manufacturer. Typically, it is incumbent on the integrated manufacturer that it have superior knowledge about component specifications, design of the component, manufacturing of the component, integration of the component into the final product, and anticipated use(s) of the final product. These are typical scenarios under which components are supplied, but frequently the component manufacturer may participate in any one of these steps, any one of which may subject the component manufacturer to additional liability. See *Welsh v. Bowling Electric Machinery, Inc.*, 875 S.W.2d 569, 574 (Mo. Ct. App. 1994) (component manufacturer not liable for component not designed and not integrated by component

manufacturer); *Sparacino v. Andover Controls Corp.*, 592 N.E.2d 431, 434 (Ill. Ct. App. 1992) (component manufacturer was never provided written specifications about component's installation or component's use in final product); *Mayberry v. Akron Rubber Machinery Corp.*, 483 F. Supp. 407, 413-14 (N.D. Okla. 1979) (component manufacturer had no duty to warn about dangers in final product in absence of control over design of final product); see also Ausness, *Learned Intermediaries and Sophisticated Users: Encouraging the Use of Intermediaries to Transmit Product Safety Information*, 46 Syracuse Law Review 1185 (1996).

4. Liability for use of raw materials falls upon the entity that made the decision to include the raw materials in the final product. Thus, if a power cord is provided by Company A to be integrated into a home appliance manufactured by Company B, Company B is liable for any final product that is defective because the power cord contained faulty wiring for conducting electrical current. Company A is not liable for defective design of the home appliance but may be liable for the power cord that is itself defective, particularly if the power cord did not meet the final product manufacturer's specifications or was made to Company A's own specifications. The *Restatement (Third)* commented on this particular liability. See *Restatement (Third)* at Comment c, § 5; see also *Apperson v. E.I. du Pont de Nemour*, 41 F.3d 1103, 1107 (7th Cir. 1994) (manufacturer not liable when inherently safe raw material became unreasonably dangerous upon integration into specialized medical prostheses); *Palmer G. Lewis Company, Inc. v. Arco Chemical Company*, 904 P.2d 1221 (Alaska 1995) (final product manufacturer sought indemnity from raw material supplier).

5. The extent to which the component manufacturer participates in the integration of the component product into the final product will determine the liability of the component manufacturer's liability. (The *Restatement (Third)* at Comment e § 5.)

6. Bulk suppliers are typically held to the same rationale and standards as component manufacturers. See *Jackson v. Reliable Paste and Chemical Co.*, 483 N.E.2d 939, 943 (Ill. Ct. App.

1985) (bulk supplier of methanol owed no duty to warn because purchaser was fully aware of methanol's flammable and explosive qualities); *Donahue v. Phillips Petroleum Co.*, 866 F.2d 1008, 1012-14 (8th Cir. 1989) (bulk supplier may avoid liability by warning its immediate purchaser with intent that such warning be passed to ultimate consumer); *Duane v. Oklahoma Gas & Electric Co.*, 833 P.2d 284, 286-87 (Okla 1992) (bulk supplier had no duty to warn knowledgeable product user about generally known dangers of product); *cf. Heifner v. Synergy Gas Corp.*, 883 S.W.2d 29, 46 (Mo. Ct. App. 1994) (bulk suppliers obligated to provide adequate instructions to distributor next in line).

7. Is the supplier of a raw material used in the manufacture of a medical device which has allegedly been defectively designed and/or defectively manufactured liable to a consumer who has allegedly been injured by the defective device? To what extent must the raw material supplier have participated in the design, integration, assembly, or final manufacturing of the completed product for liability to attach to the raw material supplier? Do the answers to these questions change if you substitute component manufacturer or bulk supplier in the place of raw material supplier?

8. Who are the purchasers of component parts or raw materials? What is the expected use of these products?

Pharmaceuticals and Medical Devices

Drugs and medical devices are subject to strict liability for any harm brought to persons by the defective manufacturing, design, or warning that is caused by any manufacturer, seller, or entity responsible for placing the drug or medical device into the stream of commerce. Pharmaceutical products are ordinarily given greater deference on a risk-benefit scale. All pharmaceutical products are generally regarded as unavoidably unsafe because the wrong drug taken at the wrong time is certain to produce harm to its user. However, the right drug taken at the right time is equally certain to produce a therapeutic benefit to its user. Accordingly, courts are frequently asked to give greater weight to the benefit of the pharmaceutical company's product, particularly with regard to the allegedly defective design of a drug or medical device or inadequate warnings given under certain circumstances. The *Restatement (Third)* requires that the drug or device *not* be regarded as reasonably safe if the prescribing health care provider would not prescribe the product to any class of patients. See § 6 *Restatement (Third), Liability of Commercial Seller or Distributor for Harm Caused by Defective Prescription Drugs and Medical Devices.* Likewise, the drugs and medical devices are not considered reasonably safe if adequate instructions and warnings are not provided to prescribing health care providers or to the patient. *Id.* In the absence of either, the drug or medical device would be considered inherently dangerous and defective.

 CASE LAW

◆ **learned intermediaries in drug and medical device litigation**

Artiglio v. Superior Court,
27 Cal.Rptr. 2d 589 (Cal.
App. 4 Dist. 1994).

Trial court dismissed coordinated plaintiffs' cause of action for strict liability in breast implant cases ruling that plaintiffs could not state a cause of action for strict liability based upon a design defect in the breast implant devices. Plaintiffs petitioned the appellate court for a reversal of the trial court's ruling.

FROEHLICH, Associate Justice.

* * *

The concept of strict liability imposes legal responsibility for injury upon the manufacturer of a product without proof of negligence based upon a determination that the product is: (1) defectively manufactured, (2) defectively designed, or (3) distributed without adequate warnings as to its potential for harm. [Footnote omitted.] *Brown v. Superior Court, supra,* 44 Cal.3d 1049, 245 Cal. Rptr. 412, 751 P.2d 470, established an exception to general products strict liability rules for prescription drugs. It was held, for policy reasons set forth at length in the opinion, that drug manufacturers could not be held strictly liable for design defects in prescription drugs. (*Id.* at p. 1069, 245 Cal. Rptr. 412, 751 P.2d 470.) The trial court held that the rationale of *Brown* was applicable to breast implant devices. We agree with the trial court and hence deny the writ petition. The explanation for our agreement is best revealed by analysis and rejection of the petitioners' several objections to the ruling.

Petitioners first contend that a condition to avoidance of strict liability is that the product has been marketed with adequate warnings of its potential risks. It is true that pre-*Brown* authorities lumped together the concepts of proper manufacture, lack of design defect and adequate warning. [Footnote omitted.] *Brown,* however, very clearly distinguished among the three concepts of fault. Liability for defective design could not be premised on strict liability, but would require proof of negligence. (*Brown v. Superior Court, supra,* 44 Cal.3d at p. 1061, 245 Cal. Rptr. 412, 751 P.2d 470.) Strict liability would continue applicable for manufacturing defects; and liability for failure to warn of known or reasonably knowable risks in the use of the product remains viable "under general principles of negligence." (*Id.* at p. 1069, fn. 12, 245 Cal. Rptr. 412, 751 P.2d 470.) Therefore, in reaching the question of strict liability based solely on design defect the court was not required to, and it did not, consider or rule upon either manufacturing fault or failure to give adequate warnings. The summary adjudication leaves these issues unresolved and available for future adjudication.

A second contention of the petitioners is that exemption from exposure to strict liability for design defects is available only for drug products which have been tested and approved by the United States Food and Drug Administration (hereafter FDA). Petitioners assert that breast implants not only have not been so tested and approved, but in fact in recent years have been disapproved by the FDA. Petitioners base their argument upon a portion of footnote 12 on page 1069, page 412 of

245 Cal. Rptr., page 470 of 751 P.2d of *Brown,* which states:

> "It should also be noted that the consumers of prescription drugs are afforded greater protection against defects than consumers of other products, since 'the drug industry is closely regulated by the Food and Drug Administration, which actively controls the testing and manufacture of drugs and the method by which they are marketed, including the contents of warning labels.' " (Quoting from *Sindell v. Abbott Laboratories* (1980) 26 Cal.3d 588, 609, 163 Cal. Rptr. 132, 607 P.2d 924.)

The weakness of petitioners' position is that nowhere in the *Brown* opinion proper is there any suggestion that FDA testing or approval is a requisite to exemption from design defect strict liability. The footnote reference is little more than a makeweight afterthought to the opinion's policy argument. Further, in its footnote the *Brown* court did not state that FDA "approval" was a condition to exemption, but merely that the drug industry in general is closely regulated. Through appellate briefing we have been educated as to the various levels of FDA testing, regulation and approval, and the years at which such came into effect. This dissection and examination of the federal regulation of the drug industry was in the main not available to the trial court, however, and the court's order granting summary adjudication does not refer to this aspect of petitioners' argument. Also, there is no suggestion in *Brown* or any other California authority that FDA approval or regulation is relevant to the determination of prescription drug exemption from design defect strict liability. On the contrary, the *Brown* court consistently speaks simply of "drug manufacturers," "drugs," and occasionally of "prescription drugs." We note, also, that Comment k to the cited Restatement provision, which is the genesis of the special treatment of prescription drugs, pertains broadly to products for which FDA review and approval could not have occurred at the time of initial distribution, as it covers "many new or experimental drugs as to which, because of lack of time and opportunity for sufficient medical experience, there can be no assurance of safety, or perhaps even of purity of ingredients. . . ." We therefore conclude that there is no authority for the proposition that FDA control or approval of a product has anything to do with its exemption from design defect products strict liability.

Conceivably the most potentially persuasive of petitioners' arguments is that based on the definitional holding of *Brown*. *Brown* establishes a rule for prescription drugs; this rule does not control the issue of strict liability for breast implants, it is contended, because the breast implant is a medical device and not a "drug." Related to this argument is the corollary contention that the exemption from strict liability should be available only for worthy prescriptions which save lives or promote health, and should be denied for medical applications which are merely cosmetic.

We are able to deal with these contentions summarily, since they have been completely addressed in *Hufft v. Horowitz* (1992) 4 Cal. App. 4th 8, 5 Cal.Rptr.2d 377. [Footnote omitted.] That case, from a sister division of our Fourth District, dealt with the potential of strict liability for design defects in penile prostheses. After ample exploration of the subject, the *Hufft* court concluded that "the rule of *Brown* . . . immunizing manufacturers of prescription drugs from strict liability for design defects, should be extended to manufacturers of implanted prescription medical devices." (*Id.* at p. 11, 5 Cal.Rptr. 2d 377.) While there are obvious differences in the devices, we apprehend that the reasoning leading the *Hufft* court to exempt penile prostheses from strict liability applies equally to breast implants. Just as drugs are injected or ingested into the body, a breast implant, as a penile prosthesis, is "plugged in" to the individual. The implant, in each case, poses the potential of harm and the possibility of required removal. (*Id.* at p. 18, 5 Cal.Rptr.2d 377.) Just as with typical prescription drugs, the public interest is served by the development of effective and affordable medical implants, such as each of these devices illustrates.

We also reject, as did the *Hufft* court, the contention that the aspect of cosmetic improvement somehow eliminates breast implants from exemption from strict liability. The *Hufft* court summarily stated in a footnote that "[i]t is irrelevant to our analysis whether a patient has obtained a penile prosthesis for procreation, alleviation of an impotency problem or cosmetic purposes." (*Id.* at p. 18, fn. 9, 5 Cal.Rptr.2d 377.) We agree, and would add that in these days of recovery of vast amounts for mental suffering and emotional distress, it seems sophistic indeed to suggest that medical devices which enhance esteem and add to life's enjoyment are somehow not as protectible as those which merely increase health or combat disease. In any event, it is clear that some substantial percentage of breast implants are for the purpose of restoring the body to natural form following cancer surgery, which presumably anyone would agree is a "medical" rather than "cosmetic" purpose. Any effort to distinguish the potential for strict liability as respects identical medical procedures, based upon the motivation for such (cosmetic in the one case as distinguished from medical reconstruction in another) would not only be fraught with extremely nice and practically difficult factual determinations, but also would be contrary to the approach dictated by *Brown*, which is to reject a case-by-case analysis in favor of protection for an entire category of procedures.

Case Notes: Drugs and Medical Devices.

1. The most prominent part of § 6 of the *Restatement (Third)* is subsection d, which retained the "learned intermediary" rule. Courts have described the rule as follows:

   [T]he purchaser's [health care provider] is a learned intermediary between the purchaser and the manufacturer. If the doctor is properly warned of the possibility of a side effect in some patients, and is advised of the symptoms normally accompanying the side effect,

   there is an excellent chance that injury to the patient can be avoided. This is particularly true if the injury takes place slowly [.]

   Wooderson v. Ortho Pharmaceutical Corp., 681 P.2d 1038, 1050 (Kan. 1984); see § 6(a), (d) of the *Restatement (Third)*; see also Green, *Prescription Drugs, Alternative Designs, And The* Restatement (Third): Preliminary Reflections, 30 Seton Hall L. Rev. 207 (1999); Cheney, *Not Just For Doctors: Applying The Learned*

Intermediary Doctrine To The Relationship Between Chemical Manufacturers, Industrial Employers, and Employees, 85 Nw. U. L. Rev. 562 (Winter 1991).

2. The learned intermediary rule is a defense for pharmaceutical and medical device manufacturers that shifts liability to the qualified health care professional who prescribed the product to the patient and presumably explained the risks, dangers, and side effects of the product at the time the prescription was given. *The Restatement (Third)* was specific in defining prescription drugs and medical devices as "one that may be legally sold or otherwise distributed only pursuant to a health-care provider's prescription," thus necessarily placing the health care provider within the scope of those individuals to whom § 6 of the *Restatement (Third)* applies. See *Krug v. Sterling Drug, Inc.,* 416 S.W.2d 143, 146 (Mo. 1967) (applying learned intermediary doctrine in a pharmaceutical context); *Donahue v. Phillips Petroleum Co.,* 866 F.2d 1008, 1013 (8th Cir. 1989) (explaining rationale for the doctrine applying in a pharmaceutical context); see also Comment b, § 6 of the *Restatement (Third); Schwartz, Prescription Products and The Proposed Restatement (Third),* 61 Tennessee Law Review 1357 (1994); Schwartz, *The Impact of the New Products Liability Restatement on Prescription Products,* 50 Food and Drug Law Journal 399 (1995); McCall, *A Survey of Law Regarding The Liability of Manufacturers and Sellers of Drug Products and Medical Devices,* 18 St. Mary's L. J. 395 (1986).

3. Certain state court litigation concerning medical devices may be preempted by federal law, which will require that the matter be litigated in federal court. See 1976 Medical Device Amendment to the federal Food, Drug & Cosmetic Act, 21 U.S.C. § 360k(a) (medical devices) and 21 C.F.R. 808.1 through 808.101 (Exemptions from Federal Preemption of State and Local Medical Device Requirements); *Chmielewski v. Stryker Sales Corporation,* 966 F. Supp. 839, 841-44 (D.Minn. 1997) (strict liability claims were preempted by the Medical Devices Amendments). The defendant manufacturer's liability will depend on its compliance with applicable federal regulations regarding the pharmaceutical or medical device. See also Sanders, *Product Liability: Getting to the Heart of the Matter: Medical Device Preemption Defense Skips a Beat as Plaintiffs are no Longer Completely Precluded From Bringing State Product Liability Claims Against Medical Device Manufacturers [Medtronic, Inc. v.* Lohr, 116 S.Ct. 2240 (1996)], 36 Washburn Law Journal 319 (1997); Wilson, *Listen to the FDA: The Medical Device Amendments Do Not Preempt Tort Law,* 19 Hamline Law Review 409 (1995); Grauberger, *Feldt v. Mentor Corporation: The Fifth Circuit Examines Preemption and the Medical Device Amendments in the Context of Penile Implant Litigation,* 70 Tulane Law Review 1182 (1996); Leflar and Adler, *The Preemption Pentad: Federal Preemption of Products Liability Claims after Medtronic,* 64 Tennessee Law Review 691 (1997); Turner, *Preemption of State Product Liability Claims Involving Medical Devices: Premarket Approval As A Shield Against Liability,* 72 Washington Law Review 963 (1997).

4. Before the *Restatement (Third)*, § 402A of the *Restatement (Second)* recognized the highly beneficial nature of pharmaceutical products. They were known as unavoidably unsafe and tolerated as such in the context of product liability suits. Many courts recognized Comment k of § 402A and incorporated it into their own state's law. The Supreme Court of California noted the following:

> Comment k to section 402A of the Restatement Second of Torts recognizes the significant risk to the public interest presented by imposing excessive liability on the manufacturer of prescription drugs. Under the heading "Unavoidably unsafe products," comment k observes that commonly used drugs, while highly beneficial, are often incapable of being made entirely safe. It then notes: "It is also true in particular of many new or experimental drugs as to which, because of lack of time and opportunity for sufficient medical experience, there can be no assurance of safety, or perhaps even of purity of ingredients, but such experience as there is justifies the marketing and use of the drug notwithstanding a medically recognizable risk." (Rest.2d Torts, § 402A, com. k, p. 354.) It concludes that a manufacturer of drugs that are sold with a proper warning "where the situation calls for it, is not to be held to strict liability for unfortunate consequences attending their use, merely because he has undertaken to supply the public with an apparently useful and desirable product, attended with a known but apparently reasonable risk." (Ibid.)

Carlin v. The Superior Court of Sutter County, 920 P.2d 1347, 1357-58 (Cal. 1996) *citing* Schwartz, *Un-*

avoidably Unsafe Products: Clarifying the Meaning and Policy Behind Comment K, 42 Wash. & Lee L. Rev. 1139 (1985); Henderson & Twerski, *A Proposed Revision of Section 402A of the Restatement (Second) of Torts,* 77 Cornell L. Rev. 1512 (1992).

5. The central issue regarding pharmaceutical and medical products is the obligation to warn and instruct about their use. Comment j of § 402A of the *Restatement (Second)* previously suggested that directions and warnings be given directly to the product consumer.

> Comment. J. Directions or warnings [.]
>
> Where, however, the product contains an ingredient to which a substantial number of the population are allergic, and the ingredient is one whose danger is not generally known, or if known is one which the consumer would reasonably not expect to find in the product, the seller is required to give warning against it, if he has knowledge, or by the application of reasonable, developed human skill and foresight should have knowledge, of the presence of the ingredient and the danger. Likewise in the case of poisonous drugs, or those unduly dan-

gerous for other reasons, warning as to use may be required. . . .

6. The *Restatement (Third)* does not ignore the manufacturer's obligation to provide warnings directly to the patient. See Comment e to § 6 of the *Restatement (Third);* see also Comment, *Bypassing The Learned Intermediary: Potential Liability For Failure To Warn In Direct-Consumer Prescription Drug Advertising,* 2 Cornell J. L. & Public Policy 449 (Spring 1993); Ridgway, *No-Fault Vaccine Insurance: Lessons From The National Vaccine Injury Compensation Program,* 24 J. Health Pol. Pol'y & L. 59 (May 1999); Schwartz & Mahshigian, *National Childhood Vaccine Injury Act of 1986: An Ad Hoc Remedy or a Window For the Future?,* 48 Ohio St. L. J. 387 (1987).

7. Under what circumstances should drug and medical device manufacturers be required to warn their product consumers instead of a learned intermediary? What items are essential to include in the warning? What parts of the warning must the learned intermediary pass on to the product consumer? Who are the purchasers of prescription drugs and medical devices? Through whom must they be obtained?

Food

Defective food is determined by evaluating the expectations of the reasonable consumer. Defective food will contain at least one ingredient that a reasonable consumer would not expect to be in that particular food product, such as a rat in a soda bottle, a grasshopper in a chocolate bar, or a snake bone in a can of green beans. Food itself can be inherently dangerous, such as with a harmful bacteria or spoilage, and rendered defective for that reason. In either instance, the defendant packaging company or food processing manufacturer may be liable in strict liability for the allegedly defective product. See § 7, *Restatement (Third), Liability of Commercial Seller or Distributor for Harm Caused by Defective Food Products.*

 CASE LAW

◆ **contaminant in candy bar was not reasonably safe for human consumption**

Gates v. Standard Brands, Inc., 719 P.2d 130 (Wash. Ct. App. 1986).

Plaintiff sued candy bar manufacturer when plaintiff bit into a snake vertebrae lodged in the product. After a jury trial, the

court entered a judgment for the defendant manufacturer. Plaintiff appealed complaining that he was entitled to a strict liability cause of action for a defective product.

MUNSON, Judge.

Edward L. Gates bit into a Baby Ruth candy bar, manufactured by Standard Brands, which contained a "snake bone." Mr. Gates subsequently brought this action, alleging breach of the implied warranty of fitness for human consumption. By special verdict, the jury found the candy bar was not "unreasonably dangerous." Mr. Gates appeals, claiming the trial court erred in: (1) ruling a cause of action for breach of the implied warranty of fitness for human consumption ceased to exist following the adoption of the Restatement (Second) of Torts § 402A (1965); (2) not finding as a matter of law the candy bar was "defective" according to section 402A; and (3) admitting testimony concerning Standard Brands' manufacturing process of candy bars.

Mr. Gates purchased a Baby Ruth candy bar. [Citations omitted.] Eating it, he bit into something which he alleged was "gristly" or "spongy"; he testified he immediately noticed a nauseating taste; he became sick and began to vomit. Mr. Gates handed his wife the remaining piece of candy bar and the object, which was later identified as a snake vertebra.

Standard Brands' expert witness, an archaeologist at Central Washington University, testified the vertebra was several hundred to several thousand years old; was odorless and tasteless; and consisted of approximately 97 percent inorganic material. A quality control expert, called by Standard Brands, testified a Baby Ruth could not contain any matter which was either foul smelling or tasting because of the manufacturing process.

* * *

Washington first recognized a cause of action for breach of the implied warranty of fitness for human consumption over 70 years ago. *Mazetti v. Armour & Co.*, 75 Wash. 622, 135 P. 633 (1913). The action was premised on the theory the law implies a special warranty that food sold is wholesome and fit for human consumption. *Pulley v. Pacific Coca-Cola Bottling Co.*, 68 Wash.2d 778, 783, 415 P.2d 636 (1966); [citations omitted].

Although the standard of liability was analogous to the standard embodied in the common law of implied contractual warranties, [footnote omitted] the theory of Mazetti and its progeny arose by implication of law and principles of tort. [Citations omitted.]

This theory of implied warranty was gradually extended to nonfood cases. [Footnote omitted.] Recovery was allowed on the rationale that no logical distinction could be drawn between those particular products and food. See generally Comment, Defective Products Liability-Tort or Implied Warranty, 1 Gonz.L.Rev. 106

(1966). Finally, in *Ulmer* [v. Ford Motor Co., 452 P.2d 729 (Wash. 1969)] the court adopted a theory of strict liability as defined by the Restatement (Second) of Torts § 402A, providing:

Section 402A, . . . is in accord with the import of our cases which have been decided upon a theory of breach of implied warranty and we hereby adopt it as the law of this jurisdiction. . . . Consequently, our decision to discard the terminology of "implied warranty" and adopt the language of strict liability contained in the Restatement (Second) of Torts § 402A, applies only to the liability of manufacturers.

Ulmer, at 531-32, 452 P.2d 729. The court explained it was discarding the label of "implied warranty" because:

[I]t is illogical to create an implied warranty but refuse to attach to it any of the customary incidents of a warranty. For examples, in this court-created warranty, there is no necessity of a contract or privity between the parties; no necessity that the purchaser rely on the warranty; no requirement of notice of the breach within a reasonable time after learning of it; and no provision for disclaimer. There is also the difficulty of reconciling the implied warranty with the Uniform Sales Act, which provides that there shall be no implied warranties other than those listed therein. (See RCW 63.04.160). *Ulmer*, at 529, 452 P.2d 729.

Notwithstanding *Ulmer*, Mr. Gates vigorously asserts that a separate cause of action for breach of the implied warranty of fitness for human consumption still exists in Washington. He contends (1) strict products liability, as defined by section 402A and adopted by Ulmer, embodies a different standard of liability, and (2) according to the Mazetti line of cases, he need only prove the candy bar was "unfit for human consumption" as opposed to "unreasonably dangerous." He concludes food may be "unfit" or "impure" without being "unreasonably dangerous" and, therefore, the court's instructions, based on section 402A, erroneously imposed on him the heavier burden of showing the candy bar was "unreasonably dangerous."

However, comparison of the two causes of action demonstrates that they are essentially the same:

(1) Under 402A, the defendant must be engaged as a manufacturer or seller of the

product which caused the injury. Restatement (Second) of Torts § 402A(1)(a) (1965). Similarly, in *Geisness v. Scow Bay Packing Co.,* 16 Wash.2d 1, 13-14, 132 P.2d 740 (1942), the court required the same element.

(2) Under both theories, the unwholesome or defective condition must exist at the time it leaves the manufacturer's hands. Compare Restatement (Second) of Torts § 402A comment g (1965) with Geisness, at 14, 132 P.2d 740.

(3) Neither the implied warranty in tort theory nor section 402A is subject to the various contractual doctrines such as privity, notice, or disclaimer; neither theory requires that the plaintiff proved the defendant was negligent. Compare *Ulmer v. Ford Motor Co.,* supra, with *Flessher v. Carstens Packing Co.,* [160 P.14 (Wash.1916)]; [footnote omitted].

(4) Finally the crucial question is whether the standards "unfit for human consumption" and "defective condition unreasonably dangerous to the user" provide the same degree of liability with respect to the sale of food.

The standard of liability provided for in section 402A is the same as that found in implied warranty. As is true in several areas of the law, the term "unreasonably dangerous" cannot be taken literally. The meaning of that phrase has spawned many conceptual problems, but *Seattle-First Nat'l Bank v. Tabert,* 86 Wash.2d 145, 152-55, 542 P.2d 774 (1975), eliminated much of the confusion. In *Tabert,* at 154, the court rejected the literal interpretation of unreasonably dangerous, and firmly established that the concept of defect in Washington, as refined by comment i to section 402A, is based on the "consumer's reasonable expectation of buying a product which is reasonably safe." Accordingly, the court held a product is defective when it is "not reasonably safe," which simply means: "it [the product] must be unsafe to an extent beyond that which would be reasonably contemplated by the ordinary consumer." *Tabert,* at 154, 542 P.2d 774. See also section 402A comments g, h, and i. Thus, under Washington's formulation of section 402A, a product is defective, notwithstanding the phrase "unreasonably dangerous," when it is "not reasonably safe . . . to an extent beyond that . . . reasonably contemplated by the ordinary consumer."

We believe the concept of consumer expectations as set out in section 402A and formulated in *Ulmer* and *Tabert* reflects the same warranty heritage found in the theory of implied warranty in tort. Thus, we conclude the concepts represented by the labels, "defective condition unreasonably dangerous" and "unfitness" are identical. [Footnote omitted.] Consequently, we hold a cause of action for breach of an implied warranty of fitness for human consumption has been succeeded [footnote omitted] by the "buyer oriented" consumer expectations test when determining whether food is defective. [Citation omitted.]

Mr. Gates next contends the court erred in refusing to hold a candy bar containing a snake vertebra is defective as a matter of law. Generally, whether a product is defective is a jury question. [Citations omitted.] Here, the court instructed the jury a product is defective if "unreasonably dangerous." Although the court correctly left the question of defectiveness to the jury, we conclude the instructions erroneously defined defect under Washington's formulation of section 402A.

The concept of defect, under our view of 402A, is the same as the standard embodied in Mazetti and its progeny. Unfortunately, the drafters of the Restatement modified the definition of defect with the phrase "unreasonably dangerous." This addition was not supposed to change the concept of defect as defined by comment i to section 402A; [footnote omitted] the practical effect, however, has been to create significant definitional problems with respect to the term.

In Washington, a product which is unreasonably dangerous is necessarily defective. [Citation omitted.] However, a product need not be unreasonably dangerous in order to be found defective. This is because: "unreasonably dangerous implies a higher and different standard than what we conceive to be the intended thrust of section 402A strict liability." *Tabert,* 86 Wash.2d at 154, 542 P.2d 774. Rather, as noted, a product is defective when it is "not reasonably safe" because of a condition which renders the product unexpectedly unsafe to the ordinary consumer. [Citations omitted.]

The difference between "not reasonably safe" and "unreasonably dangerous" is not merely a theoretical problem or simply a question of semantics. The application of one term or the other has a dramatic impact on how the issue of defect is perceived by a jury. The minimum threshold, at which point a product may be found defective, is raised or lowered depending on which phrase is chosen.

Following the lead of *Tabert* and subsequent decisions, we find the court erred by including "unreasonably dangerous" in its jury instructions rather than "not reasonably safe." Instructing a jury that a product is defective, if unreasonably dangerous, connotes to the jury that the product's deviation or flaw must create a condition of abnormal or extraordinary danger before recovery is allowed. [Footnote omitted.] Such a connotation unavoidably places upon the plaintiff a significantly increased burden of proof which does not comport with our view of Washington's products liability doctrine. It also undermines one of the fundamental rationales for adopting strict products liability; i.e., the elimination of the heavy proof problems which the plaintiff must bear under other theories.

We recognize instruction 6 also included consumer expectation language which mitigates, to some extent, the implication of extraordinary danger embodied in the phrase unreasonably dangerous. Notwithstanding, because the jury may have interpreted instructions 5 and 6 as requiring Mr. Gates to prove the candy bar was extraordinarily dangerous, rather than simply "not reasonably safe," we cannot say the error was harmless given the facts of this case. Therefore, we conclude the instructions, as given, were misleading and failed to inform the jury of the proper standard of liability under our formulation of section 402A. [Citation omitted.] Upon new trial, a defective product should be defined, for the purposes of the instructions, as a product which is "not reasonably safe" because "it [is] . . . unsafe to an extent beyond that which would be reasonably contemplated by the ordinary consumer." *Tabert,* 86 Wash.2d at 154, 542 P.2d 774. Although we reverse for a new trial,

we address Mr. Gates' final assignment of error since the question may arise again at the subsequent trial.

Mr. Gates' final contention is that the trial court erred in admitting the testimony of Harry Lawrence. Apparently, the theory of both parties was that the vertebra arrived with the peanuts. Mr. Lawrence's testimony related the manufacturing process employed by Standard Brands with respect to the processing of the peanuts used in the candy bars.

He indicated that by the time Mr. Gates bit into the Baby Ruth, the vertebra could not have been "gristly and spongy" and could not have been tasted or smelled. Mr. Gates maintains, based on *Pulley v. Pacific Coca-Cola Bottling Co.,* 68 Wash.2d 778, 783, 415 P.2d 636 (1966), that the introduction of this evidence was irrelevant and prejudicial.

In *Pulley,* at 783, 415 P.2d 636, the defendant tried to rebut the plaintiff's contention that a bottle of Coca Cola contained the remains of a cigarette by attempting to introduce evidence which demonstrated the modern bottling methods utilized to prevent contamination.

Here, on the other hand, the testimony of Mr. Lawrence was not offered to demonstrate the Baby Ruth did not contain the snake vertebra at the time it left the seller. Rather, the testimony was offered to show the condition of the vertebra at the time Mr. Gates bit into the candy bar. The court's jury instructions stated the testimony of Mr. Lawrence could only be considered for the limited purpose of the vertebra condition. Therefore, we find no error.

We reverse and remand for a new trial consistent with this opinion.

Other Considerations Concerning Food: Food as an Inherently Dangerous Product

 CASE LAW

◆ **proving food product unreasonably dangerous**

Brown v. Western Farmers Association, 521 P.2d 537 (Ore. 1974).

Plaintiff chicken purchasers brought strict liability cause of action against manufacturer of chicken feed to recover loss of chickens, cost of the defective chicken feed, and lost profits. The trial court dismissed plaintiffs' claim for lost profit. The plaintiff purchasers appealed complaining that they were entitled to lost profits under a strict liability cause of action.

TONGUE, Justice.

This is an action against the manufacturer and retailer of chicken feed for damages because the feed was defective. The complaint seeks recovery on a theory of strict liability. [Footnote omitted.] In addition to seeking damages for loss of eggs caused to taste bad, for loss of chickens caused to become valueless and which had to be replaced, and for the cost of the defective feed, the complaint seeks to recover lost profits from plaintiffs' egg business in the sum of $11,000.

The court, on motion by defendant Western Farmers Association, the manufacturer, struck the allegations of loss of profits. Plaintiffs refused to plead further and the court entered an order dismissing the case as to that defendant. [Footnote omitted.] Plaintiffs appeal. We affirm.

Restatement of Torts 2d (1965), as previously adopted by this court, [footnote omitted] should be extended to economic loss, including loss of profits from inability to use property damaged by a defective product. Plaintiffs recognize that this question has not yet been decided by this court and submit various cases and authorities in support of that contention.

It is contended by defendant, however, that regardless of whether recovery under Section 402A should be extended to economic loss, including loss of profits, there can be no recovery under Section 402A because, by its terms, that rule is limited to products which are not only "in a defective condition," but are also "unreasonably dangerous to the user or consumer or to his property." Defendant contends that plaintiffs' complaint does not allege an "unreasonably dangerous" defect.

Because of the importance of this question and because it was not raised by defendant until oral argument we called for supplemental briefs on this point.

In their supplemental brief plaintiffs state the recognized rule that when a question whether a complaint states a cause of action is raised for the first time on appeal, the complaint will be liberally construed in favor of the plaintiffs. Plaintiffs point out that the complaint, after alleging that the chicken feed was fed to the laying hens, goes on to allege:

"That the said feed so purchased was defective and such defect in the feed was such that when the feed was fed to the plaintiffs' chickens, the chickens were affected adversely and damaged thereby."

Plaintiffs contend that:

"The obvious inference from these allegations is that the feed was defective and in damaging the chicks to which it was fed it obviously was not fulfilling the reasonable expectations of the plaintiffs, because chicken feed is not expected to damage one's chickens so that their eggs taste bad and they quit laying eggs, as is also alleged in paragraph V."

Plaintiffs then quote from our decision in *Heaton v. Ford Motor Co.*, 248 Or. 467, 471, 473, 435 P.2d 806 (1967), in which we expressly adopted the rule as stated in Restatement of Torts 2d § 402A, and contend that:

"What this seems to be saying is that if a product does not meet the reasonable expectations of an ordinary consumer it is defective and in a condition unreasonably dangerous to the user."

Similarly, plaintiffs construe Comment I under Section 402A as follows:

"What this is obviously saying is that if a product has a defect and because thereof it is in a condition not reasonably contemplated by the ordinary consumer, the product is by definition unreasonably dangerous." [Footnote omitted.]

Based upon this reasoning, plaintiffs conclude as follows:

"We submit that under the Restatement and the Heaton case law this complaint has alleged facts, i.e. a defect and a condition not reasonably contemplated by the ultimate consumer which in effect says the product was unreasonably dangerous. That certainly is to be inferred from the language of the complaint. In construing it for the first time on appeal the plaintiffs should have the benefit of all reasonable inferences to be drawn from the facts alleged."

Defendant responds to these contentions as follows:

"A material and necessary element of strict liability under Section 402A of the Restatement of Torts 2d is that the property be 'unreasonably dangerous' to its user or consumer or to the user or consumer's property. [Citations omitted.]

* * *

"The defect in the feed is not specified. If the defect was, for example, ground glass, the court could state without any question that the feed itself because of the defect was unreasonably dangerous to the chickens. On the other hand, if the defect was too much of an ingredient, the feed itself might not be unreasonably dangerous, except in the manner in which it was fed or eaten by the chickens.

"Therefore, from the plaintiff's complaint it is not clear whether or not the plaintiff is claiming that the defective chicken feed was 'unreasonably dangerous' or merely that the feed was defective. Both elements are required."

In considering these opposing contentions we recognize that some authorities go even further than plaintiffs and take the position that recovery on a theory of strict liability by a consumer or user of defective goods is not dependent upon proof that such goods are "unreasonably dangerous." [Footnote omitted.] This court, however, in its development of a theory of strict liability for application in cases involving defective products, has proceeded on the basis of quite different underlying assumptions.

* * *

Since our decision in *Heaton* we have consistently held that our adoption of Section 402A as the basis for an action in strict liability in tort includes its requirement that the defect be "unreasonably dangerous to the user or consumer or to his property." [Citations omitted.]

After reviewing our previous decisions in cases involving actions in strict liability by the purchasers of defective goods, as well as other cases and authorities on this subject, [footnote omitted] we reaffirm our belief that when an action for damages by the purchaser of defective goods is brought on a theory of strict liability, rather than fault or warranty, such an action is proper only when the defective goods are "unreasonably dangerous to the user or consumer or to his property."

The complaint in this case does not, in our judgment, allege facts from which it appears, either directly or by inference, that the chicken feed involved in this case was "unreasonably dangerous," rather than merely "defective" in some manner that would not make it "unreasonably dangerous." [Footnote omitted.] We do not agree with plaintiffs' contention that "if a product has a defect and because thereof it is in a condition not reasonably contemplated by the ordinary purchaser, the product is by definition unreasonably dangerous."

Neither do we agree with the contention of the dissenting opinion by O'Connell, C. J., that "the only question is whether the damage caused by the feed was that which would be contemplated by the ordinary pur-

chaser." This, according to the dissent, would include any damage that would decrease the value of plaintiffs' property.

Under that rationale, a dog food which caused a champion show dog to lose the gloss of its coat, thus decreasing its value as a show dog, would be "unreasonably dangerous" despite the fact that the health of the dog was in no way impaired. Or inferior baking powder may cause an entire batch of bread in a commercial bakery to not "rise" in the normal manner, thus impairing the salability of the bread, although not affecting its qualities of nourishment.

The rule of strict liability as stated in Section 402A, at least as adopted by this court, had its genesis in cases involving products such as automobiles with defective wheels, so as to be "unreasonably dangerous" to human life. [Citation omitted.]

* * *

We need not decide in this case whether our adoption of the rule of strict liability, as stated in Section 402A, for application in cases involving damage to property. [Citation omitted.] We do not reach or decide that question in this case, notwithstanding the interpretation of our opinion by the dissent to the contrary.

We believe, however, that the term "unreasonably dangerous," as used in Section 402A as the basis for the imposition of strict liability, without proof of negligence, was not intended to be so "watered down" as to extend to any defect which in any way may decrease the value of property, as suggested by the dissent and as plaintiffs must contend in order to recover in this case.

For these reasons we hold that the trial court did not err in striking the allegations of the complaint alleging loss of profits or in dismissing the complaint upon plaintiffs' refusal to plead further. It follows that we need not decide in this case whether, in an action on a theory of strict liability under Section 402A by the purchaser of defective goods for the recovery of damage to property, such recovery may include loss of profits or other economic loss. [Citation omitted.]

Both the specially concurring opinion and the dissenting opinion by O'Connell, C. J., propose the adoption of a rule to the effect that the remedy for breach of warranty under the Uniform Commercial Code should be the sole remedy in this case, to the exclusion of any remedy under Section 402A. [Footnote omitted.] Because we hold that no remedy is available in this case under Section 402A it may follow that the remedy provided under the UCC for breach of warranty may be the only remedy available to the plaintiff in such a case. However, the question as to whether (and, if so, the extent to which) remedies under Section 402A and under the UCC should be mutually exclusive in actions for damage to property or for economic loss was not briefed or argued by either party. Cf. *Markle v. Mulholland's Inc.,* 265 Or. 259, 509 P.2d 529 (1973). We therefore do not decide that question in this case

For all of these reasons, we affirm the judgment of the trial court.

DENECKE, Justice (specially concurring).

Confusion was created in this field of law because commercial contract concepts covering claims of economic loss were shaped to impose liability for personal injuries. Other contract concepts had to be ignored or overcome to impose liability. Eventually, the tort of strict liability was recognized as the basis for liability for personal injuries and the contract [action] was discarded. See concurring opinion in *Redfield v. Mead, Johnson & Company,* 266 Or. 273, 285, 512 P.2d 776 (1973). This court and others are now striving logically to fill in the interstices of this new creation of strict liability.

In the present case the plaintiff is now attempting to reverse the field and use the new tort of strict liability to impose liability with facts which have been governed by commercial contract principles. For example, see *Kassab v. Central Soya,* 432 Pa. 217, 246 A.2d 848 (1968), in which plaintiff contended that defective feed lowered the value of his cows. I am of the opinion that the remedy for breach of warranty that a buyer has under the Uniform Commercial Code (UCC) is adequate and should be a buyer's sole remedy. It is unnecessary and unwise to bring the confusion of the tort of strict liability to commercial transactions.

I categorize this as a case that should be governed solely by the UCC because of two characteristics: (1) the loss claimed is purely economic, loss of profits; and (2) the loss was not an 'accidental' one such as the loss in *Wulff v. Sprouse-Reitz Co., Inc.,* 262 Or. 293, 498 P.2d 766 (1972).

The UCC requirement of notice of breach of warranty, ORS 72.6070, or the possibility of the seller putting in a disclaimer, ORS 72.3160, are not unfair or foreign under these circumstances.

In my opinion there is a need for certainly in this field that outweighs my inability to state more logically why

recovery for personal injuries or for the kind of property damages involved in *Wulff v. Sprouse-Reitz Co., Inc.,* supra (262 Or. 293, 498 P.2d 766), can be based upon the tort of strict liability and the economic loss claimed by plaintiff in this case can only be based upon the remedies provided for in the UCC.

O'CONNELL, Chief Justice (dissenting).

The majority holds that the complaint does not allege facts from which it could be found that the defective chicken feed was "unreasonably dangerous" within the meaning of Section 402A of the Restatement (Second) of Torts (1965).

The complaint alleged that the defect in the feed "was such that when the feed was fed to the plaintiffs' chickens, the chickens were affected adversely and damaged thereby." As we noted in *Heaton v. Ford Motor Co.,* 248 Or. 467, 435 P.2d 806 (1967), the term "unreasonably dangerous" in the context of § 402A "means dangerous to an extent beyond that which would be contemplated by the ordinary purchaser." It is clear that the section was intended to include the danger of damaging property as well as injuring the user or consumer. See Comment D of § 402A, Restatement (Second) of Torts. The word "dangerous" may not be the best word to describe a risk of harm to property, but it was adopted by the Restatement and I see no compelling reason for attempting to refine the language of the Section.

Since damage to property falls within the ambit of § 402A, the only question is whether the damage caused by the feed was that which would be contemplated by the ordinary purchaser. I should think that if the feed had killed the chickens, the damage would clearly be sufficient to bring the defect within § 402A. If the damage falls short of this, but disables the chickens from properly performing the function that give chickens their value as property, I am unable to see why § 402A would not be applicable.

The majority opinion reads plaintiffs' brief as arguing that a product is unreasonably dangerous under § 402A in every case where the product does not meet the reasonable expectations of an ordinary consumer. I do not so interpret plaintiffs' argument. Plaintiffs argue only that if a defective product causes damage there is a right to recover, but only if the article is found to be dangerous to an extent beyond that which would be contemplated by the ordinary consumer who purchases it.

The majority opinion would permit recovery for property damage under § 402A only if the product were found to be unreasonably dangerous to human life. This seems to be the import of the court's statement that "(t)he only two decisions by this court in which Section 402A has been applied to property damage have been cases in which the defective product also posed an unreasonable danger to human life and safety." It is not illogical to argue that recovery under § 402A should be limited to damage for personal injuries, [footnote omitted] but it is incomprehensible to me to say that a product must constitute a risk of injury to human life before recovery will be allowed for property damage, even though in the particular instance in which the property damage occurred no person suffered any harm. Apparently the court would hold that recovery would be allowed for the damage to the chickens if it could be shown that the feed contained a chemical which could, but did not, damage plaintiffs hands. This is indeed a strange doctrine. The majority denies that it has embraced this doctrine, but a careful reading of the opinion reveals that the distinction made by the court between a product which is unreasonably dangerous and one which is not either must be regarded as resting on the reasoning I have described or as being based upon no reasons whatsoever.

The trial court struck the allegations of loss of profit, apparently upon the basis of our holding in *Price v. Gatlin*, 241 Or. 314, 405 P.2d 502 (1965). For the reasons set forth in my dissent in this case, I would not preclude recovery for loss of profits in the present case.

* * *

Case Notes: Food.

1. Food cases present a reoccurring problem in that the foreign ingredient in the foodstuff is difficult to be characterized as an inherent defect in the food product itself. See Comment b to § 7 of the *Restatement (Third)*.

2. Courts faced with determining whether the unwanted ingredient in the foodstuff was foreign to the product or natural to its preparation typically chose between a foreign-natural test or a reasonable consumer expectation test. The foreign-natural test requires that the defendant manufacturer of the food product be liable for any foreign material found in the product but not for any ingredient that is natural to its preparation. The consumer expectations test is similar to that employed in other strict liability analyses. Under this test, the determination whether the product is inherently defective turns upon that which is reasonably expected by the consumer to be in the food product. A majority of courts have applied the consumer expectations test. See *Lenhardt v. Ford Motor Co.*, 683 P.2d 1097 (Wash. 1984); *Morrison's Cafeteria of Montgomery, Inc. v. Haddox*, 431 So.2d 975, 978 (Ala. 1983); *Yong Cha Hong v. Marriott Corp.*, 656 F.Supp. 445, 448 (D.Md. 1987); *Mexicali Rose v. Superior Court*, 822 P.2d 1292 (Cal. 1992). A minority of courts continue to apply the foreign-natural test. See *Harris-Teeter, Inc. v. Burroughs*, 399 S.E.2d 801, 802 (Va. 1991); *Cohen v. Allendale Coca-Cola Bottling Co.*, 351 S.E.2d 897, 899-900 (S.C. Ct. Ap. 1986); see also Comment, *Defective Products Liability—Tort or Implied Warranty*, 1 Gonz. L. Rev. 106 (1966); Spak, *Bone of Contention: The Foreign-Natural Test and the Implied Warranty of Merchantability for Food Products*, 12 J. L. & Comm. 23 (1992).

3. The dangerous nature of the food product itself must arise from an inherently defective condition. A foodstuff is unreasonably dangerous only if such a condition was beyond that contemplated by the consumer of the product. Section 402A of the *Restatement (Second)* made this point more clear in connection with food products:

   Comment i. Unreasonably dangerous.

   * * * Ordinary sugar is a deadly poison to diabetics, and castor oil found use under Mussolini as an instrument of torture. That is not what is meant by "unreasonably dangerous" in this Section. The article sold must be dangerous to an extent beyond that which would be contemplated by the ordinary consumer who purchases it, with the ordinary knowledge common to the community as to its characteristics. . . . Good tobacco is not unreasonably dangerous merely because the

effects of smoking may be harmful; but tobacco containing something like marijuana
may be unreasonably dangerous. Good butter is not unreasonably dangerous because, if
such be the case, it deposits cholesterol in the
arteries and leads to heart attacks; but bad
butter, contaminated with poisonous fish oil,
is unreasonably dangerous.

See also Wade, *On The Nature of Strict Tort Liability for Products*, 44 Miss. L. J. 825(1973).

4. What ingredients in foodstuffs would be sufficiently foreign to the product to merit the
finding of liability against the food product
manufacturer under either the majority or

the minority test? What ingredients are typically natural to the preparation of food? Can
a court hold a food product manufacturer
strictly liable without fault for a contaminant
found in a foodstuff not intended or placed
there by the manufacturer? What elements
must be present in order for plaintiff to make
a submissible case in strict liability for contaminated food? What circumstantial evidence of contaminated food is acceptable to
prove plaintiff's case in strictliability? What
use is ultimately expected of a food product?
What can the consumer expect to be included
in the product?

Used Products

A used product is generally regarded as an item that has been previously sold to a buyer
who was not in the commercial stream of commerce. The seller of a used product may
face strict liability for an allegedly defective used product if that product contains a defect
that arose because the seller did not exercise due care or because the product had been
marketed as if it were new. Such a marketing scheme does not imply deceit; it implies that
warnings may have been given about the dangerous nature of the product, none of which
were attributed to its quality of being a used product. Finally, a seller of used products may
be strictly liable if the used product was remanufactured by the seller. See § 8 *Restatement
(Third), Liability of Commercial Seller or Distributor of Defective Used Products.*

 CASE LAW

◆ **strict liability of commercial dealers in used
products**

*Harber v. Altec Industries,
Inc.,* 812 F.Supp. 954
(W.D.Mo. 1993).

*Buyers of used truck brought strict liability claim against seller.
District court decided issue whether buyer had viable strict liability claim for allegedly defective used product.*

STEVENS, Chief Judge.
Missouri Law

* * *

The question of whether a dealer in used goods may
be liable under the doctrine of strict liability is undecided
under Missouri law. See *Williams v. Nuckolls,* 644 S.W.2d
670, 674 n. 1 (Mo.Ct.App.1982) ("Because of the absence of evidence to support a finding of a defect at the
time the automobile left the seller's hands, we do not
reach the controversial question of the applicability of
[Restatement of Torts (2d)] § 402(a) to the sale of used
cars."). The question has been ducked by other courts as
well. See, e.g., *Grimes v. Axtell Ford Lincoln-Mercury,* 403
N.W.2d 781, 783 (Iowa 1987) (On certification from the
Eighth Circuit Court of Appeals the Iowa Supreme
Court declined to decide the question of strict liability
for the seller of used goods, instead decided the case on

the facts). Other jurisdictions have addressed this issue and there is no national consensus: states appear to be evenly split. [Citations omitted.] Therefore, this issue is one of first impression in Missouri and there is no clear national trend that guides our result.

Normally a Federal Court looks to established state law to decide legal issues in diversity cases, but where "the state law issue is a question of first impression, a federal district court judge must apply the law as he believes the state's highest court would declare it to be if it had the opportunity to do so." *Sell v. Bertsch & Co.*, 577 F.Supp. 1393, 1398 (D.Kan.1984). In making this analysis, this court may look to prior actions of the Missouri Supreme Court and the Missouri General Assembly, as well as decisions from other states.

The Missouri Supreme Court adopted the doctrine of strict liability in *Keener v. Dayton Elec. Manufacturing Co.*, 445 S.W.2d 362 (Mo.1969). The court specifically adopted the rule as set forth in the Restatement (Second) Torts § 402A:

* * *

The court gave three reasons for adopting this rule. First, strict liability will "insure that the costs of injuries resulting from defective products are borne by the manufacturers [and sellers] that put such products on the market." Id. at 364. Second, using this doctrine would eliminate the confusion surrounding the use of warranty language to reach similar results. Id. And third, strict liability gives direction to products liability litigation. Id.

* * *

The Missouri Legislature has not addressed the issue of sellers of used goods either directly or indirectly, but its latest pronouncement on the issue of strict liability may be relevant to its intent. The legislature defined the term "products liability claim" in relation to a seller, the state of the art defense and contributory negligence:

> The term "products liability claim" means a claim or portion of a claim in which the plaintiff seeks relief in the form of damages on a theory that the defendant is strictly liable for such damages because:

(1) The defendant, wherever situated in the chain of commerce, transferred a product in the course of business; and

(2) The product was used in a manner reasonably anticipated; and

(3) Either or both of the following:

    (a) The product was then in a defective condition unreasonably dangerous when put to a reasonably anticipated use, and the plaintiff was damaged as a direct result of such defective condition as existed when the product was sold; or

    (b) The product was unreasonably dangerous when put to a reasonably anticipated use without knowledge of its characteristics, and the plaintiff was damaged as a direct result of the product being sold without an adequate warning. Mo.Rev.Stat. § 537.760.

The next section provides that a defendant "whose liability is based solely on his status as a seller in the stream of commerce may be dismissed from a products liability claim" if another defendant, including the manufacturer, is before the court, and if full recovery may be had from the other defendants. Mo.Rev.Stat. § 537.762. These new provisions seem to cast the net of strict liability to any seller "in the stream" or "chain" of commerce. The plain language of this can be interpreted, as many courts do, to include all sellers of products—new and used.

However, the assumption underlying courts' usage of the broad term "chain" or "stream" of commerce is that the stream of commerce begins with the manufacture and ends with the sale to the first end user. See, e.g., *Welkener v. Kirkwood Drug Store Co.*, 734 S.W.2d 233, 241 (Mo.Ct.App.1987). This "chain" of commerce very well may be broken when the product is first sold to the consumer. Subsequent sales in the second-hand market may be outside of this chain. The usage of the term "chain of commerce" by the legislature should be looked at in the context of its usage by the courts.

Therefore, the court finds that the broad language of M.Rev.Stat. § 537.762 does not expressly include dealers in used goods and does not establish the intent of the legislature on the issue of strict liability for the dealer in used goods.

OTHER JURISDICTIONS

Since the position of the Missouri Supreme Court on this issue is not discernible through case law or statutory language, this court will examine approaches used by the more widely cited cases from other states that have decided this issue.

Dealers in Used Goods Not Strictly Liable

The Illinois Supreme Court was the first to address this issue. In *Peterson v. Lou Bachrodt Chevrolet Co.*, 61 Ill.2d 17, 329 N.E.2d 785 (1975), the court refused to impose strict liability on a used car dealer for defects that arose after its original manufacture because to do so would be to make the dealer an insurer for defects that arise while the car is under the control of others. The court found it decisive that the defect was not present when the car left the manufacturer.

The Oregon Supreme Court has been cited frequently for its thorough analysis of the issue in *Tillman v. Vance Equipment Co.*, 286 Or. 747, 596 P.2d 1299 (1979). In that case a dealer who sold a used crane "AS IS" without making any repairs, inspection, or modifications was held not to be strictly liable. The court reviewed the justifications for strict liability—compensation to the injured party, satisfaction of the reasonable expectations of the user, and risk reduction through pressure to market a better product—and concluded that while used products dealers may be able to compensate those injured, the other two factors were not furthered by imposing liability. The court found that other factors weighed heavily against finding liability:

We conclude that holding every dealer in used goods responsible regardless of fault for injuries caused by defects in his goods would not only affect the prices of used goods; it would work a significant change in the nature of used-goods markets. Those markets, generally speaking, operate on the apparent assumption that the seller, even though he is in the business of selling such goods, makes no particular representation about their quality simply by offering them for sale. If a buyer wants some assurance of quality, he typically either bargains for it in the specific transaction or seeks out a dealer who routinely offers it (by, for example, providing a guarantee, limiting his stock of goods to those of a particular quality, advertising that his used goods are specially selected, or in some other fashion). The flexibility of this kind of market appears to serve legitimate interests of buyers as well as sellers.

We are of the opinion that the sale of a used product, without more, may not be found to generate the kind of expectations of safety that the courts have held are justifiably created by the introduction of a new product into the stream of commerce.

As to the risk reduction aspect of strict products liability, the position of the used-goods dealer is normally entirely outside the chain of distribution of the product. As a consequence, we conclude, any risk reduction which would be accomplished by imposing strict liability on the dealer in used goods would not be significant enough to justify our taking that step. The dealer in used goods generally has no direct relationship with either manufacturers or distributors. Thus, there is no ready channel of communication by which the dealer and a manufacturer can exchange information about possible dangerous defects in particular product lines or about actual and potential liability claims. *Tillman*, 596 P.2d at 1303.

In *Wilkinson v. Hicks*, 126 Cal.App.3d 515, 179 Cal.Rptr. 5 (1981), a dealer in used machinery who sold a defective 20-year old punch press was not strictly liable. In facts similar to the case at bar, the dealer had about 20 other used presses, some of which were reconditioned, but most were sole "AS IS." The court considered several factors important in finding against strict liability: whether the dealer keeps product in stock; whether the dealer inspected, used, modified, or repaired the equipment; whether the dealer had any connection to the manufacturer; whether the dealer disclaimed any warranties; and whether the dealer had any facilities or employees to inspect repair or recondition. The court also examined several policy rationales behind strict liability. "To impose such liability would as a practical matter require all dealers in used goods routinely to dismantle, inspect for latent defects, and repair or recondition their products. Such a rule would effect a radical change in nature of the used product market, which would deprive that market of the desirable flexibility referred to in *Tauber-Arons* and *LaRosa*. It would in effect render used goods dealers as insurers against defects which came into existence after the original chain of distribution and while the product was under the control of previous consumers." *Id.* 179 Cal.Rptr. at 8. In *Tauber-Arons Auctioneers Co. v. Superior Court of Los Angeles County,* 101 Cal.App.3d 268, 161 Cal.Rptr. 789 (1980), one of the cases referred to in Wilkinson, an auction company was not held strictly liable for a defective product sold at auction, even though it was clearly a "seller."

In *Fuquay v. Revel Motors, Inc.,* 389 So.2d 1238 (Fla.Ct.App. 1980), a used car dealer was sued under strict liability for a car that burst into flames after a rear-end collision. The complaint alleged that the design and placement of the gas tank was defective. The court held that the dealer was not strictly liable because the policy rationales for strict liability[,] [which were] placing the risk on the party who makes on profits from the car and improving the safety of the product, were not furthered by imposing liability in this case:

> In the present case appellee is a seller of used cars and has no responsibility for the placement of the automobile in the stream of commerce. A vendor so removed from the original marketing chain is unable to exert any significant influence on the manufacturer, and we agree. . . . that in such circumstances the vendor should not be liable, absent additional facts, for latent design defects in the product.

Fuquay, 389 So.2d at 1240 (see also *Masker v. Smith,* 405 So.2d 432, 434 (Fla.Ct.App.1981)) ("Imposing liability on the seller of used or secondhand goods for latent defects for which he is not responsible and which he could not discover by reasonable care would make such dealer a virtual insurer against every kind of defect.")

In *Sell v. Bertsch & Co.,* 577 F.Supp. 1393 (D.Kan.1984), the district court was faced with the similar problem of having to decide whether a dealer in used goods may be held strictly liable, without the benefit of the state supreme court or legislature speaking to the issue. There, the court echoed the previously-discussed cases and found that imposing strict liability would not further the policy rationales underlying strict liability.

Dealers in Used Goods Are Strictly Liable

In *Jordan v. Sunnyslope Appliance Propane & Plumbing Supplies Co.,* 135 Ariz. 309, 660 P.2d 1236 (App. 1983), the court found that dealers in used goods may be held liable on an enterprise liability theory. The court held that the Restatement § 402A imposed liability on a

"seller" and does not require that he be the first in the chain of sellers. *Id.* 660 P.2d at 1242. The court disagreed with the Tillman court's reasoning because they believed that a buyer from a dealer in used goods would not have an expectation that the good may be unreasonably dangerous. The court also reasoned that imposing strict liability would encourage risk reduction because the dealers would increase inspection and maintenance before sale. *Id.* at 1240. The court held that the proper method by which the court could take into account the situation of the dealer in used goods is by allowing the jury to weigh the circumstances of the dealer in making a determination whether the good is unreasonably dangerous. *Id.* at 1241.

The "unreasonably dangerous" analysis was first used in *Turner v. International Harvester Co.,* 133 N.J. Super. 277, 336 A.2d 62 (1975). There, the court also held that the dealer's location in the chain of distribution was a factor to be weighed by the jury in determining whether the product was "unreasonably dangerous."

In *Nelson v. Nelson Hardware, Inc.,* 160 Wis. 2d 689, 467 N.W.2d 518 (1991), the Wisconsin Supreme Court held that a hardware store that sold a shotgun could be held strictly liable where "the defective condition causing harm to the consumer of the used product arises out of the original manufacturing process and where the other requisites for liability under sec. 402 are present." *Id.* 467 N.W.2d at 521. The court held that since the hardware store accepted used firearms as trade-ins and then sold them, it was clearly a "seller" for the purposes of strict liability. The court held that the policy reasons underlying strict liability (risk reduction, compensation and liability spreading) weigh in favor of liability in the case of dealers in used goods.

Two commentators recently proposed a replacement for Restatement § 402A, but expressly declined to address the issue of used goods.

> The liability of commercial sellers of used products has been widely debated in the courts. Every court agrees that such sellers are liable for their negligence, but whether they may be held strictly liable is disputed. A majority of courts take the position that imposing strict liability on commercial sellers of used products does not further the policies expressed in comment c. On this view, used product markets are open to such variation

that consumers are better served by freeing the market of the strictures of strict liability. A minority of courts have held that imposing strict liability pressures such sellers to improve inspection of used goods before placing them on the market, thus enhancing the safety of such consumer goods. The rule stated in this section takes no position on this issue, leaving its resolution to developing case law.

James A. Henderson, Jr. & Aaron D. Twerski, A Proposed Revision of Section 402A of the Restatement (Second) of Torts, 77 Cornell L. Rev. 1512, 1518-19 (1992) (the authors are the reporters for the ALI's drafting of the Restatement (Third) of Torts. Their article is not a reflection of the views of the ALI).

POLICY ANALYSIS

As the court noted above, the decisions of other jurisdictions are not in agreement on this issue. What they are in agreement on is that the issue should be analyzed with the goals of strict liability in mind. Therefore, this court finds that the Missouri Supreme Court would base its decision on this issue on an analysis of the policy rationales underlying strict liability. This court will identify those rationales and analyze them in light of the circumstances of this case. This court's analysis will be limited to a dealer in used goods who sells products "AS IS" and does not repair, modify or alter the product. Once a dealer in used goods takes substantial steps to change the nature of the good sold, the justifications for imposing enhanced liability change markedly.

One rationale behind strict liability is that the cost of injuries resulting from defective products can best be borne by those who market these products irrespective of fault for the cause of the defect. See Restatement (Second) of Torts § 402A cmt. c. This is not a "deep pocket" theory, but rather it recognizes that those in the distribution chain can shift the costs of such injuries to all consumers equally through increased prices. See W. Page Keeton et al., Prosser & Keeton on Torts, § 98, at 962-93 (5th ed. 1984).

This policy rationale works well with manufacturers and original sellers of products. With a new product, the price can be controlled from the manufacturer. At the beginning of the sales process, the manufacturer is able to add the extra costs to pay for future injuries caused by defective products. Under Missouri Law, a seller is entitled to indemnification from the manufacturer or may be dismissed from the lawsuit when the manufacturer is properly before the court. Mo.Rev.Stat. § 537.762. This reflects a judgment by the legislature that the manufacturer should bear the brunt of the risk whenever possible.

The manufacturer is in the best position to bear the risk because he can do it the most efficiently—he sets the original cost of the product and the extra cost of insuring the product against defects may be spread out among all the units manufactured. Retailers share in this efficient distribution of risk because of their connection to the manufacturers. The close relationship between the original distributors and retailers and the manufacturers allows them to share the risk of defective equipment with those above them in the chain. The first sellers in the chain of a product may negotiate costs with manufacturers based on the increased risk they might bear. And since they sell a number of a product, they can spread the cost of risk-protection among all their sales.

The dealer in used goods, however, must bear the entire risk itself. There is no distribution chain throughout which it can share the liability. The only parties with whom the increased cost can be shared are the consumers and the sellers of goods. Increasing the cost for consumers may drive the cost of used goods too close to the cost of new goods and drive the second-hand market out of business. If the cost of insuring the products is charged to the original owner of the goods who wishes to sell them, the lower price offered by the used-goods dealer may make it not worth their while to put the goods into the used goods market. Rather than sell for a lower price, the seller may decide to sell the goods himself. An exodus of goods from the used goods market would also shut businesses down. Shifting the cost of insurance for these goods to the sellers of used goods risks driving away the buyers or the suppliers, or both.

The goal of strict liability is not to put sellers out of business. It is to spread the risk to those who can afford it. Considering the size of many judgments, it may not be a question of spreading the cost of strict liability among customers or sellers; such judgments may close a seller down. Due to the passage of time before a product enters the second-hand market, there is more likelihood that a dealer in used goods will be the only seller or manufacturer that can be identified with the goods, and thus be left to defend the lawsuit (and pay any judgment) along. [Footnote omitted.] Or the defect in the goods may arise after the product leaves the initial stream of distribution, also leaving the dealer in used goods alone in the suit. Lawsuits that go after this type of seller usually come about because the other parties either have no money or can't be found. A dealer in used goods is rarely the first choice for a defendant. There is a good chance that by the time a lawsuit works its way to this type of defendant, the dealer in used goods may be the only defendant left to pursue.

Not only are used goods dealers more likely to be alone in a lawsuit, they are less able to deal with a judgment. Dealers in used goods tend to be much smaller operations than others in the chain of distribution and the large amounts awarded for an injury would bankrupt these smaller businesses if they are forced to pay a judgment alone.

In the present case, defendant is alone in the lawsuit. The manufacturer of the defective part is not known, and the manufacturer and seller of the original product have been judged not to be liable because the defect was not present when the equipment was manufactured originally. Defendant has no relation to the original stream of commerce, but is left to defend the suit on its own. In situations such as this, strict liability does not work to spread the risk to those who can afford it best. Instead, strict liability does not work to spread the risk to those who can afford it best. Instead, strict liability in this case will work to destroy the used-goods market. This rationale does not support imposing strict liability.

Risk Reduction through Increased Inspection

The argument that imposing strict liability will increase the safety of such goods because the dealer will use increased care in inspecting and servicing the goods [footnote omitted] is without merit in relation to latent defects, such as this one. By its very definition, a latent defect is one that "could not be discovered by reasonable care and inspection." Black's Law Dictionary 794 (5th ed. 1979). Even if a dealer in used goods were to inspect its products, latent defects would not be found and injuries would not be prevented. Defects could only be found through vigorous inspection and dismantling of the products, but that procedure would dramatically change the used-goods market. Every dealer in used goods would be forced to become a reconditioner of products. Each product would have to be taken apart and rebuilt before sale to try to avoid liability. The cost imposed would be tremendous. The used-goods market

would no longer be able to meet the needs of low-cost seeking consumers. Plaintiffs may have other remedies for discoverable defects under negligence, but imposing a rigorous duty of inspection under the aegis of strict liability would do little to prevent injuries from latent defects at the expense of the free-market nature of the used-goods market. See *Wilkinson v. Hicks*, 126 Cal.App.3d 515, 179 Cal.Rptr. 5, 8 (1981).

Risk Reduction Market Pressure

Another policy rationale is that the seller of goods can exert pressure on the manufacturer to correct defective products and discourage their marketing. This argument, too, is ineffective when applied to dealers in used goods. In the normal chain of distribution, seller or distributor have the opportunity to communicate with the manufacturer about the safety of the product. They can relay concerns and suggestions to the manufacturer either directly or through the manufacturer's sales force, or a seller can send a message to the manufacturer to correct a defect by ceasing to purchase its goods. This kind of influence is possible precisely because the normal seller of new goods deals with a product on a regular basis and has the opportunity to observe its sales and communicate with its buyers. The normal seller has adequate means to receive information on a product and relay it to the manufacturer, and the dealer has the economic influence to effect change.

On the other hand, dealers in used goods do not have the influence, and rarely have the channels of communication. *Fuquay v. Revel Motors, Inc.*, 389 So.2d 1238, 1240 (Fla.Ct.App.1980). Dealers in used goods do not buy their stock from the manufacturer, or even from a distributor—the direct link to the producer is severed. *Tillman v. Vance Equipment Co.*, 286 Or. 747, 596 P.2d 1299, 1303 (1979). Their goods come by way of resales and trade-ins. In the present case, for instance, Altec received the truck as a trade-in on another vehicle. Oftentimes, the dealer in used goods has no idea how to contact the manufacturer and sometimes, as in this case, does not even know who the manufacturer was. Meaningful communication with the manufacturer is unlikely if not impossible.

In those circumstances where the dealer can actually communicate with the manufacturer, his voice will carry little weight. Manufacturers receive no direct economic benefit from the sale of second-hand goods—they only make their money on the initial sale. Instead, manufacturers lose prospective sales of new goods to cheaper, substitute, second-hand goods. A threat by a dealer in used goods to discontinue the sale of goods until defects are corrected would be a futile gesture. Furthermore, the second-hand market often receives products that are no longer manufactured. Any comments by a seller of discontinued goods would be of little use after the fact. In the present case, the truck was 10 years old and the manufacturer is unknown. A judgment against Altec would have no discernable corrective impact on the manufacturer of this product. This rationale weighs heavily against the imposition of strict liability.

Consumer Expectations

Another rationale underlying strict liability is that consumers' reasonable expectations should be satisfied. Strict liability is based partly upon the idea "that the public has a right to and does expect . . . that reputable sellers will stand behind their goods." See Restatement (Second) of Torts § 402A cmt. c. When a person buys a new product, it is reasonable to expect that it will serve its purpose satisfactorily: the product is sold direct from the factory and usually comes with warranties and guarantees. Strict liability is justified in these circumstances to ensure that the consumer gets what is promised.

Unlike a new products market, where assurances and guarantees are freely made, the used market usually operates with no assurances and often, as was the case here, with affirmative disclaimers as to the quality of the goods. Such expectations of quality as are made in the new-goods market are not reasonable in the used-goods market [footnote omitted] where caveat emptor is generally the rule. The used product market reflects free market forces at work. Buyers go to a used market to buy something for less or to buy something that is no longer on the new product market. In exchange for the lower price or a more desirable model, buyers are willing to sacrifice some of the assurances that come with new products. In other words, the buyer of used goods is willing to take his or her chances in exchange for a cheaper price.

One important product characteristic consumers of used goods are willing to forego is that of durability. Since a product has already been used, the useful life of a product presumably has been reduced. Consumers pay less because a used product may not last as long as a new one. Consumers also pay less because a product may not work as well as a new one, either because of wear and tear or improved technology.

For our purposes the most important fact is that when buying a used product, a consumer knows that for some reason, another consumer has chosen to sell what was once new. He or she may be selling it because he wants a new item or because it doesn't work as it should but a purchaser of used goods is on notice that the used good was sold because it no longer met the seller's needs.

With these considerations in mind, the purchaser of used goods must have lower expectations of quality than a buyer of new goods. The buyer of used goods knows that there might be something "wrong" with the good—that is why it is being sold. And the better the deal, the more likely something is "wrong." If a consumer purchases a 19" color television set at a garage sale for $10 "AS IS" and with no assurance of quality, he or she should expect that the television set does not work and be pleasantly surprised if it does. Most used goods are worth what is paid for them; but consumers are willing to risk nonperformance in exchange for a good price.

Should a buyer of used goods desire more protection for the goods, that protection may be bargained for. See *Tillman v. Vance Equipment Co.*, 286 Or. 747, 596 P.2d 1299, 1303 (1979). The buyer may pay extra for a warranty or a right to return. In many retail situations, extended warranties or service contracts can be purchased to raise consumer expectations about the quality of a good.

Consumer expectations of used goods may change with the nature of the seller and the representations that the seller may make. Expectations for used goods may rise where there is no disclaimer, or there is some type of warranty or period for return. And where the product has been repaired, inspected or modified, the seller's liability should and does, increase. See *Wilkinson v. Hicks*, 126 Cal.App.3d 515, 179 Cal.Rptr. 5, 8 (1981). In the event of a product failure in those circumstances, the buyer may have an action in negligence for faulty work or failure to inspect property. [Footnote omitted.]

The way the system now stands the consumer should be protected in relation to his expectations. In this case, the truck was bought for a good price "AS IS" and the seller did not inspect, repair or modify the product. The sale contract clearly stated that the buyer accepted the product "with all faults" and after having the opportunity to inspect. Defendants took careful and deliberate steps to disclaim all warranties pursuant to Missouri law and such disclaimers were legally effective. After such warranties are disclaimed, a buyer can have no reasonable expectations that the truck will operate flawlessly and without incident. Indeed, a purchaser should expect that something might go wrong. This case amply demonstrates that the consumer expectations in a used-goods market are considerably lower than that for new goods. Therefore, strict liability is not necessary to protect the lowered expectation of consumers.

Preventing Waste

There is another policy peculiar to the used-goods market that weighs against strict liability. Used-goods markets serve the important function of preventing economic and resource waste. Many users of goods prefer to own newer, more advanced and better-performing products. When they decide to buy a new model or a replacement of an old product, there should be a place for the old product to go instead of the junk heap. In a free market, users will be free to either sell directly to another user or sell to a dealer in used goods. By selling to a dealer in used goods, the party can save time and energy and maybe get a better price (assuming it is profitable for resellers to exist). If strict liability is imposed on resellers for defective goods, the existence of a second-hand market will be threatened because dealers may not want to risk the tremendous and unpredictable expense that strict liability would impose. Without the second-hand market, the original buyers will be forced to waste time and money by selling the item themselves [footnote omitted] or waste the product by junking it. Either is an inefficient allocation of resources.

VICTIM COMPENSATION

The overriding purpose of "products liability law, essentially, is to socialize the losses caused by defective products." *Welkener v. Kirkwood Drug Store Co.*, 734 S.W.2d 233, 241 (Mo.Cto.App.1987), quoting *Lippard v. Houdaille Indus., Inc.*, 715 S.W.2d 491, 492 (Mo. banc 1986). The most important purpose of this "socialization of losses" is that innocent victims should be compensated. Strict liability was created to compensate victims

in situations where traditional common-law claims in warranty and negligence would not work. This rationale applies equally in relation to a dealer in used goods. In this case, for instance, plaintiffs have tried, and failed, to recover from the original manufacturer and seller. If Altec is allowed to escape liability, the victim will be denied recovery for his injuries from anyone connected with the product that caused the injury. Since dealers in used goods are often defendants of the last resort, removing them from strict liability may prevent many innocent victims from recovering. This factor weighs in favor of strict liability.

CONCLUSION

The court finds that the factors justifying strict liability in other situations do not warrant imposition of strict liability for a dealer in used goods. The only policy rationale that is served by imposing liability in these circumstances is that innocent victims will be compensated. Although this is an important goal of our tort system, it is not the only goal. [Citation omitted.] The tort system is based on the "fundamental principal of fairness." *Welkener*, 734 S.W.2d at 240. Fairness in strict liability is not served by imposing strict liability here. A policy with CERCLA-like tentacles of liability used against these dealers will not improve the manufacture of the goods and will not prevent latent defects from being passed on to consumers. Consumer expectations are already being met in the used-goods market. Furthermore, the dealers in used goods are not well situated to bear the cost of insuring the goods they sell. Imposing strict liability here would risk destroying one of the few truly free markets left. The policy rationales weigh heavily against strict liability in the circumstances in this case.

Based on the discussion above, this court finds that the Missouri Supreme Court would not extend strict liability to include to sellers of used goods who perform no maintenance, modification or repair on the used product and who successfully disclaim all warranties of title. Consequently, the court finds that defendant is entitled to judgment as a matter of law on Count I. All three of plaintiff's counts, therefore, do not state viable causes of action against this defendant.

Case Notes: Used Products.

1. The *Restatement (Third)* at § 8 addresses all theories under which the dealer of used products may be found liable for the harm caused by the product. Specifically, subsection (a) imposes liability on a seller of used products for his or her negligence. Subsections (b), (c), and (d) of the *Restatement (Third)* impose liability in the absence of fault under particular circumstances. Many factors will affect the consumer's expectation regarding a used product, including its safe function and performance, age, condition, and price. See comment b to § 8 of the *Restatement (Third)*. See also Korpela, Annotation, *Strict Liability in Tort. Liability of Seller of Used Product*, 53 A.L.R.3d 337 (1973 & Supp. 1992); Note, *The Application of Strict Liability in Tort to Retailers of Used Products: A Proposal*, 16 Okla. City L. Rev. 373 (1991).

2. The *Restatement (Third)* at § 8 was specific in defining used products as "a product . . . commercially sold or otherwise distributed . . . and used for some period of time." Two aspects of such a product are important here. First, such a product must have been used for some period of time before again being sold commercially. Second, the used product must have been sold by a commercial dealer of used products, such as a retailer, distributor, or wholesaler. It is not enough that a used product be sold by merely anyone. See Comment d to § 8 of the *Restatement (Third)*; see also *J.B. Jordan v. Sunnyslope Appliance Propane & Plumbing Supplies Co.*, 660 P.2d 1236, 1238-42 (Ariz. Ct. App. 1983); *Peterson v. Lou Bachrodt Chevrolet Co.*, 329 N.E.2d 785 (Ill. 1975).

3. What used products fall within the definition and liability parameters of § 8 of the *Restatement (Third)?* What test can a court engage to determine whether the product and its dealer are subject to strict liability? How does the court determine whether the product inherently contains a manufacturing, design, or warning defect? What standards or tests should the court not engage to determine the defective nature of the product given that the product is used? Assuming the participation of a commercial seller, do all used products qualify under the provisions of § 8 of the *Restatement (Third)?*

Regulation Through Litigation

Product liability lawsuits may also serve the broader purpose of preventing injury to others and, thus, offering an implied regulation of the defective product. For example, strict liability for defective products requires that the product manufacturer be liable without the finding of its fault, because it serves the public's general interest to require that the product manufacturer makes safe products. Certainly, other regulatory mechanisms are more readily available, such as legislation, market demands, and insurance constraints. But where these approaches fail to prevent a defective product from reaching the market, a product liability lawsuit may be an individual's only avenue to create change. This approach is difficult; it is slow; it requires publicity; and it requires others literally to follow by bringing their own lawsuits. But it has been successful in producing modification of defective products, which has resulted in preventing injury to others. Among the best known examples of lawsuit-induced product modification are defects in automobiles, such as the absence of airbags, shoulder harness seat belts, the width of the chassis suspension axle, and the placement of the gas tank.

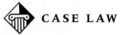

CASE LAW

♦ **regulation of handguns through vicarious liability lawsuit**

Ganim v. Smith & Wesson Corporation, et al., 1999 WL 1241909 (Conn. Super. Ct. 1999).

Plaintiffs Mayor and City of Bridgeport brought causes of action against firearms manufacturers, trade associations, and retail sellers alleging that defendants had failed to make firearms safer by incorporating locks and safety devices into products, by protecting against the flow of firearms to criminals and illegal markets, by failing to warn consumers about the dangers of firearms. Trial court decided issues whether plaintiffs had sufficient standing and whether plaintiffs had viable causes of action against defendants.

MCWEENY, J.

* * *

[T]he essential issue before this court is whether the plaintiffs can maintain that their claimed interest has been specially and injuriously affected in a way that is cognizable by law. The general rules of standing will determine the plaintiffs' ability to maintain their non-statutory claims alleged in the fourth [footnote omitted] through ninth counts. Conversely, in order to maintain the statutory claims asserted in the first through third counts, the plaintiffs must meet the statutory definition of persons intended to bring these actions.

The plaintiffs' allegation of harm as outlined above from the preface of the first amended complaint characterize their damages as including expenditures of large amounts of money on police, prisons, medical care, fire department services, emergency services, public health services, social services, pension benefits, court resources and other services and facilities. The complaint also alleges substantial losses of tax revenue, investment, economic development and productivity as a result of the defendants' actions.

The defendants contend that the plaintiffs' claims are too remote to be cognizable by law. Indeed, it is recognized at common law that a plaintiff who complains of harm resulting from misfortune visited upon a third person is generally held to stand at too remote a distance to recover. [Citation omitted.] An early Connecticut case was instrumental in the recognition of this principle. In *Connecticut Mutual Life Insurance Co. v. New York & New Haven R. Co.*, 25 Conn. 265, 276 (1856), the supreme court held that an insurance company could not recover from a third party for the death of its insured. More than a century later, the court held in *Maloney v. Pac*, 183 Conn. 313, 321, 439 A.2d 349 (1981), that standing requires a colorable claim of direct injury to the complaining party. Connecticut courts also follow the usual rule against vicarious third-party liability. [Citations omitted.]

According to the plaintiffs, they have suffered direct injury in the form of expenditures they have had to make for increased police and fire protection, as well as medical and other public services necessitated by gun injuries to persons who are not parties to this litigation. [Footnote omitted.] The court notes that they complained of misuse of firearms necessitating increased police protection and other social services are in fact acts of unidentified persons who are not named or represented as parties in this lawsuit.

In advance of their unusual theories supporting this litigation, the plaintiffs draw inspiration if not precedent from the "tobacco" cases. These are a series of suits brought by states claiming damages against tobacco companies for the cost of medical care expended by the states on behalf of sick smokers. Generally, a state's right to maintain such an action has been held cognizable by law. See *State Ex. Rel. Norton v. R.J. Reynolds Tobacco Co.*, Docket No. 3432 (Colo.Dist.Ct., October 2, 1998); *State Ex. Rel. Kelley v. Phillip Morris, Inc.*, Docket No. 84281 (Mich.Cir.Ct., May 28, 1997); *State Ex. Rel. Humphrey v. Phillip Morris, Inc.*, Docket No. 8565 (Minn.Dist.Ct., Feb. 19, 1998); *State v. Phillip Morris, Inc.*, Docket No. 744 (Vt.Sup.Ct., Mar. 25, 1998); *State v. American Tobacco Co.*, Docket No. 15056 (Wash.Sup.Ct., Nov. 19, 1996); *State Ex. Rel. Bronster v. Brown & Williamson Tobacco Corp.*, Docket No 441 (Hawaii Cir. Ct., Sept. 18, 1998). In each of these cases, state statutes authorized the state to maintain its claims against the defendant tobacco companies. [Footnote omitted.] In *Texas v. American Tobacco Co.*, 14 F.Sup.2d 956, 962-63 (E.D.Tex.1997), the unique quasi-sovereign right of the state to protect the health and welfare of its citizens afforded it standing to sue. [Footnote omitted.] The result of these cases is that states that sued tobacco companies have been promised more than $200 billion over a twenty-five year period.

When conceiving the complaint in this case, the plaintiffs must have envisioned such settlements as the dawning of a new age of litigation during which the gun industry, liquor industry and purveyors of "junk" food would follow the tobacco industry in reimbursing government expenditures and submitting to judicial regulation.

The tobacco litigation, by the states, has not succeeded in eradicating the rules of law on proximate cause, remoteness of damages and limits on justifiability. This is evidenced by a series of federal appellate decisions dismissing "me-too" cases initiated by insurers and health and welfare funds against the tobacco companies. [Citation omitted.] Just as the states had sought reimbursement for the expense of medical care on behalf of citizens affected by cigarette smoking, these cases involved claims by insurers and health and welfare funds for medical expenses paid on behalf of smokers. In all of these cases the insurer or fund claims were dismissed because, unlike the claims brought by the states, insurers and private welfare funds are not statutorily authorized to initiate direct actions against a third-party tortfeasor; nor do they enjoy a statutory right of subrogation, or possess the unique quasi-sovereign rights of the state. The Second Circuit noted in *Laborers Local 17 v. Philip Morris, Inc.*, supra, that: "Hence, in general, state cases are often distinguishable on the issue of proximate causation given the state's unique role relative to protection of its citizens, statutes governing Medicaid recoupment, and certain state statutes that permit states to maintain actions on behalf of their citizenry." Id.

The plaintiffs can cite no statute specifically authorizing them to recoup the expenditures they claim or obtain the injunctive relief they seek. Plaintiffs cite a provision of Connecticut's Home Rule Act, General Statutes § 7-148(c)(1), which essentially provides that "[a]ny municipality shall have the power to . . . (A) . . . sue and be sued, and institute, prosecute, maintain and defend any action or proceeding in any court of competent jurisdiction." Also relied upon by the plaintiffs are the other provisions of the Home Rule Act which at General Statutes § 7-148(c)(7)(H) empower municipalities to [r]egulate and prohibit the carrying on within the municipality of any trade, manufacturer, business or profession . . . prejudicial to public health . . . or danger-

ous to, or constituting an unreasonable annoyance to, those living or owning property in the vicinity . . . [p]reserve the public peace and good order . . . and do all things necessary or desirable to promote the public health." Id., (ii) through (xi).

The plaintiffs also argue in their Memorandum of Law in Opposition to Defendants' Motion to Dismiss for Lack of Subject Matter Jurisdiction, p. 7, that "[t]he defendants have pointed to no language in the Home Rule Act nor to any case law, and Bridgeport is aware of none, that provides the type of limitation that they would have the court read into the otherwise clear and broad language of Section 7-148." The plaintiffs' argument mistakes the law. In determining whether a municipality has authority for certain action pursuant to the Home Rule Act, the role of the trial court is to follow the rule of law articulated by the Connecticut Supreme Court, as follows: "We do not search for a statutory prohibition against [what is sought]; rather, we must search for statutory authority for the enactment." *Avonside, Inc. v. Zoning & Planning Commission*, 153 Conn. 232, 236, 215 A.2d 409 (1965); *Buonocore v. Bradford*, 192 conn. 399, 402, 471 A.2d 961 (1984). Again, this rule logically results from the fact that a municipality has no inherent powers of its own; it is merely a creation of the state and its actions must be authorized by the state. [Citations omitted.] The statutory authority to sue and be sued and to promote the public health fails as statutory authority to bring suit against gun manufacturers and distributors for recoupment of municipal expenditures. [Footnote omitted.]

The plaintiffs' absence of statutory authority is apparent in view of the scope of its claims for relief. The plaintiffs seek broad injunctive relief relating to the manufacture, distribution and marketing of handguns.

Connecticut law clearly maintains that a municipality is preempted from action where the legislature has demonstrated that intent to occupy the entire field of regulation on the matter, or whenever the local ordinance irreconcilably conflicts with a statute. *Dwyer v. Farrell*, 193 Conn. 7, 14, 478 A.2d 257 (1984) (fact that local ordinance does not expressly conflict with statute will not save it when legislative purpose in enacting statute is frustrated by the ordinance); [citations omitted]. *Dwyer v. Farell, supra*, 193 Conn. 7, 475 A.2d 257, involved a determination that a New Haven City ordinance regulating the retail sale of pistols and revolvers was pre-empted by state law. The court found "the New Haven ordinance removes an entire class of persons as potential sellers of handguns at retail. The state permit is rendered an illusory right because a casual seller residing in a non-business zone can have no real hope of ever conforming to the local ordinance. In this respect, the local ordinance conflicts with the legislative intent as expressed in the applicable statutes. The City has removed the right that the state permit bestows and thus has exceeded its powers." *Id.*, 14, 475 A.2d 257.

The Connecticut legislature has enacted a statutory scheme of regulation on the sale, distribution and purchase of firearms within the State of Connecticut, [footnote omitted] further evidencing the absence of plaintiffs' statutory authorization under the Home Rule Act for action that appears to conflict with state regulations. The Connecticut Supreme Court has recognized in the above referenced decisions, among many others, that municipalities have no inherent power under the Home Rule Act to act on matters of statewide concern. [Citation omitted.] Surely the scope and magnitude of the problems described by plaintiffs in their first amended complaint are serious matters of public health and safety that are of statewide concern.

In Plaintiff's Memorandum of Law in opposition to the Defendants' Motion to Dismiss for Lack of Subject Matter Jurisdiction, p. 7 n. 2, the plaintiffs concede that they do not claim nor do they need to claim parens patriae status. Nor do they or can they claim sovereign status akin to that enjoyed by the State of Connecticut. [Citation omitted.]

As the court outlined earlier, the plaintiffs' standing to bring statutory claims under the PLA and CUTPA will be dealt with separately. Thus far it has been determined in this opinion that the plaintiffs are not statutorily authorized either to initiate this action under the Home Rule Act or to recoup municipal expenditures, nor are the plaintiffs blessed with the sovereign power of the state to protect the public health and welfare. Whether the plaintiffs have standing to maintain their non-statutory claims therefore must turn on whether the common law allows them to.

The court will consider this issue by analysis similar to that relied upon by the federal appellate courts in the recent decisions affecting recoupment claims by insurance and health and welfare funds. A case recently dismissed by the Seventh Circuit Court of Appeals had been brought by the Blue Cross and Blue Shield Associations of Arkansas, Connecticut, Illinois, Kentucky, Missouri and North Dakota, joined by affiliated insurers (collectively "the Blues") against the tobacco industry, seeking "to sue directly for wrong done to their insureds." *International Brotherhood of Teamsters, Local 734 Health & Welfare Trust Fund v. Philip Morris, Inc.* (7th Cir. November 15, 1999). The Seventh Circuit noted that "[b]ecause three other appellate courts have issued comprehensive opinions on the merits of plaintiff's claims, we just hit the highlights, mentioning only our principal reasons for agreeing with these decisions." *Id.* Likewise, this court is persuaded by the same authority, in this case in which a city and its mayor seek to sue the handgun industry directly for alleged wrongs against the Bridgeport citizenry.

In dismissing the action before it, the Seventh Circuit noted that "[f]or more than one hundred years state and federal courts have adhered to the principle (under both state and federal law) that the victim of a tort is the proper plaintiff, and that insurers or other third-party providers of assistance and medical care to the victim may recover only to the extent their contracts subrogate them to the victims' rights. . . ." *Id.* The decision provides one of the rationales for that rule:

The outcome of smokers' suits is why the funds and "Blues" want to sue in their own names; they choose antitrust and RICO [instead of subrogation] because, in the Blues' [own] words, assumption of the risk, contributory negligence, and similar defenses are not pertinent. This is exactly why plaintiffs must lose. A third-party payor has no claim if its insureds did not suffer a tort; no rule of law requires persons whose acts cause harm to cover all of the costs, unless these acts were legal wrongs. The food industry puts refined sugar in many products, making them more tasty; as a result some people eat too much (or eat the wrong things) and suffer health problems and early death. No one supposes, however, that sweet foods are defective products on this account; chocoholics can't recover in tort from Godiva Chocolatier; it follows that the funds and the Blues can't recover from Godiva either. The same reasoning applies when the defendant is Philip Morris. If, as the Funds and the Blues say, the difference is that Philip Morris has committed civil wrongs while Godiva has not, then the way to establish this is through tort suits, rather than through litigation in which the plaintiffs seek to strip their adversaries of all defenses. Given the posture of these cases we must assume, as the complaints allege, that the cigarette manufacturers have lied to the public about the safety of their products. But lies matter only if the customers are deceived. Whether smokers relied to their detriment on tobacco producers' statements is a central question in tort litigation, a question that cannot be dodged by the device of an insurers' direct suit. *Id.*

Likewise, in this case the nefarious conduct of the gun industry should be addressed in a traditional tort suit in which the direct victims would have to overcome the industry's claims of proximate cause, assumption of risk and contributory negligence.

On this same issue, the Second Circuit observed that the plaintiffs "have sued in their own right for the money spent for plan participants and, in addition, for injuries and damages they insist were separate from the injuries to plan participants. . . ." *Laborers Local 17 Health & Benefit Fund v. Philip Morris, Inc.,* supra. The court dismissed the case on the basis of the direct injury requirement of proximate cause. "Because the consequences of an act go endlessly forward in time and its causes stretch back to the dawn of human history, proximate cause is used essentially as a legal tool for limiting a wrongdoer's liability only to those harms that have a reasonable connection to his actions. The law has wisely determined that it is futile to trace the consequences of a wrongdoer's actions to their ultimate end, if an end there is." *Id.* Rather, relying on *Holmes v. Securities Investor Protection Corp.,* supra, 503 U.S. 258, 112 S.Ct. 1311, 117 L.Ed.2d 532 (1992), the court realized the demand at common law for some direct relation between the injury asserted and the conduct alleged. "A plaintiff's right to sue . . . require[s] a showing that the defendant's violation not only was a 'but for' cause of his injury, but was the proximate cause as well." *Id.,* 268.

In Holmes, the Supreme Court discussed three policy concerns that courts should consider when determining whether a party may recover for injuries to a third person: (1) the difficulty of determining damages; (2) the possibility of multiple recoveries; and (3) the general interest in deterring injurious conduct and availability of other parties who are more directly injured and may be better able to vindicate this interest rather than the plaintiff. To this end, the Holmes court applied a proximate cause analysis, observing that " 'proximate cause' is used to label generically the judi-

cial tools used to limit a person's responsibility for the consequences of that person's own acts. . . . Thus, a plaintiff who complain[s] of harm flowing merely from the misfortunes visited upon a third person by the defendant's act is generally said to stand at too remote a distance to recover. . . . Although such directness of relationship is not the sole requirement of [proximate] causation, it has been one of its central elements." [Citations omitted.] *Id.,* 268-69.

This language tells us that to plead a direct injury is a key element for establishing proximate causation, independent of and in addition to other traditional elements of proximate cause. Thus, the other traditional rules requiring that defendant's acts were a substantial cause of the injury, and that plaintiff's injury was reasonably foreseeable, are additional elements, not substitutes for alleging (and ultimately, showing) a direct injury. [Citation omitted.]

The case before this court essentially is a recoupment claim pleaded in nine counts. Plaintiffs are seeking damages analogous to those sought by the Blues and the Funds discussed above, as asserted against the tobacco industry. But the plaintiffs in this case have no greater authority to pursue monetary gain than did the plaintiffs in those actions. The plaintiffs may have suffered increased costs because of the defendants' products, but that "but for" argument cannot and does not overcome the necessary finding of proximate cause, relying on direct injury. At common law, loss that is purely contingent upon harm to third parties is too remote to be recoverable. [Citation omitted.]

The plaintiffs' claim relying on diminution of property values is similar to the "infrastructure harm" case discussed by the Second Circuit: it was found that the plaintiff's business may have been damaged by the defendant's ship breaking lose, crashing into and collapsing a bridge, causing disruption of river traffic; however [p]roximate cause was lacking because those injuries were not "direct" but "occurred only because the downed bridge made it impossible to move traffic along the river"; in other words, the injuries were merely indirect and therefore too remote as a matter of law, since they were wholly derivative of an injury to the property of a third party, the bridge owner.

"[T]he critical question posed by the direct injury test is whether the damages a plaintiff sustains are derivative of an injury to a third party. If so, then the injury is indirect; if not, it is direct." *Id.* Damages that are derivative of harm suffered by third parties, being the citizens of Bridgeport in this case, are indirect and too remote to be recoverable by these plaintiffs under the common law tort principles. "Consequently, because [the] defendants' alleged misconduct did not proximately cause the injuries alleged, [the] plaintiffs lack standing to bring [their common law tort] claims against [these] defendants." *Id.*

This conclusion is consistent with the three policy considerations addressed in Holmes. The Second Circuit in applying the Holmes policy factors noted the difficulties of providing damages as between a plaintiff insurer and a defendant cigarette maker, when superimposed on any calculation is the agency of the individual smokers deciding whether and how frequently to smoke. The difficulties presented in this case by the agency of the individuals firing guns and injuring themselves or others cannot be overcome. Calculating the impact of gun marketing on teen suicide and diminution of property values in Bridgeport would create insurmountable difficulties in damage calculation. "In this light, the direct injury test can be seen as wisely limiting standing to sue to those situations where the chain of causation leading to damages is not complicated by the intervening agency of third parties . . . from whom the plaintiffs' injuries derive." *Laborers Local 17 Health & Benefit Fund v. Philip Morris, Inc.*, supra.

The benefit of recognizing early on the futility of a damage calculation in this case is supported by *Beverly Hills Concepts, Inc. v. Schatz & Schatz, Ribocoff & Kotkin*, 247 Conn. 48, 717 A.2d 724 (1998), in which the Supreme Court overturned an award of $15.9 million in lost profits, "guided by the well-established principal that such 'damages must be proven with reasonable certainty.' " *Id.*, 60, 717 A.2d 724. Plaintiffs cannot seriously maintain that reasonable certainty in calculating their damage claims is within the realm of possibility. As the Second Circuit noted in *Laborers Local 17*: "[F]or us to rule otherwise could lead to a potential explosion in the scope of tort liability, which, while perhaps well-intended, is a subject best left to the legislature." *Laborers Local 17 Health & Benefit Fund v. Philip Morris, Inc.*, supra.

The second policy factor addressed in Holmes focuses on the possibility that recognizing claims of the indirectly injured would force courts to adopt complicated rules apportioning damages among plaintiffs removed at different levels of injury from the violative acts, to obviate the risk of multiple recoveries. *Holmes v. SIPC, supra*, 503 U.S. at 269. In this instance, the State of Connecticut, insurance companies, health and welfare funds, the directly injured and others "at different levels of injury from the violative acts" would require just the type of complicated apportioning of damages which is to be avoided.

The third Holmes policy factor requires recognizing the availability of other persons (including directly injured victims) who might vindicate the law without any of the problems attendant upon suits by these plaintiffs. The directly injured victims of gun injuries would be able to proceed under traditional tort or perhaps nuisance [footnote omitted] theories of redress.

Moreover, with respect to the medical expense claim, the state through Medicaid reimbursement certainly would be in a better position than plaintiffs to seek recoupment, inasmuch as such action by the state is statutorily authorized. See General Statutes § 17b-265 and 42 U.S.C. § 1396k (concerning the State of Connecticut's right to medical reimbursement). In addition, such an action would meet the "general interest in deterring injurious conduct" standard noted in Holmes as the objective of its third policy consideration. *Holmes v. SIPC*, supra, 503 U.S. 269. [Footnote omitted.]

The plaintiffs also have asserted a claim under the PLA. General Statutes § 52-572m(c) of the PLA defines a "claimant" as: "a person asserting a product liability claim for damages incurred by the claimant or one for whom the claimant is acting in a representative capacity." General Statutes § 52-572m(b) defines a "product liability claim" as "all claims or actions brought for personal injury, death or property damage. . . ." The plaintiffs' indirect injury claims are insufficient to grant them standing under the PLA statutory requirements. The damages claimed by the plaintiffs were not incurred by them and they lack statutory authority to act for those directly injured.

The plaintiffs in this case also have asserted their own nuisance claim. In the fourth count of their first amended complaint, the plaintiffs claim that the defendants have "unlawfully facilitated, participated in and contributed to the illegal flow of handguns into Bridgeport, thereby causing damages and injury to Bridgeport's residents and Bridgeport . . . Defendants' conduct has caused and continues to cause a public nuisance in Bridgeport." (First Amended Complaint, Fourth Count, 88 and 101.) Whether the plaintiffs are the proper parties to challenge the illegal flow of handguns within and between any city of the State of Connecticut, and whether they even have the authority to do so, are questions at the heart of the defendants' motions to dismiss.

"It is settled law that as a creation of the state, a municipality has no inherent powers of its own. . . . A municipality has only those powers that have been expressly granted to it by the state or that are necessary for it to discharge its duties and to carry out its objects and purposes. . . ." [Citations omitted.] *Buonocore, supra,* 192 Conn. 401-402. "It is well established that a city's charter is the fountainhead of its municipal powers. . . . The charter serves as an enabling act, both creating power and prescribing the form in which it must be exercised. . . . [Citations omitted.] *Keeney v. Town of Old Saybrook,* 237 Conn. 135, 145, 676 A.2d 795 (1996). By what authority may the plaintiffs declare alleged illegal gun trade a public nuisance? Such authority must be found in the statutes and in the municipality's charter.

General Statutes § 7-148(c)(7)(E) grants a municipality the power to "[d]efine, prohibit and abate within the municipality all nuisances and causes thereof . . . and cause the abatement of any nuisance at the expense of the owner or owners of the premises on which such nuisance exists." The City of Bridgeport Charter ("charter"), Chapter 5, Section 8, p.11, provides that "every act . . . placing any burden upon or limiting the use of private property, shall be by ordinance." At Section 7.(a), p. 9, the charter provides that "[t]he city council shall have the power, by the concurrent vote of the majority of the whole number of council members, with the written approval of the mayor, or over the mayor's veto, as herein provided, to make, alter, and repeal ordinances not inconsistent with the law." No such power is conferred on the mayor. *See* Charter, Chapter 3, Section 1(e).

No ordinance has been passed by the Bridgeport city council to achieve the remedies sought by this lawsuit. The admission by counsel [footnote omitted] in Plaintiffs' Memorandum of Law in Opposition to Defendants' Motion To Dismiss for Lack of Subject Matter Jurisdiction, p. 15, establishes that the city counsel did not at any time enact any ordinance with respect to the remedies sought in the fourth count of the plaintiffs' amended complaint. Instead, the "specific authority to bring the action [arises from] a specific line item in the Bridgeport budget adopted by the city counsel dealing with the budget for this case." Transcript of Hearing on Motion To Dismiss, p. 88.

By circumventing the ordinance requirement contained in the charter, the plaintiffs have deprived this court of the judicial review demanded in *Dwyer v. Farrell, supra,* 193 Conn. 7, 475 A.2d 257. As discussed previously in this memorandum, the Dwyer court was faced with a preemption issue involving handgun control. A New Haven handgun ordinance was challenged for requiring that a seller hold a federal firearms dealer license, prohibiting sales from a private dwelling, and requiring that sale premises be located in business zones. General Statutes §§ 29-28 through 29-38 contained no such restrictions.

In its decision holding that the New Haven ordinance was preempted by state statute, the Connecticut Supreme Court wrote that "the statutory pattern evinces a legislative intent to regulate the flow of handgun sales and restrict the right to sell to those establishing the requisite qualifications." *Dwyer v. Farrell, supra,* 193 Conn. 13. It is clear to this court that the plaintiffs seek to act or have the court act to control the flow of handguns in a more comprehensive manner.

That the lawsuit itself is a line item in the city's budget falls far short of the requirement of the charter that action by the city council in this regard be taken in the form of an ordinance. "The charter of [Bridgeport] is its enabling act, and where the charter points out a particular way in which any act is to be done, the prescribed form must be pursued for the act to be lawful." *Food, Beverage & Express Drivers Local Union v. Shelton,* 147 Conn. 401, 405, 161 A.2d 587 (1960). As a matter of law, the court has no jurisdiction to entertain the fourth count of the first amended complaint.

Accordingly, on the basis of the above discussion, the first amended complaint is hereby dismissed for lack of subject matter jurisdiction. Judgment is hereby entered for all appearing defendants, with the exception of Lorcin Engineering Company, Inc., which defendant is subject to a stay in bankruptcy.

Case Notes: Regulation Through Litigation.

1. Given that the lawsuit against the firearm industry sought to prevent injury to others, why was the cause of action not successful? What elements were missing? Were the subject products defective? Was the City's lawsuit based solely on the argument that handguns were defective? Was the City's lawsuit a private cause of action? Was the court simply reluctant to assume a regulatory role in requiring the firearm industry to make safer products? Does the court have the power to be reluctant in assuming this role? If the City's lawsuit had been successful, could it have created sufficient change in the firearm industry?

2. Lawsuits specifically designed to gain public awareness of an allegedly defective product often have difficult standing issues. Standing requires that the complaining party be the proper party to the lawsuit, which includes a direct injury to that party and a personal stake in the outcome of the controversy. See *Ganim,* 1999 WL 124909 at *3. In *Ganim,* the court noted that the Connecticut Supreme Court had held that

> Standing is . . . a practical concept designed to insure that courts and parties are not vexed by suits brought to vindicate nonjusticiable interests and that judicial decisions which may affect the rights of others are forged in hot controversy, with each view fairly and vigorously represented . . . These two objectives are ordinarily held to have been met when a complainant makes a colorable claim of direct injury [that the complainant] has suffered or is likely to suffer, in an individual or representative capacity.

Id. citing Connecticut Associated Builders and Contractors v. Hartford, 251 Conn. 169, 178 (1999).

3. Unlike well-known automobile cases alleging defective airbags or the misplacement of the automobile's gas tank, *Ganim* sought to impose liability on the handgun industry based upon the argument that handguns have failed to serve broader societal interests because these products continue to be responsible for injury, death, and property damage. Some states have enacted legislation preventing the evaluation of societal interests in firearms. For example, California product liability statutes include the following:

§ 1714.4. Products liability; defectiveness of firearms or ammunition. (1983)

(a) In a products liability action, no firearm or ammunition shall be deemed defective in design on the basis that the benefits of the product do not outweigh the risk of injury posed by its potential to cause serious injury, damage, or death when discharged.

(b) For purposes of this section:

   (1) The potential of a firearm or ammunition to cause serious injury, damage, or death when discharged does not make the product defective in design.

   (2) Injuries or damages resulting from the discharge of a firearm or ammunition are not proximately caused by its potential to cause serious injury, damage, or death, but are proximately caused by the actual discharge of the product.

(c) This section shall not affect a products liability cause of action based upon the improper selection of design alternatives.

(d) This section is declaratory of existing law.

4. Assuming that handguns could be evaluated in the context of a product liability analysis, what is the appropriate standard for such an evaluation? Could consumers reasonably expect that handguns would not cause injury, death, and property damage? Could consumers reasonably expect that handguns would cause injury, death, and property damage? How would a court measure the societal risks and benefits of a handgun in or-

der to determine whether the product is defective? Is the court better able to evaluate the defective nature of a handgun on a case-by-case basis in which the facts of a specific incident provide the context for the evaluation? Why should that matter? Do handguns differ from other products that are considered to be unavoidably dangerous but able to provide a benefit to society? What is the appropriate risk/benefit analysis for handguns? Can that standard be appropriately applied to handguns?

5. Generally, tort litigation is viewed as one of several methods available to promulgate the societal interest that manufacturers make safe products. Two particular effects of product liability suits are compensatory (for the benefit of the injured plaintiff in the lawsuit) and preventative (for the benefit of society at large). *See* Teret & Jacobs, *Prevention and Torts: The Role of Litigation in Injury Control,* 17 Law, Med. & Health Care 17 (1985); see also Viscusi, *Toward a Diminished Role for Tort Liability: Social Insurance, Government Regulation, and Contemporary Risks to Health and Safety,* 6 Yale J. Reg. 65 (1989).

6. Given that product liability suits have some societal benefit, should jury awards in product liability suits be capped? Do such suits fuel nuisance litigation? What is the appropriate balance between aggressively useful product liability suits that contribute to the societal regulation of product manufacturers and a deluge of lawsuits that create a liability crisis? See Henderson & Eisenberg, *The Quiet Revolution in Products Liability: An Empirical Study of Legal Change,* 37 U.C.L.A. L. Rev. 479 (1990); Abel, *The Real Tort Crisis—Too Few Claims,* 48 Ohio St. L. J. 443 (1987).

7. Who are the purchasers of handguns? For what purpose are handguns used? What damages are typically caused by handguns? Suppose we can, in fact, make a blanket statement about who uses and purchases handguns or, at least, about the damages caused by handguns. Why, then, would a court not be willing to modify the liability expectations placed on handgun manufacturers and sellers? Standing issues aside, why was the court in *Ganim* reluctant to promulgate such modifications? Can we expect the same from courts considering other products that provide a less-than-favorable benefit to society, such as tobacco or liquor? Who are the purchasers of tobacco products? For what purpose is tobacco used and consumed? What damages are typically caused by tobacco? If we can, in fact, make a blanket statement about who uses and purchases tobacco products or, at least, the damages caused by tobacco products, why would a court not be willing to modify the liability expectations placed on the providers of tobacco products?

Post-Sale Obligations of the Product Manufacturer or Seller

The post-sale obligation is ordinarily a duty to warn consumers about inherent dangers of the product that became known after the sale of the product to the consumer. Strict liability attaches only where a reasonable person (in the seller or distributor's position) failed to provide such a warning.

See § 10 *Restatement (Third), Liability of Commercial Product Seller or Distributor for Harm Caused by Post-Sale Failure to Warn.*

 **CASE LAW** ──────────────────────────────────◆

◆ **manufacturer's post-sale duty to warn**

Patton v. Hutchinson Wil-
Rich Manufacturing
Company, 861 P.2d 1299
(Kan. 1993).

─────────────────────

Plaintiff was injured by field cultivator and sued manufacturer
in federal court over strict liability issue whether manufacturer
had post-sale obligations to the product purchaser.

─────────────────────

SIX, Justice.

* * *

This is a first impression products liability case. Four questions concerning a manufacturer's post-sale duties to warn of danger incident to use of its product have been certified by the United States District Court for the District of Kansas. Our jurisdiction is under K.S.A. 60-3201 (authority to answer certified questions).

The Certified Questions

The four certified questions are:

I. Whether Kansas products liability law recognizes a continuing duty to warn theory of liability requiring manufacturers who learn of a danger incident to the use of their products after the sale of those products to warn ultimate consumers who purchased the products prior to the time the manufacturers learned of the potential danger through warnings disseminated to the manufacturers' retailers who have continuing contact with the consumers.

II. Whether Kansas products liability law recognizes a continuing duty to warn theory of liability requiring manufacturers who learn of a danger incident to the use of their products after the sale of those products to directly warn ultimate consumers who purchased the products prior to the time the manufacturers learned of the potential danger.

III. Whether Kansas products liability law places a duty to retrofit upon manufacturers who learn of a potential danger incident to the use of their products after the products have been sold.

IV. Whether Kansas products liability law places a duty to recall upon manufacturers who learn of a potential danger incident to the use of their products after the products have been sold.

Answers to the Certified Questions

Because of the infinite variety of products marketed in this state, the following answers are inexorably linked to and amplified by the corresponding portions of the opinion.

We answer the four certified questions as follows:

A qualified yes.

A qualified yes.

No.

No.

* * *

The Post-Sale Duty to Warn

In *Wooderson* [v. Ortho Pharmaceutical Corp., 681 P.2d 1038 (Kan. 1984)], we undertook an analysis concerning the duty of a manufacturer of ethical drugs to warn others regarding drug side effects. As long as an ethical drug manufacturer markets a prescription product, it has a duty to warn the medical profession of dangerous side effects of which it knows, has reason to know, or should know. The duty continues as long as the marketing continues. 235 Kan. at 409, 681 P.2d 1038. We relied on and quoted extensively from three cases *(Lindsay v. Ortho Pharmaceutical Corp.,* 637 F.2d 87 [2d Cir. 1980]; *Ortho Pharmaceutical v. Chapman,* 180 Ind.App. 33, 388, N.E.2d 541 [1979]; *McEwen v. Ortho Pharmaceutical,* 270 Or. 375, 528 P.2d 522 [1974]), all of which involved ethical drug claims against Ortho Pharmaceutical Corporation, the principal defendant in Wooderson. 235 Kan. at 400, 402, 405, 681 P.2d 1038. Wooderson's rationale is limited to the ethical drug context.

The expert testimony and exhibits in Wooderson disclosed that there was an abundance of information in medical journals published prior to the years when Wooderson was taking Ortho-Novum 1/80. The information linked the use of oral contraceptives with hemolytic uremic syndrome, malignant hypertension, and acute renal failure. 235 Kan. at 408-09, 681 P.2d 1038. The abundance of information published prior to the sale to Wooderson presented a fact situation that is different from the case at bar. HWR had no knowledge at the point of sale of any hydraulic cylinder hazard associated with the farm cultivator.

* * *

Patton contends that the Court of Appeals recognized a post-sale duty to warn in *Stratton v. Garvey Internat'l, Inc.*, 9 Kan.App.2d 254, 676 P.2d 1290 (1984). However, the opinion addressed the question of the extent of a successor entity's duty to warn of defects in its predecessor's products. Stratton held that a successor corporation has a legal obligation to warn when the successor has both knowledge of the defective condition and a sufficient relationship with the predecessor's customers. 9 Kan.App.2d at 258, 676 P.2d 1290. Stratton failed to meet this two-pronged burden. Consequently, he was unable to demonstrate that the successor corporation had a duty to warn. 9 Kan.App.2d at 261, 676 P.2d 1290.

Patton observes that GAF Corp. referenced Wooderson in holding that a roofing products manufacturer had a duty to warn or take corrective action rather than continue to ignore recurring defects in its product. 242 Kan. at 156057, 747 P.2d 1326. HWR argues that GAF Corp. only establishes a duty to warn at the time of sale. GAF Corp. is a "knowledge prior to sale" case. GAF had experienced problems with its product five years before it submitted the published specifications upon which the architects relied. 242 Kan. at 153-55, 747 P.2d 1326. GAF knew its product was defective for the purpose for which it was designed and manufactured when it was sold; consequently, the case is factually dissimilar from the case at bar. 242 Kans. at 157, 747 P.2d 1326.

The questions certified limit our determination of a continuing duty to warn after sale to an ultimate consumer who purchased the cultivator prior to the time HWR learned of any potential danger. Although the HWR-Patton relationship is distinguishable from those in Wooderson, GAF Corp., and Stratton, the three cases do not signal rejection of a post-sale duty to warn.

In considering whether HWR may have a duty to warn of product hazards after the point of sale, we choose the label "post-sale" rather than "continuing". The post-sale claim is separate from the warning claim asserted with respect to the point of sale. [Citations omitted.] A post-sale warning could not be given at the point of sale because a manufacturer would not have knowledge to give it.

A distinction also should be drawn between a negligence claim and a strict liability claim. A basic negligence concept involves a risk-utility analysis in which the risk inherent in a condition or activity is balanced against the utility of the condition or conduct and the burden nec-essary to eliminate or reduce the risk. *See* Restatement (Second) of Torts §§ 291-293 (1964).

Under a negligence theory, the duty to warn may be post sale and is not keyed to the manufacture or sale of the product. The duty to warn under a theory of strict liability exists only at the time the product leaves the manufacturer's control. This distinction reflects the emphasis in strict liability upon the danger of the product rather than the conduct of a manufacturer, i.e., if a product is not rendered unreasonably dangerous by the absence of warnings when it leaves the manufacturer's control, it cannot at some later date become unreasonably dangerous due to the lack of warnings. [Citations omitted.] A negligence analysis is more appropriate than an application of strict liability in the post-sale context. [Citation omitted.] In the case at bar, Patton has asserted both negligence and strict liability claims.

A variety of courts have found that a manufacturer does not have a post-sale duty to notify product purchasers or users of changes in the state of the art concerning the safe use of the product. *Collins v. Hyster Co.*, 174 Ill.App.3d 972, 977, 124 Ill.Dec. 483, 529 N.E.2d 303 (1988), lv. to app. denied 124 Ill.2d 554, 129 Ill.Dec. 148, 535 N.E.2d 913 (1989) (forklift products liability case), recognized the duty to warn distinction in the defect at sale and new design improvement contexts: "Certainly the law does not contemplate placing the onerous duty on manufacturers to subsequently warn all foreseeable users of products based on increased design or manufacture expertise that was not present at the time the product left its control." *Lynch v. McStome & Lincoln Plaza*, 378 Pa.Super. at 440-42, 548 A.2d 1276, considered a manufacturer's duty to retrofit an escalator with a new braking system or to warn the owners of the new design. The court determined that no such duty existed. [Citations omitted.]

The state of the art may be altered by the development of a more effective safety device. For business reasons, a manufacturer may seek to bring product improvement to the attention of its past customers, and it should be encouraged to do so in a manner that does not underplay important safety developments. [Citation omitted.] Patton neither requests nor do we impose a requirement that a manufacturer seek out past customers and notify them of changes in the state of the art.

The KPLA [Kansas Product Liability Act] became effective July 1, 1981. The KPLA is based on the Model Uniform Product Liability Act, 44 Fed.Reg. 62,714 et seq. (1979). The purpose of the Model Act was to consolidate all product liability actions, regardless of theory into tone theory of legal liability. 44 Fed.Reg. 62,720. K.S.A. 1992 Supp. 60-3302(c) provides that all legal theories of recovery, e.g., negligence, strict liability, and failure to warn, are to be merged into one legal theory called a "production liability claim."

K.S.A. 60-3304 repeatedly utilizes the phrase "at the time of manufacture". The phrase does not appear in K.S.A. 60-3305. We agree with Patton's reasoning that K.S.A 60-3305 does not exclude a post-sale duty to warn. The K.S.A. 60-3305 reference is to "any duty on the part of the manufacturer . . . to warn or protect against a danger or hazard which could or did arise in the use or misuse of such product" in "any product liability claim". We find no statutory limitation nor has HWR cited precedential authority limiting a manufacturer's duty to warn to the point of sale. See *Reed v. Ford Motor Co.*, 679 F.Supp. 873, 878-79 (S.D.Ind. 1988). The three K.S.A. 60-3305 categories which exclude a duty to warn are: (a) warnings related to precautionary conduct that a reasonable user or consumer would take for protection, (b) precautions that a reasonable user or consumer would have taken, and (c) obvious hazards which a reasonable user or consumer should have known. The period beyond "the time of manufacture" is not an excluded category.

Comstock v. General Motors Corp., 358 Mich. 163, 99 N.W.2d 627 (1959), the seminal case upon which Patton relies, held that a manufacturer's duty to warn of a known latent defect exists not only at the time of sale but also when such a defect becomes known to the manufacturer. The *Comstock* facts presented a situation where the defective automobile brake was present at the time of manufacture. The Michigan court limited its holding by observing that: (1) the brake hazard became known to General Motors "shortly after" the car had been put on the market, and (2) the defect was life threatening. 358 Mich. at 177-78, 99 N.W.2d 627.

The post-sale duty to warn varies among jurisdictions. In *Cover v. Cohen*, 61 N.Y.2d 261, 275, 473 N.Y.S.2d 378, 461 N.E.2d 864 (Ct.App.1984), a duty to warn product users of discovered dangers was imposed. [Citation omitted.] In *doCanto v. Ametek, Inc.*, 367 Mass. 776, 784-85, 328 N.E.2d 873 (1975) (alleged defective commercial ironer), the Supreme Court of Massachusetts stated: "When the manufacturer of such a machine learns or should have learned of the risk created by its

fault, it has a duty to take reasonable steps to warn at least the purchaser of the risk." [Citation omitted.]

Some courts have elected to further limit the scope of the applicable duty to warn to particular contexts. For example, in *Walton v. Avco Corp.*, 530 Pa. 568, 577-78, 610 A.2d 454 (1992) (Walton II, a strict liability case) the court imposed on a helicopter manufacturer a duty to warn owners that a defective part had been incorporated into the helicopter. See also *Walton v. Avco Corp.*, 383 Pa.Super. 518, 531-32, 557 A.2d 372 (1989) (Walton I), for the lower court's analysis which draws a distinction between household consumer goods and a manufacturer of a unique product such as the helicopter. *Habecker v. Clark Equipment Co.*, 797 F.Supp. 381, 388 (M.D.Pa.1992), applied Walton I to a strict products liability action concerning a defect in a forklift and suggested:

"[W]hile forklifts are not common household goods, they are certainly much more prevalent than helicopters. Nearly any business which has a loading dock or a warehouse has a forklift, and it does not stretch the boundaries of imagination to envision frequent interbusiness transfers of this type of equipment. Accordingly, with the Walton [I] panel's own warning in mind, this court is not willing to extend that doctrine to common business appliances such as forklifts."

* * *

We recognize a manufacturer's post-sale duty to warn ultimate consumers who purchased the product who can be readily identified or traced when a defect, which originated at the time the product was manufactured and was unforeseeable at the point of sale, is discovered to present a life threatening hazard. [Citation omitted.] We agree with the Wisconsin Supreme Court in Kozlowski when it observed, after applying a post-sale warning duty to a sausage making machine under a claim of strict liability and negligence:

"We do not in this decision hold that there is an absolute continuing duty, year after year, for all manufacturers to warn of a new safety device which eliminates potential hazards. A sausage stuffer and the nature of that industry bears no similarity to the realities of manufacturing and marketing household goods such as fans, snowblowers or lawn mowers which have become increasingly hazard proof with each succeeding model. It is beyond reason and good judgment to hold a manufacturer responsible for a duty of annually warning of safety hazards on household items, mass produced and used in every American home, when the product is 6 to 35 years old and outdated by some 20 newer models equipped with every imaginable safety innovation known in the state of the art. It would place an unreasonable duty upon these manufacturers if they were required to trace the ownership of each unit sold and warn annually of new safety improvements over a 35 year period." 87 Wis.2d at 901, 275 N.W.2d 915.

We acknowledge practical problems associated with imposing a post-sale duty to warn. [Citation omitted.] The questions of whether such a duty arises in a particular case will depend on the facts of that case. The passage of time from manufacture and initial sale to the discovery of previously unknown hazards may reflect that the product has changed ownership many times. The original purchaser may have moved. The length of product life will vary. What is reasonably prudent post-sale conduct for one manufacturer and one type of product may not be reasonable for another manufacturer of an entirely different type of product. The sale of the farm cultivator was made to Patton's father on a one-time basis 13 years before the injury. What sales records will be available to the manufacturer? Notification by a manufacturer to all prior purchasers of a product may be extremely burdensome, if not impossible. In the case at bar, the manufacturer's retailer has continuing contact with the consumers. We reason that a manufacturer who was unaware of a hazard at the time of sale and has since acquired knowledge of a life-threatening hazard should not be absolved of all duty to take reasonable steps to warn the ultimate consumer who purchased the product; however, the warning of unforeseeable dangers is neither required nor possible at the time of sale. A manufacturer is to be given a reasonable period of time after discovery of the life-threatening hazard in which to issue any post-sale warning that might reasonably be required.

The imposition of liability upon a manufacturer for inadequately warning an ultimate consumer who purchased the product prior to the time the manufacturer learned of the potential danger regarding the dangers of the product is dependent upon a reasonableness test and the manufacturer's actual or constructive knowledge of the risk. [Citation omitted.] A post-sale duty to warn does not exist until either actual or constructive knowledge is acquired by the manufacturer concerning a later life-threatening hazard posed by a product when the product is used for its normally intended purpose. The alleged defect in the cultivator was unknown to HWR when it was initially sold. We do not apply a strict liability theory to the post-sale duty to warn. The cardinal inquiry is, was HWR's post-sale conduct reasonable? The reasonableness standard is flexible. [Citation omitted.] The type of notice of a problem revealed by product use that will impose a post-sale duty to warn will be a function of the degree of danger which the problem involves and the number of instances reported. Whether a prima facie case has been made for the presence of a post-sale duty will depend on the facts of each case. *Cover*, 61 N.Y.2d at 276, 473 N.Y.S.2d 378, 461 N.E.2d 864. Each plaintiff must make an initial showing that the manufacturer acquired knowledge of a defect present but unknown and unforeseeable at the point of sale and failed to take reasonable action to warn of the defect.

The nature of the post-sale warning and where and to whom it should be given will involve a case-by-case analysis. The analysis shall include but not be limited to the examination of such factors as: (1) the nature of the harm that may result from use without notice, (2) the likelihood that harm will occur (Does future continuing use of the product create a significant risk of serious harm which can be lessened if a post-sale warning is given?), (3) how many persons are affected, (4) the economic burden on the manufacturer of identifying and contacting current product users (Does the manufacturer have an ongoing relationship with the purchaser or other knowledge of the identity of the owner of the product which provides a practical way of providing a post-sale warning?), (5) the nature of the industry, (6) the type of product involved, (7) the number of units manufactured or sold, and (8) steps taken other than giving of notice to correct the problem. *See Cover*, 61 N.Y.2d at 276-77, 473 N.Y.S.2d 378, 461 N.E.2d 864. The facts may indicate that notice to all ultimate consumers who purchased the product prior to the time the manufacturer learned of a potential danger is unreasonable, if not impossible. Notice to the distributor or retail seller may, in certain contexts, meet the reasonableness standard.

The particular facts may reflect that a lack of notice was not unreasonable and that a reasonable manufacturer under the circumstances would have taken no post-sale action. Knowledge and reasonableness, as determinative factors, will provide an incentive to manufacturers to issue warnings if latent product hazards are discovered after the initial sale and a warning under the circumstances would be reasonable. We cannot fashion a "bright line" rule from a farm cultivator case that applies with interpretative ease to the infinite variety of products that inhabit the marketplace.

Each trial judge will necessarily be required to make a determination as to whether the record presents a fact question as to knowledge and reasonableness whenever a plaintiff's claim of negligent breach of a post-sale duty to warn is alleged. Generally, resolution of the issue of reasonableness, after an initial court determination that the issue is presented, will be one of fact for the jury. The trial judge, in instructing the jury on a post-sale duty to warn, shall utilize the relevant factors referenced herein, including the nature and likelihood of the injury posed by the product, the feasibility and expense of issuing a warning, whether the warning would be effective, and whether ultimate consumers who purchased the product can be identified.

Retrofitting and Recall

The answer to certified questions three and four is "no." Patton has provided no statute or case law to support the claim that HWR is subject to a duty to retrofit or recall the cultivator. We reason that product recalls are properly the business of administrative agencies as suggested by the federal statutes that expressly delegate re-

call authority. Extensive federal recall legislation deals with the post sale obligations of manufacturers of products such as automobiles, consumer products, boats, and medical devices. See Consumer Product Safety Act, 15 U.S.C. § 2064 (1988) (Consumer Product Safety Commission); National Traffic and Motor Vehicle Safety Act of 1966, 15 U.S.C. § 1414 (1988) (Secretary of Transportation); The Radiation Control for Health and Safety Act of 1968, 42 U.S.C. § 263g (1988) (Secretary of Health and Human Services); Safe Medical Devices Act of 1990, 21 U.S.C. § 360h (1988 and Supp.IV, 1992).

The recall issue in Kansas is referenced in *Johnson v. Colt Industries Operating Corp.*, 609 F. Supp. 776, 782 (D.Kan.1985) (Evidence on a duty to recall was introduced; the court did not instruct the jury that the manufacturer had a duty to recall.). Although the Johnson opinion does not precisely indicate what post sale duties were recognized for manufacturers, the Tenth Circuit on appeal clarified the fact that the district court's approach did not stand for the existence of a duty to recall or retrofit under Kansas law. [Citation omitted.]

Courts deal with the business of individual cases grounded on specific facts. The parties' contentions are developed and placed before us with specific facts in mind. The decision to expand a manufacturer's post sale duty beyond implementing reasonable efforts to warn ultimate consumers who purchased the product of discovered latent life-threatening hazards unforeseeable at the point of sale should be left to administrative agencies and the legislature. [Citations omitted.] These institutions are better able to weigh the benefits and costs involved in locating, recalling, and retrofitting products.

Case Notes: Post-Sale Obligations of the Product Manufacturer or Seller

1. The *Restatement (Third)* embraces a negligence standard as the test to determine whether a product manufacturer or seller has an obligation to provide a post-sale warning. "The standard governing the liability of the seller is objective: whether a reasonable person in the seller's position would provide a warning. This is the standard traditionally applied in determining negligence." See Comment b to § 10 of the *Restatement (Third)*. Its roots stem from the Model Uniform Products Liability

   Act. See § 104 (C)(6) of the Uniform Product Liability Act.

2. Post-sale obligations, particularly the obligation to locate and warn current users of a product, impose tremendous burdens on the manufacturer. The standard adopted by the *Restatement (Third)* is designed to weigh that burden under appropriate circumstances and on a case-by-case basis. The imposition of a post-duty to warn on the manufacturer must include an analysis of several factors, includ-

ing the degree of danger the problem involves, the number of reported incidents, the burden of providing the warning to current product users, and the ability of the manufacturer to track product users following the sale of the product. See *Cover v. Cohen,* 461 N.E.2d 864, 871-73 (N.Y. 1984); see also *Comstock v. General Motors Corp.,* 99 N.W.2d 627 (Mich. 1959) (Supreme Court of Michigan was first to recognize that the manufacturer's duty to warn users about product dangers does not end when product is sold).

3. Despite the burdens faced by manufacturers, the obligation itself arises from the manufacturer's unique position to follow the use and adaptation of its product by consumers and to track its product among users so as to distribute further information about the product and product sales, technical bulletins, and service notices. Moreover, the manufacturer typically has a superior position among product users, retailers, distributors, or wholesalers to learn about post-sale defects, dangers discovered during use of the product, available modifications, or the need for a product recall. See O'Reilly, *Product Warnings, Defects and Hazards* at § 16.01, "Criteria for a Postsale Duty to Warn" (1999); see also *Cover v. Cohen,* 461 N.E.2d 864, 871-73 (N.Y. 1984); Matula, *Manufacturers' Post-Sale Duties in the 1990s,* 32 Tort & Insurance L. J. 87 (1996).

4. Section 10 of the *Restatement (Third)* requires that four factors be met in order to determine whether a product manufacturer or seller would provide a warning. These four factors are (1) if the seller knows or should know that the product poses a substantial risk of harm to persons or property; (2) those to whom the warning would be provided can be identified and can be assumed to be unaware of the current risk; (3) a warning can be effectively communicated to and acted upon by the recipients; and (4) the risk of harm is sufficiently great to justify imposing the burden of providing a warning on the product manufacturer or seller.

5. The *Restatement (Third)* also embraces a negligence standard as the test to determine whether a product manufacturer or seller has an obligation to recall a defective product. See § 11 of the *Restatement (Third), Liability of Commercial Product Seller or Distributor for Harm Caused by Post-Sale Failure to Recall Product.*

6. "Recall" differs from a warning in that it typically refers to some form of "structured, intentional intervention between user and product, usually as a physical contact between the product and a remedial, repair, or removal actor, typically the agent of the manufacturer." O'Reilly, *Product Warnings, Defects and Hazards* at § 16.02[A], "Product Recalls and Postsale Warnings" (1999).

THEORIES OF LITIGATION

Chapter 7   Product Liability Lawsuit and Recovery

Chapter Seven

Product Liability Lawsuit and Recovery

PARTIES

Parties to the product liability lawsuit may vary as much as in any commercial litigation case. Typically, the product lawsuit will be brought by an individual who has sustained bodily injury or has incurred property damage and will be defended by the product manufacturer, the retailer, and any other entity present in the stream of commerce. Other individuals and entities can also be party to the products lawsuit. These other parties include insurance companies in subrogation suits, lessors and bailors, succession corporations that have assumed the predecessor's liability, trade associations, component part manufacturers, wholesalers and distributors, and others. To identify proper plaintiff parties, the key is to assess the real person and property damages sustained and identify the individuals who sustained this loss. To identify proper defendant parties, the key is to identify any entity that participated in the production of the subject product at any point in the stream of commerce, from production factory to the retailer's shelf. This section will assist you in identifying the proper parties to the product liability lawsuit.

Plaintiffs

Plaintiffs in product liability cases can generally be divided into three categories:

1. purchasers
2. non-purchasers who used the product
3. bystanders See Frumer and Friedman, Products Liability, Vol. 2A, § 4.01 [Matthew Bender, 1993].

Although there are some exceptions based on the person's status, purchasers and non-purchasers who use a product can sue in negligence and strict liability because privity is no longer required. Under most state statutes, a person who represents the estate of a decedent who was injured by a defective product may also pursue such an action. In addition, a person can institute suit based upon a negligence or strict liability law for a product defect that injured the decedent who is named as a person entitled to sue under a state's wrongful death statute. It is good practice to check the applicable state's product liability statute, including the definitions of plaintiff, claimant, user, or consumer, before drafting the initial pleading.

The ability of bystanders to sue using negligence and strict liability theories varies widely by jurisdiction. Section 395 of the *Restatement (Second) of Torts* contains comments to the effect that certain "foreseeable" bystanders do have a cause of action against manufacturers for negligent design and manufacture of a product. A foreseeable bystander is someone the manufacturer could expect would be endangered by the product. For example, a passenger in an automobile injured by a defect in the automobile would have a cause of action against the automobile's manufacturer.

Breach of contract theory does not encompass as broad a group of plaintiffs as negligence and strict liability. Strictly speaking, the Uniform Commercial Code (U.C.C.), limits recovery along vertical and horizontal privity lines. Vertically, the UCC limits plaintiffs to those in the stream of commerce, beginning with the immediate product buyer and extending upward. Therefore, product users who are not buyers are not included. Horizontally, potential plaintiffs are limited to the buyer, his or her family, and household members. Bystanders are generally not recognized as having a cause of action against the manufacturer or seller of a product unless the product is inherently or unreasonably dangerous. See Haig, Business and Commercial Litigation in Federal Courts, Vol. 5, § 70.4 (1998). Each state has *sales* statutes, many of which adopt the UCC to some degree. Therefore, the applicable sales law should be researched before plaintiffs are named in a breach of warranty action.

In addition to the three groups of potential plaintiffs, product liability actions can be brought by individuals who themselves were not injured but who sustained losses as a result of the injury sustained by someone else. These claims are usually limited to a spouse, a child, or a parent. The rules limiting these claims are generally the same in products liability cases as in any other personal injury case.

Business entities can also sue for injuries sustained from defective products, but their damages may not be recognized under some product liability theories, such as the economic loss doctrine. These theories are discussed in the *Damages* section of this chapter.

◆ **bystanders as plaintiffs**

 **CASE LAW**

Embs v. Pepsi-Cola
Bottling Co. of
Lexington, 528 S.W.2d 703
(Ky. App. 1975).

Plaintiff was in a self-service retail store for the purpose of "buying soft drinks for the kids" when she went to an upright soft drink cooler to remove bottles of soda. Although she did not notice it, a carton of Seven-Up was sitting on the edge of a nearby counter about one foot from where she was standing. As she turned away from the cooler, she heard an explosion that "sounded like a shotgun." When she looked down, she saw a gash and soda on her leg, green pieces of glass, and the Seven-

Up carton on the floor. Plaintiff sued the manufacturer and supplier of the soda.

LUKOWSKI, Justice

* * *

Our expressed public policy will be furthered if we minimize the risk of personal injury and property damage by charging the costs of injuries against the manufacturer who can procure liability insurance and distribute its expense among the public as a cost of doing business; and since the risk of harm from defective products exists for mere bystanders and passersby as well as for the purchaser or user, there is no substantial reason for protecting one class of persons and not the other. The same policy requires us to maximize protection for the injured third party and promote the public interest in discouraging the marketing of products having defects that are a menace to the public by imposing strict liability upon retailers and wholesalers in the distributive chain responsible for marketing the defective product which injures the bystander. The imposition of strict liability places no unreasonable burden upon sellers because they can adjust the cost of insurance protection among themselves in the course of their continuing business relationship. Anno.: Products Liability: Extension of Strict Liability in Tort to Permit Recovery by a Third Person who is Neither a Purchaser Nor User of Product, 33 A.L.R.3d 415, 417.

We must not shirk from extending the rule to the manufacturer for fear that the retailer or middleman will be impaled on the sword of liability without regard to fault. Their liability was already established under Section 402A of the Restatement of Torts 2d. As a matter of public policy the retailer or middleman as well as the manufacturer should be liable since the loss for injuries resulting from defective products should be placed on those members of the marketing chain best able to pay the loss, who can then distribute such risk among themselves by means of insurance and indemnity agreements. *Caruth v. Mariani,* 11 Ariz.App. 188, 463 P.2d 83 (1970). Any inclination to relieve the retailer must have in mind the little corner grocery store but in these days the dealer is more likely to be Safeway Stores or some other nationwide enterprise which is the prime mover in marketing the goods and the manufacturer only a small concern which feeds it to order. Prosser, The Fall of the Citadel, 50 Minn.L.R. 791, 816.

The result which we reach does not give the bystander a "free ride." When products and consumers are considered in the aggregate, bystanders, as a class, purchase most of the same products to which they are exposed as bystanders. Thus, as a class, they indirectly subsidize the liability of the manufacturer, middleman and retailer and in this sense do pay for the insurance policy tied to the product.

Public policy is adequately served if parameters are placed upon the extension of the rule so that it is limited to bystanders whose injury from the defect is reasonably foreseeable. *Elmore v. American Motors Corp.,* 70 Cal.2d 578, 75 Cal.Rptr. 652, 451 P.2d 84 (1969).

For the sake of clarity we restate the extension of the rule. The protections of Section 402A of the Restatement of Torts 2d extend to bystanders whose injury from the defective product is reasonably foreseeable.

* * *

Defendants

The tasks of every plaintiff's attorney in a products liability case are to: (1) consider the identity of all possible party defendants; (2) research the substantive law of the jurisdiction to determine who may be sued under each products liability theory; and (3) carefully determine the parties to be named as defendants. Generally, the parties named as defendants will include any entity connected with the manufacture, distribution, or sale of the product. (*Id.*) Plaintiffs' counsel should keep in mind not only the potential liability of each defendant, but also the practical ramifications of including each. Some of those considerations include the ease or difficulty of effecting service, whether personal jurisdiction can be obtained, and the effect that naming each defendant might have on other defendants. With regard to the latter, for example, some state statutes provide that sellers in the stream of commerce who did nothing to alter the product, are to be dismissed from the case unless they are the only defendants in the case. See Mo. Rev. Stat. § 537.762. Adding another defendant, no matter how bad the facts may seem to be against it, can facilitate the dismissal of perhaps the plaintiffs' *best* defendant.

Defendant Manufacturers   The development of strict liability doctrine provided plaintiffs with the primary theory to use against manufacturers of allegedly defective products. In every jurisdiction in which strict liability is recognized, there is no doubt that plaintiffs can sue the manufacturers of defective products. Manufacturers are also subject to suit in virtually every jurisdiction under the theories of negligence and breach of warranty, with the only exception being statutory protection. See Frumer and Friedman, Product Liability, Vol. 2A, § 5.05 (Matthew Bender 1993). Perhaps the most vague question that remains in this area of law is whether an entity is truly a manufacturer. A few states define a manufacturer as "the designer, fabricator, producer, compounder, processor, assembler, constructor, maker, remanufacturer, rebuilder, refurnisher, reconditioner of a product, or a person or entity which 'otherwise prepares' a product prior to its sale to a user or consumer." *(Id.)*

When drafting the complaint in a product liability case where the manufacturer is one of the defendants, the manufacturer ordinarily should be the first named party. See Haig, Business and Commercial Litigation in Federal Courts, Vol. 5, § 70.4 (1998). Naming the manufacturer first is psychologically advantageous because triers of fact, particularly juries, consider the first-named party the most responsible one. Strategically, the manufacturer may have the *deepest pocket* and may be the obviously liable party.

 CASE LAW

◆ **the extended manufacturer's liability doctrine**

**The First National Bank
of Mobile v. Cessna
Aircraft Company,** 365
So. 2d 966 (Ala. 1978).

Plaintiff sued the manufacturer of an aircraft, who demonstrated the aircraft and placed it in the stream of commerce, but did not sell it to the plaintiff.

Beatty, Justice

* * *

Nor do we consider that the Restatement of Torts 2d § 402A, on which the Extended Manufacturer's Liability Doctrine is based, limits the principle to sales situations. The Restatement does speak in terms of "one who sells" and the "seller" as being liable. Perhaps a sale is the most common situation in which application of § 402A arises, but the policy behind § 402A supports the extension of liability to situations other than sales. Comment *c.* to § 402A is instructive:

On whatever theory, the justification for the strict liability has been said to be that the seller, *by marketing his product* for use and consumption, has undertaken and assumed a special responsibility toward any member of the consuming public who may be injured by it; that the public has the right to and does expect, in the case of products which it needs and for which it is forced to rely upon the seller, that reputable sellers will stand behind their goods; that public policy demands that *the burden of accidental injuries caused by products intended for consumption be placed upon those who market them,* and be treated as a cost of production against which liability insurance can be obtained; and that the consumer of such products is entitled to the maximum of protection at the hands of someone, and the proper persons to afford it are those who market the products. (Emphasis added).

Marketing is defined as:

> An aggregate of functions involved in transferring title and in moving goods from producer to consumer including among others buying, selling, storing, transporting, standardizing, financing, risk bearing, and *supplying market information. Webster's Third New International Dictionary* (G. & C. Merriam Co., 1971). (emphasis added)

The fact that a technical sale has not taken place should not relieve a manufacturer who has placed defective merchandise on the market. Quite the contrary, the manufacturer's liability arises because *he has placed the product on the market. A fortiori*, having placed the product on the market, if the manufacturer still retains some measure of control, he should be liable under the doctrine.

The tendency of strict liability cases in other jurisdictions is to extend liability in non-sale situations: *Delaney v. Towmotor Corp.*, 339 F.2d 4 (2d Cir. 1964) (demonstration of fork lift truck); *Cintrone v. Hertz Truck Leasing and Rental Service*, 45 N.J. 434, 212 A.2d 769 (1965) (lease of a truck); *McKisson v. Sales Affiliates, Inc.*, 416 S.W.2d 787 (Tex. 1967) (free sample given to prospective customer); *Perfection Paint and Color Co. v. Konduris*, 147 Ind. App. 106, 258 N.E.2d 681 (Ind. 1970) (free lacquer reducer furnished following sale).

* * *

Not only does decisional authority emphasize the "stream of commerce" in fixing liability, but it is also the more reasonable view. When a product is placed in the "stream of commerce," the marketing cycle as it were, whether by demonstration, lease, free sample or sale, the doctrine should attach. In each of these situations the profit motive of the manufacturer is apparent whether or not a "sale" in the strict sense takes place. Moreover, the manufacturer who enters the market is in a better position to know and correct defects in his product and as between him and his prospective consumers should bear the risk of injury to those prospective consumers when any such defects enter the market uncorrected. Justification for this doctrine is founded on "broader moral notions of consumer protection and on economic and social grounds, placing the burden to compensate for loss incurred by defective products on the one best able to prevent the distribution of those products." *Atkins* at 139.

* * *

Defendant Manufacturers of Component Parts

Just as courts began to find manufacturers strictly liable for their defectively manufactured products, they also began to find manufacturers of component parts strictly liable. Indeed, there is little logical reason to exclude the manufacturer of a defective component part, while holding the manufacturer of the whole defective product strictly liable.

 CASE LAW

◆ **liability of component part manufacturers**

Carter v. Joseph Bancroft & Sons Co., 360 F. Supp. 1103 (E.D. Pa. 1973).

Plaintiff, injured when her dress caught fire while crepes suzette were being served at a dinner party, sued the licensor of the fabric from which her dress was made. Plaintiff alleged strict liability, breach of warranty, and negligence. The jury found in favor of plaintiff and awarded her damages. The Court issued the following opinion in response to defendants' motion for judgment not withstanding the verdict.

Green, J.J.

* * *

Defendants resourcefully contend that, under the evidence, they cannot be liable under Section 402A of the Restatement of Torts, Second, because they were not the "seller" within the meaning of the section. [Footnote omitted.]

* * *

It is obvious that defendants are not relieved of liability by the Comment relied upon because the tag does not clearly state that defendants had nothing to do with the goods except to distribute or sell them. Indeed, defendants clearly state on their label that the article was made according to specifications and quality standards prescribed and controlled by defendants. Thus, under Section 400, supra, the jury could have found defendants to be liable as a manufacturer and manufacturers are deemed sellers under Section 402A. n2

* * *

n2: It might be appropriate to point out that by providing the specifications and prescribing and controlling the quality standards of the Ban-Lon fabric, defendants were involved in the manufacture of a component, the Ban-Lon fabric, that went into the final product, the dress. In this regard, we note that the Pennsylvania Supreme Court has declared that a manufacturer of a defective component part of a product is liable under Section 402A for an injury to the ultimate user. *Burbage v. Boiler Engineering and Supply Co.*, 433 Pa. 319, 249 A. 2d 563, 566 (1969).

* * *

Case Notes: Liability of Component Part Manufacturers

1. Liability of a component part manufacturer is limited to situations in which the defect exists in the component part. Following that logic, the manufacturer of a non-defective hydraulic valve that was incorporated into a log splitter was found to have no duty to anticipate the dangers that might occur with respect to a finished product into which the component was incorporated. See *Childress v. Gresen Mfg. Co.*, 888 F.2d 45 (6th Cir. 1989) (applying Michigan law). An issue that can arise in component manufacturing cases is whether the item at issue is a component part or a product in itself. Such a question can be important if the state statutory law protects either the manufacturer or component manufacturer from liability.

2. Courts may also be asked to determine, between the manufacturer of the whole product and a component part manufacturer, which party was responsible for a design defect. See *e.g. Leahy v. Mid-West Conveyor Co., Inc.* 120 A.2d. 16 (N.Y. 1986). Numerous sub-issues can arise that impact that decision, including which party provided the specifications for the component part, whether specification information provided to a component part manufacturer was accurate, and whether other information important to the design and manufacture of the component part was related to its manufacturer.

Defendant Wholesalers, Retailers, and Distributors   Wholesalers, retailers, and distributors, also known as *middlemen,* are held liable by a majority of jurisdictions under negligence and strict liability theories for injuries resulting from defective products, even though they had no chance to discover the defect. See Haig, Business and Commercial Litigation in Federal Courts, Vol. 5, § 70.4 (1998). Middlemen include wholesalers, retailers, distributors, and suppliers. The justification for imposing liability on these middlemen in the stream of commerce is that they are better positioned than the consumer to prevent the distribution of defective products and to apply pressure on manufacturers to improve product safety. One exception to this rule of strict liability is that every state, after the decision below, now exempts health care providers statute from strict product liability.

 CASE LAW

◆ **other entities in a product liability suit**

Budding v. SSM Healthcare System, No. 19 S.W. 3d 678 (Mo. 2000).

Her physician, Dr. Rotskoff, who determined that since her jaw could not be rebuilt, Vita Teflon implants should be necessary, treated plaintiff, who was diagnosed with temporomandibular joint disease. Dr. Rotskoff obtained the implants from the hospital inventory, sized the implants, and surgically implanted them. The hospital never billed plaintiff for the implants themselves. For about six years, the plaintiff's condition improved. Then, she began experiencing pain, but declined to have corrective surgery, despite Dr. Rotskoff's written request that she come in for an examination and warning about the safety hazards presented by the implants. Approximately three years later, plaintiff had corrective surgeries, which were accompanied by complications. Plaintiff sued the hospital. A jury returned a verdict in favor of the hospital.

Holstein, Justice

* * *

Budding's first claim on appeal asserts the trial court erred in requiring the use of the word "sale" instead of "transfer" in the verdict directing instruction relating to products liability. This claim of error assumes that a health care provider is strictly liable for a products liability claim where the health care provider "transfers" a defective medical device to a patient. Because the Court concludes that chapter 538 forecloses any such claims for strict products liability, the Court need not reach the question presented. [Footnote omitted.]

Section 538.205(5) defines "Health care services" to include the "transfer to a patient of goods or services . . . in furtherance of the purposes for which an institutional healthcare provider is organized." [Emphasis added].

Section 538.225.1 mandates:

In any action against a health care provider for damages for personal injury or death on account of the rendering of or failure to render health care services, the plaintiff or his attorney shall file an affidavit with the court stating that he has obtained the written opinion of a legally qualified health care provider which states that the defendant health care provider failed to use such care as a reasonably prudent and careful health care provider would have under similar circumstances and that such failure to use such reasonable care directly caused or directly contributed to cause the damages claimed in the petition.

The affidavit must be filed within ninety days after the filing of the petition unless extended for good cause. *Sec. 538.225.4.* If a plaintiff fails to file such affidavit, the trial court may dismiss the petition. *Sec. 538.225.5.*

The Court's role in interpreting these statutes is to "ascertain the intent of the legislature from the language used, to give effect to that intent if possible, and to consider the words used in their plain and ordinary meaning." *State ex rel. Riordan v. Dierker,* 956 S.W.2d 258, 260 (Mo. banc 1997). In determining the legislature's intent in adopting the various provisions of chapter 538, several conclusions are obvious. First, by using the words "any action" in sec. 538.225.1, the legislature clearly demonstrated its intent that the statute not only apply to a negligence action but to a products liability action as well. Second, the legislature intended the provisions of the chapter to apply not only to services but to transfers of goods to a patient in furtherance of a health care institution's purpose. Third, the legislature intended to impose specific limitations on the traditional tort causes of action available against a health care provider. Included in these limitations is not only a cap on noneconomic damages, sec. 538.210, and structured settlements of future damages, sec. 538.220, but the requirement that the cause of action be dependent upon an affidavit by a "legally qualified health care provider" of failure to exercise reasonable care attributable to the defendant health care provider, sec. 538.225. [Footnote omitted.]

It is true that nothing in the statute specifically requires the plaintiff to prove negligence or other level of culpability in order to recover. However, in construing the statute, the Court is not to assume the legislature intended an absurd result. *Akers v. Warson Garden Apartments,* 961 S.W.2d 50 (Mo. banc 1998). It would be an obvious absurdity to require an affidavit of negligence as a condition of proceeding with the cause of action even though negligence need not be proved in order to submit the case to a jury or to obtain a judgment. On that basis alone, it is reasonable to conclude that the legislature intended to eliminate liability of health care providers for strict liability.

Further buttressing the conclusion that strict liability is not applicable to health care providers is sec.

538.300. That section provides that the provisions of sec. 537.760 to sec. 537.765, relating to products liability actions, are not applicable to actions against health care providers. Section 537.760 codifies sec. 402A of the *Restatement (Second) of Torts. Rodriguez v. Suzuki Motor Co.,* 996 S.W.2d 47, 65 (Mo. banc 1999). n5 The exception of health care providers from the provisions codifying strict products liability is yet another clear indication that the general assembly intended to abrogate such liability for health care providers. Just as enactment of sec. 537.760 codified strict products liability, the exception provided for in sec. 538.300 was intended to eliminate such statutory liability for health care providers.

* * *

Defendant Successor Corporations Product liability claims may arise after the product at issue harms the plaintiff many years after it has been manufactured. It is possible that during the years between the product's manufacture and the harm it caused, the original manufacturer has been acquired by a succeeding entity. The question each litigator in such a scenario must answer is whether the successor corporation is liable for defects in products manufactured by its predecessor. Typically, the answer is no, but most jurisdictions recognize four exceptions to this general rule:

1. an agreement, express or implied, to assume liabilities
2. the transaction amounts to a consolidation or merger of two corporations
3. the successor corporation is a mere continuation of the predecessor corporation
4. when the transaction was fraudulent, not made in good faith, or without sufficient consideration. See *Fish v. Amsted Industries, Inc.,* 376 N.W.2d 820 [Wis. 1985].

Of these four exceptions, many jurisdictions typically recognize liability of a successor corporation when there has been a continuation of the enterprise, such as when the corporation represents itself as a continuation of the seller and retains other characteristics of the predecessor corporation.

 CASE LAW

◆ **criteria for holding successor corporations liable for product liability claims**

Lacy v. Carrier Corporation d/b/a ILG Industries and ILG Industries, Inc. 939 F. Supp. 375 (E.D. Pa. 1996).

Plaintiff, while cleaning the walls of a Philadelphia fire station, inadvertently made contact with an unguarded exhaust fan, which injured his arm severely. The fan in question was manufactured by ILG Industries, Inc. some time between June 1968 and January 1972.

Padova, J.J.

* * *

Pursuant to an agreement dated December 27, 1972 which became effective in February 1973, Carrier, a Delaware corporation, acquired ILG Industries, Inc.; Carrier merged its wholly-owned subsidiary, JHG Corp., into ILG Industries, and operated the consolidated entity as a Carrier division bearing the name Ilg Industries. See December 27, 1972 Agreement and Plan of Reorganization, Carrier's Mem. Supp. Mot. Summ. J. Ex. B (hereinafter "the 1972 Agreement"). The merger was accomplished by a stock-for-stock transaction. Each share of Carrier's wholly-owned subsidiary, JHG, was converted into a share of the new common stock of ILG. Id. at P 3.1(a). In exchange, each outstanding share of the old common stock of ILG Industries was converted into four shares of Carrier common stock. Id. at P 3.1(b). The 1972 Agreement contained no provision by which Carrier assumed the liabilities of ILG Industries, Inc.

Carrier continued to manufacture the ILG Industries product line through its Ilg Industries division. Carrier operated the Ilg Industries division until December 1978, when an Illinois Corporation known as ILG Industries, Inc. purchased all of the assets, properties, and operations of the Ilg Industries division from Carrier. See December 28, 1978 Agreement, Carrier's Mem. Supp. Mot. Summ. J. Ex. C (hereinafter "the 1978 Agreement"). Under the terms of the 1978 Agreement, Carrier explicitly retained responsibility for product liability suits only with respect to items manufactured and/or sold by the Carrier Ilg Industries division during the 1973–1978 period. Id. at § 11. After the 1978 sale, Carrier ceased to produce or service the product line it had acquired from the first ILG Industries. The second ILG Industries, Inc., an entity with no connection to Carrier, operated as a distinct and separate corporate entity until it filed for Chapter 7 bankruptcy protection in 1991. [Footnote omitted.]

* * *

The *Dawejko* court described several criteria that are pertinent in deciding to apply the product line exception, including whether the purchaser: (1) acquired all or substantially all of the manufacturer's assets; (2) undertook the same manufacturing operation as the seller; (3) held itself out as an ongoing concern of the seller; (4) maintained the same product, name, personnel, property, and clients as the seller; and (5) acquired the

seller's name and good will and required the seller to dissolve. *Dawejko*, 434 A.2d at 110-11 [Citations omitted.]. *Dawejko* stated that it "will always be useful to consider whether the three-part test stated in *Ray v. Alad Corp.* . . . has been met." *Id.* at 111. Thus, the court may also consider whether the purchaser's acquisition destroyed the plaintiff's remedy; the purchaser has the ability to assume the manufacturer's risk-spreading role; and the fairness of imposing responsibility on the purchaser for a defective product that was a burden attached to the seller's good will that is being enjoyed by the successor in the continued operation of the business. Id. at 109 (*citing Ray v. Alad Corp.*, 19 Cal. 3d 22, 560 P.2d 3, 8-9, 136 Cal. Rptr. 574 (Cal. 1977).

* * *

. . . Plaintiff moves the Court to find as a matter of law that Carrier is potentially liable under the product line exception. Therefore, we must determine whether the exception's other criteria are met. I initially note that I am aware of no authority that holds that each of the criteria set forth in *Dawejko* must be met before the product line exception may be applied. See *Conway v. White Trucks*, 692 F. Supp. 442, 451 (M.D. Pa. 1988) (noting that the *Dawejko* court neither indicated what degree of weight to accord each factor nor decided whether all the factors had to be established in order to impose liability under the exception), aff'd, 885 F.2d 90 (3d Cir. 1989).

First, Article 6 of the 1972 Agreement shows that through the stock transaction Carrier acquired all of the first ILG Industries' assets. See 1972 Agreement at Art. 6. For example, the 1972 Agreement provided for the transfer of: (1) all real property owned or leased by ILG, id. at P 6.1; (2) all contracts, loan, security, distributor and license agreements, and equipment leases to which ILG was a party, id. at P 6.3; (3) lists of key suppliers to ILG and ILG's biggest customers, id. at P 6.4; and (4) ILG's intellectual property, including patents and patent applications, trademark registrations and trademark registration applications, and trade names owned by ILG. Id. at P 6.5.

Second, it is undisputed that the Carrier Ilg Industries division undertook the same manufacturing operation as the seller and continued to produce the same product line. Third, the terms of the 1972 Agreement showed that Carrier planned to hold itself out as an ongoing concern of ILG Industries. The Agreement provided that Carrier's subsidiary, JHG, would merge into ILG Industries, JHG would then cease to exist as a separate entity, and ILG would be the surviving corporation. Id. at P 1.1. The finding that Carrier held itself out as an ongoing concern of ILG is further confirmed by the 1978 Agreement, which states that Carrier was selling an entity known as the Ilg Industries division; this demonstrates that the division bore the ILG name during the five-year period of its operation by Carrier. See 1978 Agreement at p. 1.

Fourth, the above-cited sections of the 1972 Agreement demonstrate that Carrier would continue to use the ILG name and sell to ILG's customers. The Carrier Ilg Industries division carried on the same product line using the properties and assets acquired from the first ILG Industries. And with regard to personnel, the 1972 Agreement provided that the original ILG Industries' officers and directors would continue as officers and directors in the new Carrier division. See 1972 Agreement at P 2.3. Fifth, the entire structure of 1972 transaction demonstrates that Carrier intended to capitalize on the goodwill built up by ILG Industries; Carrier merged its own subsidiary into ILG so that ILG would be the surviving entity. Id. at P 1.1. Additionally, Plaintiff correctly notes that according to a document submitted by Carrier, after Carrier purchased ILG in 1973, the nameplates on fans subsequently produced by the Carrier division had the wording "Ilg Industries/Division of Carrier Corp." See Carrier's Mem. Supp. Mot. Summ. J. Ex. A at p. 2. The evidence establishes that Carrier acquired and capitalized on ILG's name and goodwill. The fifth factor also asks whether the purchaser required the seller to dissolve, and I note that the 1972 Agreement did not require the dissolution of ILG Industries but, instead, provided that ILG would be the surviving entity in the merger. See 1972 Agreement at P 1.1. [Footnote omitted.] As noted supra, however, the product line exception is less concerned with corporate formalities and emphasizes instead the nature of the successor's business operations.

I already have discussed supra how the evidence supports a finding that Carrier's acquisition contributed to the destruction of Plaintiff's remedies against the original manufacturer as a separate entity. The next factor to consider is the purchaser's ability to assume the risk-spreading role. In Nieves, as described supra, the court concluded that the intermediate successor had the ability to spread the risk of defective products because in its purchase agreement with the current successor, the intermediate successor agreed to retain liability for any personal injury or property damage suits arising out of products it sold before the sale of the business. Nieves, 431 A.2d at 831-32. As aforementioned, in this case, the 1978 Agreement provided that Carrier would retain responsibility for product liability suits with respect to products manufactured and/or sold by the Carrier Ilg Industries division prior to the 1978 sale. See 1978 Agreement at § 11, pp. 15–16. Thus, I find that Carrier has the ability to assume the risk-spreading role.

Finally, the court must consider whether it is fair to impose successor liability on Carrier given the particular circumstances of this case. I am cognizant of the argument that there is an element of unfairness in imposing liability on a company which no longer receives the benefits of the product line and sold those operations before Plaintiff was injured. At the same time, the evidence establishes that Carrier capitalized on ILG's goodwill and for a period of five years was a part of the "overall enterprise" of manufacturing the same product line, and then received a cash benefit when it sold off the division in 1978. Additionally, Plaintiff in the instant case will likely be left without a remedy for his alleged injuries if Carrier is not recognized as a successor in liability. I find that these considerations outweigh any potential unfairness to Carrier.

I find that the evidence establishes substantially all the criteria of the product line exception. Therefore, I hold as a matter of law that Carrier is potentially liable to Plaintiff as a successor corporation under this exception.

* * *

Defendant Employers   Occasionally, a defective product manufactured by a plaintiff's employer may injure an employee. Can the employee sue his or her employer for product defect? Ordinarily, the answer is no because worker's compensation laws preclude such suits and immunize the employer for liability for unintentional torts. In most states, workers are guaranteed compensation if they are injured. However, a few exceptions to the general rule exist. One exception allows an employee to sue a corporate parent. Another is the *dual capacity doctrine*, which provides that an employer who distributes products to the public assumes a responsibility to provide safe products, which is a separate responsibility from its responsibilities as an employer. See *Cole v. Fair Oaks Fire Protection Dist.*, 729 P.2d 743 (Cal. 1987). Finally, the employee might escape the bar worker's compensation poses by attempting to show that her exposure or use of the product occurred outside of the scope of her employment.

 CASE LAW ————————————————————————————————————◆

◆ **related defendant employers in product cases**

Olson v. U.S. Industries, Inc., 649 F. Supp. 1511 (D.C. Kan. 1986).

Plaintiff was instructed by his employer, Ulysses, to observe and copy a competitor's molding machine used in manufacturing. He did so and constructed the machine in 1979. Plaintiff successfully operated the machine until July 1983, when Ulysses was purchased by another company, USI. The purchase agreement provided that Ulysses disclaimed all warranties and USI acquired the assets of Ulysses "as is." Seven months after the purchase, plaintiff activated the machine, which severed his hands. Plaintiff sued USI in strict liability and negligence for its allegedly defective design and manufacture of the machine.

KELLY, J.J.

* * *

. . . In the present case, the plaintiff user was the same person who copied, modified and built this machine for the company he now seeks to hold liable for negligent design and manufacture, and plaintiff used it successfully for over four years prior to his injury. There can be no question plaintiff possessed substantial experience with, and education and special knowledge of, this machine and we note, but need not find, his expertise equaled or exceeded that of USI. Under Kansas law, to whatever extent USI was the "manufacturer" of this machine, defendant labored under no duty *to this plaintiff,*

with his special knowledge, awareness and experience, to guard or warn against the patent, open and obvious danger of activating the machine while his hands were located beneath the plunger.

* * *

Applying these standards, and viewing the parties' evidence and the totality of the circumstances, the court finds that a jury properly instructed in accordance with the foregoing standards of superseding cause could reach only one conclusion: that even if defendant USI labored under any duty to plaintiff Olson in light of his special and intimate knowledge and experience with the end-cap molding machine, the unique circumstances of the sale, Ulysses' knowledge of the disclaimer of all warranties and representations, the patent danger involved, Ulysses' affirmative duties to act for the safety of plaintiff, and the lapse of time, operated together to shift the entire responsibility for this machine from USI to Ulysses, whose failure to inspect, test and guard against the obvious danger before placing the machine in operation is a superseding cause of Olson's injuries, relieving defendant USI of any liability. Third party defendant Ulysses is the only party from which plaintiff may recover for his injuries, and Ulysses' liability has been satisfied fully by payment of workers' compensation benefits to plaintiff.

It is accordingly ordered this 29 day of December, 1986, defendant USI's motion for summary judgment is granted, and the case dismissed in its entirety.

Defendant Lessors, Bailors, and Licensors   The terms *lessor* or *bailor* are not included in §402A of the *Restatement (Second) of Torts*. Nevertheless, the majority of courts that have addressed the issue have relied on that section to impose on lessors and bailors the same obligations that section imposes on *sellers*. These courts have reasoned that there is little to distinguish between a sale, in which ownership is transferred for a price, and a lease or bailment for hire, in which possession is exchanged for a rental fee. See *Cintrone v. Hertz Truck Leasing & Rental Service, 212 A.2d 769 (N.J. 1965)*. Similarly, courts have compared lessors and bailors to manufacturers on the basis that both place products in the stream of commerce. These reasons for the similar treatment of lessors and bailors apply only in the commercial context, and the lease or bailment must be a regular part of the commercial business. As in strict liability, courts are extending the limited language of the UCC to lessors and bailors. Specifically, UCC § 2-102's phrase "transaction in goods" extends to leases and bailments. See *Bachner v. Pearson*, 479 P.2d 319 (Alaska 1970).

Practitioners should note that exculpatory language in a rental document has been held not to shield a lessor from product liability. In addition, litigants should carefully research the applicable jurisdiction's statutory and case law on the issue of the treatment of lessors and bailors. Although the weight of authority treats lessors and bailors similarly, some jurisdictions treat the two differently. See Frumer and Friedman, Products Liability, Vol. 2A, §5.08 (Matthew Bender, 1993).

Licensors have not faired much better than lessors and bailors under § 402A of The *Restatement (Second) of Torts*. The rationale is the same, in that the objective of the strict liability doctrine is to shift the risk of loss to those in the chain of distribution of defective products. See *Torres v. Goodyear Tire & Rubber Company, Inc.*, 901 F.2d 750, 751 (9th Cir. 1990). The test for whether licensors should be held liable under strict liability law focuses on the degree of control a licensor exercises over the design, manufacture, and sale of the defective product. One court stated

> As a common law matter, trademark licensors who significantly participate in the overall process by which the product reaches its consumers, and who have the right to control the incidents of manufacture or distribution, are subject to liability under the rules of Restatement § 402A as adopted and applied in Arizona. Like lessors of products, they are the functional equivalent of manufacturers and sellers. *Id.*

 CASE LAW ─────────────────────────────────◆

◆ **strict liability of a defendant lessor**

**Francioni v. Gibsonia
Truck Corp.,** 372 A.2d 736
(Pa. 1977).

Plaintiff, a truck driver, sued under negligence and strict liability theories for injuries he sustained in an accident that occurred when he was driving a tractor-trailer that his employer had leased from the defendant.

NIX, Justice

* * *

In *Escola v. Coca Cola Bottling Co. of Fresno,* 24 Cal.2d 453, 150 P.2d 436 (1944), Justice (later Chief Justice) Traynor declared in his landmark concurring opinion:

> . . . public policy demands that responsibility be fixed wherever it will most effectively reduce the hazards to life and health inherent in defective products that reach the market. *Id.* at 462, 150 P.2d at 440.

By the adoption of Section 402A, that responsibility was placed on those who, through manufacturing and distribution, intend that products "reach the market." *Bialek v. Pittsburgh Brewing Co.*, 430 Pa. 176, 187 n. 2, 242 A.2d 231, 236 n. 2 (1968); Restatement (Second) of Torts § 402A, Comments c and f. While Section 402A speaks only in terms of "sellers," the foregoing policy statement and accompanying citations demonstrate the propriety of extending its application to anyone "who enters into the business of supplying human beings with products which may endanger the safety of their persons and property, . . ." Restatement (Second) of Torts § 402A, Comment f. What is crucial to the rule of strict liability is not the means of marketing but rather the fact of marketing, whether by sale, lease or bailment, for use and consumption by the public. *Link v. Sun Oil Co.*, Ind. App., 312 N.E.2d 126, 130 (1974); *Whitfield v. Cooper*, 30 Conn.Sup. 47, 298 A.2d 50 (1972); *Delaney v. Towmotor Corp.*, 339 F.2d 4, 6 (2d Cir. 1964). Where the fundamental principles are applicable, the imposition of artificial distinctions will only frustrate the intended purpose.

The leading case to apply strict liability principles to lessors is *Cintrone v. Hertz Truck Leasing & Rental Service*, 45 N.J. 434, 212 A.2d 769 (1965). The plaintiff, a truck driver, was injured while riding in a truck leased by his employer from the defendant which was in the business of leasing motor vehicles. Plaintiff's complaint charged negligence on the part of the defendant as well as breach of defendant's warranty of fitness. The trial court, however, dismissed the warranty claim and the jury found in favor of the defendant on the issue of negligence. On appeal, the Supreme Court of New Jersey held, although no sale and purchase had occurred, that a warranty of fitness did indeed arise from the lease and reversed the lower court. It analogized the warranty of fitness to strict liability and noted a similarity of function [*368] between the seller and lessor of products which necessitated application of strict liability to both:

> A bailor for hire, such as a person in the U-drive-it business, puts motor vehicles in the stream of commerce in a fashion not unlike

a manufacturer or retailer. In fact such a bailor puts the vehicle he buys and then rents to the public to more sustained use on the highways than most ordinary car purchasers. The very nature of the business is such that the bailor, his employees, passengers and the traveling public are exposed to a greater *quantum* of potential danger of harm from defective vehicles than usually arises out of sales by the manufacturer. *Id.* at 450, 212 A.2d at 777.

Several courts have followed the lead of *Cintrone* and extended Section 402A coverage to lessors in the business of leasing products to the public. See *Lechuga v. Montgomery*, 12 Ariz.App. 32, 467 P.2d 256 (1970); *Bachner v. Pearson*, 479 P.2d 319 (Alaska 1970); *Price v. Shell Oil Co.*, 2 Cal.3d 245, 85 Cal.Rptr. 178, 466 P.2d 722 (1970); *McClaflin v. Bayshore Equipment Rental Co.*, 274 Cal.App.2d 466, 79 Cal.Rptr. 337 (1969); *Martin v. Ryder Truck Rental, Inc.*, 353 A.2d 581 (Del.1976); *Stewart v. Budget Rent-A-Car Corp.*, 52 Haw. 71, 470 P.2d 240 (1970); *Galluccio v. Hertz Corp.*, 1 Ill.App.3d 272, 274 N.E.2d 178 (1971); *Stang v. Hertz*, 83 N.M. 730, 497 P.2d 732 (1972); *Rourke v. Garza*, 530 S.W.2d 794 (Tex.1975); *George v. Tonjes*, 414 F.Supp. 1199 (W.D.Wis.1976). All have premised their holdings on these pertinent factors: (1) In some instances the lessor, like the seller, may be the only member of the marketing chain available to the injured plaintiff for redress; (2) As in the case of the seller, imposition of strict liability upon the lessor serves as an incentive to safety; (3) The lessor will be in a better position than the consumer to prevent the circulation of defective products; and (4) The lessor can distribute the cost of compensating for injuries resulting from defects by charging for it in his business, *i.e.*, by adjustment of the rental terms. We find the reasoning of these opinions to be highly persuasive and hold that all suppliers of products engaged in the business of supplying products for use or consumption by the public are subject to strict liability for injuries caused by "a defective condition unreasonably dangerous to the user or consumer or his property."

* * *

International Defendants

 **CASE LAW**

◆ **nonresident defendants**

Simon v. Philip Morris,
Inc., 86 F. Supp.2d 96
(E.D.N.Y. 2000).

Plaintiffs, who were smokers, sued the defendants, various to-bacco companies and affiliated organizations in a nationwide personal injury class action alleging that for decades the defendants conspired to deceive the American public regarding the addictiveness of nicotine and the adverse health consequences of smoking. Defendant B.A.T. Industries, a foreign holding company parent moved to dismiss based upon the court's lack of personal jurisdiction.

Weinstein, J.J.

* * *

B.A.T. Industries, p.l.c. ("BAT"), the British holding company parent of United States defendant, Brown & Williamson Tobacco Corp. ("B&W"), has moved to dismiss for lack of personal jurisdiction. It claims that it is a passive stockholding parent corporation with no connection to the fraud and conspiracy alleged by the plaintiffs. BAT's motion was denied by order dated July 19, 1999. This amended memorandum explains the basis for the denial.

BAT is a quintessential example of a sophisticated holding company presiding over a multinational corporate empire whose operations span the globe. Through the promulgation of binding company-wide policies and long distance active participation in the large-scale marketing, research, and development of cigarettes, it is regnant in the cigarette industry in the United States and throughout the world. Its sway is an aspect of to-day's global technological-commercial community, in which the click of a mouse may affect events unfolding thousands of miles away and concepts of sovereignty for jurisdictional purposes have eroded. BAT's conduct has supranational effects. It must accept the price of its international ascendancy by defending suits here in the United States, where it has allegedly been responsible for massive damage.

* * *

To establish jurisdiction over a nonresident defendant on the basis of the New York acts of a co-conspirator, the plaintiff must: (1) establish a prima facie case of conspiracy; (2) allege specific facts warranting the inference that the defendant was a member of the conspiracy; and (3) demonstrate the commission of a tortious act in New York during, and pursuant to, the conspiracy. See *Allstate Life Ins. Co. v. Linter Group Ltd.,* 782 F. Supp. 215, 221 (S.D.N.Y. 1992); *Chrysler Capital,* 778 F. Supp. at 1266.

Under New York law a prima facie showing of a conspiracy entails allegation of the primary tort and the following four elements:

1. a corrupt agreement between two or more parties,
2. an overt act in furtherance of the agreement,
3. the parties' intentional participation in the furtherance of a plan or purpose, and
4. the resulting damage or injury. [Citation omitted.]

The requisite relationship between the defendant and its New York co-conspirators is established by a showing that

(a) the defendant had an awareness of the effects in New York of its activity;

(b) the activity of the co-conspirators in New York was to the benefit of the out-of-state conspirators; and

(c) the co-conspirators acting in New York acted 'at the direction or under the control' or 'at the request or on behalf of' the out-of-state defendant.

Chrysler Capital, 778 F. Supp. at 1268-69 (quoting Dixon, 507 F. Supp. at 350).

2. Application of Law to Facts

First, it should be noted that New York state and federal courts have recognized the applicability of the conspiracy theory of jurisdiction to BAT in other tobacco litigations. [Citations omitted.]

* * *

Courts of a number of other jurisdictions have also exercised conspiracy-based jurisdiction over BAT. [Citations omitted.]

* * *

Defendant contends that a parent and its subsidiary cannot civilly conspire. Even were this contention true, it would not affect BAT's jurisdictional status since, as already demonstrated, it also conspired with non-BAT Group entities comprising essentially the entire United States tobacco industry. In any event, research, uncovers no rule in this circuit such as that defendant professes outside the special Sherman Act context. See *Copperweld Corp. v. Independence Tube Corp.*, 467 U.S. 752, 81 L. Ed. 2d 628, 104 S. Ct. 2731 (1984) (a parent and a wholly owned subsidiary could not conspire for purposes of section 1 of the Sherman Act); see also *Viacom Int'l Inc. v. Time Inc.*, 785 F. Supp. 371, 381 (S.D.N.Y. 1992) (Copperweld requires "plurality of economic actors" to support allegations of conspiracy to monopolize under section two of the Sherman Act).

The policies animating the Sherman Act can be adequately vindicated by treating a multi-corporate entity as one body even though its component corporations perform separate actions intended in total to frustrate the Act; it is the cooperation of one entity with another distinct and unrelated one which is particularly threatening to the free market competition the Act was designed to protect. See *Copperweld*, 467 U.S. at 771 ("If a parent and its wholly owned subsidiary do 'agree' to a course of action, there is no sudden joining of economic resources that had previously served different interests, and there is no justification for § 1 scrutiny.").

In the mass tort product liability area, by contrast, the dangers to be deterred can be created just as easily when two corporations that are part of the same entity cooperate to harm the public as when independent entities cooperate to the same end. As the case law of this circuit demonstrates, the component corporations of a single integrated entity may be considered separate and capable of conspiring with one another for some purposes, but not for others. Compare, e.g., *Aerotech, Inc. v. TCW Capital*, 1994 U.S. Dist. LEXIS 5086, No. 93 Civ. 1987, 1994 WL 775439, at *2 (April 20, 1994 S.D.N.Y.) (parent and subsidiary incapable of combining or conspiring for purposes of sections 1 and 2 of the Sherman Act) with *Rouse v. Rouse*, 1990 U.S. Dist. LEXIS 13879, *40, No. 89

CV 597, 1990 WL 160194, at *14 (Oct. 17, 1990 N.D.N.Y.) ("the mere fact that an alleged RICO conspiracy is intracorporate does not mean that the alleged RICO conspiracy fails as a matter of law,") and Supra *USA Inc. v. Samsung Electronic Co.*, 1987 U.S. Dist. LEXIS 10406, No. 85 Civ. 9696, 1987 WL 19953, at *14 (Nov. 10, 1987 S.D.N.Y.) (Copperweld doctrine does not apply to suits under Robinson-Patman Act). See also *Ashland Oil, Inc. v. Arnett*, 875 F.2d 1271, 1281 (7th Cir. 1989) (recognizing intracorporate RICO conspiracy); *Shearin v. E.F. Hutton Group, Inc.*, 885 F.2d 1162, 1167 (3d Cir. 1989) (same); *Curley v. Cumberland Farms Dairy, Inc.*, 728 F. Supp. 1123, 1135 (D.N.J. 1989) (recognizing "intracorporate conspiracies is more faithful to the broad purposes of RICO than a narrow reading which is modeled on antitrust law").

The nature of the danger determines the policy and its implementation by way of specific substantive and jurisdictional rules. While the goals of the Sherman Act may not be sufficiently threatened by parent-subsidiary conspiracies to warrant its applicability to such cases, the same cannot be said of the policies embodied in New York's substantive tort and jurisdictional law. The hub in this case may be said to have conspired with the integrated spokes and rim as well as with other independent wheels.

a. Prima Facie Showing of Conspiracy

Plaintiffs have alleged the primary tort of fraudulent concealment. Its elements are material false representation, intent to defraud, reasonable reliance, damages and a duty to disclose on the part of the misrepresenting party. See *Banque Arabe et Internationale d' Investissement v. Maryland National Bank*, 57 F.3d 146, 153 (2d Cir. 1995). The tobacco industry's repeated assertions that a causal link between smoking and disease had not been established were, plaintiffs contend, material, false and made with the intent to defraud and conceal from them research data confirming the health risks of cigarettes. Plaintiffs further allege that their reliance on these misrepresentations was reasonable in view of the industry's (including BAT's as a leading member) superior resources and knowledge and its public promise to fund and disseminate the results of objective smoking and health research. These same factors, it is plausibly argued, also gave rise to a duty on the part of the industry, including BAT, to disclose all relevant information. Plaintiffs claim to have suffered substantial personal injuries and damages as a result of this alleged fraud.

A corrupt agreement, the first element of a conspiracy, may be readily inferred from the tobacco companies' formation of and membership in CTR. The 1953 "Frank Statement to Cigarette Smokers" signed by, among others, the American Tobacco Company, B&W, Philip Morris, and R.J. Reynolds, informed the American people that out of its concern for their welfare, the tobacco industry would provide "aid and assistance to the research effort into all phases of tobacco use and health." Pls.' Ex. 1. Yet, as revealed by the documents, CTR's actual purpose was to place the industry in a positive light while at the same time generating research for use in supporting its deceptive position that the health hazards of smoking were unproven.

The remaining elements of a conspiracy are also satisfied. There is evidence of multiple overt acts by the tobacco companies in furtherance of the alleged conspiracy both in and outside of New York. New York acts include the formation of CTR and the covert distribution of funds through CTR "special projects" and "special account 4." See, e.g., 2004.29, 2034.01-02, 2034.06, 2015.02, 2024.02. These acts also satisfy the requirement of the commission of a tortious act in New York.

Another example of an overt New York act is the publication of the Barron's advertisement. As already pointed out, the editorial denied proof that smoking was dangerous and characterized the evidence to the contrary as part of a regulatory "crusade" by "witch doctors" and "medicine men." See *Glantz*, supra, at 177; see also Doc. No. 2101.06 (letter from B&W's vice president for advertising characterizing the Barron's campaign as a "step forward together" by the industry). The Barron's advertisement was prepared by Tiderock Corporation, a New York advertising agency, see *Glantz*, supra, at 175, and was available to New York readers.

The overt acts enumerated above also support an inference of intentional participation in furtherance of a plan of purpose. See, e.g., *Cleft of the Rock*, 992 F. Supp. at 582.

The proposed plaintiff class is composed of individuals who smoked one package of cigarettes or more per day over a twenty-year period. Their claims to have developed lung cancer as a result of the tobacco industry's conduct satisfy the final element of a prima facie case of conspiracy.

It should be emphasized that a determination that sufficient color of a conspiracy exists for jurisdictional purposes does not control the issue of whether plaintiffs will ultimately adduce sufficient evidence to prevail on the merits of their conspiracy claim at trial.

* * *

Defendant Trade Associations A trade association is ordinarily regarded as a voluntarily organized group of business concerns, all of which have similar interests. It is akin to professional associations. Most of these organizations are non-for-profit and are comprised of often-competing businesses. Although the naming of trade associations as defendants has not been common in products liability litigation, it has increased in popularity. Trade associations are named as defendants for a wide variety of reasons, most notably because they often set or help to set standards for an industry. Most suits against trade organizations are not successful, but occasionally, as demonstrated below, a case succeeds in at least putting a trade association before a jury.

 CASE LAW

◆ **alleging a cause of action against a trade association**

Snyder v. American Association of Blood Banks, 676 A.2d 1036 (N.J. 1996).

On August 23, 1984, William Snyder underwent open-heart surgery at New Jersey hospital. In 1987, he learned that he had contracted Acquired Immune Deficiency Syndrome (AIDS) from a transfusion of blood that the Bergen County Blood Center (BCBC), a non-profit blood bank, had provided to St.

Joseph's. The BCBC is a member of the American Association of Blood Banks (AABB), an association of blood banks and blood-banking professionals. This case addressed, among other issues, whether AABB owed a duty of care to Snyder.

POLLOCK, Justice

* * *

On August 23, 1984, Snyder underwent open-heart surgery at St. Joseph's Hospital in Paterson. During the surgery he received transfusions of several units of blood platelets, including unit 29F0784, which BCBC had supplied to St. Joseph's.

At the time, no direct test existed to determine whether blood was infected with Human Immunodeficiency Virus (HIV), the cause of AIDS. Other means of making that determination, however, were available. Starting in 1985, the enzyme-linked immunoabsorbent-assay-screening test (the ELISA test) enabled blood banks to screen for HIV.

* * *

Crucial to the assessment of the AABB's alleged duty of care is its role in the blood-banking industry in 1983–84. The blood-banking industry consists of a voluntary sector, which depends on voluntary donors, and a commercial sector, which depends on paid donors. Generally speaking, the voluntary sector provides whole blood and blood components, and the commercial sector provides plasma and plasma derivatives.

Central to the voluntary sector is the American Red Cross with its blood banks, community and hospital blood centers, and the AABB, which includes almost every blood bank in the United States. These voluntary blood banks rely on public-spirited donors for their blood supply. Voluntary blood banks commonly separate donated blood into three components: plasma, platelets, and red cells.

* * *

State and federal regulations apply to both sectors of the blood-banking industry. The Food and Drug Administration (FDA), an agency of the Public Health Service (PHS) in the United States Department of Health and Human Services (DHHS), inspects and licenses blood banks and other blood facilities. See 21 U.S.C.A. § 321(g)(1)(B) (broadly defining "drugs" to include "articles intended for use in the diagnosis, cure, mitigation, treatment, or prevention of disease," which includes blood and blood products); 21 U.S.C.A. § 360(b) (requiring processing establishments, including blood banks, to register with the FDA); 42 U.S.C.A. § 262(c) to (d) (requiring inspection and licensing by the FDA (as delegated by secretary of DHHS) of blood or blood-product facilities that participate in interstate commerce; 21 C.F.R. 5.10(a)(1) and (5) (1995) (delegating to FDA authority vested in the secretary, DHHS, and PHS in the Food, Drug and Cosmetic Act (21 U.S.C.A. §§ 301-95) and in 42 U.S.C.A. §§ 262 and 263); 21 C.F.R. 607.3(b) (1995) (defining blood as a drug). In New Jersey, the Department of Health (DOH) [**1040] discharges similar responsibilities. See N.J.S.A. 26:2A-1 (authorizing DOH to regulate collection, processing and distribution of blood). A blood bank in New [*277] Jersey cannot operate without licenses from both the FDA and DOH. 42 U.S.C.A §§ 262(a); N.J.S.A. 26:2A-4.

Against this background, we consider the role of the AABB. According to the AABB's certificate of incorporation, the purpose of the AABB is

> to foster the exchange of ideas and information relating to blood banks and blood transfusion services[;] . . . to advance and incorporate high standards of performance and service by blood banks[;] . . . to function as a clearing house for the exchange of blood and blood credits . . . [and] to encourage the development of blood banks through education, public information and research.

The AABB describes itself as a "professional, non-profit, scientific and administrative association for individuals and institutions engaged in the many facets of blood and tissue banking, and transfusion and transplantation medicine." It is "the only organization devoted exclusively to blood banking and blood transfusion services." In the early 1980s, the AABB centers collected about half of the nation's blood supply and transfused eighty percent of the blood to patients. Its institutional members were mainly hospitals and non-profit blood centers.

According to the AABB's executive director, Joel Solomon, the general purpose of the AABB is "to develop and recommend standards on the practice of blood banking, to help promote the public health, . . . and to conduct numerous programs for communication and education among organization members and the public at-large." The AABB discharges its educational mission by conducting workshops and seminars, and by publishing books, newsletters, pamphlets, and a peer-review journal, Transfusion. Additionally, the AABB lobbies the United States Congress and state legislatures and participates in federal and state administrative rulemaking procedures.

Significantly, the AABB annually inspects and accredits member institutions. It conditions accreditation on compliance with standards published in its Standards for Blood Banks and Transfusion Services and procedures outlined in its Technical Manual. According to the annual report, AABB standards often become FDA standards. As the AABB has declared, it "leads the industry in setting policy and establishing standards of practice for its member blood banks in excess of the FDA."

Both the state and federal government, as well as the blood-banking industry, generally accept AABB standards as authoritative. Consequently, blood banks throughout the nation rely on those standards. For example, BCBC relied on the AABB standards in developing its own operating procedures. In the words of Anthony Passaro, Executive Director of BCBC, the AABB's standards in 1984 "were basically the Bible of the blood center."

AABB's inspections complement the annual inspection by the FDA. If a blood bank loses its AABB accreditation but retains its FDA and New Jersey licenses, it can continue to operate, but only with significant practical problems. Hospitals and other blood banks prefer to work with AABB accredited institutions.

* * *

By words and conduct, the AABB invited blood banks, hospitals, and patients to rely on the AABB's recommended procedures. The AABB set the standards for voluntary blood banks. At all relevant times, it exerted considerable influence over the practices and procedures over its member banks, including BCBC. On behalf of itself and its member banks, the AABB lobbies legislatures, participates in administrative proceedings, and works with governmental health agencies in setting blood-banking policy. In many respects, the AABB wrote the rules and set the standards for voluntary blood banks.

* * *

The risk also was foreseeable. Epidemiologists at the CDC believed as early as 1982 that the AIDS virus could be transmitted by blood and blood products. In January 1984, Dr. Curran's article in the New England Journal of Medicine confirmed that belief. Thus, before Snyder received his transfusion, the AABB should have foreseen that a blood transfusion could transmit AIDS.

* * *

Defendants That Have Alternative, Enterprise, or Market Share Liability   Product liability litigation sometimes presents plaintiffs' counsel with the seemingly unanswerable question of "Who manufactured this product?" The problem is exacerbated when the product no longer exists in its original form, such as food or drugs. When the identity of a product's manufacturer is unknown, the plight of the potential plaintiff may seem doomed, especially if she or he cannot name any defendant. Creative plaintiffs' lawyers have developed legal theories of alternative and enterprise liability that attempt to solve that problem. These theories attempt to hold liable all manufacturers who have a substantial share of the product's market.

The theory of alternative liability shifts the burden of proof to the defendants in circumstances in which the plaintiff alleges that one of the defendants is the liable party but the party responsible for the defective problem cannot be identified. The seminal case on this theory is *Summers v. Tice,* 199 P.2d 1 (Cal. 1948), in which the plaintiff was shot by one of two hunters who fired their guns at the same time. The court, relying on §433B(3) of the *Restatement (Second) of Torts,* ruled that the burden was on each hunter to prove that he was not the party at fault. The consequences of failing to meet that burden is the imposition of joint and several liability.

Alternative liability can be applied to cases that meet the following criteria:

1. a limited number of suppliers or manufacturers supplied such products and all were joined as defendants
2. all defendants possessed joint knowledge of the risks inherent in the product and a joint capacity to reduce the risks
3. each defendant delegated the responsibility to set safety standards to a trade association that failed to reduce the risks associated with use of the product

See *Hall v. E.I. Du Pont de Nemours & Co.*, 345 F. Supp 353 (E.D.N.Y. 1972).

Logically, cases based on the theory of alternative liability cannot be brought against industries that are large or not self-regulated.

Market share liability does not require a small and self-regulated industry. Rather, it is a theory that allows the plaintiff to identify all the manufacturers who made a substantial portion of the defective product that injured her or him. Then, the burden shifts to the manufacturer to prove that the plaintiff's injuries could not have been caused by its product. If a defendant cannot successfully do so, it will be found liable for its share of the market. A defendant can escape *market share* suits if it can prove that it possessed only a small share of the market, such as 10 percent. See *Murphy v. E.R. Squibb & Sons, Inc.*, 710 P.2d 247 (1985). Some jurisdictions recognize this theory only in connection with negligence claims, and not in connection with strict liability claims.

 CASE LAW

♦ **alleging market share liability in a product liability suit**

Morris v. Parke, Davis & Co., 667 F. Supp. 1332 (C.D. Cal. 1987).

Plaintiff, who allegedly was injured as a result of the administration of Diptheria-Pertussis-Tetanus vaccine ("D.P.T.") sued five vaccine manufacturers that he claimed manufactured the vaccine. He could not identify the entity that actually produced the vaccines administered to him. He proceeded under a theory of market share liability.

KELLEHER, J.J.

* * *

Plaintiffs contend that they fall outside the scope of *Sheffield,* and that *Sindell* controls because plaintiff David Morris' injury was caused by a manufacturing defect which *was* present in all of the defendants' D.P.T. products. Said contention is based upon plaintiffs' allegations that defendants' respective D.P.T. products, and each of them, "shared common inadequacies" in manufacturing, testing, storage and marketing.

Plaintiffs' legal theory is correct. The *Sheffield* Court expressly based its holding that the *Sindell* market share liability theory did not apply upon two factors: (a) the assumption that only one manufacturer produced the vaccine that had the manufacturing defect; and (b) the resulting unfairness of imposing the costs of injury against a manufacturer whose product is not harmful. *Sheffield,* 144 Cal.App.3d at 594-595, 599, 192 Cal.Rptr. at 876-877, 880; *see also: Pena v. W.H. Douthitt Steel & Supply Co.,* 179 Cal.App.3d 924, 929-930, 225 Cal.Rptr. 76, 79 (1986) ("*Sheffield* held that the *Sindell* theory did not apply unless the plaintiff could show that all defendants acted tortiously, i.e., manufactured the same defective product.").

Assuming for the purpose of determining the validity of plaintiffs' legal theory that their allegations are true, neither such factor is present in this case. There is no unfairness [footnote omitted] in holding a given defendant manufacturer liable for the proportion of a judgment represented by its share of the market when: (a) the plaintiff establishes that (i) his injuries were caused by a particular product defect or combination of defects, (ii) the product marketed by the given defendant manufacturer had said defect or combination of defects, (iii) he has joined in the action the manufacturers of a substantial share of the product; *and* (b) the given manufacturer fails to establish that it could not have made the product which caused the plaintiff's injuries. *See: Sindell,* 26 Cal.3d at 594, 611-613, 163 Cal.Rptr. at 135, 144-146. It is irrelevant under such circumstances whether the defect which caused the plaintiff's injuries is common to the products of all the defendant manufacturers because it was a design defect or because it was a manufacturing defect resulting from common (perhaps for reasons of economy) substandard means of production, storage, transportation, or marketing. Conversely, unlike the case in *Sheffield,* the plaintiffs will have established that each defendant held liable for its "market" share of the judgment acted tortiously; i.e., manufactured a defective product that could have caused plaintiff David Morris' injury. *See: Sheffield,* 144 Cal.App.3d at 594-595, 599, 192 Cal.Rptr. at 876-877, 880; *See also: Pena v. W.H. Douthitt Steel & Supply Co.,* 179 Cal.App.3d at 929-930, 225 Cal.Rptr. at 79.

It is, however, important to recognize a critical procedural and evidentiary distinction between *Sindell* and the present case. [Footnote omitted.] In *Sindell* it could not be contested that the DES products of each defendant manufacturer had the injury causing defect because said defect was inherent to DES; i.e., a design defect. Such is not the case here. In order to recover damages from a given defendant in the present case, plaintiffs bear the initial burden of proving that the D.P.T. said defendant manufactured *might* have caused plaintiff David Morris' injuries; i.e., that said D.P.T. had the *same* defect as that which caused his injuries. This is necessary in order to satisfy the requirement that said defendant acted tortiously. *See: Sheffield,* 144 Cal.App.3d at 594-595, 599, 192 Cal.Rptr. at 876-877, 880; *Pena v. W.H. Douthitt Steel & Supply Co.,* 179 Cal.App.3d at 929-930, 225 Cal.Rptr. at 79. This is also necessary in order to justify shifting the burden of proof to each defendant to prove that it could not have made the vaccine that was in fact administered to plaintiff David Morris, causing his injuries. *See, Murphy v. E.R. Squibb & Sons, Inc.,* 40 Cal.3d 672, 684, 221 Cal.Rptr. 447, 455, 710 P.2d 247 (1985) ("[In Sindell we] held that if the plaintiff joined in the action the manufacturers of a substantial share of the DES *which her mother might have taken,* the injustice of shifting the burden of proof to defendants to exonerate themselves would be significantly diminished."); *Sindell,* 26 Cal.3d at 612, 163 Cal.Rptr. at 145 ("If the Plaintiff joins in the action the manufacturers of a substantial share of the DES *which her mother might have taken,* the injustice of shifting the burden of proof to defendants to demonstrate that they could not have made the substance which injured plaintiff is significantly diminished."). Thus, in order to recover against a given defendant, plaintiffs must initially prove as a part of their above-described *prima facie* case that: (i) a particular D.P.T. defect or combination of defects caused David Morris' injuries; and (ii) the given defendant's D.P.T. had the same defect or combination of defects. Plaintiff failure to discharge said burden of proof against a given defendant necessarily means that the action against said defendant must be dismissed. The plaintiffs will be able to proceed against those defendants against whom they have discharged said burden of proof. n9 Conversely, once plaintiffs have established their *Sindell prima facie* case, the burden shifts to each defendant to prove that it could not have produced the particular D.P.T. product that was in fact administered to plaintiff David Morris.

* * *

Third Party Defendants   Because products liability law is premised on the concept of liability based on participation in the stream of commerce, third party practice is an integral defense tactic. Third party complaints are filed by a defendant against a party that the plaintiff failed to name, but which the defendant believes may be liable wholly or in part. In the products liability context, the third-party defendant is ordinarily a party in the stream of commerce, which of course can include the manufacturer, designer, supplier, component part manufacturer, designer, or trade organization. Practitioners should think strategically before filing a third-party complaint. The empty chair is sometimes a more inviting co-defendant than a named party.

Case Notes: Parties

1. Under the *Restatement (Third) of Torts,* is a business liable for defects in free samples of products given away for promotional purposes? Why should a manufacturer be more liable than others in the stream of commerce for product defects? What policy reasons justify the exclusion of health care providers from strict products liability? What policy reasons argue against that exclusion?

2. Are there any aspects of the leasing, bailment, and licensing businesses that mitigate against the imposition of strict liability? Why might the imposition of liability on trade association not have the same effect as it would on business entities? What are the advantages and disadvantages of each theory of liability available to plaintiffs who cannot identify the defendant?

PROVING THE DEFECT

Evidentiary law is "the system of rules and standard by which the admission of proof at the trial of a lawsuit is regulated." See 1 J. Strong, McCormick on Evidence § 1, at 2 (West 4th ed. 1992). Although only a small number of lawsuits ever go to trial, and fewer still ever reach a jury, the impact of evidentiary law is tremendous, particularly on products liability suits. The large number of suits that are settled or dismissed, either voluntarily or judicially can be explained in large part by the evidence that the parties anticipate presenting at trial. The practitioner should begin analyzing each case by applying the pertinent evidentiary law to the known facts and formulating an appropriate discovery and litigation strategy. From the initial stages, both parties to a products liability case must analyze the evidence with an eye towards the ultimate issue at trial: can plaintiff prove the defect.

Spoliation

Spoliation, in its simplest terms, is the destruction of evidence. It can include actual physical destruction, alteration, or concealment of evidence. Some argue that spoliation includes attempting, by use of threats or coercion, to prevent or alter witness testimony. Generally, courts grant the following four remedies for spoliation: (1) an evidentiary inference, (2) sanctions, (3) dismissal of plaintiff's complaint, or (4) an independent tort of spoliation.

 CASE LAW

◆ **spoliation as evidence at trial**

Schneider v. G. Guilliams, Inc., 976 S.W.2d 522 (Mo. App. 1998).

Plaintiff, personal representative for Carolyn Schneider's estate, sued the contractor who built Carolyn Schneider's home, *as well as the sub-contractor who installed a wood-burning furnace in the home. About four years later, the house burned, incurring substantial damage. Plaintiff alleged negligence and breach of warranty of fitness for a particular purpose. Defendants filed a motion for summary judgment based on spoliation of evidence.*

Dowd, Robert G., Jr., Judge

Defendants urged in their motions that no genuine issues existed as to any of the following facts: The Schneiders were insured by the Republic Insurance Company, which paid the Schneiders under the terms of its policy for the damage caused by the fire; having paid the Schneiders, Republic Insurance Company became subrogated to the rights of the Schneiders against Defendants; the Schneiders alleged in their petition against Defendants that they negligently installed the wood-burning furnace, and in particular, negligently installed the components of the flue system, including the flue base, the pipe connector and the flue, which remove combustible materials from the furnace and through the roof of the Schneiders' residence; after the fire, the Schneiders' residence remained under the possession and control of the Schneiders and their insurance carrier; at some point during either the clean-up or during the inspection after the fire, the flue base was discarded and Defendants have never inspected the flue base; the Schneiders and the Republic Insurance Company retained the services of two experts, Mr. Wysong and Mr. Richardson, who were both able to inspect the flue, the pipe connector and the flue base; after Mr. Richardson examined the flue and pipe connector, these pieces remained exclusively in his possession and under the Schneiders' and Richardson's control; at some point during 1995, Mr. Richardson disposed of the pipe connector and the flue, which were the remaining portions of the furnace system; and, although [**6] they requested to inspect the remaining two portions of the system, Defendants alleged that they were unable to examine the pieces because the Schneiders had destroyed, or intentionally spoliated the evidence.

In support of their motions for summary judgment, Defendants asserted that since Republic, the real party in interest, and its retained expert were in control of the flue components, and such expert had intentionally discarded these components, the spoliation doctrine applied, giving rise to an adverse inference against the spoliator. Defendants argued that the proper application of an adverse inference precluded the Schneiders from proving an element of causation necessary for recovery, namely that the cause and origin of the fire was attributable to Defendants.

* * *

In their first point on appeal, the Schneiders allege that a grant of summary judgment in favor of Defendants on Counts I, II and V for negligence and breach of implied warranty of habitability based on spoliation of evidence was improper. Specifically, they argue the spoliation [**8] doctrine does not apply when a non-party accidentally destroys evidence. Moreover, the Schneiders argue that even if a party had intentionally destroyed evidence, at most Defendants would only be entitled to an adverse inference and not summary judgment. Furthermore, the Schneiders urge that the unavailability of the flue components is not "substantially prejudicial" to Defendants' defense in light of the fact that before the pieces were destroyed, they were photographed and examined by experts.

* * *

" 'Spoliation' is the destruction or significant alteration of evidence. *Baugher v. Gates Rubber Co., Inc.*, 863 S.W.2d 905, 907 (Mo. App. E.D. 1993). If a party intentionally spoliated evidence, indicating fraud and a desire to suppress the truth, that party is subject to an adverse evidentiary inference." Id. (citing *Brown v. Hamid*, 856 S.W.2d 51, 56057 (Mo. 1993) (emphasis ours). Not concerned with whether the opposing party suffers prejudice as a result of the destroyed evidence, the doctrine works only to punish the spoliator. See *Pomeroy v. Benton*, 77 Mo. 64, 86 (1882). It is because of the very fact that the evidence of the plaintiff, the proofs of his claim or the muniments of his title, have been destroyed, that the law, in hatred of the spoiler, baffles the destroyer, and thwarts his iniquitous purpose, by indulging a presumption which supplies the lost proof, and thus defeats the wrong-doer by the very means he had so confidently employed to perpetrate the wrong. Specifically, the spoliation doctrine and the resulting adverse inference punishes the spoliators by holding them to admit that the destroyed evidence would have been unfavorable to their position. The adverse inference, however, does not prove the opposing party's case. Instead, the spoliator is left to determine whether any remaining evidence exists to support his or her claim in the face of the inference. [Citations omitted.]

Since the doctrine of spoliation is a "harsh rule of evidence, prior to applying it in any given case it should be the burden of the party seeking its benefit to make a prima facie showing that the opponent destroyed the missing [evidence] under circumstances manifesting fraud, deceit or bad faith." *Moore v. General Motors Corp.,* 558 S.W.2d 720, 735 (Mo. App. E.D. 1977). "Mere negligence is not enough." *Brissette v. Milner Chevrolet Co.,* 479 S.W.2d 176, 182 (Mo. App. E.D. 1972). However, under certain circumstances, the spoliator's failure to satisfactorily explain the destruction of the evidence may give rise to an adverse inference against the spoliator. *Brown v. Hamid,* 856 S.W.2d 51, 57 (Mo. 1993). In other circumstances, "it may be shown by the proponent that the alleged spoliator had a duty, or should have recognized a duty to preserve the evidence." *Morris v. J.C. Penney Life Ins. Co.,* 895 S.W.2d 73, 77-78 (Mo. App. W.D. 1995). [emphasis omitted].

Defendants urge that since an expert retained by Republic discarded the flue components, and that expert should have recognized a duty to preserve the components, the spoliation doctrine applies. Defendants also contend that the unavailability of the flue components for their inspection, in light of the fact that Appellant's experts have examined the components, is so prejudicial to them that the only fair result is the application of an adverse inference. We disagree.

Defendants have failed to cite and we could not find any Missouri case which applied the spoliation doctrine to facts in which a non-party destroyed evidence. In his treatise, Wigmore on Evidence, Mr. Wigmore explains, by way of example, the reasoning behind limiting the spoliation doctrine to the acts of a party:

When A, the defendant in an action by B for slander, bribes a witness to assist in proving a plea of truth as to B's misdoing, A's conduct is some evidence of consciousness that his cause is a weak one; and yet A ordinarily has no personal knowledge, one way or the other, of B's misdeed, so that his belief or consciousness is ordinarily not a mark or a trace of his own past act, but is an impression founded on all that he has been able to learn by inquiry. Thus if A were a third person, the evidential use of his conduct would amount to little more than using his hearsay assertion, . . . Consequently, such evidence would have to be confined to the conduct of parties in the cause, since for them it would at any rate be receivable as an admission; for any assertion by an opponent in the cause may be offered against him as an applied admission.

2 John H. Wigmore, Wigmore on Evidence, Section 277 (Chadbourn rev. 1979) [emphasis omitted]. While

Mr. Wigmore recognizes that certain circumstances in which the spoliator is not a party but a third person or agent of a party may give rise to the spoliation doctrine, he cautions that in those situations the act must be brought home to the party's connivance or sanction, express or implied, in order to use it as indicating any consciousness on his part of a weak cause. In thus connecting it with the party, it is to be noted, on the one hand, that no more [sic] technical theory of agency will suffice to charge him; for it is not a question of legal liability, but of actual moral connivance. On the other hand, no mere technical deficiencies of proof should be allowed to exonerate him; due regard to the common probabilities of experience should be paid.

* * *

Guided by these standards governing the spoliation doctrine, we find that Defendants were not entitled to summary judgment as a matter of law. Defendants failed to show that either Appellant, the Schneiders, or Republic intentionally destroyed or discarded the flue components. Neither did Defendants present any evidence that a party in bad faith directed, encouraged, or in any other way took part in destroying evidence. Instead, they alleged only that Republic's retained expert, Mr. Richardson, discarded such evidence. In the deposition offered by Defendants, Mr. Richardson stated that the disposal of the evidence was unintentional and that he was not directed to dispose of the evidence. Without any evidence in the record manifesting bad faith or intent to defraud on the part of a party, application of the spoliation doctrine is inapplicable. We note, however, that our holding does not preclude Defendants from offering evidence indicating bad faith on remand if such evidence exists. If, however, Defendants succeed in proving spoliation and become entitled to an adverse inference, Appellant must be allowed to pursue her claim and attempt to overcome the adverse inference as she may determine remaining evidence allows.

Accordingly, the trial court's decision with regard to summary judgment is reversed and remanded for proceedings consistent with this opinion.

* * *

Circumstantial Evidence

Circumstantial evidence may support the inference of a product defect and may infer that the harm sustained by plaintiff was brought about by the alleged defect. This evidence is sufficient to prove plaintiff's cause of action in the absence of proof of a specific defect. In many states, courts have treated this approach as a malfunction theory, under which plaintiff is required to prove only that the product was defective and that a resulting harm took place within the same time and space. This theory has many of the same characteristics as that of a res ipsa loquitur claim. *See also § 3* Restatement (Third), *Circumstantial Evidence Supporting Inference of Product Defect.*

 **CASE LAW** ────────────────────────────────────

◆ **circumstantial evidence**

Dietz v. Waller, 685 P.2d
744 (Ariz.1984).

Plaintiffs purchased a supposedly new "jet" boat from a retailer, defendant Waller. Plaintiffs immediately experienced a variety of problems with the boat, including an electrical wiring problem, and a leak so severe and continuous that the boat had to be returned to Waller's shop at least six times. Evidence was introduced that the engine appeared to be from another boat that had previously been run, and that the boat's seats were not the original ones, but were used.

Evidence was also submitted that the boat was in a minor accident while being towed by one of the plaintiffs, but defendant Waller inspected the boat after the accident and found no resulting structural damage.

─────────────────────

Holohan, Chief Justice

* * *

On July 4, 1978, appellants took the boat, which up to that date had been operated less than ten hours, to Lake Pleasant. The lake was calm with no wind, and only a few other boats were in the water. After running the boat for a short while, Dietz, also an experienced boatman, accelerated the boat until it planed out at about 45–50 m.p.h. After going about 100 yards, Dietz testified, "the left pickle fork blew off" and the boat broke apart, with the forward half of the boat essentially breaking off from the back half. Dietz testified that he had seen no large boat wake or debris in the water prior to this occurrence and that he did not know why the boat broke apart. Dietz sustained personal injuries in the accident which required medical attention and resulted in his missing one week's work.

* * *

We think reasonable minds could differ over the conclusions to be drawn from the evidence presented by appellants. While no single item of evidence is conclusive, there are several items that point to changes being made in the boat by Waller. The boat was shown to leak substantially from the moment it was placed in the water, and the leak(s) could not be stopped. While there was no direct evidence that the leak(s) actually caused the disintegration of the boat, we think it could be reasonably inferred that they were an indication of a structural problem. Moreover, no specific defect need be shown if the evidence, direct or circumstantial, permits the inference that the accident was caused by a defect. *Franks v. National Dairy Products Corp.,* 414 F.2d 682 (5th Cir.1969); *Hale v. Advance Abrasives Co.,* 520 S.W.2d 656 (Mo.App.1975); *Moraca v. Ford Motor Co.,* 66 N.J. 454, 332 A.2d 599 (1975); *Pearson v. Franklin Laboratories, Inc.,* 254 N.W.2d 133 (S.D.1977). The stipulation that the boat was free of defects at the time of manufacture, in conjunction with the existence of the leak, the installation of used seats, the engine's appearance of previous use, and the electrical and engine problems, could lead a reasonable jury to infer that Waller or someone else had mishandled or tampered with the boat prior to sale, or had negligently modified it. This inference, when combined with the evidence that the boat had seen only approximately ten hours of use and was being properly operated by an experienced boatman on a clear, calm day, could lead the jury to conclude the boat's sinking was due to a defect in the boat that existed at time of sale.

Admittedly, there was sharp dispute over the material facts and the inferences to be drawn therefrom. In addition to the stipulation, evidence was presented from which to infer that the defect might not have existed at time of sale—namely the boat's accident while being trailer-towed by appellants, and Waller's assertion that, prior to sale, he only waxed the boat, put it on the showroom floor, and installed the flip-throttle to match the length of his customer's legs. Nevertheless, considering all the facts and circumstances, there was a reasonable likelihood that reasonable people might reach different conclusions from the competing inferences. To prove a product defective, a plaintiff is not required to eliminate with certainty all other possible causes of an accident, but rather to present evidence sufficient to allow the trier of facts to reasonably infer that it was more probable than not that the product was defective. *Daleiden v. Carborundum Co.,* 438 F.2d 1017 (8th Cir.1971); *Schmidt v. Plains Electric, Inc.,* 281 N.W.2d 794 (N.D.1979); 63 Am.Jur.2d *Products Liability* § 224 (1984). Thus it was for the jury to decide the truth of the matter. *Reader, supra.*

* * *

Expert Witnesses

Most products liability cases require the retention of experts to prove a prima facie case that the product was defective at the time it left the manufacturer. Expert witnesses in products liability cases play two major roles. First, experts educate counsel, evaluate the merits of the case, assist counsel in determining practical liability theories, and assist in formulating discovery and trial strategy.

Second, experts testify at trial on specific ultimate issues, including the standard of care, the allegedly defective nature of the product, and causation. An expert's trial testimony may also educate the jury and the judge about the science or technology associated with the product. The search for the right expert must begin as soon as practicable because several difficulties may hinder it, such as the newness of the scientific or technical field, the number of experts in the field, conflicts of interest, budgetary constraints, the availability of individual experts, problems with the expert's personal or professional background, and the expert's willingness to be retained. Experts are often found in many of the following locations:

- local universities and teaching hospitals
- companies within the same industry as the defendant
- advertisements in bar publications
- national trade and professional organizations
- authors of leading scientific, technical, or medical articles on the subject of the case
- reports of other litigation involving similar product defects or injuries
- private consulting firms, which often advertise in bar journals and newspapers
- bar associations and trial lawyer groups, such as the American Trial Lawyers Association (ATLA) for plaintiffs and the Defense Research Institute (DRI) for defendants
- seminars and seminar materials on the same or similar areas of litigation
- government agencies, although in many instances government personnel may be prohibited from testifying as experts in private civil litigation. Former agency employees may also be a good source for experts.

The admissibility of the expert's testimony at trial is governed by applicable state or federal evidentiary rules or state common law regarding admissibility. Evidentiary law has become remarkably homogenized, given the promulgation of the federal rules of evidence and the adoption of relatively similar codes of evidence by the large majority of states. See Frumer and Friedman, Products Liability, Vol. 2A, §18.01 (Matthew Bender, 1993). So when the U.S. Supreme Court had addressed a nonconstitutional, evidentiary issue, its influence spread far beyond the federal courts.

A trilogy of cases decided by the U. S. Supreme Court have carved out more precise requirements for the admission of expert testimony. Before the first of the trilogy was decided in 1993, the prevailing test for the use of expert testimony was embodied in the 1924 case, *Frye v. U.S.*, 293 F. 1013, 1014 (D.C. Cir. 1924). *Frye* reflected a serious effort to exclude novel scientific theories by requiring that expert testimony be based on scientific principles that are accepted in the relevant scientific community. The trilogy reflected the Supreme Court's clear determination to provide clearer and stricter requirements than *Frye*. The trilogy, *Daubert v. Merrell Dow Pharmaceuticals, Inc.*, 509 U.S. 579 (1993), *General Electric Company v. Joiner*, 522 U.S. 136 (1997), and *Kumho Tire Company, Ltd. V. Carmichael*, 526 U.S. 137 (1999) are built upon well-reasoned, evidentiary principles, all of which are based upon the Federal Rules of Evidence §§702, 703 and 704.

Federal Rule of Evidence 702. Testimony by Experts

If scientific, technical, or other specialized knowledge will assist the trier of fact to understand the evidence or to determine a fact in issue, a witness qualified as an expert by knowledge, skill, experience, training, or education, may testify thereto in the form of an opinion or otherwise, if (1) the testimony is based upon sufficient facts or data, (2) the testimony is the product of reliable principles and methods, and (3) the witness has applied the principles and methods reliably to the facts of the case.

Federal Rule of Evidence 703. Bases of Opinion Testimony by Experts

The facts or data in the particular case upon which an expert bases an opinion or inference may be those perceived by or made known to the expert at or before the hearing. If of a type reasonably relied upon by experts in the particular field in forming opinions or inferences upon the subject, the facts or data need not be admissible in evidence in order for the opinion or inference to be admitted. Facts or data that are otherwise inadmissible shall not be disclosed to the jury by the proponent of the opinion or inference unless the court determines that their probative value in assisting the jury to evaluate the expert's opinion substantially outweighs their prejudicial effect.

Federal Rule of Evidence 704. Opinion on Ultimate Issue

(a) Except as provided in subdivision (b), testimony in the form of an opinion or inference otherwise admissible is not objectionable because it embraces an ultimate issue to be decided by the trier of fact.

(b) No expert witness testifying with respect to the mental state or condition of a defendant in a criminal case may state an opinion or inference as to whether the defendant did or did not have the mental state or condition constituting an element of the crime charged or of a defense thereto. Such ultimate issues are matters for the trier of fact alone.

Federal Rule of Evidence 705. Disclosure of Facts or Data Underlying Expert Opinion

The expert may testify in terms of opinion or inference and give reasons therefor without first testifying to the underlying facts or data, unless the court requires otherwise. The expert may in any event be required to disclose the underlying facts or data on cross-examination.

* * *

 CASE LAW

◆ **establishing factors that determine the admissibility of expert witness testimony**

Daubert v. Merrell Dow Pharmaceuticals, Inc.,
509 U.S. 579 (1993).

Two minor children and their parents sued a drug company which had marketed the prescription drug Bendectin. Plaintiffs alleged that the children's birth defects were caused by the mothers' ingestion of Bendectin while they were pregnant. The company moved for summary judgment, relying in part on the affidavit of an epidemiologist to the effect that no published human study (statistical) had demonstrated a statistically significant association between Bendectin and birth defects. To counter that argument, plaintiffs submitted expert opinion testimony based on (1) test-tube and live-animal studies that had allegedly found a link between Bendectin and birth defects; (2) pharmacological studies that allegedly showed similarities between the chemical structure of Bendectin and that of substances known to cause birth defects; and (3) the recalculation, of previously published epidemiological studies. The Court agreed to hear the case to determine the standard for admitting expert scientific testimony in a federal trial.

Blackmun, Justice

* * *

Petitioners Jason Daubert and Eric Schuller are minor children born with serious birth defects. They and their parents sued respondent in California state court, alleging that the birth defects had been caused by the mothers' ingestion of Bendectin, a prescription anti-nausea drug marketed by respondent. Respondent removed the suits to federal court on diversity grounds.

After extensive discovery, respondent moved for summary judgment, contending that Bendectin does not cause birth defects in humans and that petitioners would be unable to come forward with any admissible evidence that it does. In support of its motion, respondent submitted an affidavit of Steven H. Lamm, physician and epidemiologist, who is a well-credentialed expert on the risks from exposure to various chemical substances. Doctor Lamm stated that he had reviewed all the literature on Bendectin and human birth defects—more than 30 published studies involving over 130,000 patients. No study had found Bendectin to be a human teratogen (i.e., a substance capable of causing malformations in fetuses). On the basis of this review, Doctor Lamm concluded that maternal use of Bendectin during the first trimester of pregnancy has not been shown to be a risk factor for human birth defects.

Petitions did not (and do not) contest this characterization of the published record regarding Bendectin. Instead, they responded to respondent's motion with the testimony of eight experts of their own, each of whom also possessed impressive credentials. These experts had concluded that Bendectin can cause birth defects. Their conclusions were based upon "in vitro" and "in vivo" animal studies that found a link between Bendectin and malformations; pharmacological studies of the chemical structure of Bendectin that purported to show similarities of the drug and that of other substances known to cause birth defects; and the "reanalysis" of previously published epidemiological studies.

The District Court granted respondent's motion for summary judgment. The court stated that scientific evidence is admissible only if the principle upon which it is based is "sufficiently established to have general acceptance in the field to which it belongs." [Citations omitted.] The court concluded that petitioners' evidence did not meet this standard.

* * *

The United States Court of Appeals for the Ninth Circuit affirmed. . . . [In] *Frye v. United States,* 54 App.D.C. 46, 47, 293 F. 1013, 1014 (1923), the court stated that expert opinion based on a scientific technique is inadmissible unless the technique is "generally accepted" as reliable in the relevant scientific community.

* * *

We granted certiorari [in order to discuss] the sharp divisions among the courts regarding the proper standard for the admission of expert testimony. [Citations omitted.]

* * *

The merits of the *Frye* test have been much debated, and scholarship on its proper scope and application is legion. [Footnote omitted.] Petitioners' primary attack, however, is not on the content but on the continuing authority of the rule. They contend that the *Frye* test was superseded by the adoption of the Federal Rules of Evidence. [Footnote omitted.] We agree.

* * *

Nothing in the text of this Rule establishes "general acceptance" as an absolute prerequisite to admissibility. Nor does respondent present any clear indication that Rule 702 or the Rules as a whole were intended to incorporate a "general acceptance" standard. The drafting history makes no mention of *Frye,* and a rigid "general acceptance" requirement would be at odds with the "liberal thrust" of the Federal Rules and their "general approach of relaxing the traditional barriers to 'opinion' testimony." *Beech Aircraft Corp. v. Rainey,* 488 U.S. at 169 (citing Rules 701 to 705). See also *Weinstein,* Rule 702 of the Federal Rules of Evidence is Sound; It Should Not Be Amended, 138 F.R.D. 631 (1991) ("The Rules were designed to depend primarily upon lawyer-adversaries and sensible triers of fact to evaluate conflicts"). Given the Rules' permissive backdrop and their inclusion of a specific rule on expert testimony that does not mention "general acceptance," the assertion that the Rules somehow assimilated *Frye* is unconvincing. *Frye* made "general acceptance" the exclusive test for admitting expert scientific testimony. That austere standard, absent from, and incompatible with, the Federal Rules of Evidence, should not be applied in federal trials. [Footnote omitted.]

* * *

That the *Frye* test was displaced by the Rules of Evidence does not mean, however, that the Rules themselves place no limits on the admissibility of purportedly scientific evidence. n7 Nor is the trial judge disabled from screening such evidence. To the contrary, under the Rules the trial judge must ensure that any and all scientific testimony or evidence admitted is not only relevant, but reliable.

* * *

The primary focus of this obligation is Rule 702, which clearly contemplates some degree of regulation of the subjects and theories about which an expert may testify. *"If scientific, technical, or other specialized knowledge will assist the trier of fact* to understand the evidence or to determine a fact in issue" an expert "may testify *thereto."* [Emphasis added.] The subject of an expert's testimony must be "scientific . . . knowledge." [Footnote omitted.] The adjective "scientific" implies a grounding in the methods and procedures of science. Similarly, the word "knowledge" connotes more than subjective belief or unsupported speculation. The term "applies to any body of known facts or to any body of ideas inferred from such facts or accepted as truths on good grounds." Webster's Third New International Dictionary 1252 (1986). Of course, it would be unreasonable to conclude that the subject of scientific testimony must be "known" to a certainty; arguably, there are no certainties in science. [Citations omitted.] But, in order to qualify as "scientific knowledge," an inference or assertion must be derived by the scientific method. Proposed testimony must be supported by appropriate validation—*i.e.,* "good grounds," based on what is known. In short, the requirement that an expert's testimony pertain to "scientific knowledge" establishes a standard of evidentiary reliability. [Footnote omitted.]

* * *

We note that scientists typically distinguish between "validity" (does the principle support what it purports to show?) and "reliability" (does application of the principle produce consistent results?) . . . In a case involving scientific evidence, *evidentiary reliability* will be based upon *scientific validity.*

* * *

Rule 702 further requires that the evidence or testimony "assist the trier of fact to understand the evidence or to determine a fact in issue." This condition goes primarily to relevance. . . . The study of the phases of the moon, for example, may provide valid scientific "knowledge" about whether a certain night was dark, and if darkness is a fact in issue, the knowledge will assist the trier of fact. However (absent creditable grounds supporting such a link), evidence that the moon was full on a certain night will not assist the trier of fact in determining whether an individual was unusually likely to have behaved irrationally on that night. Rule 702's "helpfulness" standard requires a valid scientific connection to the pertinent inquiry as a precondition to admissibility.

* * *

Faced with a proffer of expert scientific testimony, then, the trial judge must determine at the outset, pursuant to Rule 104(a), n10 whether the expert is proposing to testify to (1) scientific knowledge that (2) will assist the trier of fact to understand or determine a fact in issue. n11 This entails a preliminary assessment of whether the reasoning or methodology underlying the testimony is scientifically valid and of whether that reasoning or methodology properly can be applied to the facts in issue. We are confident that federal judges possess the capacity to undertake this review. Many factors will bear on the inquiry, and we do not presume to set out a definitive checklist or test. But some general observations are appropriate.

* * *

Ordinarily, a key question to be answered in determining whether a theory or technique is scientific knowledge that will assist the trier of fact will be whether it can be (and has been) tested. "Scientific methodology today is based on generating hypotheses and testing them to see if they can be falsified; indeed, this methodology is what distinguishes science from other fields of human inquiry." [Citations omitted.]

* * *

Another pertinent consideration is whether the theory or technique has been subjected to peer review and publication. Publication (which is but one element of peer review) is not a *sine qua non* of admissibility; it does not necessarily correlate with reliability . . . The fact of publication (or lack thereof) in a peer reviewed journal thus will be a relevant, though not dispositive, consideration in assessing the scientific validity of a particular technique or methodology on which an opinion is premised.

Additionally, in the case of a particular scientific technique, the court ordinarily should consider the known or potential rate of error. . . . [Citations omitted.]

Finally, "general acceptance" can yet have a bearing on the inquiry. A "reliability assessment does not require, although it does permit, explicit identification of a relevant scientific community and an express determination of a particular degree of acceptance within that community." *United States v. Downing,* 753 F.2d at 1238. See also 3 Weinstein & Berger P702[03], pp. 702–41 to 702–42. Widespread acceptance can be an important factor in ruling particular evidence admissible, and "a known technique which has been able to attract only minimal support within the community," *Downing,* 753 F.2d at 1238, may properly be viewed with skepticism.

* * *

The inquiries of the District Court and the Court of Appeals focused almost exclusively on "general acceptance," as gauged by publication and the decisions of other courts. Accordingly, the judgment of the Court of Appeals is vacated, and the case is remanded for further proceedings consistent with this opinion.

* * *

Case Notes: Daubert and Establishing Criteria to Verify the Reliability of Experts

1. In 1997, the U.S. Supreme Court granted certiorari in *General Electric Company v. Joiner,* 522 U.S. 136 (1997), seizing the opportunity to clarify two points of law related to expert testimony left unclear after its *Daubert* decision.

First, *Joiner's* single issue on which certiori was sought was "What is the standard of appellate review for trial court decisions excluding expert testimony under *Daubert?*" The court answered this question by ruling that appellate courts should apply the "abuse of discretion" standard in reviewing a trial court's decision to admit or exclude expert testimony under *Daubert.*

2. The court went beyond that question to examine the merits of the appellate court's review of the trial court's decision to exclude expert testimony. That question arose in the following context: Plaintiff had been a cigarette smoker for eight years in his twenties, and contracted lung cancer when he was thirty-seven years old, after working in an environment that exposed him, without his knowledge, to massive doses of PCBs for nearly twenty years. The plaintiff did not dispute that smoking may have initiated the cell damage that led to his lung cancer, but took the position that it is unusual for anyone— even one who smoked far more than plaintiff— to suffer the actual onset of lung cancer at such an early age. Plaintiff contended that the onset of his cancer was accelerated by his exposure to PCBs. He also contended that dioxins and furans, to which he was also exposed regularly in his work environment, contributed to the acceleration of his lung cancer. The district court ruled that plaintiff had failed to identify evidence that would permit a jury to find that he had been exposed to dioxins or furans and granted summary judgment on these claims without addressing the admissibility of plaintiff's expert testimony that furans and dioxins promote lung cancer. The Court of Appeals reversed this ruling, holding that the record contained evidence of exposure to furans and dioxins.

The defendants moved for summary judgment, contending that plaintiff could not show that PCBs cause or accelerate the onset of lung cancer. Thus, defendants placed the issue of "general causation," that is, whether the challenged substance causes or promotes cancer in anyone in issue. The plaintiff countered the summary judgment motion with affidavits of two distinguished scientists, both of whom opined that likelier than not PCBs generally promote lung cancer and, specifically, likely accelerated the onset of Mr. Joiner's lung cancer. The U.S. Supreme Court addressed the question of whether the animal studies upon which plaintiffs' expert's relied could be used to support their conclusions that PCB's cause or accelerate the onset of lung cancer in humans.

3. Rather than explaining how and why the experts could have extrapolated their opinions from these seemingly far-removed animal studies, respondent chose "to proceed as if the only issue [was] whether animal studies can ever be a proper foundation for an expert's opinion" (*Joiner,* 864 F. Supp. at 1324). Of course, whether animal studies can ever be a proper foundation for an expert's opinion was not the issue. The issue was whether *these* experts' opinions were sufficiently supported by the animal studies on which they purported to rely. The studies were so dissimilar to the facts presented in this litigation that it was not an abuse of discretion for the District Court to reject the experts' reliance on them. (*General Electric Company v. Joiner,* 522 U.S. at 145.)

4. Thus, the Court mandated that the trial court must examine the conclusions of expert witnesses and ensure that they logically connect the facts of the case to the science or tests upon which they rely.

5. *Joiner* provided more guidance about how trial courts should analyze expert testimony to determine whether it should be admitted is admissible and about whether *Daubert* extended to non-scientific expert testimony. The federal courts of appeals were split on the issue. In 1999, the U.S. Supreme Court definitively answered the question in *Kumho Tire Company, Ltd. v. Carmichael,* 119 S.Ct. 1167.

Further Consideration of Expert Witnesses

 **CASE LAW**

◆ **evaluating the reliability of expert testimony**

**Kumho Tire Company,
Ltd. v. Carmichael,** 526
U.S. 137 (1999).

Plaintiff sued the manufacturer and distributor of a tire, claiming that a defect in the tire caused the tire's steel-belted membrane to separate from its tread, which in turn, caused the tire to blow out. Plaintiffs offered the testimony of a tire failure analyst to support their claims. He based his testimony on the following theory: (1) that, ordinarily, separation is caused by either a defect in the tire or overdeflection (the generation of heat within the tire due to underinflation or excessive weight); (2) that the degree of overdeflection necessary to cause a separation is marked by physical symptoms; and (3) that the inability to detect at least two of the physical symptoms of over deflection meant that a defect caused the separation. He based his conclusions on his visual and tactile inspection of the tire. The trial court excluded the expert's testimony, relying on Daubert. *The Eleventh Circuit reversed, holding that* Daubert *only applied to opinions based on scientific theory, as opposed to opinions based on knowledge gained by experience.*

Breyer, Justice

* * *

We agree with the Solicitor General that "the factors identified in *Daubert* may or may not be pertinent in assessing reliability, depending on the nature of the issue, the expert's particular expertise, and the subject of his testimony." Brief for United States as *Amicus Curiae* 19. The conclusion, in our view, is that we can neither rule out, nor rule in, for all cases and for all time the applicability of the factors mentioned in *Daubert,* nor can we now do so for subsets of cases categorized by category of expert or by kind of evidence. Too much depends upon the particular circumstances of the particular case at issue.

Daubert itself is not to the contrary. It made clear that its list of factors was meant to be helpful, not definitive. Indeed, those factors do not all necessarily apply even in every instance in which the reliability of scientific testimony is challenged. It might not be surprising in a particular case, for example, that a claim made by a scientific witness has never been the subject of peer review, for the particular application at issue may never previously have interested any scientist. Nor, on the other hand, does the presence of *Daubert's* general acceptance factor help show that an expert's testimony is reliable where the discipline itself lacks reliability, as, for example, do theories grounded in any so-called generally accepted principles of astrology or necromancy.

At the same time, and contrary to the Court of Appeals' view, some of *Daubert's* questions can help to evaluate the reliability even of experience-based testimony. In certain cases, it will be appropriate for the trial judge to ask, for example, how often an engineering expert's experience-based methodology has produced erroneous results, or whether such a method is generally accepted in the relevant engineering community. Likewise, it will at times be useful to ask even of a witness whose expertise is based purely on experience, say, a perfume tester able to distinguish among 140 odors at a sniff, whether his preparation is of a kind that others in the field would recognize as acceptable.

We must therefore disagree with the Eleventh Circuit's holding that a trial judge may ask questions of the sort *Daubert* mentioned only where an expert "relies on the application of scientific principles," but not where an expert relies "on skill- or experience-based observation." 131 F.3d at 1435. We do not believe that Rule 702 creates a schematism that segregates expertise by type while mapping certain kinds of questions to certain kinds of experts. Life and the legal cases that it generates are too complex to warrant so definitive a match.

To say this is not to deny the importance of *Daubert's* gatekeeping requirement. The objective of that requirement is to ensure the reliability and relevancy of expert testimony. It is to make certain that an expert, whether basing testimony upon professional studies or personal experience, employs in the courtroom the same level of intellectual rigor that characterizes the practice of an expert in the relevant field. Nor do we deny that, as stated in *Daubert,* the particular questions that it mentioned will often be appropriate for use in determining the reliability of challenged expert testimony. Rather, we conclude that the trial judge must have considerable leeway in deciding in a particular case how to go about determining whether particular expert testimony is reliable. That is to say, a trial court should consider the specific factors identified in *Daubert* where they are reasonable measures of the reliability of expert testimony.

* * *

Case Notes: Expert Witnesses

1. Both sides of the bar have developed helpful tips to practitioners as to how best to proffer expert testimony in light of the U.S. Supreme Court's trilogy. Counsel for both sides can follow these suggestions:
   a. Hire an expert in a recognized field of expertise.
   b. Be certain that your expert's qualifications are appropriate for his or her profession.
   c. Research your expert and her or his methodology, asking questions about whether your expert's methodology has been admitted into evidence in the past and whether there are any published or unpublished opinions commenting on the expert or his methodology.
   d. Discuss methodology at the start of the engagement. Ask the following questions:
      ◆ Is your expert relying upon a theory or technique that cannot be tested?
      ◆ Is the methodology the expert has employed accepted within the expert's professional community?
      ◆ If applicable, has the expert's theory or methodology been subjected to peer review or any recognized standards?
      ◆ Is the expert's methodology so subjective that one cannot verify the expert's conclusions except by placing faith in the expert's judgment?
   e. Monitor your expert's work.
   f. Treat a motion to exclude expert testimony seriously.
   g. Be mindful of Rules changes.
   h. Be aware that state courts may use the same or similar analysis as those reflected in *Daubert, Joiner,* and *Kumho.*

   See also Solovy and Africk, Use of Experts in Federal Courts in the Wake of *Kumho Tire,* The Practical Litigator, p. 23 (January, 2000).

2. To what degree must the plaintiff negate causes other than product defect under subsection (b)? Compare *Szubinski v. Stanton Trading Corp.,* 1994 WL 1113353 (E.D. Pa.) (ruling that bottle manufacturing cannot rely on inference in impleading a bottle manufacturer where there is no proof that the bottle did not break because of the opener or some other cause), and *Bruther v. General Electric Co.,* 818 F. Supp. 1238, 1242 (S.D. Ind. 1993) (finding no requirement that plaintiff produce an expert to bolster his allegation).

3. What are the four indicia of unreliability for scientific expert testimony outlined in *Daubert?* Must all of them be used by federal judges in every case? If not, how many would suffice? See *Watkins v. Telsmith, Inc.,* 121 F.3d 984, 999-91 (5th Cir. 1997) (stating that "not every guidepost in *Daubert* will necessarily apply to expert testimony based on engineering principles and practical experience. . . .")

4. What does the court mean when it says in *Daubert* that the scientific status of a theory depends on its "falsifiability?" How much expert opinion testimony can be analyzed as to its falsifiability? Must scientific expert testimony be known to a certainty?

5. Does *Daubert* teach that the federal trial judge should evaluate the final conclusions of experts? If not, what is the judge to evaluate concerning the expert testimony? What standard of review should federal appellate courts apply to a trial court's decision as to whether to admit or exclude expert testimony?

6. What are the benefits of empowering federal judges to decide whether the underlying science or tests upon which expert witness testimony purportedly relies in fact is logically connected to the conclusions reached by the expert about the case before her court? What are the problems inherent with the exercise of that power?

7. Practitioners and judges can ask the following questions about expert testimony in the product liability area:

a. Did the expert try to reconstruct or create design drawings?

b. Did the expert try to build a product differently?

c. Did the expert test the design changes?

d. How do other manufacturers test design and/or performance?

See *e.g. Dancy v. Hyster Company,* 127 F.3d 649, 651-652 (8th Cir. 1997).

Why are the foregoing questions not suitable for all types of products liability cases? How can they be modified to fit other types of cases, such as a case in which the defect is alleged to be a faulty weld?

DAMAGES

Types of Damages

Plaintiffs can claim three types of damages caused by defective products: personal injury, property damage, and economic loss of the product itself. Interestingly, the laws of negligence, warranty, and strict liability do not treat all three types of damage the same. Their treatment is based upon the idea that "damages available in negligence or strict liability are those available in tort." See Haig, Business and Commercial Litigation in Federal Courts, Vol. 5, § 70.15 (1998). A product liability plaintiff who pleads negligence and strict liability theories may claim compensatory damages and, depending on the facts in each case, punitive damages. Compensatory damages include damages for physical injury, including medical expenses, property damage, pain and suffering, emotional or mental distress, death, loss of actual earnings, loss of earning capacity, and the loss of a spouse's consortium. Punitive damages are levied as a penalty against a defendant that exercised willful, wanton, or grossly negligent conduct in manufacturing, designing, or warning about a product. Plaintiff must have specific evidence about the defendant's intent in order to meet the burden of proof for punitive damages.

In contrast, damages awarded in warranty claims are more closely concerned with the product itself, as opposed to a plaintiff's personal injuries or property damages. Warranty damages are governed by UCC § 2-714(2). This section of the UCC provides the following:

The measure of damages for breach of warranty is the difference at the time and place of acceptance between the value of the goods accepted and the value they would have had if they had been as warranted, unless special circumstances show proximate damages of a different amount (*Id.*)

UCC § 2-715(2)(a) provides that a buyer may also recover consequential damages where the facts of a case support the finding of the award of such damages. Personal injury, property damage, and lost profits are damages that may be considered consequential damages.

Economic Loss

Economic loss is the diminution in the value of the product, including the cost of repairs or the cost of replacement. Lost profits may be considered economic loss, although they are generally excluded from the economic loss doctrine, which applies only to the product itself. Under tort theory, a plaintiff's loss of earnings and reduction in earning capacity are common forms of economic loss flowing from the plaintiff's personal injuries. They are included under subsection (a). A type of economic loss that plaintiffs can claim under subsection (a) is damage to a store's reputation as a result of a fire as in the example given previously. The store could recover for the economic loss resulting from its damaged reputation, since it is recoverable in tort from the seller of the defective air conditioning unit. However, if the manager of the store was killed in the fire caused by the defective air conditioning unit and the store suffered substantial economic loss as a result of the manager's death, the store would not be able to recover that economic loss from the seller under negligence or strict liability theories. An employer does not have a tort cause of action against a third party for deprivation of the employee's services arising from personal injuries to the employee. Interestingly, under a breach of contract theory, the store could recover lost profits as a result of the fire. Some courts will not allow a plaintiff who does not have privity, to claim lost profits under a breach of warranty theory.

The economic loss doctrine in products liability claims bars recovery in tort when a plaintiff claims purely economic damages unaccompanied by physical injury to persons or damages to other property. It is based on the theory that parties to a contract may allocate the risks within their agreement, so they do not need the protection of tort law to provide damages for breach that are not allowed under their agreement. The seminal case on the economic loss doctrine is *East River Steamship Corp. v. Transamerica Delaval, Inc.*, 476 U.S. 858 (1986). In *East River,* the court held that, under admiralty law, a cause of action in tort does not lie "when a defective product purchased in a commercial transaction malfunctions, injuring only the product itself and causing purely economic loss" (*Id.* at 859, 871). The court drew a further distinction between damage caused to the "product itself" and damage caused to a "person or other property." See 476 U.S. at 870. It ruled that when the product itself is damaged, the "resulting loss is purely economic" and losses such as "repair costs, decreased value, and lost profits . . . essentially [involve] the failure of the purchaser to receive the benefit of its bargain—traditionally the core concern of contract law" (*Id.*)

◆ **damages as the basis for the economic loss doctrine**

Saratoga Fishing Co. v.
J.M. Martinac & Co., 520
U.S. 875 1997.

The purchaser of a ship added a skiff, a fishing net, and spare parts before reselling it to Saratoga Fishing. A faulty hydraulic system caused an engine room fire, which in turn caused the ship to sink. Saratoga sued the manufacturer of the hydraulic system and the company that built the vessel. The court addressed the question of whether the economic loss doctrine precluded recovery for the added equipment.

* * *

When a Manufacturer places an item in the stream of commerce by selling it to an Initial User, that item is the "product itself" under *East River.* Items added to the product by the Initial User are therefore "other property," and the Initial User's sale of the product to a Subsequent User does not change these characterizations.

* * *

Indeed, the denial of recovery for added equipment simply because of a subsequent sale makes the scope of a manufacturer's liability turn on what seems, in one important respect, a fortuity, namely whether a defective product causes a foreseeable physical harm to the added equipment before or after an Initial User (who added the equipment) resells the product to a Subsequent User. One important purpose of defective-product tort law is to encourage the manufacture of safer products. The various tort rules that determine foreseeable losses are recoverable aim, in part, to provide appropriate safe-product incentives. And a liability rule that diminishes liability simply because of some such resale is a rule that, other things being equal, diminishes that basic incentive. That circumstance requires a justification. That is to say, why should a series of resales, after replacement and additions of ever more physical items, progressively im-

munize a manufacturer to an ever greater extent from the liability for foreseeable physical damage that would otherwise fall upon it?

The *East River* answer to this question—because the parties can contract for appropriate sharing of the risks of harm—is not satisfactory in the context of resale after initial use. That is because, as other courts have suggested, the Subsequent User does not contract directly with the Manufacturer (or distributor). Cf. *Peterson v. Idaho First Nat. Bank,* 117 Idaho 724, 727, 791 P.2d 1303, 1306 (1990); *Tillman v. Vance Equipment Co.,* 286 Ore. 747, 755-756, 596 P.2d 1299, 1304 (1979). Moreover, it is likely more difficult for a consumer—a commercial user and reseller—to offer an appropriate warranty on the used product he sells akin to a manufacturer's (or distributor's) warranty of the initial product. The user/reseller did not make (or initially distribute) the product and, to that extent, he normally would know less about the risks that such a warranty would involve. Cf. *Tillman, supra,* at 755, 596 P.2d at 1303-1304; *Peterson,* 117 Idaho at 726-727, 791 P.2d at 1305-1306. That is to say, it would seem more difficult for a reseller to warrant, say, a ship's engine; as time passes, the ship ages, the ship undergoes modification, and it passes through the hands of users and resellers.

* * *

We conclude that the equipment added to a product after the Manufacturer (or distributor selling in the initial distribution chain) has sold the product to an initial User is not part of the product that itself caused the physical harm. Rather, in *East River's* language, it is "other property." (We are speaking of course, of added equipment that itself played no causal role in the accident that caused the physical harm.) Thus the extra skiff, nets, spare parts, and miscellaneous equipment at issue here, added to the ship by a user after initial sale to that Initial User, are not part of the product (the original ship with the defective hydraulic system) that itself caused the harm.

* * *

Case Notes: Economic Loss Doctrine

1. What is the general rule as to whether economic damages can be claimed under warranty, negligence, and strict liability theories? The court in *East River Steamship Corp.* justified

denying purely economic damages in a commercial setting when a product damages only itself, by the fact that such losses can be insured. Which party must then purchase insurance to protect against those losses? How would the outcome of a case differ if the economic damages were sustained by an individual rather than a commercial user? Would all torts exclude claims for economic damages (*i.e.,* conversion and misrepresentation)? Also consider the relationship between a commercial buyer and the manufacturer of a component part. How familiar are they with each other? Are they always free to *bargain* with one another?

2. What is *economic loss?* Courts generally refer to economic loss as a situation in which the plaintiff has suffered neither personal injury nor damage to tangible property. In such an instance, as demonstrated by the *East River,* most courts are opposed to recovery on a negligence or strict liability theory. State laws often conflict as to the classification of a loss as economic, which a plaintiff could not claim, or property damage, which a plaintiff generally could claim. Can the same loss be classified as both?

3. Does the economic loss doctrine assume that interference with economic integrity is not as significant as interference with physical integrity? If so, is that assumption justified, and what is that justification? What are the strongest counter-arguments?

4. Consider whether damages for the delimber unit in the following example should be allowed, using the lessons from *East River* and *Saratoga:*

Plaintiff acquired a delimber, which is a piece of forestry equipment used in its logging business. A delimber must be mounted onto some motorized carrying equipment, such as an excavator, which is precisely what was done in this case. An excavator is used to dig dirt. To convert the excavator into the delimber, the boom, arm, and bucket of the excavator, which are typically used for digging, were removed and the delimber was attached.

Defendants moved for summary judgment . . . contending that plaintiff's tort claims were barred because the only damage, when the unit caught fire, was to the delimber unit itself. Thus, it claimed it had no duty to plaintiff under a negligence or strict liability claim. Plaintiff responded by claiming that the delimber attached to the excavator constituted "other property." Because plaintiff claimed the fire started in the excavator portion of the equipment, it argued that the fire in the excavator damaged "other property" when it burned and destroyed the attached delimber unit.

See *Hutton v. Deere & Co.,* No. 99-8052, 2000 U.S. App. LEXIS 6285 at*9-11 (10th Cir. April 5, 2000).

Punitive Damages

The possibility of punitive damages often sparks heated debates, especially among non-litigants. Although an understanding of the debate can enlighten litigants in product liability cases, they must expeditiously move beyond the debate to the practical implications of punitive damages. The possibility of gaining or losing potentially huge punitive damages should spark strategic planning from the early stages of a case through its appeal because punitive damages pose the potential of monumentally changing otherwise unremarkable results.

The debate is tantalizing, though. Perhaps most hotly debated is whether and to what degree plaintiffs can obtain punitive damages when they bring product liability cases. Those who favor punitive damage reform claim, among other concerns, that punitive damages threaten business competition, detrimentally affect the economy, and violate the Constitution. See Pace, Kimberly A., *Recalibrating The Scales of Justice Through National Damage Reform,* The American U. L. Rev. (1997) (Footnotes omitted.) From a practical perspective, punitive damage reformers believe that the purpose of punitive damages, which is to punish and deter, does not fit the behavior of product manufacturers. See Owen, *Problems In Assessing Punitive Damages Against Manufacturers Of Defective Products,* U. Chi. L. Rev. 1, 15-25 (1982).

Conversely, punitive damage proponents accuse reformers of relying on myths and unrepresentative anecdotes that distort reality. They believe that products liability is a small and declining area of litigation and that, of the millions of individuals injured by defective products, very few of them sue and win because product liability suits are long and expensive, and defendants are usually major companies with seemingly endless resources. Testimony, April 10, 1997, Joan Claybrook, President Public Citizens House Judiciary Product Liability Revision, Federal Document Clearing House, Inc., Copyright 1997. (internal citations omitted.) In addition, they claim:

> The argument for limitations on punitive damage awards also is not supported by jury verdict data and appellate court records. According to research conducted by Professor Michael Rustad of the Suffolk University School of Law and published in the Iowa Law Review, in the 25-year period between 1965 and 1990, only 355 punitive damages were awarded in state and federal product liability lawsuits nationwide—an average of 14 per year. Of these awards, only 35 were larger than $10 million. All but one of these $10 million-plus awards were reduced; eleven of the 35 were reduced to zero (*Id.*).

The prospect of punitive damages bring practical considerations into the litigation of a products liability case, not to mention the incentive they provide defendants to settle a case earlier than if punitive damages were not available. See Schwartz, Teresa Moran, *Punitive Damages and Regulated Products,* 42 Am. U. L. Rev. 1335 (Summer, 1993).

In the midst of the debate, litigators must deal with the reality that punitive damages are obtainable in product liability cases. The prospect of punitive damages in any products liability case should be considered before either plaintiff or defense counsel embark very far down the discovery road. Every case should be evaluated against the applicable legal standard of liability for punitive damages for products liability cases.

The standard for punitive damages has been recently addressed by the United States Supreme Court. In reaction to the award of $2 million in punitive damages to a customer who purchased a "new" car that had been re-painted at a cost of $601.37, the Court established the general guideposts for the imposition of punitive damages in *BMW of North America, Inc. v. Gore,* 517 U.S. 559 (1996). The Court declared:

> Elementary notions of fairness enshrined in this Court's constitutional jurisprudence dictate that a person receive fair notice not only of the conduct that will subject him to punishment but also of the severity of the penalty that a State may impose. Three guideposts, each of which indicates that BMW did not receive adequate notice of the magnitude of the sanction that Alabama might impose, lead to the conclusion that the $2 million award is grossly excessive: the degree of reprehensibility of the nondisclosure; the disparity between the harm or potential harm suffered by Dr. Gore and his punitive damages award; and the difference between this remedy and the civil penalties authorized or imposed in comparable cases (*Id.,* 575).

Significantly, the Court criticized the method by which the jury was allowed to calculate the punitive damage award because the jury verdict reflected a computation of the amount of punitive damages based largely on conduct that happened in other states. The problem with computing damages based on occurrences in other states was that the jury was not instructed as to the law in the other states, so it could have been awarding damages for conduct that was legal in those states. The Court explained that the principles of state sovereignty and comity do not allow the jury to apply Alabama law so as to sanction the tortfeasors' lawful conduct in other states. *Id.*

How, then, are practitioners to interpret and use *BMW* when dealing with a punitive damages case? The Court drew few bright lines in *BMW,* but a few important considerations can be absorbed and used by practitioners from both sides of the bar.

Defense counsel can argue that *BMW* entitles them to a jury instruction cautioning the jury that it may not try to change, through its punitive damages award, the defendants' behavior outside of the state whose law the jury is applying. See McKee, *The Implication of BMW v. Gore for Future Punitive Damages Litigation: Observations from a Participation,* 48 Ala. L. Rev. 175 (Fall 1996). In that instruction, the jury could be further instructed that it may not use nationwide sales figures or cost data as a multiplier to arrive at a punitive damages award. Another jury instruction that defense counsel can request based on *BMW* is one that tells the jury that administrative fines and penalties can be used as a benchmark to establish punitive damages. Defense counsel should strongly consider fighting for the suggestion of such fines and penalties, since they are relatively low compared to the potential for punitive damage awards. In essence, this argument highlights the third guidepost established in *BMW,* which considers the civil penalties authorized or imposed in similar cases. Finally, it would likely be advantageous for a defendant in an economic loss case to stress the first of the three *BMW* guideposts, which is the degree of reprehensibility. When a jury is asked to compare the reprehensibility of economic loss compared to the loss of human safety or life, the jury will likely treat the defendant less harshly. If the jury does not respond to that argument, defense counsel could argue in post-verdict motions and on appeal that large punitive damage awards in economic loss cases must be reduced as a matter of law, since they violate constitutional due process protections because the defendant could not have prior notice of such punishment.

The Court in *BMW* did not leave plaintiffs' counsel without weapons. Although the Court instructed that the defendants' out-of-state conduct cannot be used in calculating punitive damages unless the law of those states is provided to the jury, that same evidence can arguably be used in evaluating the reprehensiveness of that conduct. It is intellectually difficult even for experienced litigators and jurists to separate the use of such damaging evidence for each guidepost, much less for untrained jurors. Consequently, the use of that evidence by the jury is difficult to control and will generally be helpful to plaintiffs. In addition, plaintiffs' counsel can get the defendants' out-of-state conduct into evidence if the jury is also instructed on the applicable law for each of the states in which the conduct is considered by the jury. The practical implications of such instructions appear overwhelming. However, plaintiffs' counsel can reduce the sheer number of jury instructions by combining in one instruction, the law of several states that have the same law on the relevant legal issue. Plaintiffs' counsel can also reduce the number of instructions by choosing to limit the number of states whose laws the jury is to consider by selecting only those states where large damages are available. In essence, it may be more beneficial for plaintiffs to forego damages based on some out-of-state conduct committed in states where damages are low, in favor of obtaining large damages based on the same conduct in other states. This strategy eliminates the Court's concern with punishing defendants for conduct that is legal in states other than the one in the trial court's jurisdiction, and it simplifies the jury's task.

Outside of the general guideposts provided in *BMW*, practitioners must consult the applicable state statutory law and the case law interpreting it, particularly as it applies to product liability and wrongful death actions. Very little can be generalized about these statutes. They may or may not address the specific questions of whether punitive damages are recoverable in product liability cases, or perhaps in actions alleging strict liability, negligence, or breach of warranty. They may or may not attempt to place limits on punitive damages awards or to channel a certain percentage of punitive damages to the state or state agencies. Moreover, a state's wrongful death statute may be a consideration as to whether and under what circumstances punitive damages may be awarded. The case law interpreting those statutes presents a myriad of analysis and results. For example, in 1999, the Missouri Supreme Court accepted the defendants' argument in a product liability case that the court had jurisdiction to determine whether the Missouri statute providing that 50 percent of all punitive damages must be paid to a state tort victim's compensation fund violated the excessive fines or takings clause of the constitution. *Rodriguez v. Suzuki Motor Corp.*, 996 S.W.2d 47, 53 (Mo. 1999). The practitioner should research the applicable state statutes and interpretive case law well in advance of most discovery, since the approach to written and oral discovery should be tailored accordingly.

Emotional Distress Damages

Plaintiffs in products liability cases can claim intentional and negligent infliction of emotional distress damages, each of which is controlled by its own legal tests. These damages have been claimed in product liability cases involving car accidents, train accidents, gas explosions, street car collisions and tobacco smoking. Those damages are only available with certain fairly narrowly drawn strictures that vary somewhat on a state-by-state basis.

 CASE LAW ─────────────────────────────────◆

◆ **emotional distress damages**

Masepohl v. American Tobacco Company, Inc.,
974 F. Supp. 1245 (D.C. Minn. 1987).

Plaintiff Masepohl sued tobacco distributors and companies contending that they, over the course of several decades, manufactured, promoted, and sold cigarettes to him and thousands of Minnesota residents while knowing, but denying and concealing, that such cigarettes contain the highly addictive drug nicotine. He also alleged that the Defendants, without public knowledge, controlled and manipulated the nicotine levels in cigarettes in order to create and sustain addictions to their products. Among other damages, plaintiff claimed damages for intentional infliction of emotional distress and negligent infliction of emotional distress.

─────────────────────────

MAGNUSON, J.J.

* * *

Masepohl included in his Complaint a claim for intentional infliction of emotional distress directed generally at "the Defendants" as well as at the Tobacco Companies, but he makes no attempt in either of his memoranda of law to argue that this claim is colorable as to the Distributors. To succeed on his claim of intentional infliction of emotional distress, Masepohl must prove that: (1) the Distributors' conduct was extreme and outrageous; (2) the conduct was intentional or reckless; (3) the conduct caused emotional distress; and (4) the distress was severe. See *Hubbard v. United Press Int'l, Inc.,* 330 N.W.2d 428, 438-39 (Minn. 1983). The conduct alleged must be "so atrocious that it passes the boundaries of decency and is utterly intolerable to the civilized community," and the distress inflicted must be so severe that "no reasonable man could be expected to endure it." Id. at 439.

At best, Masepohl alleges that the Distributors acted in an extreme and outrageous manner toward him and the other members of the class by remaining silent about the addictive properties of nicotine. (See *Compl.* P 67.) Under no set of facts could this conduct, if true, be construed as extreme or outrageous or "so atrocious that it passes the boundaries of decency. . . ." *Hubbard,* 330 N.W.2d at 439. Masepohl has failed to assert a colorable claim against the Distributors for intentional infliction of emotional distress.

* * *

Masepohl alleges claims of negligence and negligent infliction of emotional distress. As with his intentional infliction claim, Masepohl does not address these negligence claims in his memoranda of law.

A person may recover damages for negligent infliction of emotional distress if he: "(1) was within a zone of danger of physical impact; (2) reasonably feared for his own safety; and (3) suffered severe emotional distress with attendant physical manifestations." *K.A.C. v. Benson,* 527 N.W.2d 553, 557 (Minn. 1995). Whether the plaintiff was in a zone of danger is an objective question. See id. at 558. The Minnesota Supreme Court has determined that actual physical impact is not a required element of a claim for emotional distress. See id. at 557-58.

The Court first adopted the zone of danger test in *Purcell v. St. Paul City Railway Co.,* in which a woman suffered a miscarriage after a narrowly avoided cable car accident. 50 N.W. 1034 (Minn. 1892). In finding for the plaintiff, the Court noted that the impending cable car collision "seemed so imminent, and was so nearly caused, that the incident and attending confusion of ringing alarm-bells and passengers rushing out of the car caused to plaintiff sudden fright and reasonable fear of immediate death or great bodily injury." Id.; see also *Okrina v. Midwestern Corp.,* 282 Minn. 400, 165 N.W.2d 259, 261 (Minn. 1969) (finding woman who, while in a department store dressing room, heard a noise like an explosion and witnessed the collapse of a wall, although she herself merely got dusty, to be within a zone of danger); *Quill v. Trans World Airlines, Inc.,* 361 N.W.2d 438, 440 (Minn. Ct. App. 1985) (determining that man who experienced a sudden 34,000-foot drop in elevation due to the out-of-control tailspin of the commercial aircraft in which he was a passenger was within a zone of danger).

Masepohl has not alleged a single incident that could even remotely be construed as placing him in a zone of danger. The doctrine of negligent infliction of emotional distress simply does not cover the type of conduct that Masepohl asserts. Cf. *K.A.C.,* 527 N.W.2d at 558 (holding that defendant must have placed plaintiff in "a situation where it was abundantly clear that plaintiff was in grave personal peril for some specifically defined period of time" for negligent infliction claim to be actionable).

* * *

Case Notes: Damages from Emotional Distress

1. What damages are available if the plaintiff is not in the "zone of danger?" The results are mixed. Many jurisdictions allow damages to be recovered by bystanders to a serious accident affecting an immediate family member. In *Smith v. Bell Sports, Inc.,* 934 F. Supp. 70, 77 (W.D.N.Y. 1996), the court outlined the test for recovery of emotional distress damages, in this case, claimed by her companion, her co-plaintiff who alleged that he was injured as a result of a defective motorcycle helmet. That outline consisted of four elements:

a. the death or serious physical injury of another caused by defendant's negligence

b. a marital or intimate, familial relationship between plaintiff and the injured person

c. observation of the death or injury at the scene of the accident

d. resulting severe emotional distress

2. Interestingly, the court in *Smith* recognized the claim for damages by one other than a *family* member, based on the closeness of the relationship between the non-married cohabitants, reasoning, "[g]iven the widespread reality and acceptance of unmarried cohabitation, a reasonable person would not find the plaintiff's emotional trauma to be 'remote and unexpected.'" (*Id.*) (Citation omitted.) In this case, the damages for emotional distress were claimed by a woman who alleged that she had cohabited in a close relationship with the injured party for fourteen years, was at the race-

track at the time of the accident, and had witnessed the injured parties' pain and suffering that resulted from the accident. (*Id*, 78.)

3. What problems arise in applying the "more probable than not" standard to increased risk cases? What is the thinking of courts that apply the minority view? See, for example, *Valori v. Johns-Manville Sales Corp*, 1985 US Dist LEXIS 12921, *8-9 (D NJ) (concluding that a plaintiff, claiming to suffer from asbestosis, showed reasonable probability of contracting cancer by offering statistical evidence that he was a member of a class of which 43 percent would contract cancer); *Brafford v. Susquehanna Corp*, 586 F Supp 14, 17-18 (D Colo 1984) (concluding that plaintiffs could recover for increased risk because proof of probable injury from exposure demonstrated that they had "suffered a definite, present physical injury").

Damages in Toxic Tort Cases

Some plaintiffs do not exhibit symptoms of physical injury, yet seek to recover in toxic tort cases for damages they claim arise from their exposure to a toxic agent. Three types of damages claims have emerged from these cases: (1) damages from the anxiety or worry over contracting a disease in the future, or fear of future pain, suffering, and harm; (2) damages from the increased risk of contracting a disease as a result of exposure to the toxic agent; and (3) damages from the cost of medical monitoring for the onset of the feared disease. See Miller, *Note, Toxic Torts and Emotional Distress: The Case for an Independent Cause of Action for Fear of Future Harm*, 40 Ariz. L. Rev. 681, 684 (Summer, 1998).

The U.S. Supreme Court provided some guidance on the question of whether plaintiffs can recover damage claims based on the fear of contracting illness after being exposed to toxic or deleterious substances and the cost of medical monitoring, at least in the context of a F.E.L.A. claim.

 CASE LAW

CASE LAW

◆ **toxic tort damages**

Metro-North Commuter Railroad Co. v. Buckley, 521 U.S. 424 (1997).

Plaintiff Buckley sued his employer under F.E.L.A., a statute that permits recovery for railroad workers who have suffered injury resulting from their employers' negligence. He claimed damages for his emotional distress caused by his negligent exposure to asbestos by his employer. He manifested no signs or symptoms of illness caused by asbestos. The trial court dismissed

Buckley's claim on the basis of insufficient evidence that would allow a jury to find that he had suffered real emotional distress and Buckley's lack of any "physical impact." On appeal, the Second Circuit reversed, holding that Buckley's contact with the insulation dust that contained asbestos satisfied the "physical impact" requirement because his exposure was "massive, lengthy, and tangible." It also found that Buckley's workplace statements of worry about becoming ill due to asbestos sufficient to send his emotional distress claim to a jury.

BREYER, J.J.

* * *

The case before us, as we have said, focuses on the italicized words "physical impact." The Second Circuit interpreted those words as including a simple physical contact with a substance that might cause a disease at a future time, so long as the contact was of a kind that would "cause fear in a reasonable person." 79 F.3d at 1344. In our view, however, the "physical impact" to which *Gottshall* referred does not include a simple physical contact with a substance that might cause a disease at a substantially later time—where that substance, or related circumstance, threatens no harm other than that disease-related risk.

First, *Gottshall* cited many state cases in support of its adoption of the "zone of danger" test quoted above. And in each case where recovery for emotional distress was permitted, the case involved a threatened physical contact that caused, or might have caused, immediate traumatic harm. *Keck v. Jackson,* 122 Ariz. 114, 593 P.2d 668 (1979) (car accident); *Towns v. Anderson,* 195 Colo. 517, 579 P.2d 1163 (1978) (gas explosion); *Robb v. Pennsylvania R. Co.,* 58 Del. 454, 210 A.2d 709 (1965) (train struck car); *Rickey v. Chicago Transit Authority,* 98 Ill. 2d 546, 457 N.E.2d 1, 75 Ill. Dec. 211 (1983) (clothing caught in escalator choked victim); *Shuamber v. Henderson,* 579 N.E.2d 452 (Ind. 1991) (car accident); *Watson v. Dilts,* 116 Iowa 249, 89 N.W. 1068 (1902) (intruder assaulted plaintiff's husband); *Stewart v. Arkansas Southern R. Co.,* 112 La. 764, 36 So. 676 (1904) (train accident); *Purcell v. St. Paul City R. Co.,* 48 Minn. 134, 50 N.W. 1034 (1892) (near streetcar collision); *Bovsun v. Sanperi,* 61 N.Y.2d 219, 461 N.E.2d 843, 473 N.Y.S.2d 357 (1984) (car accident); *Kimberly v. Howland,* 143 N. C. 398, 55 S.E. 778 (1906) (rock from blasting crashed through plaintiffs' residence); *Simone v. Rhode Island Co.,* 28 R.I. 186, 66 A. 202 (1907) (streetcar collision); *Mack v. South-Bound R.*

Co., 52 S.C. 323, 29 S.E. 905 (1898) (train narrowly missed plaintiff); *Gulf, C. & S. F. R. Co. v. Hayter,* 93 Tex. 239, 54 S.W. 944 (1900) (train collision); *Pankopf v. Hinkley,* 141 Wis. 146, 123 N.W. 625 (1909) (automobile struck carriage); *Garrett v. New Berlin,* 122 Wis. 2d 223, 362 N.W.2d 137 (1985) (car accident). Cf. *Deutsch v. Shein,* 597 S.W.2d 141 (Ky. 1980) (holding that exposure to x-rays was "physical contact" supporting recovery for emotional suffering where immediate physical harm to fetus was suspected).

Second, *Gottshall's* language, read in light of this precedent, seems similarly limited. *Gottshall,* 512 U.S. 532 at 555 ("zone of danger test . . . is consistent with FELA's central focus on physical perils"); *id.,* at 556 (quoting *Lancaster v. Norfolk & Western R. Co.,* 773 F.2d 807, 813 (CA7 1985), cert. denied, 480 U.S. 945, 94 L. Ed. 2d 788, 107 S. Ct. 1602 (1987)) (FELA seeks to protect workers "from physical invasions or menaces"); 512 U.S. 532 at 556. (employer should be liable for "emotional injury caused by the apprehension of physical impact"); *id.,* at 547-548 (quoting Pearson, Liability to Bystanders for Negligently Inflicted Emotional Harm—A Comment on the Nature of Arbitrary Rules, 34 U. Fla. L. Rev. 477, 488-489) (1982) ("Those within the zone of danger of physical impact" should be able to "recover for fright" because "a near miss may be as frightening as a direct hit").

Taken together, language and cited precedent indicate that the words "physical impact" do not encompass every form of "physical contact." And, in particular, they do not include a contact that amounts to no more than an exposure—an exposure, such as that before us, to a substance that poses some future risk of disease and which contact causes emotional distress only because the worker learns that he may become ill after a substantial period of time.

Third, common-law precedent does not favor the plaintiff. Common law courts do permit a plaintiff who suffers from a disease to recover for related negligently caused emotional distress, see *supra* at 4, and some courts permit a plaintiff who exhibits a physical symptom of exposure to recover, see, *e.g.,* *Herber v. Johns-Manville Corp.,* 785 F.2d 79, 85 (CA3 1986); *Mauro v. Owens-Corning Fiberglas Corp.,* 225 N.J. Super. 196, 542 A.2d 16 (App. Div. 1988). But with only a few exceptions, common law courts have denied recovery to those who, like Buckley, are disease and symptom free. *E.g., Burns v. Jaquays Mining Corp.,* 156 Ariz. 375, 752 P.2d 28

(Ct. App. 1987), review dism'd, 162 Ariz. 186, 781 P.2d 1373 (1989); *Mergenthaler v. Asbestos Corp. of Am.*, 480 A.2d 647 (Del. 1984); *Eagle-Picher Industries, Inc. v. Cox*, 481 So. 2d 517 (Fla. App. 1985), review den., 492 So. 2d 1331 (Fla. 1986); *Capital Holding Corp. v. Bailey*, 873 S.W.2d 187 (Ky. 1994); *Payton v. Abbott Labs*, 386 Mass. 540, 437 N.E.2d 171 (1982); *Simmons v. Pacor, Inc.*, 543 Pa. 664, 674 A.2d 232 (1996); *Ball v. Joy Technologies, Inc.*, 958 F.2d 36 (CA4 1991); *Deleski v. Raymark Industries, Inc.*, 819 F.2d 377 (CA3 1987) (Pennsylvania and New Jersey law); *Adams v. Johns-Manville Sales Corp.*, 783 F.2d 589 (CA5 1986) (Louisiana law); *Wisniewski v. Johns-Manville Corp.*, 759 F.2d 271 (CA3 1985) (Pennsylvania law); *In re Hawaii Federal Asbestos Cases*, 734 F. Supp. 1563 [*433] (Haw. 1990) (Hawaii law); *Amendola v. Kansas City So. R. Co.*, 699 F. Supp. 1401 (WD Mo. 1988) (FELA); see also *Potter v. Firestone Tire & Rubber Co.*, 6 Cal. 4th 965, 863 P.2d 795 (1993) (en banc) (no recovery for fear of cancer in a negligence action unless plaintiff is "more likely than not" to develop cancer).

Fourth, the general policy reasons to which *Gottshall* referred—in its explanation of why common law courts have restricted recovery for emotional harm to cases falling within rather narrowly defined categories—militate against an expansive definition of "physical impact" here. Those reasons include: (a) special "difficulty for judges and juries" in separating valid, important claims from those that are invalid or "trivial," *Gottshall*, 512 U.S. at 557; (b) a threat of "unlimited and unpredictable lia-

bility," *ibid.*; and (c) the "potential for a flood" of comparatively unimportant, or "trivial," claims, *ibid.*

To separate meritorious and important claims from invalid or trivial claims does not seem easier here than in other cases in which a plaintiff might seek recovery for typical negligently caused emotional distress. The facts before us illustrate the problem. The District Court, when concluding that Buckley had failed to present "sufficient evidence to allow a jury to find . . . a real emotional injury," pointed out that, apart from Buckley's own testimony, there was virtually no evidence of distress. App. 623-625. Indeed, Buckley continued to work with insulating material "even though . . . he could have transferred" elsewhere, he "continued to smoke cigarettes" despite doctors' warnings, and his doctor did not refer him "either to a psychologist or to a social worker." Id., at 624. The Court of Appeals reversed because it found certain objective corroborating evidence, namely "workers' complaints to supervisors and investigative bodies." 79 F.3d at 1346. Both kinds of "objective" evidence—the confirming and disconfirming evidence—seem only indirectly related to the question at issue, the existence and seriousness of Buckley's claimed emotional distress. Yet, given the difficulty of separating valid from invalid emotional injury claims, the evidence before us may typify the kind of evidence to which parties and the courts would have to look.

* * *

Case Notes: Damages in Toxic Tort Cases

1. The court in *Gottshall* made a similar point:

   "Testing for the 'genuineness' of an injury alone . . . would be bound to lead to haphazard results. Judges would be forced to make highly subjective determinations concerning the authenticity of claims for **emotional** injury, which are far less susceptible to objective medical proof than are their physical counterparts. To the extent the genuineness test could limit potential liability, it could do so only inconsistently" (*Gottshall*, 512 U.S. at 552).

2. Some of the policy concerns impacting the restriction of emotional distress claims are (1) the proliferation of "fear of cancer" and similar claims in the absence of meaningful restriction might compromise the availability and affordability of liability insurance for toxic liability risks; (2) the unduly detrimental impact that unrestricted fear liability might have on the health care field, including the impact of suits for the fear of becoming ill as a result of taking prescribed medications; (3) the concern that allowing recovery to all victims who have a fear of cancer may detrimentally affect those who sustain actual

physical injury and those who ultimately develop cancer as a result of toxic exposure; and (4) the establishment of a clear limitation on recovery would establish a definite and predictable threshold for recovery, so as to permit consistent application from case to case. See *Potter v. Firestone Tire and Rubber Co.*, 863 P.2d 795, 812-815 (Cal. 1993).

3. From the plaintiffs' perspective, courts should not draw lines that leave people who live in fear of the traumatic and devastating effects of defendants' products with no remedy because plaintiffs could prove no revelation of illness. Plaintiffs' counsel can question why corporate polluters should be allowed to expose their workers, their workers' families, and their neighbors to toxic materials such as asbestos, trichloroethylene, and dioxin, yet be protected from civil liability. They can also argue that corporate polluters can act with impunity in causing people to fear for their health if they do not have to pay.

4. Increased risk of disease is one of the theories plaintiffs can use to avoid the seemingly difficult hurdles that accompany damages claims based on fear of disease. To prevail on an "increased risk" claim, most courts require plaintiffs to prove to a "reasonable medical probability." See *Sterling v Velsicol Chemical Corp*, 855 F2d 1188, 1204 (6th Cir 1988) (requiring, in an increased risk of cancer claim, with no disease present, "the predicted future disease must be medically reasonably certain to follow from the existing present injury"); *Herber v. Johns-Manville Corp*, 785 F2d 79, 82 (3d Cir 1986) (holding that a future injury, to be compensable, must be shown to be a reasonable medical probability). Therefore, the plaintiff must overcome a standard of "more probable than not" or greater than "fifty per cent" using reliable medical and statistical evidence to show that the disease will occur as a result of exposure.

5. Finally, plaintiffs in toxic torts have successfully begun to claim damages for the cost of medical monitoring, specifically the cost of medical examinations to facilitate early detection and treatment of disease caused by a

plaintiff's exposure to toxic agents. The argument for these damages is based on the reasonable certainty that the plaintiff needs medical monitoring, even in the absence of physical injury, due to defendants' tortious conduct in negligently exposing the plaintiff to toxic substances. The court in *Potter v. Firestone Tire & Rubber Co.*, 863 P.2d 795, 823 (Cal. 1993) quoting *Friends for All Children, Inc. v. Lockheed Aircraft Corp.*, 746 F.2d 816, 826 (D.C. Cir. 1984), explained that the reasonable need for medical examinations is itself compensable, without proof of other injury because:

> It is difficult to dispute that an individual has an interest in avoiding expensive diagnostic examinations just as he or she has an interest in avoiding physical injury. When a defendant negligently invades this interest, the injury to which is neither speculative nor resistant to proof, it is elementary that the defendant should make the plaintiff whole by paying for the examinations.

6. Most courts that allow medical monitoring claims generally require plaintiffs to show only the following:
   a. exposure to hazardous substances
   b. the potential for injury
   c. the need for early detection and treatment
   d. the existence of monitoring and testing procedures that make early detection and treatment possible and beneficial

The threshold for proving a medical monitoring case is therefore less onerous than an "increased risk" case. See *Merry v. Westinghouse Electric Corp.*, 684 F Supp. 847, 850 (M.D. Pa. 1988) (stating the first three requirements); *In re Paoli*, 916 F2d 829, 851–52 (adding the fourth requirement).

7. Although the Supreme Court has ruled neither in favor nor against medical monitoring claims in general, it recently refused to allow a medical monitoring claim under F.E.L.A. in the same *Metro-North Commuter Railroad Co.*, 521 U.S. 442-444 (1997), excerpted earlier.

The Court reasoned that monitoring costs "will sometimes pose special difficulties for judges and juries, due to "uncertainty among medical professionals about just which tests are most usefully administered and when." The Court acknowledged that millions of individuals may have suffered exposure to substances that might justify some form of substance-exposure-related medical monitoring. However, it expressed concern about the uncertainty as to liability, which could cause the Courts to be flooded with minor cases, and the defendants to be subjected to the threat of unpredictable and possibly unlimited liability. Also, the Court pointed out that for many plaintiffs the costs of medical monitoring might already be covered by employers or outside insurance.

8. Assuming we are all somewhat aware of and worried about the hazards posed by toxic agents, we are all potential "fear of cancer" plaintiffs. How, then, is a court to restrict the number of "fear of cancer" plaintiffs, particularly if *Metro-North Commuter Railroad Co.* is construed to apply only to F.E.L.A. cases. Consider, *Wilson v. Key Tronic Corp.*, 701 P.2d 518 (Wash. App. 1985). Plaintiffs were five

owners of property near a landfill in which a defendant disposed of a cleaning byproduct containing a toxic substance (1-1-1 trichloroethane). Plaintiffs were advised by the State Department of Energy (DOE), after testing water wells in the area, that they should not use the well water for drinking or cooking. Plaintiffs presented no proof of objective disease symptoms. Regardless, the Court ruled: "Fears of present and future health problems stemming from actual ingestion of the chemical by family members are not remote and fanciful, but rather are reasonable and therefore compensable." See *Id.*, 524.

But see, *Leaf River Forest Products, Inc. v. Ferguson*, 662 So.2d 648 (Miss. 1995) (rejecting emotional distress damages claims until "any disease caused by alleged exposure to dioxin manifests itself" and *Potter v. Firestone Tire and Rubber Co.*, 863 P.2d 795, 816 (Cal. 1993) (rejecting emotional distress damages claims because the plaintiff failed to present reliable medical or scientific opinion that he or she harbors a serious fear that the toxic ingestion or exposure is of such magnitude and proportion as to likely result in the feared cancer).

Table of Cases

Principle cases appear in bold typeface

C

Resources

American National Standards Institute (ANSI)
www.ansi.org

American Society for Testing and Materials
www.astm.org

Code of Federal Regulations
www.access.gpo.gov/nara/cfr/index.html

Consumer Information Center
www.pueblo.gsa.gov

Consumer Product Safety Commission
www.cpsc.gov

Federal Register
www.access.gpo.gov/su_docs/aces/aces140.html

Federal Register Table of Contents
www.access.gpo.gov/su_docs/aces/fr-cont.html

General Product Liability
www.productslaw.com

Mine Safety and Health Administration
www.msha.gov

National Institutes of Health
www.nih.gov

National Highway Traffic Safety Administration
www.nhtsa.gov

National Transportation Safety Board
www.ntsb.gov

National Climatic Data Center
www.ncdc.noaa.gov

Occupational Safety & Health Administration
www.osha.gov

Underwriters Laboratories
www.ul.com

U.S. Food and Drug Administration
www.fda.gov

Index

S